Between Dreams and Reality

The Military Examination in Late Chosŏn Korea, 1600–1894

Harvard East Asian Monographs 281

Between Dreams and Reality

The Military Examination in Late Chosŏn Korea, 1600–1894

Eugene Y. Park

Published by the Harvard University Asia Center
Distributed by Harvard University Press
Cambridge (Massachusetts) and London 2007

Printed in the United States of America

The Harvard University Asia Center publishes a monograph series and, in coordination with the Fairbank Center for East Asian Research, the Korea Institute, the Reischauer Institute of Japanese Studies, and other faculties and institutes, administers research projects designed to further scholarly understanding of China, Japan, Vietnam, Korea, and other Asian countries. The Center also sponsors projects addressing multidisciplinary and regional issues in Asia.

Library of Congress Cataloging-in-Publication Data

Park, Eugene Y.

Between dreams and reality : the military examination in late Choson Korea, 1600–1894 / Eugene Y. Park.

p. cm. -- (Harvard East Asian monographs ; 281)

Includes bibliographical references and index.

ISBN 978-0-674-02502-8 (hardcover : alk. paper)

1. Military education--Korea--History. 2. Korea--Armed Forces--Examinations--History. 3. Sociology, Military--Korea--History--1392–1910. 4. Korea--History--Choson dynasty, 1392–1910. I. Title. II. Title: Military examination in late Choson Korea, 1600–1894.

U635.K6P37 2007

355.2'234--dc22

2007002975

Index by the author

♾ Printed on acid-free paper

Last figure below indicates year of this printing

17 16 15 14 13 12 11 10 09 08 07

To my parents

Acknowledgments

My interest in history goes back to the years of earliest childhood, but only after entering college did I think seriously about becoming a historian. I recall the joy and excitement of my first quarter as a history major at UCLA after changing my major from electrical engineering. Then along came John Duncan. His first lecture was impressive, as he went down the list of Japanese colonialist distortions of Korean history, critiquing them one by one. It was not only that I enjoyed the course, but also that he gave me a real sense of the profession and life-style of a historian, and encouraged me to seek advanced training in Korean history. I went off to Harvard for graduate study, but John has remained my mentor to this day.

I learned so much from other scholars I met at Harvard. My advisor, the late Ed Wagner, was a patient teacher who was reassuring on whatever concerns I had and guided me to progress at my own pace. His untimely illness and passing deprived me the honor of getting my dissertation read by a true founding figure of Korean studies in North America, but fortunately his disciple and successor, Milan Hejtmanek, enabled me to complete my doctoral training. Along with Carter Eckert, who was the secondary reader and offered so much positive criticism, Milan helped me hone the skills that laid the foundation for this book.

During the various stages of book writing, John Duncan, Martina Deuchler, Anne Walthall, Kathy Ragsdale, Ken Pomeranz, and Bin Wong read different parts, if not the entirety, of the manuscript. Their valuable feedback helped sharpen the focus of my argument and present it more effectively. I thank Anne and Kathy in particular for subjecting themselves to the regimen of ploughing through the manuscript in a summer, aiding me tremendously in implementing the valuable suggestions for revision provided by anonymous reviewers.

Over the years, scholars in Korea have inspired and helped me, not only to mature as a historian, but also to access necessary source documents. I am grateful toward Ahn Byung Woo, Chu Chin-Oh, Chung Doo Hee, Kim In-Geol, Kim Yong Sun, Lee Hoon Sang, and Yi Tae-Jin; I have always felt that if I could somehow go back in time I would have loved to take their seminars as a graduate student. On matters more directly related to the Chosŏn military examination system, I was able to discuss various issues and obtain sound advice from Chung Hae Eun and Shim Seunggu.

Studying Korea with friends and colleagues has been an integral part of my learning experience, and many are now established scholars at research institutions. On various subjects I brainstormed with Avram Agov, Jongchol An, Jai-Keun Choi, Kyung Hwan Choi, John Frankl, Seunghyun Han, Kyung Moon Hwang, Chong Bum Kim, Kyu Hyun Kim, Mike Kim, Tae Yang Kwak, Kirk Larsen, John Woo Chung Lee, Tae-Gyun Park, Ken Robinson, Chiho Sawada, Jae-hoon Shim, and David Sokolove, both in and outside classroom settings.

My research received invaluable assistance from various institutions and their staff. For archival support, I am especially indebted to Choong Nam Yoon, Bill Wong, Sook Hyun Lee, and Seunghee Paek. Also, I thank Harvard-Yenching Library, Korea University Museum, Kyujanggak Library, Samsung Museum of Art, and Tenri University Library for granting me photograph permissions. In completing the book, the one-year Advanced Research Grant from the Korea Foundation allowed me to go on leave and focus on writing.

Many graduate students helped me with research, writing, and editing. I asked Hyun Choe, Younshik Chung, Jungwon Kim, Sachiko Kotani, Junghwan Lee, Kate Merkel-Hess, and Mike Wert to perform tasks of varying degrees of onerousness, ranging from tedious data entry to searching through volumes of traditional Korean genealogy to preparing digital maps to obtaining permissions for photo reproduction.

Last but not least, I thank my family. I am grateful toward my parents, Brian and Irene Park, and my sisters, Elisa and Heather, without whom I would not be where I am today. My parents-in-law, Sung Hwan Oh and Seong Bae Kim, have rooted for me. My daughter Lauren will not remember much about my book-writing odyssey, but since her birth in September 2002 she has been a blessing, helping my wife Seri and me to put all this in perspective. My gratitude goes to Seri for loving support.

Contents

List of Maps, Figures, and Tables xiii
List of Abbreviations xv
Introduction 1
1 The Early Military Examination System 15
Koryŏ Antecedents and the Founding of Chosŏn 16
A Military to Serve the State 19
The New Military Examination System 25
The Declining Political Stature of Military Examination Graduates 33
Continuing Aristocratic Domination of the Military Examination 38
Summation 47
2 The Rise of a Military Aristocracy 49
The Military Examination System after 1592 50
Late Chosŏn Critiques of the Military Examination System 60
The Emergence of Central Military Official Descent Lines 68
Why Specialization? 73
The Military Aristocracy and Politics 79
Summation 84
3 Local Elites and the Military Examination 86
Southern Local Yangban *88*
The Kaesŏng Elite 100

The Northern Elites of P'yŏngan and Hamgyŏng Provinces *105*
Summation *114*

4 *Yangban* Cohesiveness and the Chosŏn Dynasty 117
Marriage Ties *119*
Adoption *123*
Branch Affiliation Diversity *125*
The Government Sale of Ranks and Offices *128*
The Sacrosanct Aristocracy *132*
Summation *141*

5 Nonelites and the Military Examination 143
Anecdotal and Legal Evidence of Nonelite Participation in the Seventeenth Century *144*
The Actual Extent of Nonelite Participation: The Examination Roster Data *149*
Nonelites and Late Chosŏn Social Mobility *154*
The Limitations of the Military Examination as a Ladder of Success *158*
Nonelite Aspirations *162*
Military Ethos and Popular Culture *168*
Summation *177*

Conclusion: The State and the Military Examination System 179

Appendixes

A Highest Achievements of Military Examination Passers from Elite Military Lines, 1592–1894 188
B New Local Military Competitions from the Reigns of Sukchong through Yŏngjo, 1674–1776 190

Reference Matter

Notes 193
Works Cited 235
Character List 253
Index 263

List of Maps, Figures, and Tables

Maps

1.1 Eight Provinces of Chosŏn Korea 23

3.1 Elite Zones in Late Chosŏn Korea, ca. 1800 89

Figures

1.1 Polo as Illustrated in an Eighteenth-Century Manual on Martial Arts 27

1.2 Annual Frequency of Military Examinations, 1402–1608 29

1.3 Military Examination Degree Holders Produced Annually, 1402–1608 29

2.1 Late Chosŏn Factional Lineage 63

3.1 Regional Representation among Military Examination Passers, 1608–1894 87

3.2 Military Examination Passers from Chŏlla and Kyŏngsang Provinces, 1608–1894 98

3.3 Military Examination Passers from P'yŏngan and Hamgyŏng Provinces, 1608–1894 109

4.1 Cho I-ryang as Recorded in the 1672 Special Military Examination Roster 121

4.2 Portrait of Yi Chu-guk at 64 *Se* (1784) 138

4.3 Portrait of Sin Hŏn at 61 *Se* (1870) and Photograph at 67 *Se* (1876) 139
5.1 Scene of Degree Ceremony for the 1795 Suwŏn Courtyard Examination 165
5.2 Portrait of Im Kyŏng-ŏp Depicting Him as an Official 173
5.3 Shaman Painting Depicting Im Kyŏng-ŏp as a Deity 175

Tables

2.1 Military Examinations Producing 1,000 or More Passers, 1608–1894 57
2.2 Types of Military Examination and Number of Passers, 1608–1894 61
2.3 Descent Group Representation among Military Examination Passers, 1608–1894 71
2.4 Kyujŏnggong Branch Miryang Pak Civil Examination Passers with Degree Holding Relatives, 1393–1894 77
2.5 Kyujŏnggong Branch Miryang Pak Technical Examination Passers with Degree Holding Relatives, 1393–1894 77
2.6 Military Division Commanders from Civil Examination Backgrounds, 1593–1882 81
4.1 Intraprofessional Marriages among Nineteenth-Century Military Examination Passers 120
4.2 Intraprofessional Marriages among Nineteenth-Century Interpreter Examination Passers 120
A Highest Achievements of Military Examination Passers from Elite Military Lines, 1592–1894 188
B New Local Military Competitions from the Reigns of Sukchong through Yŏngjo, 1674–1776 190

List of Abbreviations

HMMTS	*Han'guk minjok munhwa taebaekkwa sajŏn* (Encyclopedia of Korean national culture)
MT	*Mansŏng taedongbo* (Comprehensive genealogy of ten thousand surnames)
PT	*Pibyŏnsa tŭngnok* (Records of the Border Defense Command)
SI	*Sŭngjŏngwŏn ilgi* (Daily records of the Royal Secretariat)
SW	*Ssijok wŏllyu* (Origins of descent groups)
YK	*Yŏllyŏsil kisul* (Narratives of Yŏllyŏsil [Yi Kŭng-ik])

Between Dreams and Reality

The Military Examination in Late Chosŏn Korea, 1600–1894

Introduction

For a span of two hundred years, from the mid-seventeenth to the mid-nineteenth century, Korea enjoyed freedom from external threat. Nonetheless, millions of men from all walks of life honed the archery, musket-shooting, and other combat-related skills that—along with a knowledge of the classics—were necessary to pass the military examination (*mukwa*) designed to recruit military officials. This era, the late Chosŏn period, saw the total dominance of civilian Confucian scholar-officials in politics, yet the frequency and scale of military examinations increased dramatically. Though most politically influential officials had passed the civil examination (*munkwa*), which usually entitled them to a civil office in the central bureaucracy, only a minority of the military examination degree holders received an appointment. When the state finally needed the military—during nineteenth-century conflicts with enemies from both within and without—the effectiveness of its military men was minimal.

Why was it that the number of aspirants who succeeded in passing the military examination increased as the state's rewards for that success diminished? Why did the state maintain extensive mechanisms for staffing the military when there was little actual need to employ it? Why did the military ultimately fail to perform its function of protecting the state?

The answers to such questions lie in the nature of the military examination system. In the late Chosŏn period, increasing domination of the civil branch of central government by a small number of aristocratic descent groups based in the capital, Seoul, led to the political marginalization of other aristocrats (*yangban*).[1] Through the military examination, some of these marginalized families transformed themselves into a military aristocracy functioning as a junior political partner of the civil aristocracy. In exchange, military officials enjoyed the support of the state and the patronage of civil officials. Many local aristocrats of the south also chose military careers as they struggled to maintain a presence in the central political arena.[2] Despite the process of differentiation, however, the local aristocratic lineages of the south and the civil and military official descent groups of the center continued to recognize one another as bona fide members of the aristocracy. Meanwhile, local elites of other regions, as well as nonelites, began to participate en masse in the military examination. Still retaining prestige in large part thanks to the aristocrats who held it, the degree served to satisfy their aspirations for higher social status and to win recognition in their social circles, but it did not lead to political power or membership in the aristocracy. Overall, the late Chosŏn military examination assumed a dual role: as a political institution it guaranteed a place in the power structure for one segment of the aristocracy, and as a sociocultural medium, it released the tensions engendered by the rigid status hierarchy.

The story of the expansion and reshaping of the military examination reveals a larger apparent contradiction: it was political, social, economic, and cultural change that enabled the stability and longevity of the Chosŏn dynasty (1391–1910) even well into its final century. In general, late Chosŏn saw changes in the structure of central authority, shifts in the relationship between central and local aristocracies, liberalization of the economy, upward mobility among socioeconomically prominent nonelites, and pointed criticism of the existing system by nonelites increasingly conscious of the aristocracy's Confucian moral values and lifestyle.[3] The balanced narrative of change in late Chosŏn that is revealed through an account of the military examination system does not end in stability. It charts as well the trends that eventually contributed to the uprisings of the nineteenth century and to Korea's ultimate weakness vis-à-vis the West and a modernizing Japan.

The subject of Chosŏn military examination graduates remains underresearched. Unlike the other examinations for which extant comprehensive rosters (*pangmok*) record all, or a good majority of, the successful candidates, the military examination records are spotty.[4] The majority of individual examination rosters are lost, and the extant specimens account for only about 24,000 out of some 150,000 to 170,000 degree holders.[5] Moreover, military officials are vastly underrepresented in comparison to civil officials in primary sources such as court histories and private literary collections (*munjip*).[6]

Source limitations so hampered research on the military examination system that historians working prior to the late 1980s had only a limited understanding of the institution. Consider, for example, the 1974 introduction to a reprinted primary source on the military examination, which, while noting that passers of the civil examination held most of the important posts in the government, claimed that the military examination enabled those of humble background to join the aristocracy as military officials.[7]

The assumption that the military branch of the Chosŏn central bureaucracy was a conduit for social mobility began to be questioned in the 1980s, with the appearance of more studies on the military examination. Although not all South Korean historians were ideologically or politically driven, many younger scholars became frustrated with decades of authoritarian rule and turned to Marxist history as a framework that could explain fluctuations in Korea's history. In this sense, many progressive South Korean historians empathized with their North Korean peers, who had long been employing Marxist historiography; greater academic freedom in South Korea, however, also allowed its historians to interpret Chosŏn social change from other perspectives. Furthermore, over roughly the last two decades there has appeared an almost overwhelming amount of new material on the Chosŏn period (and especially its latter half). This overall increase in sources and information has fostered a diversity of viewpoints.

Interpretations of the late Chosŏn military examination based on studies of this new material can be divided into three groups. The first, appearing even before the 1980s, focuses on the increased number of passers and the consequences of this increase for social order.[8] The earliest of these works were pioneering in that they explained the social significance of the late Chosŏn military examination. Their characterization of the institution as degenerate also set the tone for subsequent work. More recent scholarship has tried to understand the greater frequency of military examinations and the increasing number of examination passers by situating these phenomena in the political context of the late Chosŏn period, rather than viewing them as mere outgrowths of institutional mismanagement or corruption.[9]

The second group of studies on the late Chosŏn military examination generally seeks to understand the institution in a broader social context.[10] Some works even address the issue of whether mid-dynasty crises—such as the Korean-Japanese war (1592–98) and the Korean-Manchu wars (1627, 1637)—resulted in a wholesale reorganization of the earlier social order, a change assumed by older scholarship to have facilitated upward social mobility for nonelites.[11] These studies utilize previously neglected sources—the military examination rosters—for a more empirical analysis of the degree holders' social backgrounds. Unfortunately, each of these studies deals with a limited stretch of time in late Chosŏn, and thus tends to fall short of presenting the big picture.

The third group focuses on the roles of the military examination passers in the central bureaucracy.[12] These studies are important in that they seek to measure the political stature of military examination graduates. By raising this issue, scholars signaled that they were no longer content to characterize the military examination as a mismanaged institution, devolved from an aristocratic recruitment test for military officials into a tool used by commoners to achieve status. Instead, such scholars have emphasized how the military examination continued to facilitate the presence of a segment of the aristocracy in the central political arena.

Studies of the military examination to date have contributed to a better understanding of the institution's functions and the characteristics of degree holders from specific periods and backgrounds. Yet the issue of how to effectively frame findings on the military examination system within a paradigm that can explain the patterns of social change in premodern Korea remains contested. Rather remarkably for a field still small considering the international stature of South Korea alone today, scholars in Korean history are still debating over this paradigm.

In general, many historians have explained change in Korean social history in terms of social stratification and relations between groups enjoying different degrees of status. Although rarely defining its meaning, scholars doing research on premodern Korea have struggled to delineate an underlying and self-reproducing "structure." A common bias of structural analysis has been the tendency to look outside for agents of change, whether to the 1592–98 Korean-Japanese war, or to late nineteenth-century Western imperialism. Thus, it is noteworthy that in the last twenty years, the majority of historians researching late Chosŏn—especially South Korean scholars who have destroyed the colonial Japanese portrayal of Korean history as stagnant—have sought vigorously to identify agents of change within the structure itself.[13]

In challenging the stagnation view, scholars have discovered two long-term trends that were at work at different times in Korean history. One is the widening of the social base for political participation, a process that unfolds both in reality and in the popular belief shaped by aristocratic ideology. The second is the exercise of central political power by a narrowing segment of the society.[14] The apparent fluctuation of the membership base for the aristocracy is one interesting facet of these long-term trends. That base was restricted in Silla during the eighth and ninth centuries, then broadened in the Koryŏ period (918–1392), and contracted again thereafter. According to most historians, Korean and non-Korean alike, the state's inability to accommodate the growing number of social elements that desired more meaningful political participation seems to have contributed to the demise of Silla and the ultimate weakness of the Chosŏn regime.

Interpreting these long-term changes in Korean history requires a fuller understanding of the Chosŏn social hierarchy, and this has posed a special challenge to scholars. Though it is almost universally agreed that the early and late Chosŏn societies were different, there remains no consensus on the nature of the transformation separating the two eras. Depending on one's point of view, certain social groups became either more sharply defined or more amorphous. My study will show that while existing Chosŏn social categories became more clearly delineated, each also became subdivided into smaller groups that negotiated their claims to status to varying degrees. Of course, whether a modern study on Chosŏn should employ "status" rather than "class" as an analytical category is debatable. The term used in Chosŏn for the social hierarchy was *sinbun*—generally understood to mean status. What follows is my rationale for employing status over class in discussing late Chosŏn society throughout the book.

Class can be said to refer to a group of people—for example, landlords, small holders, tenants, landless peasants, slaves, and so forth—in the sense that they share similar living and working conditions. In contrast to Marxian, Weberian, and other discussions of class, E. P. Thompson's definition assigns stronger human agency to people through their actions and thoughts. Criticizing both the classical Marxist understanding of class as an inevitable offspring of the capitalist mode of production and the functionalist view of class as a component of capitalistic systems, Thompson argues that though class experience is determined by the production relations to which an individual is bound regardless of free will, such experience manifests as class consciousness. To Thompson, class arises when a group of people realizes, through transmitted tradition, values, ideology, institutions, and shared experiences, that their situation and interests differ from those of others, and thus class reflects lived, material relations instead of an idealized category.[15]

According to Max Weber's seminal formulation, "status" can be differentiated on the basis of noneconomic qualities such as honor, prestige, and religion.[16] Along with social class (determined by an economic relationship to the market) and party class (a group of people who can be distinguished by their political affiliations and their capacity to influence others' decisions), status group (or status class) is one of the three conceptually distinct embodiments of social inequality. More precisely, and more germane to the situation of Chosŏn Korea, Weber understands status as founded on differentials in hereditary prestige, formal education, occupational prestige, appropriate social interactions, and overall lifestyle. Based on these characteristics, an elite status group, for example, consists of people who effectively and monopolistically claim a special social esteem for themselves, whereas slaves, in contrast, constitute a status category with no prestige.

The late Chosŏn social order clearly illustrates why status is a more appropriate analytical tool than class. By the late seventeenth century (if not earlier), Korea's social pyramid consisted of four main status groups. At the top was the aristocracy (*yangban*), the ascriptive status elite comprising both office and non-officeholding members, rich and poor, and perhaps numbering no more than 5 percent of the total population.[17] Just below this stratum was a presumably larger, yet still relatively small, group, the *chungin* ("middle people"). The wealthiest and most prominent members of this group were government technical specialists, but it also more broadly encompassed noncommissioned military officers (*kun'gyo, changgyo*), administrative functionaries (*isŏ, sŏri*), and the illegitimate sons (*sŏŏl*) of aristocratic fathers by concubines (*ch'ŏp*).[18] The third group (and by far the largest) was made up of commoners (*yangin, yangmin, sangmin*) of widely varying occupations and degrees of wealth, who were mostly peasants but also artisans and merchants. The commoners bore most of the tax and service burdens to the state. At the very bottom were the lowborn (*ch'ŏnmin, ch'ŏnin*), a group consisting of chattel slaves (*nobi*) and some socially stigmatized people such as shamans and female entertainers (*kisaeng*).

Although I will use the concept of status throughout this study, late Chosŏn Korea was certainly not a classless society. Government slaves and poor commoner farmers, on the one hand, and high-ranking aristocratic landowners, on the other, lived in qualitatively different worlds. There is a correlation between status, related to differentials in prestige, and class-based economic conditions of wealth and poverty. For example, landholding was concentrated in the hands of aristocracy, while the tenancy rate was highest among commoners (although exceptions to this were not unheard of). Moreover, with the liberalization of the Chosŏn economy and the resultant marked increase in commerce and manufacturing, social stratification intensified.

All the same, to employ the concept of class for this period poses problems. Above all, late Chosŏn commercial and manufacturing capabilities proved woefully inadequate when subjected to Western imperialism in the late nineteenth century. Noting this, many scholars argue that the late Chosŏn economic system was qualitatively different from genuine capitalism. The established consensus locates the emergence of a fully capitalistic mode of production and its intensification no earlier than the late nineteenth century, if not in the Japanese colonial period.[19] Before the late nineteenth century the degree of correspondence between status and class—however well the latter may have been defined—remained relatively low. Thus, an individual of the highest social status could be a landlord, a smallholder, or even a part-owner and part-tenant; he could be a slave owner or possess no slave at all. We can define class in other ways, using criteria such as income and occupation (as in the modern United States), but this does not take the prestige factor into account.[20]

Well into the nineteenth century, the structure of inequality in Korea continued to be based on legally and socially recognized status, although the two did not always correspond to each other. This meant that the relations among various status groups had significant noneconomic dimensions. Not until the final decades of Chosŏn did the external impact of imperialism and capitalism accelerate social stratification and create more sharply delineated classes in an economy that fundamentally had been based on a landlord-tenant system. This situation is not part of my main story; accordingly, I choose to discuss late Chosŏn society in terms of various strata or shades of social status while avoiding an attempt to demarcate class boundaries. As will become apparent in the course of this study, political power was even less crucial in defining social status in late Chosŏn.

Any discussion of shifts within and among status groups in late Chosŏn necessarily involves an analysis of the dynamics of social change over the longer course of Korean history. Such an analysis, needless to say, also has been approached from a variety of angles.[21] The following will attempt to sketch overall trends, rather than to repeat a full historiographical discussion.

Older Korean historiography regarded the Japanese and Manchu invasions as a destructive force that shook the early Chosŏn system at its foundation and created room for a more liberalized economy that provided more opportunities to social newcomers. According to this view, advances in agricultural technology enabled many nonelites to accumulate wealth and attain aristocratic status, while the fortunes of traditional aristocrats suffered. Works in this tradition highlight the expanding capitalistic economy, the dissolution of the rigid social order, and an increase in social mobility.[22]

Though they disagree on the nature of Chosŏn society, more recent studies appearing in the last two decades or so have emphasized how political power was increasingly concentrated in a small number of aristocratic descent lines based in the capital.[23] Some view early Chosŏn as already having a clearly defined aristocracy, carried over from Koryŏ, that continued to enjoy rights and privileges sanctioned by law.[24] In contrast, others see the early Chosŏn system as a relatively open one, in which the only legally meaningful social boundary was that distinguishing the lowborn from the rest of the population, the latter group possessing the potential to enter central officialdom by passing the examination. Advocates of this view assert that the highest status group—which was more like a hereditary aristocracy—did not establish itself as such until late Chosŏn, prior to which scholar-officials were more commonly recruited on the basis of merit than birth.[25]

I agree more with those historians who view the top status group of early Chosŏn as a continuation of the Koryŏ aristocracy. Even though the civil examination gained greater prestige and importance, the Chosŏn aristocracy that virtually monopolized it was stricter than its Koryŏ predecessor in excluding hereditary local functionaries (*hyangni*) and other groups from the power structure. Chosŏn aristocratic status depended upon birth, and a descent group that had not attained it by 1392 could not do so afterward. Those who had joined top ranks before the dynastic change perpetuated themselves as an ascriptive status group for which examination degrees, ranks (*kwanp'um*), or offices (*kwanjik*) were not requirements for membership. Admission to the examinations and the holding of office were important as aristocratic credentials, but could not confer aristocratic status on those who did not already have it. This also meant that the Chosŏn aristocracy included a variety of descent lines: those producing high-ranking officials for generations, those putting forth only minor officials, and those with no presence in the central bureaucracy.[26]

Recent historians studying late Chosŏn have turned away from the center toward the periphery, but they remain divided over the importance of new social elements in relation to the old aristocracy. Though a majority of historians in Korea tend to view the emergence of social newcomers, especially wealthy commoners, as an integral part of the dissolution of the feudal order, Western scholarship generally stresses the continuity of the old aristocracy and the overall stability of the Chosŏn system—at least up to the early nineteenth century. In short, the two groups of historians disagree on the magnitude and scope of late Chosŏn social change, and the difference boils down to the question of whether the local aristocracy lost power in any meaningful sense before the arrival of imperialism. I find merits and demerits in both arguments, as I explain in Chapter 3.

Understanding the military examination's place in late Chosŏn society can help us analyze social change because the degree was accessible to a far more diverse pool of candidates than any other examination. I have taken several steps to ground my conclusions firmly in empirical evidence. First, I developed a database of 32,327 military examination passers, accounting for about a fifth of all Chosŏn military examination graduates. My database is not a statistically representative sample, since no one knows the exact distribution of various attributes among all military examination passers. At the same time, it is not a random sample either, since I put together the database using extant sources that have survived for reasons other than pure chance. This constitutes the largest sample ever to be analyzed for a study on the military examination, and we can reasonably hope that the findings based on it give us meaningful insights into the nature of late Chosŏn society.

Second, I have taken a more critical, comprehensive approach to previously more neglected documents related to the military examination system. Accordingly, I have examined new and relevant primary sources such as court records, household registers, local gazetteers, private memoirs, examination rosters, and genealogies. Reflecting source preferences of individual scholars, previous studies have underutilized or even omitted these sources.

Third, this study considers how the military examination system was reflected in popular culture. Although the original role of the military examination—as the state's primary instrument for recruiting central military officials—persisted until the end of the examination system in 1894, both the written and the oral traditions of late Chosŏn clearly show that ordinary people came to see the examination, which tested archery and horseback riding among other skills, as an exciting avenue through which the talented could transcend their more mundane existence. Its appeal came chiefly from the hope of moving up in life, a yearning exemplified by exciting, fictionalized heroes and heroines who offered stories far more dramatic than those lived by real-life military men (and women, of whom none in Korea were known).

Fourth, this book considers methodological and theoretical issues often overlooked in previous studies on the military examination system. Like most social historians, I am interested in identifying the underlying structures that can explain the way a social system functions.

I share with many the difficulty of balancing the structure's inherent tendency to reproduce itself with the agency of human actors struggling to negotiate their daily challenges and surroundings. This study seeks to explain how certain late Chosŏn institutions, such as the military examination, helped to realize the growing ambition of upwardly mobile nonelites and to contribute to the longevity of the dynasty—but only so long as other chronic problems, such as government corruption and impoverished farmers, remained under control.

In analyzing the potentials and limits of the late Chosŏn system, I found particularly useful the way William Sewell adapts Anthony Giddens's theory of the duality of structure and Pierre Bourdieu's notion of habitus.[27] Giddens's dual model of "rules" and "resources," Sewell argues, explains how actors influence structures but cannot establish how and what such actors know. Sewell finds a better treatment of this problem in Bourdieu's notion of habitus, or the set of "schemas" (Sewell prefers this term over "rules," which he finds more "proscriptive") that actors use and the way that behavior is enacted. The problem is that habitus also resists change. Sewell's solution is a notion of structure that has, on the one hand, a virtual existence in actors' minds as schemas that are applied in the enactment or reproduction of social life, and, on the other hand, a real existence in the world of resources that can serve as a source of power over materials or people. Schemas are transposable—they can be actualized in a potentially wide range of situations across time and space—as well as virtual, in that they are only manifested through practices. Such a structure is inhabited by actors who have knowledge of transposable schemas, and access to some resources. Structure is most vulnerable to transformation when little depth (the schema dimension) and power (the resource dimension) are at its disposal. All members of society exhibit a measure of agency in their daily lives, but the nature and strength of that agency are determined by the actor's social environment, which may or may not give them access to resources and the knowledge, or schemas, to use them.

Among the multiple structures of late Chosŏn Korea, political arenas, socially and culturally distinct regions, and genres of popular culture are important for this study. The schemas that reproduced or modified these structures range from aristocracy-dominated Confucian discourse to popular accounts—written or oral—of heroes and heroines who inspired ordinary people. These schemas were actualized by various resources: aristocratic pedigree; education based largely on Confucian classics; rituals drawing on a mix of Confucianism, Buddhism, and shamanism; degrees, ranks, and offices granted by the state; personal relationships that entailed political, intellectual, or kinship ties; and wealth deriving from landholdings and, increasingly, commercial profits. The effect of a schema or a resource depends on the structure in which it functions, and thus this study explains how, for example, a military examination degree conferred varying magnitudes of agency on status groups and individuals in different circumstances. The late nineteenth century witnessed the diminishing potency of late Chosŏn schemas, such as Confucian rhetoric and popular cultural narratives, as well as resources such as a government army strong enough to put down uprisings. Schemas and resources at work in the nineteenth century were not new, but some had been transposed to different structures, generating actors who demanded from the aristocracy and the state what can be called a conservative reform. Working within the system, they called for good governance by a diligent Confucian king who employed all men of talent regardless of pedigree, rather than pushing for, say, a Western- or Japanese-style constitutional monarchy or republican government.

Within the context of Sewell's structural theory, some of Bourdieu's more specific ideas—in particular that of "cultural capital"—are useful for understanding late Chosŏn practices. According to Bourdieu, cultural capital is the sum total of noneconomic assets, such as family background, social class, and education, that together can generate success.[28] Employing this notion for my study requires considering two more of Bourdieu's concepts, namely "autonom" and "hysteresis." According to the hysteresis effect, status-conscious and upwardly mobile social elements seek out diplomas or certificates (in the case of Korea, this meant the military examination degree) that have already been devalued as essential markers of social standing among aristocrats. The world within the larger society, where such trappings continue to enjoy high prestige, is the autonom. The diploma's potency is such that in the autonom, some nonelites who achieve it may choose deliberate unemployment rather than pursuing realistically obtainable work that they deem beneath them.[29]

Applying Bourdieu's insights to Korea helps us to understand the late Chosŏn context, and furthermore suggests a necessary modification to Bourdieu's theory in order to fit a different historical moment. Even though the Chosŏn social system continued to define status by birth, the military examination degree became a source of cultural capital for those negotiating the status hierarchy. The military examination's prestige declined during the half millennium of its existence, and its function of recruiting military officials benefited mainly those from the aristocracy, but the late Chosŏn hysteresis mobilized more nonelites to the contest. To attain the degree still entailed processes of education and acculturation; even if he was not accepted into the ranks of existing aristocracy, the degree holder, as certified by the state, assumed an aura that garnered social respect in his autonom beyond the locus of power. Well into the nineteenth century, the prestige of the degree for nonelites, and even for some marginalized local elites, was such that many were content with their station in life as unappointed military examination graduates. At the same time, the importance of central military official descent lines in defining the late Chosŏn aristocracy lends a gravity to Korean cultural capital that is lacking in the French homologue analyzed by Bourdieu.

As preparation for understanding the changes that took place in late Chosŏn, Chapter 1 gives an overview of the Koryŏ aristocracy, bureaucracy, and military, before explaining how the Chosŏn dynasty established the military examination system, the system's historical context, and the early signs of change affecting the examination and its degree holders. Chapters 2 through 5 analyze the place of the military examination in late Chosŏn politics, society, and culture. These chapters are organized topically to reflect the expanded social base of military examination candidates. Chapter 2 discusses the formation of central military official descent lines as distinguished from central civil official lines, both based in western central Korea. This was a pattern that departed from the less internally differentiated aristocracy of early Chosŏn. What contributed to this subdivision, and what was the political stature of military officials?

To answer these questions, the next two chapters turn to the periphery. Chapter 3 delineates the local elites in different regions and explores the significance of the military examination for each. The discussion identifies three historically and socially meaningful regional groups: (1) the local aristocracy of the south; (2) the local elite of the previous dynasty's capital, Kaesŏng, which played a vital commercial role throughout Chosŏn; and (3) the northern local elites who attained a higher level of Confucian cultural competence than previous generations but did so rather late in comparison to other elites. Among the three, the central aristocracy accepted only the southern aristocrats as a social equal. Acknowledging the existence of various types of local elites differentiated by their residence patterns, local influence, cultural orientation, and degree of participation in central politics, Chapter 4 stresses that the central civil officials, central military officials, and southern aristocrats continued to constitute a cohesive aristocratic status group. The military examination spurred the subdivision of the aristocracy into groups with distinct political functions; its members nevertheless maintained a common sociocultural identity as a whole.

Of course, not all military examination graduates were aristocrats, although the fact that the latter continued to hold the degree helped it retain its prestige. Chapter 5 considers what the military examination meant for nonelites in their pursuit of elevated status. The more socially and economically influential among them accumulated cultural capital and gained state-sanctioned markers of status, such as a military examination degree, without winning full acceptance as social equals by the existing aristocracy. Rather than ending the discussion there, as many previous studies of late Chosŏn social history have done, Chapter 5 explores the popular cultural dimensions of the military examination by assessing the aspirations of nonelites.

In the concluding chapter, I bring my findings to bear on a range of issues from social change to systemic crisis. I intend this book to initiate a reevaluation of the relation between the military and civil aristocracies, of the connections between center and periphery, and of the development of popular culture in late eighteenth- and early nineteenth-century Korea. More broadly, I hope to make a contribution to the study of military systems by raising questions about where military men come from, how the military interfaces with the rest of society, and in what ways military values resonate with those of civilian culture.

ONE

The Early Military Examination System

The ongoing process of defining and securing aristocratic status complicated civil-military relations from early Koryŏ through Chosŏn. As the role of the military waxed and waned in accord with its utility to the state, the relative power and status-value of civil and military posts shifted: sometimes they were comparable, at other times one or the other was clearly superior. In later centuries, membership in the aristocracy became increasingly circumscribed while the privileges associated with it continued to expand.

As the internal and external threats that bedeviled late Koryŏ gradually subsided, the administrative system of the succeeding Chosŏn state, dominated by civil officials, assertively absorbed the military. The state brought private armies under direct control and, as we shall see, transformed the military branch of the central government into a bureaucracy that carried out the dictates of the king and his highest-ranking statesmen.

We should understand such calculated bureaucratic restructuring as but one component of the basic changes introduced by the Chosŏn state that shaped the socioeconomic context within which the military examination system evolved. Of particular importance were alterations to the nature of aristocratic status. The *yangban* persisted as a closed ascriptive status group with special privileges. No family that was not *yangban* at the beginning of Chosŏn attained that status thereafter. Confucianism and pedigree complemented each other as constituent elements of a hegemonic discourse that allowed the aristocracy to distinguish itself from the rest of the population. Not only did the more self-conscious aristocracy emphasize rigorous education, correct moral values, and proper rituals, it also grappled with issues of economic stability and military staffing in ways that would defend its position.

This chapter traces the early Chosŏn process that defined an appropriate structure for the military and the proper status of military men. Reorganizing the military, the state introduced a new military examination and later subjected it to much fine-tuning. In spite of the perceived inferiority and numerous institutional problems of the military examination, as well as the declining political stature of military examination graduates as a whole, *yangban* dominated the military examination, as they did with the civil examination, and used it as a way of reaffirming their aristocratic status.

Koryŏ Antecedents and the Founding of Chosŏn

History rarely reveals a definitive beginning, but there is little question that the aristocracy that effectively ruled Korea until the modern era, the institutions it used to its advantage, and the underlying ideology it practiced and theorized all date back to early Koryŏ. During the tenth century, kings and statesmen fashioned a complex central bureaucracy. In 958, the government adopted a Chinese-style examination system ostensibly geared toward selecting talented men to serve in that bureaucracy.[1] Though it took centuries—arguably until the fourteenth century—for the institution to become the primary method of state recruitment of new central officials, throughout much of Koryŏ the members of the capital aristocracy, as well as the top-ranking functionaries who made up the local elite, more commonly entered central officialdom through examination.[2]

The mature central bureaucracy of Koryŏ included the civil and military officials—the "two orders" (*yangban*) of the aristocracy. An office-holder in the central bureaucracy, whether he was serving in the capital or in the countryside, was labeled a civil official (*munban*) or a military official (*muban*) based on how he entered the service, although at any given moment he might hold a military post as a civil official or vice versa. Alternative means of attaining central official posts persisted: protection appointees (*ŭmgwan*) received their posts as the kinsmen or descendants of mid-level or higher officials through the protection appointment (*ŭmsŏ*) system; some entered officialdom as clerks, others as recipients of honorary (*kŏmgyo*) offices. Over the course of Koryŏ, the examination system assumed greater importance than the more strictly ascription-based protection appointment system, though it also turned into an instrument by which the existing aristocracy perpetuated itself and restricted others' access to official positions. *Yangban* central officials made it increasingly difficult for others to enter the officialdom to the extent that by the time of the Koryŏ-Chosŏn dynastic change, if not earlier, the *yangban* formed an ascriptive status group. It comprised all those belonging to the ruling aristocracy regardless of actual degree or office holding.[3]

In contrast to the *yangban* of later centuries, the early Koryŏ *yangban* were more strictly delimited; by definition they encompassed both civil and military officials.[4] At the same time, military officials were inferior in both political stature and social standing to their civil counterparts. Since the state examination was geared toward recruiting civil officials, military officials were drawn from officers of the army, which was open to the general population. Thus, military officials tended to have more modest social backgrounds than civil officials. In fact, the backbone of early Koryŏ military organization was hereditary commoner soldiers economically supported by the state in exchange for military service.[5]

In early Koryŏ, the military successfully fought off invading Khitan armies and even played major roles in succession disputes, but civil officials nonetheless discriminated against military officials. A military examination set up in 1109, for example, soon had to be abolished due to criticisms from the civil aristocracy, which could not tolerate a military recruitment system of institutional standing equal to its own examination system. In 1170, after decades of escalating civil-military tension, the military staged a successful coup and commenced a century of military rule. Military leaders neither discarded the existing bureaucratic structure nor purged all civil officials. Instead, military strongmen began assuming prestigious civil posts for themselves, collaborating with civil officials and forming marriage alliances with them.[6] During the thirteenth century, the old social distinction between civil and military official descent groups blurred, and it became common for aristocratic families to produce both types of officials.[7]

In the meantime, the state military organization lost much of its effectiveness. The decay of the government military system began even before the Mongol subjugation of Korea in the mid-thirteenth century, occasioned by both the prolonged peace during the eleventh and twelfth centuries and the importance of commanders of personal troops. As military offices lost their original functions and existed in name only, the court filled them with little consideration for the occupants' qualifications. During the suzerainty of the Mongol Yuan dynasty (1271–1368), which followed the military rule, the Koryŏ military organization and personnel were further subjected to tight Yuan control.[8]

From the mid-fourteenth century, Korea again had to deal with various foreign invaders. The most troublesome were the *wakō*, mostly Japanese pirates raiding coastal regions. Also breaching the border were the punitive armies of the declining Yuan empire (from which Koryŏ had reasserted its independence), the Red Turbans in rebellion against Yuan, and the Jurchen tribesmen of Manchuria. Such military exigencies gave the Koryŏ state no choice but to rely on its military commanders; generally high-ranking central officials, civil or military, that were dispatched to trouble spots as inspecting commissioners (Chŏlchesa), they recruited their troops from the local population. Not surprisingly, the inspecting commissioners' troops took on the characteristics of private armies (*sabyŏng*), especially when they served the more personal needs and ambitions of their commanders.[9]

During the final decades of Koryŏ, many military officeholders were indistinguishable from the rest of central officialdom in terms of social background and career patterns. Rather than belonging to distinct social status groups of civil and military officials, a member of the central bureaucracy generally received both types of appointment in the course of his career. Prominent *yangban* descent groups tended to produce both civil and military officeholders, although some commanders were military men, pure and simple. Among the latter, Yi Sŏng-gye (1335–1408) led his northeastern comrades in arms in cooperating with more radical reformist Confucian scholar-officials. In 1392, this coalition toppled the Koryŏ and elevated Yi as the founder of the Chosŏn dynasty. Thus, the military entered the Chosŏn era in a strong position soon reinforced by the necessity of dealing with both violent internal political struggles and external military conflicts with the Japanese and Jurchens.[10]

A Military to Serve the State

The abolition of private armies and the standardization of recruitment procedures via the establishment of a permanent military examination system were two key objectives of the new regime. In this regard, the process of bringing the military under the state's full control was slow and laden with obstacles, but it was largely successful. The result was a restructured, centralized military organization built on the principle of universal military service. Military manpower was no longer the private resource of an influential general but instead an instrument of state power generally exercised by the king and his civilian bureaucracy.

At the beginning of Chosŏn, inspecting commissioners retained their late Koryŏ functions. Mostly royal kinsmen and merit subjects (*kongsin*)—enfeoffed officials receiving land and slaves from the state for extraordinary service to the throne during critical political events—they recruited their own soldiers from their respective provinces of jurisdiction. Although their troops periodically had to serve in rotation as duty soldiers (*siwip'ae*) in the capital, inspecting commissioners maintained separate draft registers.[11] Two months after the dynasty's inauguration, the court decided that inspecting commissioners could recruit soldiers only after notifying the Supreme Council of State (Top'yŏngŭisasa), the highest deliberative organ in the central government, and obtaining the king's authorization.[12]

At the same time, the government searched for ways to staff the military branch of central officialdom through a standardized test. Such a military examination had already been instituted on paper during the closing years of Koryŏ, but only with the official pronouncement by the dynastic founder Yi Sŏng-gye, also known as King T'aejo (r. 1392–98), did it assume the status of a military counterpart for the existing civil examination. A general who gained the throne with the support of Confucian scholar-officials and northeastern military officers, T'aejo valued literary and martial virtues equally.[13] For that reason he stressed that military examination graduates had to be equipped with both adequate martial skills and a good knowledge of the classics.

A few days after the accession in August 1392, he entrusted the Board of War (Pyŏngjo) with the responsibility of implementing all measures related to the military.[14] The court, grounded in an ideology that stressed the importance of both the civil and military branches of officialdom, pressed ahead with an effort to bring the military more firmly under its control. In the following year, the Righteousness Flourishing Three Armies Office (Ŭihŭng Samgunbu) was created to oversee military regulations, administration, finance, and field operations. Through this office, a select few senior officials came to exercise military command at the top level, replacing the authority of the much larger Security Council (Chungch'uwŏn).[15] All the same, the Three Armies Office had under its actual command the relatively small number of northeastern soldiers who were personally loyal to T'aejo and served in the Righteousness Flourishing Royal Guards of Left and Right (Ŭihŭng Ch'in'gun Chwauwi) that constituted the bulk of the capital army.[16] Sizable provincial armies still remained under the control of inspecting commissioners. Not until 1397 was the court able to replace the latter with garrison commanders (Chin'gwan Ch'ŏmjŏlchesa). Charged with managing military supplies at the local level, the new garrison commanders reported directly to their respective civilian provincial governors.[17]

Throughout T'aejo's reign, tension persisted between the central military command and the remaining private armies, as individual generals sought to exert influence on military matters. The mastermind behind the court's effort to strengthen the real authority of the Three Armies Office was Chŏng To-jŏn (?–1398), T'aejo's trusted advisor and essentially the author of the master plan for the new dynasty. Chŏng found further justification for the centralization effort in the looming prospect of military confrontation with China when, in 1398, Emperor Taizu (r. 1368–98), the founder of the Ming dynasty (1368–1644), took offense at a diplomatic document Chŏng had authored and demanded his extradition. Fully trusted by T'aejo, Chŏng advocated a preemptive strike against China with the Three Armies Office functioning as the agency of supreme military command. At the same time, Chŏng's military preparations and the ever-increasing power of the Righteousness Flourishing Three Armies Office aroused much opposition from the various military commanders who disliked him.[18]

Chŏng's plan to attack China was derailed later in the year when Yi Pang-wŏn, T'aejo's fifth son, who had played an instrumental role in helping his father ascend the throne, killed Chŏng for supporting another candidate for royal succession. Upon the abdication of the distraught T'aejo, Pang-wŏn's unambitious second elder brother became the next ruler—King Chŏngjong (r. 1398–1400)—but Pang-wŏn was now the real holder of power. Pang-wŏn continued centralizing the military in accordance with Chŏng's reorganization plan. At his urging, Chŏngjong dismissed some less trustworthy commanders. Those loyal to Pang-wŏn came to control most of the remaining private armies.[19]

The next major step toward a completely centralized military organization came two years later, in 1400, when the royal house split in another conflict. Attacked by the fourth elder brother, Pang-wŏn prevailed in the end, enabling him to consolidate his power. Afterward, on Pang-wŏn's recommendation, Chŏngjong ordered the abolition of the remaining private armies. In consequence, the court transferred the control of all men and supplies from inspecting commissioners to garrison commanders placed under the direct command of the Three Armies Office. Later in the year, when Chŏngjong tactfully abdicated, Pang-wŏn finally ascended the throne.[20]

As king, T'aejong (Pang-wŏn's temple name, r. 1400–18) completed the transformation of provincial military authorities from de facto military governors into commanders now subordinate to civilian provincial governors. He further augmented royal power by creating two elite royal guards: the Special Attendant Guards (Pyŏlsiwi), in 1400, and the Inner Forbidden Guards (Naegŭmwi), in 1407. Both comprised young men from *yangban* families recruited through weaponry tests.[21] Ultimately, though, T'aejong put more emphasis on the candidates' loyalty than on their skills.[22]

During this period, T'aejong also reorganized the capital army. Originally consisting mostly of T'aejo's personal troops, the army's size increased in 1400, when it absorbed the soldiers of abolished private armies. The units divided the responsibilities of guarding the palace and patrolling the city. In 1457, after undergoing numerous changes in name, organization, and scale, the capital army assumed the form of the Five Guards (Owi), effectively completing the early Chosŏn military reorganization process.[23] Overseen by the Five Guards Headquarters (Owi Toch'ongbu), twelve rotating guard generals (Wijang)—also known as the Five Guards generals (Owijang)—led the troops.

The post was a high military office of the junior second rank in the system of nine court ranks and offices and certainly reflected the importance of the officeholder's responsibilities.[24] Whereas the Headquarters were under the charge of a commander (Toch'onggwan, senior second rank)—who was usually a royal kinsman, a royal son-in-law, or a high-level civil official reporting directly to the king—the generals were more likely to be military men. All the same, the highest-ranking civil officials could hold commander and general posts concurrently, a practice which reflected the principle of civil supremacy.[25]

Outside the capital, the provincial army and navy commanders (Pyŏngma Chŏltosa and Sugun Chŏltosa, respectively junior second- and senior third-rank offices) controlled garrison (*chin'gwan*) troops. By the mid-fifteenth century, the state completed the military reorganization process, and these commanders reported directly to Seoul.[26] Throughout most of the Chosŏn period, Korea had eight provinces (Map 1.1), each with one to three army headquarters (*pyŏngyŏng*) and one or two navy headquarters (*suyŏng*). Each headquarters supervised a number of garrisons (*kŏjin*) or ports (*p'ojin, p'o*). The nearest district magistrate controlled the garrison army. Either a civil or a military official, this magistrate was appointed by the central government to administer a county and to command troops from his county as well as some neighboring jurisdictions. In contrast, port commanders (Ch'ŏmjŏlchesa) and small-port commanders (Manho), in charge of local naval forces, were military officials, though still appointed by the central government.[27]

The king and the highest-ranking civil officials headed up the military command structure that oversaw the provincial and capital armies. In reality, the extent to which the king controlled the troops depended on his actual authority over the various officials in the command hierarchy. Strong, effective monarchs such as T'aejong and Sejo (r. 1455–68) were real commanders-in-chief, whereas the boy-king Tanjong (r. 1452–55), for example, exercised only nominal authority. The fact that coups deposed two Chosŏn monarchs—one in 1506 and another in 1623—illustrates that effective authority over the military could shift from the king to powerful statesmen.[28] The latter were mostly civil officials, because the highest two of the nine office ranks in the central bureaucracy were all in the civil branch. In fact, all high-ranking positions in the deliberative council that handled military and security matters were civil offices, including that of the minister of war (Pyŏngjo P'ansŏ),

Map 1.1
Eight Provinces of Chosŏn Korea

and they were usually occupied by civil officials. Even the field command posts often went to civil officials. Below these positions, military officials mostly staffed the military branch, which consisted of over four thousand posts, including the top tier of the army officer corps.

The early Chosŏn army recruited from the entire adult male population ranging in age from 16 up to 60 *se* (Ch. *sui*; an individual's age is one *se* during the first year of life and gains a year upon the new lunar year). A draftee served in the Five Guards in Seoul on a rotating basis. When his service term at the capital ended, he was assigned to the provincial troops in or near his home locale. Except central officials and officially recognized students, every male of qualified age had to serve as either an active-duty soldier or a support taxpayer (*poin*). The latter's obligation entailed providing for the former's expenses by submitting a prescribed amount of cloth to the government each year.

In early Chosŏn, commoners and aristocrats alike provided military service. Commoner men were typically drafted as infantrymen (*chŏngbyŏng*) or marines (*sugun*), in either case serving two months per year, or as frontier garrison troops (*yubanggun*) serving three months. The elite (such as royal kinsmen and in-laws, merit subjects, and other *yangban*) served in the special guard units that escorted the king or defended the capital. According to one estimate, the total number of men officially registered to perform military duty increased from 370,000 in 1406 to somewhere between 800,000 and one million by the 1460s; among them, one-third were soldiers and two-thirds were support taxpayers.[29] Considering that the anti-Ming expedition army fielded by the Koryŏ in 1388 numbered some 30,000, the estimates seem high. In fact, even among those who were supposed to be on duty, the number of men actually serving at any given moment represented only a fraction of the total troop strength, because the frequency of service depended on the number of groups into which the soldiers were divided.

Since the adult males performing military duty of one sort or another numbered in the hundreds of thousands, yet no more than some four thousand men filled the posts in the military branch of officialdom, the question arises: what was the relationship between the central bureaucracy's military branch and the army as a whole? In other words, did military officials represent those who had risen through the ranks from the bottom of the army hierarchy, or did they represent an inherently distinct group in terms of their social origins? In early Chosŏn, both civil and military officials tended to be from *yangban* families. In contrast, noncommissioned military officers and common soldiers were not members of the military branch of central officialdom and generally were not *yangban*. Addressing these important issues regarding the connection between status and the military in Chosŏn society requires a better understanding of the nature of the military examination system, which, established in 1402 to recruit new members for central officialdom's military branch, remained intact until 1894.

The New Military Examination System

The early Chosŏn state fine-tuned the overall examination system to better meet the needs of a civilian-controlled central bureaucracy. In addition to the civil and technical examinations (*chapkwa*) that respectively recruited men for appointments to civil and technical offices, the new military examination standardized the way in which the new members of the military branch would be recruited. In contrast to the technical offices regarded as requiring merely narrowly focused, petty skills, *yangban* held the knowledge and preparation required for the civil and military examinations in higher esteem, to the extent of labeling them "grand examinations" (*taekwa*). In reestablishing the military examination in 1402, the Chosŏn state recognized the dual means available to the ruler for governing his people: moral persuasion and force.[30] The civil and military branches of central officialdom became avenues for each method of governance.

Tracing the early Chosŏn history of the military examination calls for a basic understanding of the overall state examination system. Throughout much of the dynasty there were three main categories of examination, the passing of which, at least in principle, made the degree holder eligible for an office. These competitions entitled passers to, respectively, a civil, military, or technical post in the central bureaucracy. Depending on whether an individual passed the civil or the military examination, he was labeled a "civil official" (*munban*) or a "military official" (*muban*) for the rest of his career, even though a civil official could concurrently hold both civil and military posts—or even just a military office—at any given moment. The same could be true for a military official.[31]

The career paths and perceived prestige of examination passers varied according to the subject. In early Chosŏn, the standard procedure for an aspiring civil official was first to pass a licentiate examination (*saengwŏn-chinsasi, samasi*)—either the classics licentiate (*saengwŏn*) or the literary licentiate (*chinsa*) examination, together regarded as the "lesser examinations" (*sokwa*). This entitled a degree holder to enroll in the capital's Confucian Academy (Sŏnggyun'gwan) to prepare for a future civil examination administered by the Board of Rites (Yejo). The military examination was given by the Board of War, and, unlike its civil counterpart, did not involve a licentiate stage. The less prestigious technical examinations served to fill various specialist posts in the central government.[32]

The state generally administered regular civil, military, technical, and licentiate examinations every three years. Civil and military competitions involved three stages: first, the local preliminary examination (*ch'osi*), which was held throughout the country and subject to regional quotas; second, the metropolitan examination (*hoesi, poksi*) administered in Seoul; and third, the palace examination (*chŏnsi*) given in the king's presence to rank all the successful candidates from the metropolitan stage. In contrast, both the technical and licentiate examinations involved only the first two stages. The regular finalist quotas for a triennial examination (*singnyŏnsi*) were 33 civil, 28 military, 48 technical, and 200 licentiate (100 each for classics and literary tests) graduates. In addition to the triennial competitions, the government administered a variety of irregular "special examinations" (*pyŏlsi*), such as the "augmented examinations" (*chŭnggwangsi*) given on felicitous occasions for the royal family.[33]

Administration of the dynasty's first military examination in February 1402 more or less completed the overall Chosŏn examination system.[34] Regular triennial competitions generally entailed the dual components of classics exposition (*kanggyŏng, kangsŏ*) and martial skills. During a triennial examination's preliminary stage, candidates were tested on six martial skills: (1) wooden arrow archery (*mokchŏn*); (2) iron arrow archery (*ch'ŏlchŏn*); (3) light arrow archery (*p'yŏnjŏn*); (4) horseback archery (*kisa*); (5) horseback lance-wielding (*kich'ang*); and (6) polo (*kyŏkku, kigyŏk*; see Figure 1.1).[35] In the second stage, the candidates

Figure 1.1 Polo as Illustrated in an Eighteenth-Century Manual on Martial Arts. Source: *Muye tobo t'ongji* 4: 52b. Courtesy of Kyujanggak Library, Seoul National University.

were not only tested on these martial skills again but also had to perform an exposition demonstrating knowledge of the classics as well as of the *Great Code of State Administration* (*Kyŏngguk taejŏn*), the Chosŏn law code promulgated in 1469.[36] Whereas the *Great Code* was a requirement for everyone, a candidate could choose his classics by selecting one from each of the three groups: (1) the Confucian canon, comprising the Four Books and Five Classics; (2) the Seven Military Classics; and (3) miscellaneous others. For each exposition the candidate had to recite and explain the meaning of a passage that his examiner chose from the candidate's designated text. During the palace examination stage, the finalists displayed polo and field hockey (*pogyŏk*) skills to a royal audience.[37]

Irregular special competitions were comparatively less rigorous. An augmented examination had the same requirements as the triennial examination, except for the third classics text and the *Great Code.* Other special competitions omitted a stage—or even two—and tended to emphasize martial skills over classics exposition.[38] As we shall see, such irregular competitions would become more frequent in the course of the Chosŏn period.

Almost from the outset, the government held military examination candidates to lower standards than their civil examination counterparts, testing the former on just two or three classics and martial skills of their own choosing. Court discussions of the military examination's contents centered around the issue of a minimum standard on the classics exposition, debating the premise that in spite of the institutional equality between the civil and military examinations, literary virtue was superior to martial virtue for a Confucian ruler and his officials. In contrast to King T'aejo, T'aejong established a military examination on an institutional footing equal to that of the civil examination, reflecting the necessity of strengthening the newly centralized military organization rather than an admiration for martial virtue.[39]

During the reign of T'aejong's son, Sejong (1418–50), the state scrutinized the details of various martial skill requirements. Archery prompted more purely technical discussions; the merits of polo provoked heated debate. In the end, Sejong's strong belief in the virtues of polo prevailed over some officials' fear of the indecent behavior associated with it, such as drunkenness and lechery among merry spectators. A polo requirement was officially adopted in 1425, and during the remainder of Sejong's reign it was a regular component of the triennial competitions.[40] Polo was often omitted from the various irregular special examinations that became more frequent at mid-century, but in 1470 it was restored upon a petition from the Board of War.[41]

Despite government efforts, the goal of maintaining a high standard for both martial skill and classics exposition proved elusive. The military examination continued to be widely regarded as the easier contest; contemporary accounts abound with complaints that young men from *yangban* families flocked to the military examination because they found its classics requirements easier.[42] Consequently, the Board of War recommended in 1430 that *both* the classics exposition and martial skill requirements be toughened.[43] Coupled with a strong Confucian bias in favor of literary over martial virtue, the perception of the military examination's comparative ease ensured almost from the outset that it would be less prestigious than its civil counterpart. By the end of the fifteenth century, the state had become more or less resigned to acknowledging that the former could not compare to the latter as a filter for men of talent.[44]

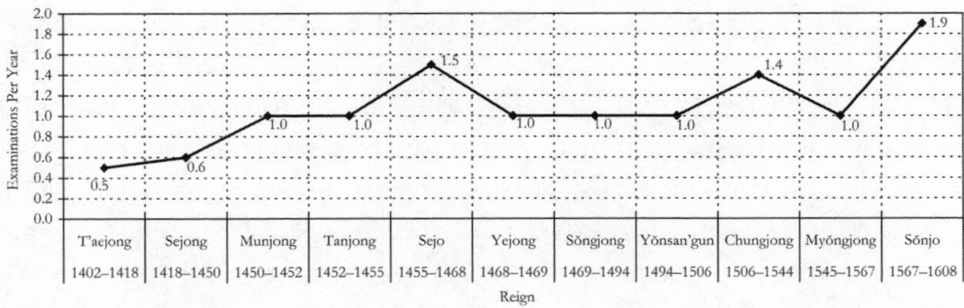

Figure 1.2 Annual Frequency of Military Examinations, 1402–1608. Source: Military examination rosters, *Sillok, Mukwa ch'ongyo, Kyonam kwabangnok,* and Sim, "Chosŏn ch'ogi mukwa chedo."

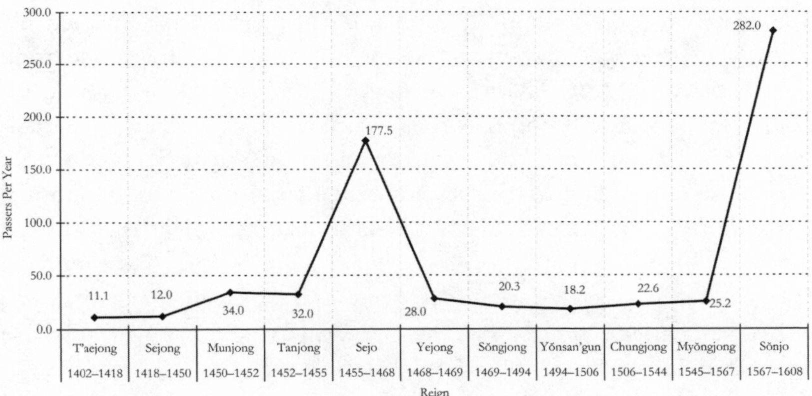

Figure 1.3 Military Examination Degree Holders Produced Annually, 1402–1608. Source: Military examination rosters, *Sillok, Mukwa ch'ongyo, Kyonam kwabangnok* and Sim, "Chosŏn ch'ogi mukwa chedo."

Just as the ongoing debate about the contents of the military examination drew to a close in the late fifteenth century, kings and officials had to grapple with the problems created by its increased frequency and scale. Both trends had held more or less steady during the preceding decades. Only toward the century's end does the government seem to have viewed them as a threat to the integrity of the military examination, and the relevant numbers are telling. Up to the end of Sŏnjo's reign (1567–1608), the frequency of military examinations increased from once every two years to every six months (Figure 1.2), while the number of degree holders produced per year also increased dramatically, from about 11 to 282 men per year (Figure 1.3).

Responsible for this proliferation was the variety of special, non-triennial contests, which were not bound by regular quotas and were given more frequently for political reasons. When, for example, the special recommendation examination of 1519 conferred the civil examination degree on younger Neo-Confucian reformists, the state also held a parallel military examination. Another form of special examination, the palace courtyard examination (*chŏngsi*), began during this period and came to be offered more frequently as the dynasty grew older. Beginning in 1489, the government had tested the Confucian Academy students every spring and autumn, rewarding the best candidates by exempting them from the early examination stages of the upcoming civil examination. This test soon became the courtyard civil examination that actually awarded degrees, and the corresponding courtyard military examination was in place by 1506.[45] Using abbreviated procedures, the courtyard examinations were held on felicitous occasions that were less important to the royal family than those warranting an augmented examination. Such courtyard and other irregular examinations also help to account for the more frequent, larger-scale military examinations: unlike the fifteenth century, which witnessed only two military examinations that produced one hundred passers or more, there were at least six such examinations in the sixteenth century before the Korean-Japanese war—all of these conducted during the century's latter half.[46]

The primary political factor seems to have been the effort by those in power to protect themselves by recruiting loyal men as court factionalism worsened. Though the reformist Neo-Confucian scholar-officials generally criticized frequent examinations, both civil and military, as merely an expedient tool for placating the people by doling out degree certificates, the conservative merit-subject statesmen and the king generally supported and sought to extend the practice. Throughout Chungjong's reign (1506–44), the most powerful officials—especially those who had put Chungjong on the throne through a coup in 1506—made sure that every civil examination was accompanied by a parallel military competition. They justified such arrangements with the ideological rationale expressed in the formula, "oneness of literary and martial virtues" (*munmu ilch'e*).[47]

The inclination of the king and his more senior officials toward frequent military examinations and a large number of graduates became stronger as political turmoil continued. After Chungjong's death in 1544, two rival families of royal in-laws engaged in a struggle that realigned the earlier divide between the conservative merit subjects and the reformist Neo-Confucian scholar-officials. After the brief reign of Chungjong's eldest son, when his maternal kinsmen held sway, a younger son, Myŏngjong (r. 1545–67), ascended the throne. During and after Myŏngjong's minority, his mother and regent, Queen Munjŏng (1501–65), along with her brothers, exercised real power. Until her death in 1565, they recruited and rewarded their allies, protégés, and cronies through various means, including the military examination. Enjoying the support of the highest-ranking officials, and especially the members of the State Council (Ŭijŏngbu), Myŏngjong persisted in approving frequent examinations in spite of the censorate's (*taegan*) criticism.[48]

As the state administered more frequent and often abbreviated special military examinations, the caliber of the graduates declined. From 1559 onward, it sometimes even recognized the participants of a simple archery competition as military examination graduates.[49] Unsurprisingly, sixteenth-century sources are replete with worries over a shortage of martial talent.[50]

The early Chosŏn military organization also broke down on more fundamental levels during the prolonged period of peace that prevailed from the late fifteenth to the mid-sixteenth century. Beginning in the late fifteenth century, aristocratic men started to avoid the military service, to which they had ostensibly contributed as members of elite guard units and support taxpayers. Though I have yet to discover a law that explicitly exempts aristocrats from military service, it seems that they regarded their avoidance of military duty as a part of their exemption from taxes in general. Their withdrawal was part of a general trend that ended the real military duties of trained, battleworthy soldiers during this period. Commoners drafted as infantrymen or marines increasingly bartered bolts of cloth, received from their support taxpayers, to hire substitutes (*taerip, korip*). Usually a private slave or a vagabond, the substitute then performed corvée labor instead of real military duties.[51] For most farmers who had to find substitutes, the cost was a heavy financial burden and many farmers ran away. In order to maintain paid troops, the government in 1537 instituted a military cloth (*kunp'o*) tax on all males subject to military obligation, but overall state finances continued to deteriorate.

Recourse to the military cloth tax was itself evidence of not only the difficulties the government faced in staffing the military but also the overall weakness of the state's financial base. The early Chosŏn state maintained a three-part tax system in which a grain tax on land, a service tax on labor, and an in-kind tribute tax (*kongnap*) levied on special local village products were all kept to a minimum to guarantee the peasantry's subsistence.[52] For a while, this system worked well: aided by advances in agricultural technology, the total amount of cultivated land registered for taxation peaked in the mid-fifteenth century.[53]

In the late fifteenth century, however, the tribute tax system began to break down. Because it was often difficult to obtain a sufficient quantity of necessary local goods in time, various offices in charge of procurement began to buy them in advance. The new tribute contracting (*pangnap*) system used multiple levels of middlemen and created more room for private commercial activities as well as administrative corruption.[54] As tribute contractors, profiteering tribute middlemen (*kongin*) collected an amount greater than the actual taxes.[55] Support taxpayers were supposed to pay their military cloth tax to fortify duty soldiers, but other taxes also weighed heavily on them, especially with the *yangban* aristocracy's increasing evasion of responsibility for the military draft and even the military cloth tax.

Throughout the sixteenth century, a fundamental concern for the state was the impoverishment and even enslavement of commoner peasants on such a scale that, despite a rapid population increase, not enough conscripts could be found to fill the military ranks.[56] Generally speaking, the founding of Chosŏn and its centralization process in the fifteenth century had benefited both the state and the aristocracy at the expense of intermediate-level social elements such as hereditary local functionaries. With the new socioeconomic developments of the sixteenth century, the aristocracy began to profit at the expense of both the state and commoner taxpayers.[57]

By the sixteenth century, these trends prompted the state to use the military examination as a quick-fix measure for manning frontier garrisons. For a better understanding of this development, we need initially to consider the issue of the deteriorating employment prospects faced by passers of the military examination. This trend presaged the late

Chosŏn pattern, according to which only a small minority of military examination graduates had meaningful careers in central officialdom.

The Declining Political Stature of Military Examination Graduates

Though the military examination's prestige had traditionally been lower than that of the civil examination, in the fifteenth century military examination graduates as a whole fared well. They generally could expect to receive military posts in the central bureaucracy, and many even attained important high civil offices. During the sixteenth century, however, increased court factionalism and the patronage politics dominated by royal in-laws favored those military men who had proper connections, leaving others struggling to receive an appointment. What follows is an assessment of the evidence demonstrating a decline in the overall political stature of military examination degree holders.

When the military examination was set up in 1402, it had an institutional status equal to that of the civil examination. The Board of Personnel (Ijo) and the Board of War respectively handled civil and military personnel recruitment.[58] The Board of War remained a vital organ handling security-related matters until the early sixteenth century, when the newly created Border Defense Command (Pibyŏnsa) brought together the senior officials of the various agencies that handled security-related issues. Prior to the emergence of the Border Defense Command, the minister of war was one of the most important among the highest officials. Those with a good knowledge of military affairs generally won the position.[59]

In the early Chosŏn climate of general appreciation for military knowledge, military examination graduates, like their civil examination colleagues, even enjoyed some of the privileges usually due officials. In 1430, for example, King Sejong followed a recommendation of the Board of Rites to treat examination passers and incumbent officials equally when they were charged with a crime, that is, to entitle them to an initial interrogation by the State Tribunal (Ŭigŭmbu).[60] The privilege granted to an examination graduate remained virtually unchallenged until the seventeenth century, when the problem of criminals and the lowborn taking the military examination became widespread.

Naturally, military examination graduates enjoyed greater prestige and respect in comparison to nondegreed military men among officers and rank-and-file conscripts. A military examination graduate worth his salt had to possess adequate martial skills, but what truly distinguished him from ordinary military men was his potential not only as a soldier but also as a commander and official.[61] As is suggested by the fact that the top (*changwŏn*) passers received a sixth-rank civil office rather than a military post, these degree holders were meant to be military administrators with a broad knowledge based on military classics, other canonical writings, and law codes.[62]

The greater honor and respect enjoyed by military examination passers compared to nondegreed military men was reflected in the former's stature in early Chosŏn central officialdom and court politics. Over the course of the dynasty, only seven military examination graduates reached a high state councillor post—that is, the chief, the second, or the third state councillor (Yŏngŭijŏng, Chwaŭijŏng, Uŭijŏng)—and three of the seven are fifteenth-century cases. This clearly suggests that the political stature of military examination degree holders was at its highest level during this period.[63]

Such military examination graduates of course represent a small minority of the several hundred Chosŏn high state councillors, and thus we also need to consider how well military men were represented in central officialdom as a whole. Among those who passed the military examination between 1402 and 1494, two-thirds of the passers whose career data are known reached a post of at least junior fourth rank. The majority of passers attained military or military-related posts such as the provincial army commander or the defense command magistrate (Pusa). In early Chosŏn, the military examination was functioning as was intended, and the institution staffed the military branch of the bureaucracy, which included centrally-appointed provincial officials. It is also noteworthy that the last known office held during the bureaucratic careers of nearly half of the military examination graduates was a civil office. Many were important, prestigious posts, including those of chief state councillor, minister of war, second counselor (Chikchehak), inspector-general (Taesahŏn), and provincial governor. In fact, among those degree holders whose career information is available, 22 men (a little under 10 percent) held such a post. Clearly, opportunities for advancement among the fifteenth-century military examination graduates were not limited to military offices.[64]

In the first half of the fifteenth century, military examination passers even enjoyed faster promotions than their civil counterparts. Besides the frequent northern military campaigns that gave them opportunities to serve the state with distinction, incompleteness of the nine-rank bureaucratic hierarchy—not all levels of it had a military post available—often enabled those being promoted to receive whatever higher military office was available. All this changed in the latter half of the fifteenth century, when the northern border situation had settled and, with the completion of the Five Guards system, all the military posts were in place. The pace of promotion for military examination graduates began to slow.[65]

Though the state sought to remedy a situation in which an increasing number of military examination graduates found their careers stymied, opportunities continued to narrow from the late fifteenth century. Worse yet, successful military examination candidates as a whole found it increasingly difficult to get even an initial appointment after earning their degrees.[66] Slightly more than half of the known degree holders from 1495 to 1591 attained a post of at least junior fourth rank—representing a noticeable decline from the previous century's figure.[67] Given that the percentage of passers for whom there is any appointment information also declined sharply, it seems that the appointment prospects for the sixteenth-century graduates dimmed significantly. On the other hand, the percentage of passers whose last known offices were civil posts changed little from the previous century. This suggests that military examination graduates who managed to join officialdom enjoyed political stature comparable to that of their predecessors.[68]

These trends make more sense when considered in conjunction with broader demographic changes; Korea's population increased from some four to five million at the dynasty's beginning to between seven and nine million in 1500.[69] As we have already seen, the number of military examination passers also increased during the same period, probably as a reflection of overall population growth. In contrast, the number of positions in the central government remained essentially fixed throughout the whole Chosŏn period, comprising 1,779 civil and 3,826 military posts at the time of the compilation of the 1469 *Great Code of State Administration*.[70]

As the overall competition for offices intensified, military examination graduates became more dependent on the patronage of influential statesmen. In 1548, an Office of the Censor-General (Saganwŏn) official criticized Chief State Councillor Yi Ki (1476–1552)—who was a powerful political ally of the king's maternal uncles—and his son, Yi Wŏn-u (1512–70; passed the military examination in 1549), accusing them of corruption and claiming that many military men flocked to them for favors.[71] And in a lengthy memorial submitted to the throne in 1557, the censor-general (Taesagan) noted that district magistracies went to the relatives of the powerful or to fortune seekers.[72] In 1564, when the government investigated some provincial army commanders for allowing their sons to compete in the military examination's preliminary tests held in their respective jurisdictions, the king pardoned them upon advice from senior officials. An official historian noted in the *Veritable Records* (*Sillok*) that the outcome reflected the king's maternal uncle's intervention on behalf of one of the commanders, all of whom were his underlings.[73]

In January 1543, problems associated with the military examination led to the nullification of the results. Involved officials indicated the following: (1) the examiners in Ch'ungch'ŏng Province helped their relatives and associates pass the examination; (2) other examination candidates, angered by this, rioted; (3) the examiners in Seoul favored certain individuals during the archery test; and (4) individuals of ineligible social status groups attempted to compete.[74] All four complaints involved western central Korea, suggesting that corruption in the military examination administration was more common where central officials and their kinsmen generally resided.[75]

These complaints, along with other similar contemporary observations, suggest that major political players maintained a client network of military examination passers. Of course, military men were important in insuring their patron's physical security during a period of political conflict. Although violent struggle subsided after the victory of a royal in-law faction over its rival in 1545, the victors nonetheless had to protect themselves against conspiracy, if not a countercoup. In this poisoned atmosphere, the dominant faction recruited a large number of military men loyal to it through the military examination. At the same time, many rapacious frontier military officials, such as garrison or port commanders, lacked the prescribed qualifications as military examination passers or elite royal guards; a good number of them got their positions through political connections while many better qualified military examination graduates and former elite guards remained jobless.[76]

The problem of spreading unemployment among military examination graduates was also linked to changes in the kinds of appointments available to them. In the fifteenth century, new degree holders were commonly appointed as commander's staff officers (*kun'gwan*), but this was no longer true by the mid-sixteenth century, when provincial army and navy commanders are said to have filled the slots with well-connected street thugs and illegitimate sons. In the early sixteenth century, the government decided to appoint jobless graduates as commander's staff officers so they could gain necessary experience before becoming border military officials, but the employment prospects for the new degree holders did not improve.[77]

Other types of appointments that military examination passers had once received became less available. Supernumerary (*kwŏnji*) assignments at various government agencies became so scarce that by the mid-sixteenth century only the Military Training Agency (Hullyŏnwŏn) assignments were still available.[78] The growing perception that military examination graduates were unsuitable as magistrates also hindered their promotion. Despite the state's efforts during the previous century, they came to be viewed as narrowly trained soldiers rather than as potential commanders or administrators with broad knowledge.[79]

The generally decreased political stature of military examination passers was reflected in their exclusion from the diplomatic missions Korea dispatched to China. Yi Su-gwang (1563–1628), an eminent scholar-official who frequently visited China, noted that from the dynasty's "middle period" (*chungse*) one could not be included in the entourage unless he was a civil official.[80] He could have meant some point midway between the beginning of the Chosŏn period and his own time, perhaps the early sixteenth century, but we cannot be sure. To be more exact about when the exclusion of military officials became standard practice, we can turn to a relevant statement by Ŏ Suk-kwŏn, who was a talented literary figure of illegitimate son–descent, and was active into the early sixteenth century. According to him, Cho Yun-son, who passed the military examination in 1502 and became the minister of war in 1536, was still included in a Korean diplomatic mission to Beijing.[81] We can then surmise that it was sometime in the mid-sixteenth century or thereafter that the court stopped assigning such duties to military men.

In spite of narrowed career opportunities and lowered prestige, military examination graduates continued to be regarded as men of martial skills specially trained for security-related tasks. Many not only became border region magistrates but even gained appointment as the magistrates of whatever districts that had special policing concerns. Since banditry was more common during the sixteenth century than in the previous decades, such districts were predictable destinations for many military examination passers.[82]

At the same time that the number of military examination graduates increased, the number of deployable troops decreased. Regional command garrisons disintegrated not only because *yangban* men were avoiding military duties, but also because commanders opted to use commoner draftees and substitutes for corvée labor rather than actual military functions.[83] Rather than relying on military examination graduates, from the mid-sixteenth century—when the Japanese and Jurchen raiders created more troubles—the central government resorted to dispatching civil officials entrusted with concurrent military command responsibilities to the flash points. Such officials were given only a small number of troops and were expected to recruit more on the way. Considering that the power of provincial army and navy commanders, usually military examination graduates, had also been reduced by this period, it is not surprising that the overall political stature of military examination passers decreased markedly.[84]

Continuing Aristocratic Domination of the Military Examination

Beginning in the late fifteenth century, the breakdown of the early Chosŏn military organization and growing external military pressure exposed conflicts between the state's interests and those of the *yangban.* Even though the state gradually eased restrictions against excluded groups, and despite the diminishing prestige of the military examination, the aristocracy sought to maintain its dominance among graduates. Incumbent officials designed policies that effectively excluded the non-*yangban* social elements wielding the greatest potential to compete successfully. Although no specific legal restrictions barred commoners, most could not invest years in rigorous preparation. This meant that the aristocracy continued virtually to monopolize both the civil and the military examinations, and thus to ensure control of the state by its members. For this reason, early Chosŏn *yangban* did not specialize in one type of examination.[85]

Throughout the first two centuries of Chosŏn rule, earning an examination degree had social implications, and the state regulated the availability of such degrees. In theory, both the civil and military examinations were open to any man not forbidden by legal constraint. The *Great Code of State Administration*, promulgated in the late fifteenth century, prohibited the following from the examination: (1) enfeoffed members of the royal family (*chongch'in*); (2) *hallyang*, the countryside descendents of Koryŏ central officials; (3) elite guards married to a non-*yangban* wife; (4) illegitimate sons and their descendants; (5) sons and grandsons of remarried mothers and other women deemed lacking in the cardinal Confucian virtue of chastity; (6) state criminals permanently barred from holding an office; and (7) the lowborn, including slaves and holders of certain socially despised occupations.[86] Though these restrictions imply that the majority of the population could participate in the examination, in reality this was not the case.

Why did the *Great Code* bar the king's descendants? Fifteenth-century court debates over the question of participation in the examination by enfeoffed members of the royal family expose the conflict between ruler and the aristocracy over this issue. Enfeoffed royal kinsmen, defined by law to include a monarch's direct male descendants down to the great-great-grandson's generation, enjoyed guaranteed income and even exemptions from the stigma of illegitimacy, regardless of the mother's social status. When kings occasionally allowed favorites to take the less rigorous military examination, with its promise of official appointment, *yangban* officials protested. At issue was the potential threat of permitting royal kinsmen—rapidly increasing in number due to the many sons produced by some early Chosŏn monarchs—to enter the regular bureaucracy. The concerns that drove the *yangban* protest were twofold: they worried about greater competition for positions and feared that a larger segment of officialdom would come to represent the interests of the royal family.[87]

A fundamental basis for the virtual *yangban* monopoly over the state examinations lay in the legal restrictions that barred other capable competitors, including illegitimate sons and hereditary local functionaries.[88] Although regulations changed constantly, the general logic behind excluding illegitimate sons seems to have been a moral one; the stigma of the mother's low social status and the less-than-respectable nature of her tie to the *yangban* father disqualified their offspring and descendants from holding an office.

In contrast, more practical concerns drove the exclusion of local functionaries. The state, bent on ensuring a steady supply of manpower for local administrative duties, shortly after the 1392 dynastic change forced functionary obligations upon central officials of the third rank or below who had formerly been local functionaries and lacked an examination degree or special merit.[89] Even though they had to perform often onerous administrative duties in the headquarters of provincial governors and district magistrates, functionaries received neither salary income nor the rank land (*kwajŏn*) that constituted a prebendal grant for a central bureaucratic rank holder. These policies made it virtually impossible for local functionaries to compete in the state examination.[90]

Yet another social group with the potential to pass the examination but who nevertheless were barred from it were *hallyang*. They seem to have been the descendents of late Koryŏ central officials who had relocated to the countryside and established themselves as locally influential figures, thereby effectively replacing rural functionaries as the local elite. Toward the end of Koryŏ, some of their descendants managed to acquire ranks and offices through military merit or the examination, and the newly instituted rank land law of 1391 allocated a minimal prebendal grant for them.[91] Beginning in the early fifteenth century, the government sought to cultivate the *hallyang* martial character by instituting local military competitions (*tosi*).[92] The special treatment accorded them, along with the members of the royal house, civil and military officials, soldiers, and other petty officials providing service to the state, shows that the state viewed *hallyang* as marginal members of a more broadly defined ruling aristocracy, if not quite as unemployed *yangban*.[93] By the late fifteenth century, they tended to be men who, generally from families of significant socioeconomic means, possessed some literacy and martial talent and yet were unrecorded on the household, army, or student registers.[94] It was on account of their failure to perform an officially recognized service to the state that *hallyang* were barred from the examination.

As legal constraints effectively excluded other groups that commanded literacy or martial talent, bona fide *yangban* were the only ones with a realistic chance of competing successfully in the military examination. Most commoners may have been legally eligible to sit for an examination, but their lack of resources effectively prevented their participation; this, despite the state's token efforts, described in the all-too-common lip service of *yangban* officials, to support public schools and avoid scheduling examinations during planting or harvest seasons. Even if a candidate acquired sufficient erudition for a military examination, the martial skill component involving horsemanship favored those who were wealthy enough to possess, train, and bring their own horses to the competition.

Available data shows that the majority of military examination passers tended to be protection appointees, acting or former military officials, or elite royal guards at the time they received the degree.[95] In fact, the father of a military examination passer could well be a high-ranking civil official, a politically prominent figure, or even an enfeoffed member of the royal family who had to be a king's great-grandson or closer. Since even less distinguished fathers still tended to be licentiates or degreeless scholars (*yuhak*)—both generally *yangban* status categories—it is clear that fifteenth-century military examination graduates were likely to be from *yangban* backgrounds.[96]

Yangban status itself was not a uniform guarantee of success, for an individual's descent group (*pon'gwan ssijok*) and, in earlier years, region of origin, were also significant factors. A descent group comprises consanguineal kin presumed to share common lineal descent. Identified by a surname and an ancestral seat (*pon'gwan*), each descent group boasts an established narrative that generally glorifies the achievements of *yangban* scholar-official ancestors, real or not. In early Chosŏn, the most successful descent groups produced a disproportionately large number of degree holders, and they tended to have their respective ancestral seats in two southernmost regions, Chŏlla and Kyŏngsang Provinces.[97] The latter was home to many localized descent groups known for the scholar-officials who joined central officialdom in late Koryŏ by passing the examination. Located in the warmer part of Korea, these provinces were traditionally the most fertile agricultural regions. Thus, the predominance of southern-origin descent groups among the military examination graduates may be explained, at least in part, by the significant advances made in agrarian technology and the consequently expanded socioeconomic base in the late Koryŏ–early Chosŏn periods.[98]

An early Chosŏn descent group could be diverse in its social composition, thus rendering it difficult to determine how closely related were the military examination passers among members, or whether they had any civil examination graduates among their relatives. The concept of lineage is not useful for this period, because the early Chosŏn *yangban* did not yet subscribe to this notion of a strictly patrilineage-oriented kinship organization.[99] Prevalent in Koryŏ was not so much a lineage as a cognatic kinship group with a more flexible structure, as agnates, affines, and matrilateral kinsmen could all be important, depending on changing needs. Reflecting these patterns was the persistence of the ancient uxorilocal marriage practice, which persisted well into early Chosŏn, and according to which children often grew up in their mother's natal homes.[100]

Despite these ambiguities, for the sake of convenience we can define a "close" patrilineal kinship group with a boundary set at the third-cousin (*p'alch'on*) radius, since it circumscribed the formal Confucian mourning group (*tangnae*).[101] Using this approach to analyze the descent groups represented among the fifteenth-century military examination graduates reveals several trends. First of all, even though a degree holder might still live in the locale of his ancestral seat, the place generally was not his family's only place of residence, because a powerful *yangban* could maintain multiple residences or estates throughout the country. Second, some descent groups consisted of segments that were geographically dispersed and genealogically distant from one another, with some unable even to demonstrate a relationship. Third, many degree holders came from prominent *yangban* descent lines encompassing both conservative merit subjects and reformist Neo-Confucian scholar-officials.[102] Considering that we are only looking at the close patrilineal kinsmen of a military examination passer, we can expect even greater diversity if matrilateral and non-agnatic kinsmen were to be considered.

The early Chosŏn pattern of *yangban* domination of the military examination continued into the sixteenth century. Even as the northern border crisis was renewed during the second half of the century, military examination passers tended to be from *yangban* backgrounds.[103] In fact, in 1525 the sons and grandsons of military examination graduates, civil examination passers, or licentiates, and those having an official of at least junior fifth rank among the "four ancestors" (father, grandfather, great-grandfather, and maternal grandfather) were all exempted from being shipped off to to the frontier region—even if they were convicted of crimes and sentenced to serve hard time.[104] Thus, the sixteenth-century military examination degree holders not only tended to be *yangban* but were also regarded by the state as members of the privileged aristocracy.

All the same, during this period the government began allowing an important new social element to compete in the military examination: the *hallyang*.[105] What prompted the state to let these *hallyang* compete in the military examination was the acute shortage of manpower for the new Jurchen Quelling Guards (Chŏngnowi) established in 1512.[106] For the hardship and danger associated with this assignment, the recruits received an incentive: after first serving as Jurchen Quelling Guards in the north, they were allowed to transfer to the more highly regarded royal guard units based in the capital. The arrangement provided a welcome new opportunity for *hallyang* to achieve the background necessary to compete in the military examination.[107]

This then begs the question: in whose interest was it that formerly barred *hallyang* were allowed to participate in the military examination? After all, why would the state let them in if the ranks—that is, the corps of military examination degree holders—were already swollen? The breakdown of the early Chosŏn military organization founded on the principle of universal military service was clearly in evidence by the early sixteenth century, and thus the state must have seen in *hallyang* a potential supply pool for the military. It could hold out the status attendant to a military examination degree as an incentive without letting such degree holders overcrowd central officialdom: after all, a military examination degree in the sixteenth century still entitled even a non-*yangban* passer, with or without an office, to treatment as a government official, and in this sense the prestige was comparable to that of the civil examination. For the *hallyang,* perhaps, the degree itself continued to appeal to those who wanted to maintain social status. Such an appeal must have been especially strong among those of lower *yangban* standing, as well as the commoners of means.

Due to the growing external threat, even illegitimate sons won permission to compete in the late sixteenth century examinations albeit, again, without receiving meaningful access to officialdom. This breakthrough came in 1583—a few days after a massive Jurchen attack—with a new measure that made those who had served garrison duties in the north for three years eligible for the civil and military examinations.[108] Thus, the primary catalyst for the change was the growing external security threat presented by the Japanese and Jurchens. The latter had been increasing for several decades and created a sense of crisis in Chosŏn Korea as well as Ming China.[109]

The growing Japanese threat from the sea also spurred the Chosŏn state to lure men into the military. For over a century the Japanese had been permitted by the Chosŏn government to engage in a limited, tightly regulated trade at designated ports in southern Korea.[110] The arrangement hardly satisfied the needs of Japanese traders, who could sometimes turn into raiders. In 1556, a year after a massive raid, the alarmed Chosŏn government administered a special military examination that recruited two hundred men. This was the first time since the two large-scale competitions in 1460 that a military examination produced more than one hundred graduates. Additional military examinations of this sort followed in the latter half of the sixteenth century.[111]

Throughout this period of escalating military crisis, the Chosŏn government enjoyed little success in strengthening the country's military defense, much of which it geared toward meeting the Jurchen challenge from the north. From about 1550, the Jurchen tribesmen began raiding the northeastern frontier regions of Ming China with greater audacity, and soon began making forays into northeastern Korea. Their attacks culminated in 1583, with a large-scale offensive that, after some initial setbacks, the Koreans managed to repulse. The perceived urgency of the situation in the north led to more frequent, larger-scale military examinations that recruited men for northern garrisons.[112]

Although desperation led the government to ease restrictions on *hallyang,* illegitimate sons, and even slaves taking the military examination, the degree continued to lure *yangban* men.[113] In fact, the majority of sixteenth-century military examination passers tended to be protection appointees, acting or former low-level military officials, or elite royal guards at the time of the degree.[114] Also present were degreeless scholars (*yuhak*) and registered provincial school students (*kyosaeng*).[115] In contrast to the fifteenth-century graduates, though, this group also includes members who clearly were not *yangban,* including the Jurchen Quelling Guards, hereditary government functionaries (*sŏri, hyangni*), students of local functionary background who had permission to study for the examination (*kongsaeng*), and even commoner infantrymen (*chŏngbyŏng*).[116] All the same, non-*yangban* elements still did not represent a significant segment of the body of military examination graduates of this period.

Most degree holders' fathers were *yangban.* Among them we find civil or military officials, enfeoffment title recipients, rank holders, elite guardsmen, civil or military examination graduates, licentiates, and degreeless scholars.[117] Though all these men most likely were *yangban* in social status, some clearly non-*yangban* fathers are to be found too, such as township headmen (*hojang*), who were upper-stratum local functionaries, and commoner infantrymen.[118] Overall, the fathers were more likely than the sons to have performed a service unequivocally indicative of *yangban* status. This pattern suggests that as far as a particular descent line over several generations is concerned, intergenerational downward mobility was a social reality in the sixteenth century, as *yangban* fathers continued to produce children by concubines of a lower social status. Of course such children were not *yangban* by birth.[119]

Descent group information too shows that sixteenth-century military examination passers tended to be *yangban.* The scant ancestral seat information, available for just 216 out of the 1,060 passers recorded on the ten extant rosters of this period, still speaks to several salient characteristics. A large number of successful military examination candidates came from a relatively close-knit kinship group descended from a recent apical figure. Second, such men were likely to be from a descent line with a history of military examination success during the previous century. Third, the sixteenth-century passers were somewhat less likely than their fifteenth-century predecessors to have a civil examination passer within the third-cousin radius. In fact, the sixteenth-century passers hailed from less politically prominent descent lines, although some did have merit subjects and the members of various political factions among their relatives. Fourth, the most successful descent groups represented among the passers from the south were likely to have their ancestral origins in the south, although those with ancestral seats in Kyŏngsang Province typically enjoyed better success in the military examination than did those based in Chŏlla Province. Regardless of the province of ancestral origin, however, a descent group could comprise segments dispersed over a wide geographical area as well as genealogically distant branches. Finally, a line that had clearly been established in the capital for several generations could still have its members recorded in the local agency officer registers (*hyangan*) for the countryside locale from which the descent group originated.[120]

As the capital of the new Chosŏn dynasty, Seoul remained the political center of the country. Although the two southern provinces still fared well during this period, passers residing in the capital dominated the military examination. This is because the military examination graduates hailed from the same Seoul-based descent lines that were producing *yangban* officials in general. In fact, the consistently strong representation of residents of western central Korea (Kyŏnggi, northern Ch'ungch'ŏng, southern Hwanghae, and western Kangwŏn regions) among the passers suggests that the central aristocracy based in and around Seoul continued to dominate the military examination.[121]

One might expect that northerners, presumably hardened by the harsher climate and Jurchen raids, would be the most successful among the provincial candidates for the military examination. On the contrary, the two northernmost provinces of Hamgyŏng and P'yŏngan fared worse than the two southernmost provinces of Chŏlla and Kyŏngsang, even though their combined populations were comparable. Though by the mid-fourteenth century the Koryŏ state had reclaimed all the northern territories annexed earlier by the Mongols, no major influx of Korean population into the region commenced until the fifteenth century. At that time, the Chosŏn government initiated a policy, continuing throughout the sixteenth century, of massive transfer of southern peasants. As relatively new settlers, northern residents of this period still may have been less capable of competing successfully in the *yangban*-dominated military examination due to economic and cultural shortfalls.[122]

Moreover, as discussed in Chapter 3, the central aristocracy deemed the north devoid of *yangban* and discriminated against the residents for their alleged cultural backwardness. Beginning in the seventeenth century, the native sons would become more competitive in the civil and military examinations, due to the region's attainment of cultural sophistication and the efforts of various kings who sought to tap into local talent in order to bolster royal power. Nonetheless, the central *yangban* prejudice continued to exclude them from more important positions in the government.

No indications in the records of the sixteenth-century military examination passers, regardless of their region, suggest that there were separate civil and military aristocracies among *yangban* in terms of their adoption and marriage practices. A *yangban* was not hampered by any civil-military divide in considering his or his male kin's bureaucratic branch affiliation, a candidate for adoption, or a family with which to contract marriage.[123] What fundamentally mattered was not so much the career orientation as the *yangban* social status itself. In other words, early Chosŏn Korea did not differentiate between civil and military aristocracies in any meaningful sense.

Summation

In tenth-century Koryŏ, the state established a complex central bureaucracy in which the personnel of civil and military branches made up the *yangban*. Initially, civil officials were superior to military officials in power and status, but after the 1170 military revolt they merged into a single *yangban* aristocracy that by the end of Koryŏ became an ascriptive status group comprising not just the officials but also their relatives and descendants. Military men became politically prominent again in the 1350s due to the state's reliance on their private armies in dealing with renewed military crisis. Although by then the examination system assumed greater importance as the state's primary recruitment method, it also became a tool by which the aristocracy reaffirmed its prestige and privileges.

In the decades after the 1392 dynastic change, the early Chosŏn state successfully reorganized the military and brought it under full control. In addition to abolishing private armies in 1400, the effort also entailed the establishment, in 1402, of the military examination system in order to recruit candidates equipped with a good knowledge of the classics and competency in martial skills. Balancing the two proved to be difficult, and the aristocracy did not regard military examination graduates as highly as their civil counterparts. Nevertheless the northern military campaigns and internal political instability of the mid-fifteenth century created a demand for capable military men. They generally received appropriate military posts, and many even attained important, high-level civil offices. Since the state effectively barred the *hallyang,* illegitimate sons, and hereditary local functionaries from the military examination, and since legally eligible commoners lacked the means to invest years of rigorous study, the aristocracy dominated the military examination. Not yet specializing in just one examination subject, *yangban* descent groups produced both civil and military officials, and marriage ties between civil and military officials were common.

In the sixteenth century, military examination graduates continued to receive appointments and even achieve important, high-ranking civil posts, but their overall employment prospects deteriorated. In the mid-sixteenth-century political climate, dominated by royal in-laws and their associates, those with powerful connections were more likely to get offices and enjoyed faster promotions. In part due to the desire of regimes to recruit loyal military men in an era of intensifying factional strife, the state more or less gave up on a serious effort to insure that military examination graduates thoroughly mastered the classics in addition to martial skills. Moreover, the renewed security crisis provoked by Jurchen and Japanese military pressures in the second half of the century spurred the government to hold larger-scale military examinations more frequently; the examinations served as an expedient means, after the collapse of the early Chosŏn system of universal military service, of raising an army. In a departure from the policy of the previous century, the increasingly desperate state eased restrictions on competition in the military examination by the *hallyang,* illegitimate sons, and even slaves. Nonetheless, the contest continued to be dominated by *yangban* who did not concentrate on just one type of examination and still formed marriage ties without making any civil-military distinction. As we will see, all these patterns changed in the seventeenth century.

TWO

The Rise of a Military Aristocracy

In Chosŏn Korea, the highest status group, the *yangban,* whose membership was determined by birth, was virtually synonymous with ruling officialdom. To secure its hold on the country's complex bureaucracy, the *yangban* sought to ensure that their members attained expertise in various areas of knowledge and thus occupied at least all the decision-making positions throughout the state machinery. The civil and the military branches mattered most. The Confucian *yangban* generally held literary virtue in higher esteem than martial virtue. However, due to the late Koryŏ merger of previously distinct civil and military elites, and the equal institutional status of the civil and military examinations, Chosŏn *yangban* could consider both branches as potential career tracks. Thus, an aristocratic descent group of early Chosŏn generally produced both civil and military officials and, as we saw in the previous chapter, made no civil-military distinction when contracting marriage ties within the status group.

All the same, the division of roles even among the ranks of the *yangban* continued throughout the Chosŏn period. If the 1392 dynastic change marked the effective exclusion of local functionaries from the central power structure and produced a sharp status boundary that demarcated the *yangban,* then the subsequent centuries witnessed the emergence of other, more finely differentiated, status groups and subgroups. By the late Chosŏn period, we see not only distinct technical specialist *chungin* descent lines, but also various subcategories of *yangban* that differed from one another in terms of their civil-military branch affiliation and the extent of their participation in the central political arena.

No laws dictated that a *yangban* family or individual choose a particular career or affiliation, and yet the late Chosŏn aristocracy came to consist of politically and functionally distinct subgroups. One segment of the aristocracy specialized in military careers for generations, while others mostly produced civil officials or, in the case of southern local aristocracy, no officials. By the late Chosŏn, the consequences of a descent group's affiliation were marked: central military officials were subordinated to their civil counterparts. Not only did a glass ceiling limit promotions, but, especially during periods of violent factionalism, the military official descent groups had to play supporting, albeit still important, political roles. Though scholars have tended to attribute increased opportunities for nonelites to various institutional changes to the military examination, of comparable importance was the interaction between these changes and the evolving position of the *yangban* military descent groups. This chapter thus analyzes two seemingly contradictory but ultimately interrelated trends: the simultaneous rise of a military aristocracy and the devaluation—only to an extent—of the military examination system as it became more open to nonelites.

The Military Examination System after 1592

Korea was unprepared for Japanese attack in 1592. Unlike the Jurchens, whose increasingly frequent, larger-scale border raids had forced King Sŏnjo's court to take action in the north, the Japanese threat caused disagreement among Sŏnjo's most influential officials over how to interpret the limited body of reports on the wars of unification in Japan and the ambitions of the unifier, Toyotomi Hideyoshi (1536–98). The massive Japanese forces initially overwhelmed what remained of the early Chosŏn military organization, which was being transformed from a system of universal military service into a smaller, mixed army of professional and drafted soldiers. The desperate state relied on local militia forces organized by *yangban* who were eager to defend their positions and who lacked confidence in government troops. Under the capable leadership of Yi Sun-sin (1545–98), the navy won one battle after another and prevented the Japanese navy from providing better logistical support for long-term operations in central and northern Korea. But the Chosŏn army, even after it became more effective under the generalship of Kwŏn Yul (1537–99), suffered from limited manpower and court factionalism that often hindered effective leadership. When Ming troops came to Chosŏn's aid, their arrival was marred by incompetence and mutual jealousy; however, this intervention was crucial in ultimately driving the Japanese out of Korea in 1598.[1]

Despite obvious exigencies, policymakers were able to enact only modest military reforms during the war and the subsequent decades. It had been years since the troop strength of the early Chosŏn Five Guards (Owi) and provincial garrison armies declined to the point of rendering them ineffective, but the political factionalism that had roiled court politics prior to the war compromised the state's ability to carry out a military reform based on a rational system of tax levies and manpower mobilization.[2] Although Sŏnjo had been presented with a pair of muskets in the summer of 1589 by the Lord of Tsushima, his court did not order the large-scale manufacture of muskets—nor instruction in firing them—until after the outbreak of the war. It was only in late 1593 that musket shooting replaced wooden arrow archery in the military examination.[3] Moreover, in 1593 the Military Training Administration (Hullyŏn Togam) was set up to train the "three skills army" (*samsubyŏng*)—musketeers (*p'osu*), bowmen (*sasu*), and close-combat "killers" (*salsu,* comprising swordsmen, pikemen, and spearmen)—under the influence of the Ming military strategies of Qi Jiguang (1528–88). The subsequent establishment of the Royal Division Command (Ŏyŏngch'ŏng, 1623), the Anti-Manchu Division Command (Ch'ongyungch'ŏng, 1624), the Namhan Fort Defense Command (Suŏch'ŏng, 1626), and the Forbidden Guard Division (Kŭmwiyŏng, 1682) completed what came to be known as the Five Military Divisions (Ogunyŏng), replacing the by-then defunct capital army of Five Guards. This organizational structure lasted until the dynasty's final decades.[4] Except for the Military Training Administration army, which consisted of permanent, professional soldiers paid by the government, the rest, beginning with the Royal Division Soldiers (Ŏyŏnggun), maintained rotating-duty soldiers and support taxpayers whose military cloth tax paid for the former's expenses, probably by making the payment to the soldiers' commanders.[5]

In the provinces, the government set up the *sogo* (Ch. *shuwu*) army, based on Qi Jiguang's late Ming military organization, the so-called

Zhejiang system. Designed to counter piracy, the Zhejiang system relied on small units—the *shuwu*—and a hierarchical organization that incorporated soldiers trained in firearms into the ranks of regular troops. Adopting these same principles, the Chosŏn *sogo* army drew heavily from nonelites. Commoner recruits tended to be those who could not buy their way out of military obligation; illegitimate sons and slaves—or their masters in some cases—were lured by various incentives. After their service, illegitimate sons were eligible for the state examination whereas public slaves were manumitted. The government recruited private slaves by compensating their owners with ranks or substitute slaves. The slaves themselves received no benefits. The provincial *sogo* soldiers paid their own expenses, unlike the central army soldiers who, when on duty, were supported by the government or support taxpayers.[6]

In principle, all adult males except slaves were responsible for the military cloth tax to support the army soldiers in the capital, but in reality the tax system suffered from much inefficiency and corruption as well as increasingly common evasion by *yangban*. The unreliability of tribute contractors in delivering promised goods finally prompted the government to undertake a tax reform. In 1608, the Uniform Land Tax Law (*taedongpŏp*) began replacing tribute with a surtax on land, province by province, and by 1708 it had been put into effect throughout the whole country. Designed to make peasants pay a fixed amount of tax based on the productivity of land, the reform shifted some of the burden from peasants to large landlords, and government revenue increased.[7]

Geared toward improving the financial health of the state and the livelihood of the people, the general levy system reform culminated in 1750 with the Equal Service Law (*kyunyŏkpŏp*). At the center of the debate that preceded it was whether to levy the military cloth tax also on the *yangban*, most of whom by then had come to view the exemption as a hereditary marker of their status. King Yŏngjo (r. 1724–76) first agreed to tax *yangban*. Faced with opposition from his officials, he yielded and settled for simply cutting the rate for commoners in half. The law replicated the practice of garrison commanders who had already reduced the rate as a means of inducing more commoners to pay the cloth tax. The government tried to make up the shortfall by requiring upper-class commoners with ranks or offices to pay as well—formerly they enjoyed what amounted to a tax-exemption benefit—while still exempting bona fide *yangban*. In the end, state revenue was reduced, but not by half, because Yŏngjo added new taxes to offset the loss.[8]

In spite of all the tax and military reforms meant to make military organization more effective, one form of seemingly persistent inefficiency was the steady increase in both the frequency of military examinations and the number of passers. Whereas 7,785 men passed the military examination from 1402 to 1591, anywhere from more than 20,000 to some 40,000 candidates did so from 1592 to 1607, and 121,623 from 1608 to 1894.[9] This last figure is more than fifteen times greater than the number in early Chosŏn prior to 1592. Many late Chosŏn military examinations resulted in awarding the degree to hundreds—occasionally even thousands—of candidates at a time. Whereas from 1402 through 1591 the military examination was administered probably around 160 times, from 1592 to 1894 it was held at least 535 times—the frequency increasing from roughly once every fifteen months to once every six months.

The earliest signs that the military examination was producing far more degree holders than the military branch of officialdom could absorb were visible well before the Korean-Japanese war. As discussed in the previous chapter, the number of military examinations producing one hundred passers or more increased markedly; this happened just twice in the fifteenth century but at least six times during the sixteenth century prior to the war—in 1556, 1583 (twice), 1584, 1589, and 1591.[10] This increase pales in comparison to that which took place during the war, when the government held at least three military examinations, each recruiting over one thousand candidates. Wartime military examinations were held without matching civil examinations, a practice which had no known antebellum precedent.

All these trends can be explained in some part by the cataclysmic military crisis posed by the war. Desperate to mobilize manpower, the government even promised a military examination degree to anyone presenting a specified number of enemy heads and capable of passing a simplified martial skills test.[11] During the four years that elapsed between the recovery of Seoul from the Japanese in 1593 and the renewed major Japanese offensive in 1597, all those who could hit the archery target even once are said to have been awarded the degree without being tested on classics exposition.[12] According to the censorate's report in the summer of 1592, requirements for the military examination were so lax that among the candidates were many who had never even held a bow, as well as large numbers of elderly men and frail children.[13]

Far from diminishing the prestige of a degree, such easy requirements inflated the number of aspirants and bolstered the ideology supporting their aspirations. The famous scholar-official Sŏng Hon (1535–98), for example, suggesting ways to increase recruits during the war, explained that receiving an examination degree was a great honor for the people.[14] Indeed, the appeal was such that the desperate government could use the military examination to round up a large number of men on short notice. For example, in the summer of 1592 while taking refuge in Ŭiju, Sŏnjo's court held a military examination to recruit fighters from neighboring districts, and thanks to these men the security inside the city walls is said to have improved.[15] The military examination degree was so coveted that in spite of a widespread famine that saw corpses piled along the roads, those from the south who took the military examination are said to have bought the degree certificate with five *toe* (equivalent to 50 dry measures) of rice each.[16] Contemporary observations vividly describe the reality of the wartime military examination administration:

> As the recruitment through the military examination was large-scale during the Korean-Japanese war, a single examination roster recording a great number of graduates could include thousands of those who had competed without mastering archery. All together they numbered several tens of thousands, including some who were lowborn. For the most part, the military examination was given to raise popular morale, and it was of no practical use. Moreover, the stature of the examination was lowered. Whether he was a public slave or a private slave, anyone presenting a Japanese head was permitted to proceed to the examination. Some even cut off the head of those who had died from starvation, claiming that it was a Japanese head, and demanded a reward. In Yŏngnam [Kyŏngsang Province], one individual earned his military examination degree by cutting off a head, and the district magistrate of his locale hosted a party to celebrate the feat.[17]

As soon as the war was over, Korea had to confront the Jurchen military threat in the north, with yet further consequences for the military examination system.[18] Escalating tension in the north prompted the government to administer the military examination even more frequently in order to recruit a large number of candidates. Reflecting the desperate situation, military examinations were again occasionally held without a corresponding civil examination.[19] The menace itself was not new, but by Kwanghaegun's reign (1608–23) various Jurchen tribes had become united under a dynamic new leader, Nurhaci (1559–1626). In 1616, he founded a new empire, Later Jin (renamed Qing in 1636), and pursued ambitions beyond Manchuria that included Ming China.

Kwanghaegun did his best to stay out of the escalating conflict between the Later Jin and Ming empires, but once Nurhaci formally declared war on Ming in 1618, the latter's persistent demand for military aid became difficult to ignore. Consequently, Kwanghaegun was compelled to order Korea's first military action since the Korean-Japanese war. In the following year, his army of thirteen thousand was routed in Manchuria during a joint military action with Ming, and the Korean commander surrendered to the enemy after losing half his troops.[20] Logistical and tactical problems in working with inept Ming commanders were partially to blame, but the outcome also revealed that neither the Chosŏn military reorganization effort after 1592 nor the frequent military examinations had produced a quick dividend.

Nonetheless, military examinations, sometimes recruiting hundreds of men or more, became established practice. In the same year, the Border Defense Command—which had increased its power during the Korean-Japanese war at the expense of the Board of War—estimated the necessary troop strength for the northern border at about 40,000, and Kwanghaegun ordered the dispatch of tens of thousands of military examination passers recruited during and since the war.[21] He furthermore calculated—on the basis of a large-scale courtyard military examination that had recruited some 3,200 candidates in the previous year—that it would not be difficult to obtain a trained army of some 100,000 if every province were to recruit men through a less rigorous military examination.[22] Escalating tension along the northern border prompted the court in 1619 to dispatch to all provinces royal secretaries (Sŭngji) conveying the king's order for an emergency military examination. Consequently, in 1620, more than 10,000 candidates are said to have been recruited, giving rise to what contemporaries termed "10,000-men examinations" (*mankwa*).[23] Another courtyard military examination recruited 4,031 men in 1621. In 1636, the government, which by then was faced with a second Manchu (formerly known as

Jurchen) invasion, held a military examination in P'yŏngan Province for any man desiring to take to the battlefields, regardless of whether he was from the region; 10,000 men were recruited in this way.[24] All in all, the scale of the military examinations given to reinforce northern defenses exceeded that of any of the competitions held for the same purpose before 1592.

Just as the antebellum military examinations did little to enhance Korea's initial military capability against the Japanese invaders in 1592, the postwar examinations contributed little to battlefield effectiveness against the Manchus and show how the nature or purpose of the examinations had changed. Besides the disastrous dispatch to aid Ming in Manchuria in 1619, the successive Manchu invasions of Korea in 1627 and 1637 demonstrated that the government had failed to turn the thousands of passers of frequent military examinations into battle-worthy soldiers. In August 1636, for example, King Injo (r. 1623–49) received a progress report from his officials that claimed that 7,000 troops would be needed to defend the border town of Ŭiju, at the mouth of the Yalu River, against the expected Manchu invasion. Since the latest military examination had recruited 6,000 men from the northwest to supplement the 1,000 already in the available army, defense was feasible.[25] At the end of the year, however, before the court could station all the recent recruits at strategic locations and have the supplies in place, the Manchus invaded with an army of 120,000. Bypassing all the defensive strongpoints, they penetrated Korea with lightning speed, reaching Seoul in just thirteen days.

Given the government's dependence on fortress-oriented resistance and, during the second invasion, on the armies raised by provincial governors, we have to wonder about the purpose of the military examination system's expansion during this period. As was true before the Japanese invasion of 1592, frequent military examinations seem to have resulted from a desperate government's search for an expedient means of mobilizing enough military manpower while putting together the new *sogo* army and various units of the greater capital area—all of which together did not yield enough troop strength to stop the invaders.

Even after Korea's submission to the Manchus in 1637, the practice of frequent, large-scale military examinations saw no end. In fact, the

Table 2.1
Military Examinations Producing 1,000 or More Passers, 1608–1894

Year	Examination type	Passers	Reason for holding examination
1618	Courtyard	3,200	Troop request from Ming China
1620	Courtyard	3,000 +	Troop request from Ming China
1621	Courtyard	4,031	Troop request from Ming China
1637	Courtyard	5,536	Expected Manchu invasion
1651	Special	1,236	Northern Expedition
1676	Courtyard	17,652	Northern Expedition
1784	Courtyard	2,692	Crown prince's enfeoffment
1882	Special	2,600 +	Queen's recovery from illness
1889	Royal Visitation	2,513	King's visit to Confucian Academy
1894	Triennial	1,147	Regular triennial competition

SOURCE: Military examination rosters, *Sillok, Sŭngjŏngwŏn ilgi, Mukwa ch'ongyo, Kyonam kwabangnok,* and Chŏng Hae-ŭn, "Chosŏn hugi mukwa kŭpcheja yŏn'gu."

"10,000-men examination" phenomenon continued throughout late Chosŏn. From the beginning of Kwanghaegun's reign in 1608 to the abolition of the examination system in 1894, 254 out of 477 total military examinations (53 percent) awarded the degree to at least one hundred candidates. In fact, over the whole course of the military examination system's existence from 1402 to 1894, there were fourteen military examinations that each produced more than one thousand successful candidates. Of those fourteen, ten were held during the period from 1608 to 1894 (Table 2.1).

Was the late Chosŏn state seeking to maintain preparedness in the face of a foreign military threat? After the Korean-Japanese war, the two sides maintained peaceful, if not amicable, relations until the mid-nineteenth century, and their periodic exchange of envoys (*t'ongsinsa*) even facilitated cultural interaction.[26] The northern power, Qing China, however, loomed large in the minds of kings and statesmen after Korea's defeat by the Manchus in 1637. As Table 2.1 shows, large-scale late Chosŏn military examinations were given in 1651 and 1676, as part of the Northern Expedition (*pukpŏl*) policy formulated during the reign of King Hyojong (1649–59), which entailed a secret preparation for attacking Qing.[27] To test the mettle of his fighters as well as to observe the state of Qing military capability, Hyojong also responded to Qing requests for troops—with the mission of driving the Russian explorers from Manchuria—by dispatching some 150 musketeers in 1654 and over 260 mixed troops in 1658.

After Hyojong's death, his immediate successors and officials discussed the Northern Expedition on an occasional basis but still maintained some hope of vengeance. The court carefully monitored the situation in China and felt especially encouraged by the massive Rebellion of the Three Feudatories (1673–81), which the Qing government took eight years to suppress. During the rebellion, the Chosŏn government could only wonder if Qing power was now in decline, and as part of an overall preparation for battle, administered in 1676 the largest military examination ever held. The court discussions as documented in the *Veritable Records* show that it was not until the Qing state crushed the rebellion (in 1681) and finally brought Ming-loyalist Taiwan under control (in 1683) that the Chosŏn government, despite anti-Manchu sentiment that persisted well into the eighteenth century, became fully resigned to the fact that the Qing empire was too powerful to confront.

Though hope of attacking Qing waned, the late Chosŏn state continued to administer frequent large-scale military examinations. As Table 2.1 shows, four of the ten between 1608 and 1894 that produced at least one thousand passers were held in the eighteenth and nineteenth centuries (in 1784, 1882, 1889, and 1894), when the government clearly had no intention of fighting against China or Japan. The French and American attacks in 1866 and 1871 spurred the government to strengthen musketeer and artillerymen units, and on each occasion the technologically superior enemy withdrew after stiff Korean resistance. By the early 1870s, however, the court seems to have concluded that Korea had successfully repelled the Western "barbarians."

If the perception of foreign military threat does not explain the frequent, large-scale military examinations in late Chosŏn, does one explanation lie in the state's concern over internal security? The government did confront possible coups and rebellions during this period, even though the only successful challenge was the 1623 coup that deposed the reigning king. The new king and his successors managed to suppress all subsequent challenges to the regime, including the rebellions by Yi Kwal (1624), Yi In-jwa (1728), Hong Kyŏng-nae (1812), and the Tonghak ("Eastern Learning") religious leaders (1894)—to cite only the major attempts.[28] Compared to the 1624 and 1728 rebellions, which were more like power struggles among *yangban* political players and were crushed within a month, both nineteenth-century uprisings were rooted in more fundamental social problems affecting the lives of the marginalized and nonelites, with each taking months to neutralize. In fact, the 1894 Tonghak uprising—an organized internal revolt of unprecedented scale that fielded well over one hundred thousand fighters—could possibly have forced the government to accept all its demands had the Japanese army not intervened to crush it. It seems possible, then, that although the frequent, large-scale military examinations of late Chosŏn may have helped the government maintain and field armies capable of defeating small rebel forces, that capability had clearly reached its limit by the late nineteenth century, when social discontent rose to a critical level.

In order to understand the possible link between the military examination and social discontent, we need to consider the process wherein examinations and degree holders proliferated. There were three major factors: the frequency of large-scale examinations in general and irregular special examinations in particular; the number of men, especially those from Seoul, who were allowed to proceed straight to the final stage of the examination; and the participation by nonelite social elements. Let us examine the first, returning to the last two in Chapters 3 and 5.

The rise in the number of "augmented examinations" (*chŭnggwangsi*), which were given on felicitous occasions for the royal family, and other types of irregular special examinations partially accounts for the increased frequency of the examination. The number of regular triennial examinations, augmented examinations, and other special examinations held from 1402 to 1607 were, respectively, 67, 13, and 150, whereas the corresponding figures from 1608 to 1894 were 93, 54, and 338. From early to late Chosŏn, the regular triennial examination continued to be given every three years, but augmented examinations that had previously been held once every fifteen to sixteen years came to be administered every five to six years. Other special examinations became even more frequent, with the average interval decreasing to just ten months, instead of ranging from one to two years, as it had previously.

Among the irregular competitions, the augmented examinations held on joyous occasions for the royal house became especially more frequent. In early Chosŏn, augmented examinations were held only when a new king ascended the throne, but from 1589 on, the list of possible occasions steadily expanded to include the following: the king's recovery from an illness; longevity celebrations for the king, queen, and queen mother; the birth of a royal heir; the heir's entry into school; the official designation of the heir apparent as crown prince; and the renovation of a royal palace.[29] An augmented examination thus publicized felicitous occasions for the royal family and ultimately enhanced the dignity of the dynasty. This was, of course, a political objective of fundamental importance for a monarchical system.

Besides the augmented examinations, other irregular special examinations also became more frequent in late Chosŏn. Listed in order of frequency, these included 194 palace courtyard examinations, 56 royal visitation examinations (*alsŏngsi*), 53 unspecified special examinations, 32 regional special examinations (*oebang pyŏlsi*), 23 Ch'undangdae examinations (*ch'undangdaesi*), 10 special provincial examinations (*tokwa*), and 9 miscellaneous competitions.[30] Courtyard examinations in particular were especially frequent in comparison to early Chosŏn, as were the royal visitation and regional special examinations. In contrast, regional special examinations and special provincial examinations were administered in specific locales or provinces. The locations varied in early Chosŏn, but in the later period these examinations tended to be given most frequently in either P'yŏngan or Hamgyŏng Province, the two regions least well represented in central officialdom.[31]

The government generally administered the regular triennial examinations in a more consistent manner. The type of military examination that granted degrees can be determined for 120,845 passers from 1608 to 1894; Table 2.2 shows the breakdown according to the examination category.[32] Although both the augmented and triennial contests technically were subject to quotas and set procedures, contemporaries regarded the actual martial skill requirements of the former as the least rigorous among all types of military examinations. Presumably, the triennial competition was thus the most highly regarded among the military examinations.[33]

Late Chosŏn Critiques of the Military Examination System

Various problems associated with the military examination after 1592 elicited more detailed, lengthier critique from policymakers than ever

Table 2.2
Types of Military Examination and Number of Passers, 1608–1894

Examination type	Passers	Percentage
Courtyard	69,809	57.76
Special	16,616	13.75
Triennial	13,064	11.81
Augmented	6,587	5.45
Regional Special	6,178	5.11
Royal Visitation	5,507	4.56
Ch'undangdae	1,902	1.57
Special Provincial	1,089	0.90
Others	93	0.08

SOURCE: Military examination rosters, *Sillok, Sŭngjŏngwŏn ilgi, Mukwa ch'ongyo, Kyonam kwabangnok,* and Chŏng Hae-ŭn, "Chosŏn hugi mukwa kŭpcheja yŏn'gu."
NOTE: Due to rounding, percentages may not total 100.00.

before. Critics argued that overly frequent military examinations produced more degree holders than could be accommodated in state positions, and that social problems would arise from a surplus of uncommissioned military examination graduates. Passers, these critics suggested, needed to be potential military commanders, equipped with a broad knowledge of the classics as well as martial skills. Sensitive to the vital importance of good military men to the state's well-being, some critics preferred even a recommendation system to the existing military examination system, which was plagued with abuses. Nonetheless, *yangban* continued to take and pass the military examination, and some began specializing in military careers. In addition to exploring these issues raised by contemporary observers, this section also explains how the aristocracy—in fact, an emerging body of central military official descent lines—continued to use the military examination system to its advantage in spite of the institution's seemingly lowered prestige.

In the seventeenth century, many policymakers called for military examination reform. The civil official Ch'oe Myŏng-gil (1586–1647) was particularly specific in describing the harm of producing too many military examination graduates. A key figure in the dominant Westerner (Sŏin) faction (see Figure 2.1) that had engineered the 1623 coup and gained power, Ch'oe listed the following problems: (1) a decrease in the number of actual soldiers; (2) increasing complaints directed at the government by unemployed degree holders; and (3) the lowered integrity associated with an official career. He noted that the fundamental reason the military examination had come to recruit men indiscriminately—that is, without regard to the adverse effects of large-scale recruitment—had to do with the urgency of manning the frontier garrisons.[34]

One of the most influential figures of the time to comment on the issue was Song Si-yŏl (1607–89). Leader of the Westerners and, later, the Patriarchs (Noron), Song was an intellectual titan of his era who defended the conservative positions of earlier Neo-Confucian scholars of China and Korea. Coming of age during the era of Manchu invasions and the subsequent humiliation of his country, Song provided the ideological foundation for advocates of revenge against Qing, especially as articulated through King Hyojong's Northern Expedition preparation. He saw military examination reform as an urgent matter, as is evident in one of his memorials to the throne:

> The 10,000-men examination of military men has become a chaotic abuse. With their number approaching twenty thousand, these passers all flock to Seoul in search of an official appointment; upon failing to obtain a post, they resent the state. The scarcity of rice in Seoul arises from this problem [of so many passers sojourning in the city] as well, and the number of farmers is dwindling [due to the large number of provincials who are wandering around in Seoul after passing the military examination]. In your servant's humble opinion, . . . if each district magistrate were to test the men of his locale and recommend the most outstanding among them to his provincial army commander, then the commander could bring them together, test them again, select the outstanding, and recommend them to the Board of War. The Board could then select the outstanding among them for an official appointment. In this way, since tens of thousands of men can each return to the countryside to farm the land on the one hand and hone their martial skills on the other, the public and the private alike, as well as both the capital and the countryside, will benefit.[35]

Taken at face value, Song's proposal is an overly idealistic formula that is merely a variant of the recommendation (*ch'ŏn'gŏ*) system that Confucianists had favored over an examination system through the ages. But Song was far from being a Neo-Confucian recluse with no understanding of the reality of the military recruitment system of his time. Like Ch'oe Myŏng-gil and other influential Westerner faction civil

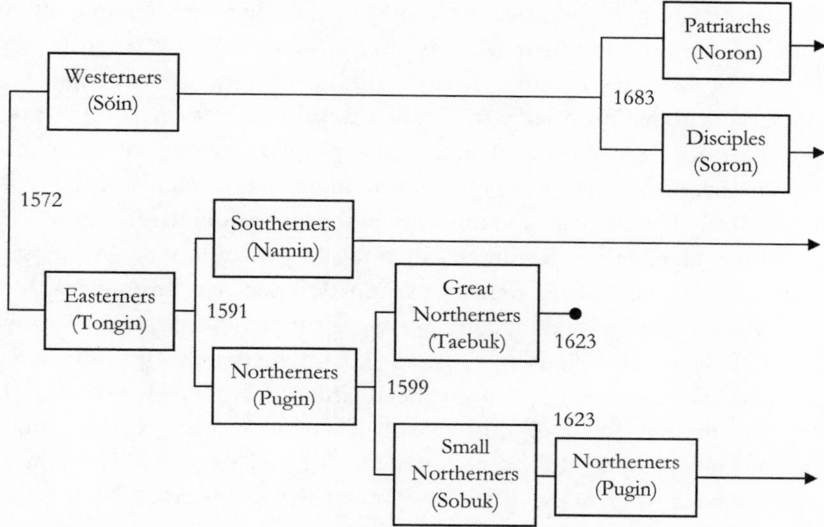

Figure 2.1 Late Chosŏn Factional Lineage. This is a simplified chart showing the factions mentioned in the text. The Easterners and the reconstituted post-1623 Northerners are not discussed in this study and are shown only for reference.

officials, Song associated with military men who, themselves Westerners, had taken part in the coup that brought the faction to power in 1623 and had provided security for the regime ever since.[36]

Song's affinity with military men and understanding of military matters compelled him in 1669 to oppose the prevalent view at court, which advocated appointing the P'yŏngan provincial army commander from among the ranks of civil officials. This proposal was advanced on the grounds that the greater prestige of a civil official over a military official would better insure that subordinates would carry out the provincial army commander's orders. Song agreed with the reasoning itself, but he expressed concern that the measure would demoralize military officials. Instead, he suggested a compromise approach of alternating between civil and military officials, stressing that what mattered was not so much the civil-military distinction as the appointee's abilities. King Hyŏnjong (r. 1659–74) followed Song's recommendation.[37]

One problem with the military examination that concerned Song and other influential statesmen derived from the particulars of the political context after 1623. Considering that the Westerner faction's grip on power was not entirely secure, and that during Injo's reign it needed the cooperation of a group of moderate Southerners (Namin) as a junior coalition partner, it is likely that influential Westerner officials like Ch'oe Myŏng-gil were alarmed by the proliferation of unemployed military examination passers, many of whom were not loyal to the ruling faction.[38] As is discussed later in this chapter, creation of and control over various military regiments were important elements of the factional struggle that peaked in intensity in the late seventeenth century.

At any rate, as the comments by Song Si-yŏl and Ch'oe Myŏng-gil imply, the prestige of the military examination declined throughout this period, and royal policies sought to reverse the trend. Injo, for instance, appointed *yangban* military men of outstanding martial talent to the mid-level or even third-rank posts of the Board of Revenue (Hojo), Board of Punishments (Hyŏngjo), or Board of Public Works (Kongjo), and bestowed bows and horses on martially talented *yangban*.[39] The king's appointment of military officials to more civil posts must have been driven also by his determination to expand the military's role in society in preparation for attacking the Manchus, but the policy continued into Hyŏnjong's reign even after the Northern Expedition preparation had been abandoned.

Arguably the most active military examination reform efforts were undertaken during the subsequent reign of Sukchong (1674–1720). In 1676, a military examination recruited for a possible attack against Qing generated an unprecedented number of 17,652 passers. This was such an unmanageable number that the degree ceremony had to be conducted *outside* one of the palace gates, even though the tradition was to honor the candidates in the royal palace courtyard in the presence of the king.[40] As discussed in detail in Chapter 5, this particular military examination not only contributed to the serious social problem of unemployed military examination graduates, some of whom committed crimes to survive in Seoul, it further lowered the prestige of the military examination in the eyes of *yangban*. In 1686, after hearing that *yangban* passers numbered not even a score among some 17,000 graduates of the 1676 examination, Sukchong stressed the importance of both literary and martial virtues for the state and ordered that any officials with several sons have some of them learn martial skills. He even punished at least one official for flagrantly refusing the royal command.[41]

Some of Sukchong's most influential officials claimed that the aristocracy and the military examination were incompatible. A military examination graduate and military official hailing from a prominent military *yangban* family, Sin Yŏ-ch'ŏl (1634–1701) explained that ever since the advent of the 10,000-men examinations, many military examination passers had grown old while unemployed and that such graduates were even looked down upon by protection appointees—to the extent that the sons of *yangban* scholar-officials preferred to remain poor literati rather than take the military examination. Examining the problem from another angle, the senior civil official Nam Ku-man (1629–1711) noted that, whereas the Chinese military examination recruited only a small number of candidates, truly employable by the state and tested on martial skills and strategies for defending the country against internal and external enemies, the Korean military examination had a couple of fundamental problems. On the one hand, its classics exposition component was so easy that even commoners could get by; on the other hand, the sons of *yangban* scholar-officials, who were more capable of explaining the classics, tended to lack adequate martial skills. Accordingly, Nam advocated raising the recruitment standard while reducing the number of degrees awarded.[42]

In spite of these observations on the problems of the military examination, and despite Sukchong's apparent dedication to reform, no fundamental change took place. Frustrated, Sukchong lamented in 1690 that though literary and martial virtues were one when it came to an official's loyalty to the state, the recent military examination rosters did not include any sons of *yangban* scholar-officials. He took this as a clear sign that *yangban* did not devote themselves to martial endeavors (*muŏp*).[43] The king then ordered the restoration of the then-defunct Office for Promotion of Martial Education (Kwŏnmuch'ŏng), which his father Hyŏnjong had set up in 1662.[44] Such a program supplemented the earlier measure of 1679, which stipulated a system of "Confucian general recommendation" (*yujangch'ŏn*) for selecting civil officials with the potential to become good commanders in the provincial army or navy.[45]

This had little effect. Various problems associated with the military examinations persisted into the eighteenth century. The Practical Learning (*Sirhak*) scholar Chŏng Yag-yong (1762–1836), in his famous early nineteenth-century reform treatise entitled *A Book from the Heart on Gov-*

erning the People (*Mongmin simsŏ*), identified five problems that apparently continued to plague the military examination of his time: (1) assaults by candidates from influential Seoul families on those from the countryside in order to prevent them from competing in an upcoming examination; (2) widespread unemployment among degree holders; (3) the government's registration of such men on the army draft register (*kunjŏk*) and its burdening them with a military cloth tax; (4) the excesses of 10,000-men examinations; and (5) the hiring of substitutes by the candidates to take the examination in their places.[46] An especially common form of the last problem was to hire a substitute archer (*taesa*) for the archery test—arguably the most important component of the military examination during much of the dynasty.

In evaluating Chŏng's allegations, Song Chun-ho rightly asks *why* the late Chosŏn government recruited so many military examination graduates and *who* these degree holders were.[47] As we have already seen, the diminishing foreign military threat does not explain the frequent, often large-scale military examinations throughout the late Chosŏn period. More fundamental reasons were the need to suppress any internal uprisings and to keep the population content. At the very least, the state had to maintain a pool of capable military men large enough to suppress internal rebellions, which it did with success even into the nineteenth century. However, the 1812 Hong Kyŏng-nae rebellion in the northwest made clear that although the state could still suppress such a rebellion, social discontent remained unresolved if not more intense.

Indeed, contemporary observations that refer to the social function of the military examination are numerous. In 1663, for example, Second Censor (Sagan) Min Yu-jung (1630–87), a powerful Westerner figure and also a royal in-law, noted that the remote northeast was not benefiting adequately from the virtues of royal grace and that what few military examination passers the region could claim had only recently passed a 10,000-men military examination.[48] In 1677, when Seventh State Councillor (Uch'amch'an) Hong U-wŏn (1605–87), a reputable Southerner statesman with a strong interest in issues related to government institutions, submitted a memorial to the throne, he noted that 10,000-men examinations were intended to make the people happy.[49] And in 1773, when King Yŏngjo asked a man from remote Cheju Island what had brought him from afar, the latter explained that he wanted to participate in a 10,000-men military examination in celebration of his majesty's advanced age.[50] These and countless similar comments throughout late Chosŏn clearly show that large-scale military examinations during times of peace served the social function of publicizing felicitous occasions for the royal house in particular and uplifting the spirit of the people in general.

The question of who earned the degrees is no less important. All the seventeenth-century observations we have considered so far seem to demonstrate that the military examination did not appeal to most *yangban.* Song Chun-ho, however, has contradicted this assumption by suggesting that the passers actually may have been from influential *yangban* descent lines in Seoul after all.[51] Both Chŏng Hae-ŭn and I have been following this lead for some time. As is discussed later in this chapter, we have found that a certain segment of the military examination passer population did continue to hail from aristocratic central military official descent lines based in the capital.

If nothing else, the average age at the time of the degree suggests that, for example, teenaged peasants of good health could not easily pass the military examination. For the military examination passers in my database, the average age at the time of the degree was 32.5 *se.*[52] This is similar to the civil examination passers. It represents a slight increase from 31.1 *se* for the period before 1608. The military examination requirements may have been substantially downgraded, but, along with other forms of evidence, the average degree-earning age in the early 30s still shows that passing the military examination was an achievement. Considering that most late Chosŏn men married as teenagers and could easily have several children—natural or adopted—by the age of 30 *se,* we can surmise that a typical military examination passer had to devote more than a decade to adequate study and training to earn the degree—a feat that certainly was more difficult for those struggling to make ends meet. Even more telling is that the average age for the roughly 5,500 men who passed the 1637 courtyard examination was 37.7 *se,* and the average for the 2,692 men passing the 1784 courtyard examination was 34.0 *se.* Since both competitions are known for their large representation of nonelite passers, we can infer from this high average age that the military examination definitely favored men of means.

The Emergence of Central Military Official Descent Lines

The late Chosŏn aristocracy did not abandon the military examination. Not only did the military examination continue to function as a recruitment system for bringing new members into the military branch of officialdom, the main supply pool from which it drew was the aristocracy. Though the social base of military examination candidates was broader in late Chosŏn than in earlier periods, a relatively limited number of capital-based *yangban* descent groups produced the bulk of the successful military examination candidates as well as the majority of those who went on to have more meaningful careers in the central bureaucracy. The continued value of the military examination as a route to officialdom for *yangban* made it critical to define precisely who was eligible to participate in this genuine competition.

Because the late Chosŏn military examination system was a venue in which successful *yangban* candidates demonstrated their social status, increased participation by nonelites—many even competing illegally—was vexing for aristocrats. Seventh State Councillor Hong U-wŏn observed in 1677: "Abuses stemming from the 10,000-men examinations are truly troubling. Commoner scoundrels try to pass themselves off as members of the scholar-official group, and even the scholar-officials lacking in skills all try to obtain an office."[53] Late Chosŏn local gazetteers (*ŭpchi*) that document the success of native sons in the military examination record the degree holders on a much more selective basis than the civil examination graduates and licentiates, who were practically all *yangban*. They almost invariably omit military examination graduates of non-*yangban* status.[54]

Despite the military examination's lowered prestige and increased nonelite participation, *yangban* still made up a sizable block among the late Chosŏn military examination passers. According to Chŏng Hae-ŭn, 24.1 percent of late Chosŏn military examination passers were central office or rank holders. The rest were military regiment affiliates (*kunjik*, 33.3 percent), *hallyang* (34.1 percent), and members of miscellaneous groups (8.5 percent).[55] Of course, none of these four categories was homogeneous in terms of its constitution, and each requires more detailed analysis.

Defining the position of *hallyang* is crucial for assessing the degree of aristocratic participation in the military examination system. As we saw in Chapter 1, by the sixteenth century the *hallyang* had become men of means who were trained in the military arts, and thus the label allowed some ambiguity as far as the ascriptive status of the individual was concerned. In other words, not all *hallyang* were bona fide *yangban* at that point. In 1696, the state tried to clarify the definition, defining *hallyang* as dutyless *yangban* men who prepared for the military examination without performing any obligation to the state—including those who had previously been registered as degreeless scholars (*yuhak*). At the same time, the government redefined the service title of *ŏmmu*, which at that point had been degraded, to mean illegitimate sons with martial talent.[56] I will discuss the issue of devalued status categories in greater detail in Chapter 5.

In addition to *hallyang*, another sizable group among late Chosŏn military examination passers, the military regiment affiliate category, absorbed more and more social elements of non-*yangban* origin. Distinct from those who held court rank or an office in the central bureaucracy, regiment affiliates were purely army officers and soldiers. Such a military officer or soldier could potentially receive a court rank or an office as recognition for distinguished service, and the length of the "waiting period" tended to be short for the regiment affiliates of higher social status—not to mention the kind of court ranks or offices they received. At any rate, the military regiment affiliate data suggests even more clearly than the *hallyang* data that the social backgrounds of military examination degree holders were becoming more diverse. Again, Chapter 5 will focus more on this development.

Besides the officers and soldiers from various military units, court rank holders and officials consistently accounted for a large share of military examination passers throughout late Chosŏn. According to Chŏng Hae-ŭn, 3,988 out of the 16,575 late Chosŏn military examination graduates she analyzed were central office or rank holders at the time of receiving the degree (24.1 percent); this group may be broken down as follows: military office (53.6 percent), civil rank only (24.7 percent), military rank only (18.7 percent), and civil office (2.7 percent). Among military officeholders, 85.7 percent held a post in the Five Guards, which was defunct as the capital army by the end of the sixteenth century and existed in name only after the establishment of the Five Military Divisions. For those holding just a civil rank at the time of receiving the degree, their ranks tended to be strictly honorary in nature.[57]

Chŏng's data on central government rank holders and officials demonstrates that compared to early Chosŏn, many *yangban* marginalized in the central political structure were turning to the military examination. In particular, those who claimed to be *yangban*, without any obligation to the state while preparing for the military examination (a group that included *hallyang*), were becoming more common, whereas social elements that could not make such a claim were being squeezed out. In fact, those in the "miscellaneous" category in Chŏng's analysis decreased from 20.8 percent in the early seventeenth century to none in the late nineteenth century.[58]

Official complaints that no *yangban* were competing in the military examination were more a reaction to the perceived change from the early Chosŏn pattern than to the actual absence of *yangban* candidates. In fact, other types of evidence suggest that by the eighteenth century many *yangban* descent groups chose to send their sons to the military examination and a military official career. Thus, in 1784, a century after King Sukchong voiced his concern, his great-grandson, King Chŏngjo (r. 1776–1800), expressed satisfaction upon learning that the latest military examination roster recorded the names of young men from many distinguished *yangban* families.[59] And, in 1800, Chŏngjo was enormously pleased when a man from a family of "literacy and purity" (*munch'ŏng*) was reported to have abandoned his ink brush in favor of preparing for and passing the military examination.[60]

Contemporary observations and Chŏng Hae-ŭn's data together suggest that by the late eighteenth century, *yangban* were participating actively in the military examination. At this point in our discussion, we may very well ask: what kind of descent lines were represented among the successful examination candidates? One way to answer this question might be to look at the passers' surnames and ancestral seat (*pon'gwan*) designations. Together, the two labels ostensibly identify the bearer as a member of a descent group (*pon'gwan ssijok*) united by presumed direct, but not necessarily lineal, descent from the same apical ancestor.[61] The problem with this approach, however, is that any given late Chosŏn "descent group" could easily comprise many lineages or segments varying tremendously in political stature and social status. Just looking at the most commonly represented descent groups among the

Table 2.3
Descent Group Representation among Military Examination Passers, 1608–1894

Descent group	Known passers	Percentage
20 most successful descent groups		
Kimhae (Kim)	1,443	5.06
Chŏnju (Yi)	1,349	4.73
Miryang (Pak)	1,128	3.95
Kyŏngju (Kim)	626	2.19
Ch'ŏngju (Han)	466	1.63
Kyŏngju (Yi)	399	1.40
Chinju (Kang)	385	1.35
P'yŏngsan (Sin)	369	1.29
Namyang (Hong)	341	1.20
Kwangsan (Kim)	288	1.01
Haeju (O)	278	1.00
P'ap'yŏng (Yun)	262	0.97
Sunhŭng (An)	248	0.86
Chŏnju (Kim)	244	0.86
Chŏnŭi (Yi)	242	0.85
Kwangju (Yi)	240	0.84
Chŏnju (Ch'oe)	232	0.84
Andong (Kwŏn)	217	0.76
Kyŏngju (Ch'oe)	213	0.75
Andong (Kim, "Old" and "New")	204	0.72
Other 1,680+ descent groups	19,357	67.85
All 1,700+ descent groups	28,531	100.11

SOURCE: Examination rosters, *Mukwa ch'ongyo, Sillok, Kyonam kwabangnok, Honamji, Chosŏn sidae sach'an ŭpchi, Han'guk kŭndae ŭpchi, Chosŏn hwanyŏ sŭngnam,* other local gazetteers, and genealogies.
NOTE: Descent groups consist of ancestral seats followed by surnames in parentheses. Due to rounding, percentages do not total 100.00.

late Chosŏn military examination graduates makes this clear. Of the 28,531 who earned their degrees from 1608 to 1894, an incredible 4,546 men (15.9%) claimed membership in one of the four most successful descent groups (out of more than 1,700 different surname-ancestral seat combinations represented among the late Chosŏn passers). The top four were clan-like "umbrella" descent groups that encompassed members of diverse social position, from *yangban* down to the lowborn, as documented in late Chosŏn census registers. The twenty most successful descent groups account for 9,174 out of the 28,531 (32.2%) late Chosŏn military examination graduates (Table 2.3).

Since the highest-order descent group information is not all that useful, we need to look at the particular descent group segment or lineage from which the degree holder hailed. In late Chosŏn, many such passers came from a patrilineal kinship group that was clearly a lineage in the sense that it descended from an apical ancestor going back no more than ten to fifteen generations, continued to be based in a particular locale, and maintained a common political identity. In contrast, other military examination passers were from a larger descent group segment that was characterized by greater diversity in terms of its members' sociopolitical orientation and descended from an apical ancestor living much farther back in time. Accordingly in discussing late Chosŏn central military officials and their patrilineal kinship groups, I choose the more general concept of descent line while noting some unique characteristics of a particular case when appropriate.

The most useful sources for identifying prominent military lines of late Chosŏn are military examination graduate genealogies (*mubo*) that record the passers from eminent *yangban* descent lines. At their most complete, the genealogies record the successful candidate's given name, courtesy name (*cha*), examination type and year, and offices held after the degree, as well as the names, examination degrees, and offices of his patrilineal ancestors to eight generations, father-in-law, and maternal grandfather.[62] The underlying attitude behind the source, of course, is elitist.

Such genealogies, along with examination rosters and other sources, demonstrate that some descent lines enjoyed extraordinary success in the military examination.[63] Just a few of them account for a large portion of the late Chosŏn military examination passers hailing from the prominent descent lines of central military officials. For example, a total of 464 out of some 1,500 passers recorded in various military examination graduate genealogies (covering the period from about 1780 to 1894) comprise the following: 103 Tŏksu Yi passers descended from Admiral Yi Sun-sin; 96 Chŏnŭi Yi descended from Sixth State Councillor (Chwach'amch'an) Yi Chun-min (1525–90), a civil examination passer, who was a nephew of famous Neo-Confucian scholar Cho Sik (pen name Nammyŏng, 1501–72) and an admirer of another famed Neo-Confucian worthy, Yi I (pen name Yulgok, 1536–84); 72 Nŭngsŏng Ku descended from Kongju Magistrate (Moksa) Ku Yang (ca. 1380–?);

80 P'yŏngsan Sin descended from Ch'ungch'ŏng Provincial Governor Sin Cha-jun (ca. 1400–?), who was a minor merit subject (*wŏnjong kong-sin*) aiding Sejo's enthronement; 73 P'yŏngyang Cho descended from Cho In (ca. 1570–?), who deliberately refrained from government service during Kwanghaegun's reign and never held more than just a junior ninth-rank civil post; and 40 Suwŏn Paek descended from Prince's Tutor (Wangja Sabu) Paek Ik-kyŏn (?–1498), also a classics licentiate.[64] In other words, 6 out of more than 50 descent groups represented in these genealogies account for about 30 percent of the *yangban* military examination graduates recorded in them for the entire period.

Even more amazingly, the examination success of the six eminent descent lines of military men became more pronounced through late Chosŏn; roughly half of their graduates earned the degree during the nineteenth century.[65] Among the prominent military lines, especially remarkable are the Tŏksu Yi descended from Yi Sun-sin, and the P'yŏngyang Cho descendants of Cho In. Both were clearly cohesive lineages: 215 and 146 military examination graduates, respectively, descended from relatively recent genealogical apex figures, that is, from an ancestor living no earlier than the sixteenth century. Such genealogical distance is comparable to that typical of a prominent late Chosŏn central official family affiliated with a particular political faction.[66] In other words, it took less than three hundred years for the capital aristocracy to produce families associated with a particular branch of the officialdom.

Why Specialization?

Many factors contributed to the emergence of a military aristocracy. Those who were descended from famed military commanders of the Japanese and Manchu campaigns, along with those who were on the winning side of a political conflict, were encouraged by successive monarchs and ruling parties to pursue military careers. Other central official military lines arose due to political setbacks suffered by ancestors in mid-Chosŏn. Of course, a *yangban* descent line could be totally ruined by being on the losing side, but, when possible, it might subsequently concentrate on military careers. The phenomenon is best explained by the stature—both real and perceived—of the military examination and a military career in the eyes of the civil aristocracy.

Several cases illustrate how political setbacks affected a descent line's choice of examination type and career orientation. The *Veritable Records'* melodramatic account of the dying moments of Im Hyŏng-su (1504–47), a prominent Confucian scholar and a victim of factional strife, reports the following admonition: "Looking at his sons, he [Im] said: 'Although I did not do anything wrong, I have ultimately come to face this predicament. Do not take the examination.' Afterward, he spoke again: 'As for the military examination, take it if feasible; do not take the civil examination.' There was no hint of even the slightest loss of composure on his part."[67]

The motivations behind Im's urgings are not fully clear. It seems, though, that initially judging that his sons should avoid government service entirely, a moment later he deemed a military career, if feasible, worth pursuing. Perhaps he saw it as a less perilous career path than its civil counterpart. Interestingly, I have found no examination graduate, civil or military, among Im's direct male descendants in the genealogy, whereas his brother's line continued to produce civil examination passers for the remainder of Chosŏn.[68]

For an example of a political setback that forced a *yangban* descent line to become more strictly oriented toward the military branch, we might consider the case of a Miryang Pak descent group segment, known as the Kyujŏnggong "branch" (*p'a*). Descended from a mid-level late Koryŏ civil official, Pak Hyŏn (ca. 1250–1336), the branch's most politically influential line, based in Seoul, enjoyed impressive civil examination success in the early and mid-Chosŏn periods.[69] This came to an end in 1623, when two Small Northerner (Sobuk) statesmen—Chief State Councillor Pak Sŭng-jong (1562–1623) and his son, Kyŏnggi Provincial Governor Pak Cha-hŭng (1581–1623), who was also the father-in-law of Kwanghaegun's crown prince—committed suicide shortly after the Westerner-led coup and the king's dethronement. Both Sŭng-jong and Cha-hŭng were civil examination graduates, and six out of eight direct male ancestors of the father had passed the civil examination. After 1623, however, not a single civil examination passer is known among the son's direct male descendants. Like some Small Northerners that survived the 1623 coup, Sŭng-jong's collateral descendants became Westerners and also passed the military examination in large numbers for the remainder of the dynasty.[70] Cha-hŭng's father-in-law, Yi I-ch'ŏm (1560–1623)—who as a leader of the Great Northerners (Taebuk) had urged Kwanghaegun to kill three princes and put the queen mother under house arrest—was executed after the coup along with all of his sons that had passed the civil examination. In stark contrast to the Pak, only a few military examination passers (but no civil examination passers) and minor officeholders are known among their descendants.[71] In sum, the Great Northerners were totally eliminated from power after 1623, as illustrated by the case of Yi I-ch'ŏm's descendants, whereas the more moderate Small Northerners survived, albeit as military officials, in the case of Sŭng-jong's collateral descendants.

In contrast to these cases of political setbacks that forced a descent line to change its career orientation is the situation of the Tŏksu Yi lineage descended from Yi Sun-sin. Although Yi himself was not from a descent line known for military officials, his legendary naval victories against the Japanese between 1592 and 1598 seem to have encouraged his descendants to continue serving the state as military men, and the state reciprocated by giving them advancement opportunities. Almost all the direct male descendants of Yi Sun-sin who passed an examination chose the military examination and military careers. Most of them became high-level military officials and commanders during the remainder of Chosŏn period.[72]

The P'yŏngsan Sin military line descended from Sin Cha-jun is an analogous case. The majority of the late Chosŏn P'yŏngsan Sin military examination passers were descended from several sixteenth-century cousins, including a famous military commander, Sin Rip (1546–92), who committed suicide after failing to fight off the advancing Japanese army at the Battle of T'an'gŭmdae in 1592. After his death, the court appointed his son, Sin Kyŏng-jin (1575–1643), as a royal messenger (Sŏnjŏn'gwan), an entry-level assignment of bright prospects most often given to military examination candidates or recent graduates from prominent descent lines.[73] Besides his father's loyal service to the state, Kyŏng-jin had the right political connections: not only was his sister married to King Injo's paternal uncle, his father's sister was Injo's maternal grandmother.[74]

In general, the state encouraged descendants of meritorious military men to pursue military careers.[75] In 1764, for instance, King Yŏngjo instituted the "examination for the loyal and the good" (*ch'ungnyangkwa*) as a martial talent competition to test the descendants of those enshrined at the Hyŏnjŏlsa and Ch'ungyŏlsa, as well as the descendants of the Ming Chinese émigrés. He allowed the winners to proceed straight to the palace examination.[76] And, in 1774, Yŏngjo held a special examination for the descendants of loyal officials, followed in the next year by an "autumn extension examination" (*ch'ugaengsi*) for the descendants of merit subjects who had helped quell the Yi In-jwa rebellion in 1728.[77] Each of the aforementioned military lines of Seoul produced at least one military man who assisted the court in putting down this rebellion directed against Yŏngjo and his Patriarch faction supporters.

The emergence of a military aristocracy reflected the general late Chosŏn social trend toward specialization.[78] As we saw in Chapter 1, early Chosŏn *yangban* descent groups did not produce degree holders or officials in one particular part of central bureaucracy. The late Chosŏn trend toward specialization becomes more evident when we analyze a large patrilineal kinship group's pattern of examination success, and an instructive case is that of the largest Miryang Pak descent group segment, the Kyujŏnggong branch, which we examined earlier. The data on the percentage of Kyujŏnggong branch civil examination graduates for various types of degree holders among the patrilineal kinsmen of third-cousin distance or closer (Table 2.4) shows that in the course of Chosŏn, the likelihood of a civil examination passer having an examination passer among his close kinsmen decreased at different rates, depending on the examination subject. By the seventeenth century, it was unusual for a successful civil examination candidate to have a technical examination graduate among his close kinsmen. In comparison, it was not until the eighteenth century that less than half of the Kyujŏnggong branch civil examination graduates could claim a military examination passer among their close relatives. These patterns suggest that a distinctly military aristocracy was not clearly visible until the eighteenth century—the period when Chŏngjo would observe that many candidates from *yangban* families were taking the military examination.

The case of the Kyujŏnggong branch of the Miryang Pak shows that the pattern of a patrilineal kinship group concentrating on one examination subject was most pronounced for the technical examinations (Table 2.5). All but three technical examination passers from the branch

Table 2.4
Kyujŏnggong Branch Miryang Pak Civil Examination Passers with Degree Holding Relatives, 1393–1894

Period	All CE passers	With CE passer relative	With ME passer relative	With LE passer relative	With TE passer relative
1393–1500	13	13 (100.0%)	13 (100.0%)	13 (100.0%)	12 (92.3%)
1501–1600	9	9 (100.0%)	9 (100.0%)	9 (100.0%)	7 (77.8%)
1601–1700	21	21 (100.0%)	15 (71.4%)	19 (90.5%)	3 (14.3%)
1701–1800	30	24 (80.0%)	9 (30.0%)	21 (70.0%)	0 (0.0%)
1801–1894	24	8 (33.3%)	3 (12.5%)	6 (25.0%)	0 (0.0%)
TOTAL	97	75 (77.3%)	49 (50.5%)	68 (70.1%)	22 (22.7%)

SOURCE: Edward W. Wagner and Song Chun-ho, *CD-ROM Poju Chosŏn munkwa pangmok*; military examination rosters; Edward W. Wagner and Song Chun-ho, "Yijo sama pangmok chipsŏng"; Yi Sŏng-mu, Ch'oe Chin-ok, and Kim Hŭi-bok, eds., *Chosŏn sidae chapkwa hapkyŏkcha ch'ongnam*; *Chosŏn sidae sach'an ŭpchi*; *Han'guk kŭndae ŭpchi*; *Chosŏn hwanyŏ sŭngnam*; other local gazetteers; and genealogies.
NOTE: Key to abbreviations: CE = Civil Examination, ME = Military Examination, LE = Licentiate Examinations, TE = Technical Examinations

Table 2.5
Kyujŏnggong Branch Miryang Pak Technical Examination Passers with Degree Holding Relatives, 1393–1894

Period	All TE passers	With TE passer relative	With ME passer relative	With CE passer relative	With LE passer relative
1393–1500	0	n/a	n/a	n/a	n/a
1501–1600	6	6 (100.0%)	6 (100.0%)	6 (100.0%)	6 (100.0%)
1601–1700	13	12 (92.3%)	13 (100.0%)	0 (0.0%)	1 (7.7%)
1701–1800	9	9 (100.0%)	8 (88.9%)	0 (0.0%)	0 (0.0%)
1801–1894	12	12 (100.0%)	5 (41.7%)	0 (0.0%)	0 (0.0%)
TOTAL	40	39 (97.5%)	32 (80.0%)	6 (15.0%)	7 (17.5%)

SOURCE: Edward W. Wagner and Song Chun-ho, *CD-ROM Poju Chosŏn munkwa pangmok*; military examination rosters; Edward W. Wagner and Song Chun-ho, "Yijo sama pangmok chipsŏng"; Yi Sŏng-mu, Ch'oe Chin-ok, and Kim Hŭi-bok, eds., *Chosŏn sidae chapkwa hapkyŏkcha ch'ongnam*; *Chosŏn sidae sach'an ŭpchi*; *Han'guk kŭndae ŭpchi*; *Chosŏn hwanyŏ sŭngnam*; other local gazetteers; and genealogies.
NOTE: Key to abbreviations: CE = Civil Examination, ME = Military Examination, LE = Licentiate Examinations, TE = Technical Examinations

came from *chungin* descent lines: all three appear in the *Record of Surname Origins* (*Sŏngwŏnnok*), a nineteenth-century genealogical work recording technical specialist *chungin* lines. Among them, two continued to produce technical examination passers throughout late Chosŏn, whereas just one did so only in the seventeenth century. As for the three exceptions, they all earned their degrees in the early sixteenth century, and none apparently produced a descendant who passed a technical examination. Actually, two of the three men were illegitimate sons fathered by high-ranking civil officials enrolled as merit subjects, whereas the third passer was an illegitimate grandson of one of these two officials. Considering that none of these three illegitimate sons founded a technical specialist *chungin* line, it seems clear that descent groups focused in technical specialties arose only in late Chosŏn.[79]

An illustrative example of apparent segmentation within the Kyujŏnggong branch is a descent line that, by the eighteenth century, had assumed capital *chungin* status and come to specialize in military service. The line originated with Government Arsenal Third Secretary (Kun'gisi Pujŏng) Pak Ki-jong (?–?), a military examination passer. According to my military examination passer database and the *Record of Surname Origins* which leaves the majority of *chungin* descent lines untraced beyond mid-Chosŏn, Ki-jong was a first cousin of aforementioned High State Councillor Pak Sŭng-jong. Perhaps hinting at an illegitimate son somewhere in the intervening generations, however, Ki-jong and his descendants do not appear in any late Chosŏn or modern edition Kyujŏnggong branch genealogies that I have checked. At any rate, a great-grandson of his, Pae-wŏn (?–?), was one of the famous Eight Robust Ones (P'al Changsa) escorting King Hyojong during his captivity as a hostage in Shenyang. Interestingly, Pae-wŏn's younger brother, Hŭng-wŏn (1614–?), passed the famous 1637 Namhan Fort courtyard military examination that awarded degrees to some 5,500 men, a significant portion of whom were manumitted slaves and other nonelites who had taken part in the defense of the fort against the Manchus as we shall see in Chapter 5. Including the founder of the line, Ki-jong, 12 military examination passers are known from this military *chungin* descent group. They formed marriage ties to technical specialist or military *chungin* lineages, but certainly not to *yangban* officials—civil or military.[80]

Likewise, *yangban* descent lines of Seoul that specialized in the military examination and military careers did so for generations. In the case of the aforementioned Seoul military *yangban* lines, less than 10 percent of their eighteenth- and nineteenth-century military examination graduates could claim any civil examination passer among close agnates of third-cousin distance or less, although generally some licentiates could be found before 1800. The late Chosŏn Tŏksu Yi lineage descended from Yi Sun-sin, for example, produced only a single civil examination graduate, a tenth-generation descendant of the famed ancestor. Surrounded by a throng of military examination graduates, including a brother and seven generations of forefathers, this lone civil examination graduate earned his degree in 1875.[81] In contrast, the P'yŏngsan Sin descended from Sin Cha-jun and the Nŭngsŏng Ku descended from Ku Yang produced more civil examination graduates and licentiates, reflecting the political connections strengthened by both descent lines during the 1623 coup that brought Injo—their relative—to the throne.[82]

The Military Aristocracy and Politics

Although representing the upper echelon of all military examination passers in terms of family backgrounds and career prospects, the central military officials' political stature was inferior to that of their civil counterparts. Most military aristocrats received more strictly military-related offices, and the highest and the most prestigious civil offices were generally beyond their reach. Members of powerful civil official descent lines even got a significant share of the military division commander (Taejang, Yŏngjang) offices, the highest realistically attainable posts for military examination passers from renowned military *yangban* lines. Even the most influential military officials played a largely supporting role in court politics, although violent struggles entailed the competing factions' employment of their armed might.

The career paths of military examination passers varied. We saw earlier that although new military examination graduates were supposed to be assigned to supernumerary (*kwŏnji*) positions in various government agencies, many from mid-Chosŏn on remained unemployed, or at best were affiliated with one of the Five Military Divisions. Unlike common soldiers, however, the successful military examination candidates serving in the Five Military Divisions could hope eventually to receive an office, according to Chŏng Hae-ŭn's analysis of the military examinations' graduates from 1674 to 1800.[83]

The military examination graduates who managed a significant career in central officialdom tended to have a distinctive background. According to Kenneth Quinones's study, an overwhelming majority of military officials from 1864 to 1910 hailed from western central Korea, the *yangban* crescent, home to more than half of all central officials at the time.[84] Though a military examination degree alone far from guaranteed an official appointment, those military examination passers who actually became military officials were most likely to be from the prominent military lines based in and around Seoul.

Toward the end of their careers, such military examination graduates might even obtain the unlikely promotion to important, high-ranking civil posts. Whereas four military examination passers attained one of the top state councillor posts from 1402 to 1591, only three military men did so from 1592 to 1894.[85] All three cases after 1592 date from the seventeenth century: Chief State Councillor Sin Kyŏng-jin (degree earned in 1600, became Councillor in 1642), Second State Councillor Ku In-hu (degree in 1603, Councillor in 1653), and Third State Councillor Yi Wan (degree in 1624, Councillor in 1674). Both Sin and Ku were relatives of King Injo and commanded troops during the 1623 coup; Ku also suppressed a rebellion in 1644. As for Yi, he was actively involved in the Northern Expedition preparation of King Hyojong. Without a doubt, all three military men were powerful defenders of the ruling Westerner faction in general and the throne in particular.[86]

The achievements of other military examination passers from the central military aristocracy were not as impressive. Using various editions of military examination passer genealogies and other genealogical sources, I compiled a list of the highest known achievements—mostly actual official posts—of military examination graduates from the top military lines of the Tŏksu Yi, the Nŭngsŏng Ku, the P'yŏngyang Cho, and the Suwŏn Paek descent groups (Appendix A). Central and provincial military posts, as well as the border region magistracies (*pyŏnji*), were the most important, realistically attainable achievements for the majority of degree holders from the four prominent military lines. For those who advanced further, the high-level central civil offices attained by the passers tended to be no more than a viceministership, even in the Board of War, or one of the high-level—yet largely honorary—positions in the Office of Ministers-without-Portfolio (Chungch'ubu).[87]

Table 2.6
Military Division Commanders from Civil Examination Backgrounds, 1593–1882

Years	King	New MDC appointments	CE graduate appointees	Percentage
1593–1608	Sŏnjo	3	0	0.0
1608–1623	Kwanghaegun	11	1	9.1
1623–1649	Injo	13	1	7.7
1649–1659	Hyojong	5	0	0.0
1659–1674	Hyŏnjong	8	3	37.5
1674–1720	Sukchong	26	7	26.9
1720–1724	Kyŏngjong	2	1	50.0
1724–1776	Yŏngjo	30	7	23.3
1776–1800	Chŏngjo	18	6	33.3
1800–1834	Sunjo	23	5	21.7
1834–1849	Hŏnjong	14	3	21.4
1849–1864	Ch'ŏlchong	12	4	33.3
1864–1882	Kojong	33	8	24.2
TOTAL		198	46	23.2

SOURCE: "Tŭngdannok."
NOTE: Key to abbreviations: MDC = Military Division Commander; CE = Civil Examination

The military officials' limited share of military division commander appointments illustrates the overall situation. Although the aristocratic military men serving as division commanders were also members of the important deliberative organ, the Border Defense Command, its key commissioner (Chejo) appointments tended to be held concurrently by influential civil officials, who often served as the military division commander as well.[88] Table 2.6 shows that from the late seventeenth to the late nineteenth century, civil examination passers held 20 to 50 percent of the military division commander posts during a given reign.[89]

Of course, the military officials who received the remaining military division commander posts represented a tiny minority of all military examination passers. Considering that roughly one hundred thousand men passed the military examination from 1608 to 1882, during which period the court made just 195 new military division commander appointments, there can be no question that the late Chosŏn military division commanders were those who had most successful careers among their military examination passer peers.[90]

Compared to a military division commander appointment, a district magistracy was much more easily obtainable, especially for the members of the central military aristocracy. For most of the Chosŏn period, the coastal and border region magistrate appointments went to graduates of the civil or the military examination, whereas the inland assignments were given mostly to civil examination passers as well as some protection appointees. By the first half of the nineteenth century, however, the practice had changed: even protection appointees were being appointed as coastal and border region district magistrates, hence edging out the military examination graduates. This new pattern was symptomatic of the trend by which local magistrates in general were being drawn from Seoul's most politically influential descent lines. This was the period of court politics being dominated by oligarchic civil official descent lines, especially the likes of the royal in-law Andong Kim and P'ungyang Cho. Due to bribery, short tenures in office, and competition among the candidates, the successful bidders for magistrate positions tended to be from more prestigious descent lines, and went on to rapaciously milk their districts as much as possible.[91]

Considering that even the more easily obtainable post of magistrate increasingly went to men from top *yangban* descent groups, it is hardly surprising that the post-degree careers of military examination graduates varied tremendously depending on their social status.[92] We can divide their career paths into three categories: (1) those who had to be content with a devalued court rank or office, if not just the degree certificate itself; (2) those who became army officers either by serving a prescribed term of military duty or by doing well on various martial talent competitions held by individual regiments and possibly ending their careers with largely honorary court ranks or high-level offices; and (3) those who, in their late teens or early 20s, were registered with the Office of Royal Messengers for future appointment as a royal messenger through the so-called "special recommendation" (*pyŏlch'ŏn*), and, after passing the examination, received a series of provincial and military posts before attaining higher-ranking civil offices or military division commander posts.[93] The evidence we have considered so far, as well as plain common sense, tells us that the group of military examination graduates belonging to the third category must have been the smallest in number.

With the state's support, Seoul's military aristocracy continued to play an important role in late Chosŏn politics. Although this role was limited in comparison to that of the powerful central civil aristocracy, military examination passers nonetheless had to take sides in the factional strife.[94] For example, the highly politicized issue of whether Queen Inmok (1584–1632) should be stripped of her rank during Kwanghaegun's reign not only involved civil officials and literati with factional ties but also many military men, such as Yi Si-ŏn (?–1624), who submitted a pro-Great Northerner memorial urging the throne to remove the hapless lady from her position.[95]

It was especially during violent, armed political struggles that military men provided more specialized services befitting their training, and numerous are such examples from late Chosŏn. For example, the 1728 Yi In-jwa rebellion, organized by some extremists from the Disciple (Soron) and Southerner factions, forced military men to take sides. Yi Su-ryang (1673–1735) was one of many renowned military officials serving under civil official superiors who were generally Patriarchs. A military examination graduate from a central official descent line, he served as a cavalry (*mabyŏng*) Special Officer (Pyŏlchang) while putting down the rebellion. For this service he was subsequently enrolled as a third-class merit subject, received an enfeoffment title, and held top military posts for the remainder of his career.[96]

Other military men such as Nam T'ae-jing (?–1728) fought with the rebels. From an elite central official family, Nam was widely regarded as a henchman of the Disciple civil officials. Thus, upon Yŏngjo's accession in 1724, when many of the Disciples were purged by the Patriarchs, he too was dismissed. Later he was reappointed when Yŏngjo reinstated some of the Disciples, only to be executed in 1728, on dubious charges, at the time of the Yi In-jwa rebellion.[97]

At any given moment, a faction's control of various military divisions and allied military officers could be so thorough that a new faction gaining power had to carry out a wholesale change in military personnel, sometimes even creating an entirely new division. For example, during their brief period of ascendancy in the late seventeenth century, the Southerners created the Military Training Special Cavalry Unit (Hullyŏn Pyŏltae) to counter the Westerner-controlled divisions. Then, in the late eighteenth century, King Chŏngjo and his political supporters established the Robust Brave Guards (Changyongwi) as a new military unit free of the Faction of Principle (Pyŏkp'a) elements. During the previous reign, when Chŏngjo's grandfather King Yŏngjo had ordered the death of Prince Sado (1735–62), many officials continued to justify Yŏngjo's action and went on to constitute a powerful new political force, the Faction of Principle. Thus when Chŏngjo, the son of Sado, succeeded Yŏngjo, he could only view the faction as the potential source of challenge against his legitimacy as the ruler.[98]

Summation

The late Chosŏn state held military examinations frequently, even after the Japanese and Manchu military threats vanished. The contest often awarded the degree to hundreds, if not thousands, of candidates at one sitting, a radical departure from earlier practice. As a consequence, the prestige of the military examinations declined, and they elicited criticisms and reform proposals from policymakers.

All the same, the late Chosŏn military examination continued to legitimate officeholding in the military branch of the bureaucracy. In fact, the increasing domination of the civil branch of central government by a relatively small number of capital civil official descent groups of the *yangban* aristocracy resulted in the political marginalization of other *yangban*. Among the latter, some in Seoul turned to the military examination and careers in the military branch, reproducing themselves as a military aristocracy. The civil-military distinction became sharper, and by the eighteenth century it was uncommon for a *yangban* examination passer to have an immediate ancestor or a close relative (within third-cousin radius) passing a type of examination different from his own.

Military examination graduates from the central military aristocracy tended to receive only those appointments that were most directly related to military responsibilities. Access to the highest levels of central bureaucracy was restricted, and a significant share of even the military division commander posts went to the members of powerful central civil official descent groups. Instead, the military aristocrats enjoyed the patronage of oligarchic central civil aristocrats to whom they owed their political allegiance. Also, the state encouraged them to continue the legacy of their military hero ancestors, although some military descent lines emerged after the mid-Chosŏn political struggles that victimized their ancestors and marginalized their descendants. In sum, late Chosŏn witnessed the internal differentiation of the *yangban* status group into central civil official, central military official, and generally non-officeholding southern *yangban* lineages—to which we shall turn in Chapter 3.

THREE

Local Elites and the Military Examination

Beginning in the seventeenth century, degrees of political participation differentiated central and local elites in Korea. The former increasingly dominated the civil examination and politically meaningful central government offices at the latter's expense. The local elites responded variously, the circumstances differing from one region to another and from one period to the next. By the end of the eighteenth century, the elites based outside western central Korea generally managed to maintain elevated social status at the local level despite being effectively shut out at the center. For some, this meant turning to the military examination and military careers.

By "local" elite, I mean those who belonged to local resident kinship groups that occupied the highest position in the social hierarchy. Within individual counties, or groups of counties constituting larger sociocultural spheres, locally prominent descent groups exerted paramount influence. I am deliberately avoiding the terms *yangban* or "aristocracy" in favor of "elites," because the question of whether the local elites of Kaesŏng and the northern provinces can be lumped together with the local aristocracy of the south requires a more nuanced explanation, an issue central to this chapter.

The following information provides necessary background to this discussion. In late Chosŏn, no massive migration depleted or swelled the population of any particular region, and yet the degree of military examination success fluctuated by locality. Figure 3.1, showing the

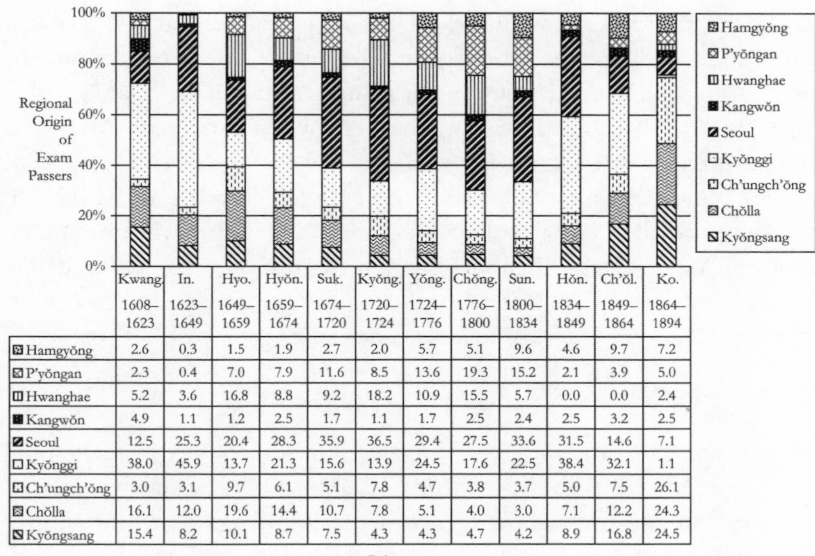

	Kwang. 1608–1623	In. 1623–1649	Hyo. 1649–1659	Hyŏn. 1659–1674	Suk. 1674–1720	Kyŏng. 1720–1724	Yŏng. 1724–1776	Chŏng. 1776–1800	Sun. 1800–1834	Hŏn. 1834–1849	Ch'ŏl. 1849–1864	Ko. 1864–1894
Hamgyŏng	2.6	0.3	1.5	1.9	2.7	2.0	5.7	5.1	9.6	4.6	9.7	7.2
P'yŏngan	2.3	0.4	7.0	7.9	11.6	8.5	13.6	19.3	15.2	2.1	3.9	5.0
Hwanghae	5.2	3.6	16.8	8.8	9.2	18.2	10.9	15.5	5.7	0.0	0.0	2.4
Kangwŏn	4.9	1.1	1.2	2.5	1.7	1.1	1.7	2.5	2.4	2.5	3.2	2.5
Seoul	12.5	25.3	20.4	28.3	35.9	36.5	29.4	27.5	33.6	31.5	14.6	7.1
Kyŏnggi	38.0	45.9	13.7	21.3	15.6	13.9	24.5	17.6	22.5	38.4	32.1	1.1
Ch'ungch'ŏng	3.0	3.1	9.7	6.1	5.1	7.8	4.7	3.8	3.7	5.0	7.5	26.1
Chŏlla	16.1	12.0	19.6	14.4	10.7	7.8	5.1	4.0	3.0	7.1	12.2	24.3
Kyŏngsang	15.4	8.2	10.1	8.7	7.5	4.3	4.3	4.7	4.2	8.9	16.8	24.5

Figure 3.1 Regional Representation among Military Examination Passers, 1608–1894. Abbreviations: Kwang. = Kwanghaegun, In. = Injo, Hyo. = Hyojong, Hyŏn. = Hyŏnjong, Suk. = Sukchong, Kyŏng. = Kyŏngjong, Yŏng. = Yŏngjo, Chŏng. = Chŏngjo, Sun. = Sunjo, Hŏn. = Hŏnjong, Ch'ŏl. = Ch'ŏlchong, Ko. = Kojong. Source: Military examination rosters; *Chosŏn sidae sach'an ŭpchi*; *Han'guk kŭndae ŭpchi*; *Chosŏn hwanyŏ sŭngnam*; *Kyonam kwabangnok*; *Honamji*; other local gazetteers; and genealogies.

reign-by-reign change in the representation of various regions among the late Chosŏn military examination passers, illustrates a significant contrast between central and local participation. Above all, the representation of Chŏlla and Kyŏngsang Provinces, together making up the most populous and agriculturally productive region in Korea, generally decreased until a resurgence in the nineteenth century. Second, the north, represented by P'yŏngan and Hamgyŏng Provinces, enjoyed increasing success in the military examination in the seventeenth and eighteenth centuries, before a sudden drop in the nineteenth century. And third, the combined share of Seoul and Kyŏnggi Province stayed at roughly 50 percent for each reign until a sharp decline in the second half of the nineteenth century.

I offer these general observations here as a way to differentiate historically and socially meaningful groups of local elites in the late Chosŏn era. I propose three by no means rigid categories: (1) the local *yang-*

ban of mostly rural communities in the southern half of the Korean peninsula, including the eastern central region; (2) the urban, commercially engaged elite of the city of Kaesŏng and its vicinity; and (3) the northern elites based in P'yŏngan and Hamgyŏng Provinces (Map 3.1). This chapter analyzes the varying degree of each local elite's military examination success in the broader context of their relations with both the agents of the central political structure and the newly prominent actors in local society. Regional variation is important: it assured the central aristocracy that difference in history, attitudes, and behavior would maintain the cleavage that sustained its hegemony.

Southern Local Yangban

When it comes to the *yangban*-dominated social hierarchy in the south, scholars of late Chosŏn local history disagree about the relative importance of continuity versus change. Nonetheless, all agree that the southern aristocracy became excluded from the central political arena and increasingly faced challenges to its local political hegemony from social newcomers. Before this challenge, southern *yangban* wielded political clout by assisting the centrally appointed magistrate in governing the county while maintaining proper social mores in the local community. As their connection to the center weakened and the number of civil examination passers and officeholders declined, some turned to the military examination. The phenomenon did not last long for many descent groups, because the general exclusion of local aristocrats from central politics made them focus more on manifesting their ascriptive status through cultural literacy beyond the reach of nonelites. In this way, they managed to compensate for state-sanctioned trappings of status.

From mid-Chosŏn onward, the percentage of local *yangban* candidates from the south holding an examination degree or office declined sharply. By "local *yangban*" I mean those of aristocratic pedigree who enjoyed elevated social status at a strictly local level for generations, rather than those who merely maintained a local residence as an alternative to their primary residence in the capital. The distinction is important, because in various locales of western central Korea outside Seoul, a large number of *yangban* officials, along with their kinsmen and descendants, were based in the capital but kept alternate residences and possessed land used as farms and ancestral grave sites.[1]

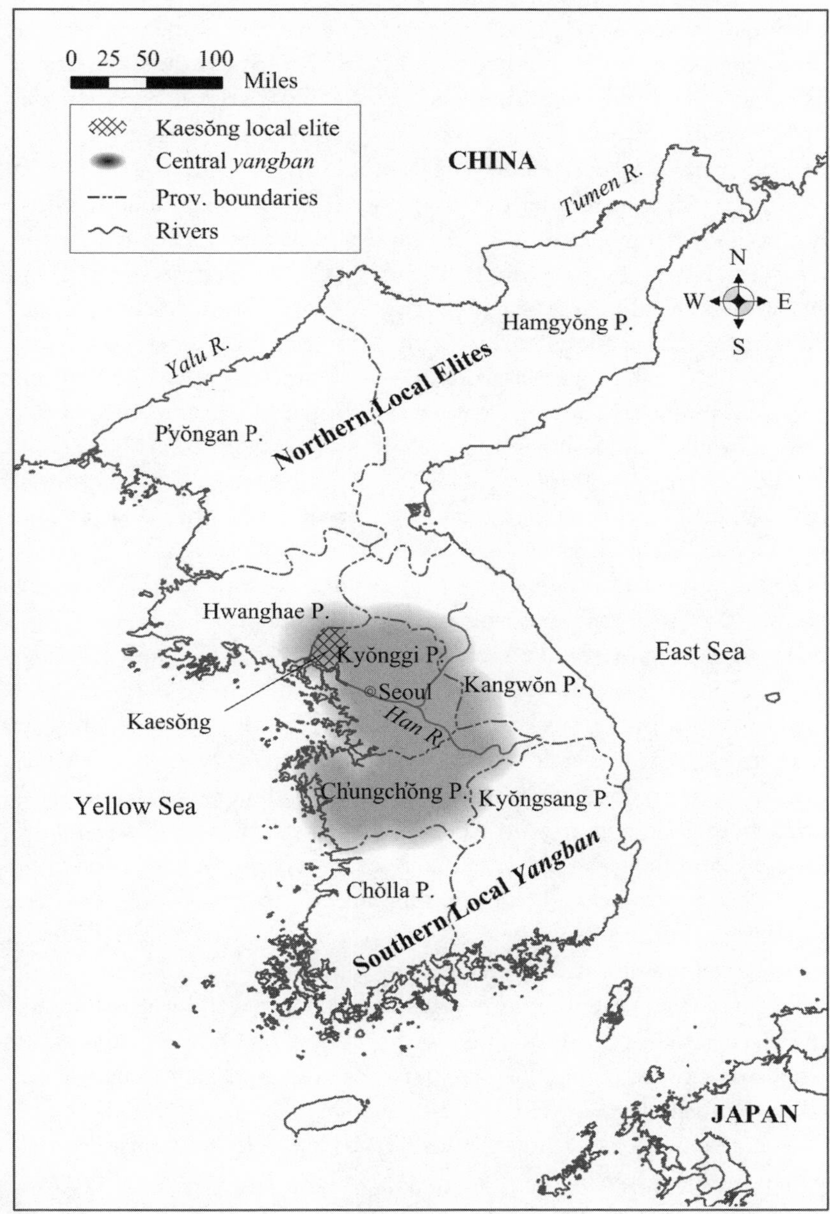

Map 3.1
Elite Zones in Late Chosŏn Korea, ca. 1800

The strong presence of Seoul-based *yangban* lineages among the civil examination degree holders and central civil officials helped perpetuate their paramount political power, because they filled the most important positions.[2] The first milestone event in the Seoul aristocracy's consolidation of its power was the 1623 coup—engineered by the Westerner faction members based largely in western central Korea—in which it overthrew the Northerner-dominated regime, an event that signified the political marginalization of the largely Northerner *yangban* based in southern Kyŏngsang Province. The next key developments were the Westerners' final victory, in 1694, over the Southerner faction, which had strong connections to northern Kyŏngsang Province, and King Yŏngjo's official exclusion from the policy-making processes of the so-called public discourse (*kongnon*), which ostensibly was an open forum for policy discussion among all.[3] In a section of his *Ecological Guide to Korea* (*T'aengniji*) devoted to Kyŏngsang Province, Yi Chung-hwan (1690–1752), who was from a capital-resident Southerner descent line, points out that the chasm between Seoul and the provinces had widened since the enthronement of Injo and the triumph of the Westerners in 1623. Since then, Yi explains, high officials from Kyŏngsang had dwindled in number while men from "hereditary [aristocratic] families of the capital" (*kyŏngsŏng sega*) were favored for official appointments.[4]

Also contributing to the dominance of Seoul was the growing number of men, generally from the capital, who earned their military degrees without going through one or more of the pre-palace examination stages. These men, who received special permission to advance to the third and final stage of the military examination, thus bypassing one or more of the previous stages that involved tests in weaponry skill and classics exposition, came to account for about half of all late Chosŏn military examination passers. Since the final stage, the palace examination, entailed just the weaponry skill demonstrations and was conducted merely for the purpose of ranking those who had made it that far, a person exempted from the pre-palace examination stages was essentially assured a degree.

Such exemptions can be traced back to the early sixteenth century, when the government adopted the practice as a way to strengthen various royal regiments comprising martially talented soldiers who had been chosen through weaponry tests.[5] The granting of exemption privileges became more regular after 1623, consistent with Injo's hatred of the Manchus and desire to someday avenge Korea's humiliation. Candidates exempted from pre-palace examination stages initially could participate only in the triennial competitions, but as the state sought to acquire and promote better-trained soldiers for new military units in the seventeenth century, it opened up various special examinations. The percentage of military examination degree holders who did not undergo preliminary examination increased steadily, from just 30.3 percent in the seventeenth century, to 54.9 percent in the eighteenth century, to 60.3 percent in the nineteenth century. In fact, in many later military examinations, more than 90 percent of graduates had been spared any of the pre-palace examination stages.[6]

As exemptions broadened in scope, they became more popular and more problematic. Originally, only the qualifying officers and soldiers of the royal regiments tended to receive exemptions. Eventually, however, a variety of martial talent competitions, held for the Five Military Regiments of Seoul as well as for all the provincial governors' and provincial army commanders' troops, came to grant the exemption to officers and soldiers who received either a perfect score in any one weapon subject during the test or the highest score overall.[7] More and more provincial residents skipped preliminary stages, mainly because the candidates for locally-held regimental martial talent competitions could receive a perfect score on one weaponry subject more easily than getting the highest overall score. Before long, though, many policy critics began to view favoring those earning a perfect score on just one weaponry test as a serious affront to the integrity of the whole military examination system.[8]

Beginning in the late seventeenth century, the government wavered between continuing and banning the practice. Persistent debate on the issue did nothing more than convince most policymakers that these rewards constituted a serious abuse and arouse efforts to limit it. Consequently, in the late eighteenth century, the government began limiting the privilege for provincial candidates. A typical measure called for selecting just the best man among all those earning perfect scores on a weaponry test at a given regimental martial talent competition and allowing only him to advance to the palace examination.[9]

The late Chosŏn southern aristocrats did not win strong representation in the civil branch of central officialdom. Thus, as early as the seventeenth century, some local *yangban* descent groups that no longer enjoyed success in the civil examination turned to the military examination. An observation made in 1633 by Minister of Personnel (Ijo P'ansŏ) Ch'oe Myŏng-gil is insightful. According to him, "the reason why the sons of eminent families have read diligently" is due to their need to pass the state examination: "Those who failed to pass the civil examination gave up on it and chose the military examination, and only after failing to pass either the civil or the military examination did they proceed to protection appointment."[10] Though commoner participation increased during this period, politically marginalized *yangban* continued to regard passing the military examination as a respectable way to acquire an office and manifest their social status, according to Chŏng Hae-ŭn's study of military examination graduates between 1674 and 1800.[11] It seems, then, that many local *yangban* descent lines turned to the military examination despite its declining prestige, often after failing for generations to produce a civil examination passer.

My investigation of the aristocratic lineages recorded in the registers of local agency (*hyangch'ŏng*) officers of various Kyŏngsang Province counties provides additional evidence, and the case of the Namp'yŏng Cho lineage of Kimhae is illustrative. Descended from Minister of Personnel Cho Yu-in (1370–1434), a 1396 civil examination passer, the Namp'yŏng Cho lineage had, prior to the mid-seventeenth century, produced only minor central officeholders without an examination passer; its success at the military examination was inaugurated by Cho Kang (1622–66), who earned his degree in 1656.[12] What is also noteworthy is that sometime in the eighteenth century, the lineage members changed their ancestral seat name from Namp'yŏng to Ch'angnyŏng—a move they apparently justified by asserting that the Namp'yŏng Cho had originally branched off from the Ch'angnyŏng Cho, the latter by then much more populous and, more importantly, politically powerful.[13] Regardless of the historicity of such claims or the sincerity of the claimants' belief in the connection, this type of behavior became common in late Chosŏn when descent groups put out increasingly more detailed genealogies claiming ancient, illustrious ancestries that could even originate in China.[14]

The Suwŏn Paek lineage of Chinju also illustrates the pattern by which a local *yangban* descent group marginalized from central politics turned to the military examination. Descended from Paek Sa-su, a 1454 civil examination degree holder, in the eighteenth century the Suwŏn Paek of Chinju began to produce successful military examination candidates only after several generations of examination failure. The lineage's fortunes changed after the adoption of a son brought in from a collateral line based in Seoul. (Descended from the same fifteenth-century civil examination graduate, the capital branch is one of the prominent central military official lines discussed in Chapter 2.) The adopted son's son, Paek Ik-chin (1757–1818), went on to pass the military examination in 1777.[15] His success suggests, without serving as proof, that capital connections constituted an unspoken ingredient in passing examinations.

Yet another revealing case is that of the Andong Kwŏn local *yangban* lineage of Tansŏng. The first man to pass the military examination from the lineage was Kwŏn P'il-ch'ing (1721–?), great-great-grandson of Kwŏn To (1557–1644), a censor-general and two-time minor merit subject during Injo's reign. The family's reputation for intellectual and literary accomplishments is demonstrated by the latter's posthumous enshrinement at two private academies (*sŏwŏn*), and P'il-ch'ing initially sought to carry on the tradition by passing the classics licentiate examination. He gave up the attempt after repeated failures and ultimately turned to the military examination, which he passed in 1750 at the age of 30 *se*. During the three years he spent preparing for the military examination, Kwŏn had to justify his course of action to his disapproving kinsmen and other local *yangban* who did not have a high regard for the military examination. Arguing that both literary and martial virtues were important for serving the country, he also stressed his obligation to serve his widowed elderly mother by becoming an official via whatever route was feasible.[16]

The local aristocracy's view that the military examination could be chosen as an alternative career path was not limited to Kyŏngsang Province. Hailing from a local Chinju Kang *yangban* lineage of Mujang in Chŏlla Province that had last produced a civil examination graduate in 1656, Kang Ŭng-hwan (1735–95) chose a military career. Reflecting the lower prestige associated with the military vocation by many literati, his father initially disapproved.[17] At this juncture, the son expressed his lofty ambition through "Song of a Martial Hero" (Muhoga) composed in the form of "sung lyrics" (*kasa*), a poetic genre typically sung to extant melodies.[18] He expressed his aspirations as follows:[19]

> To a great man (*taejangbu*) who dwells between heaven and earth. . .
> and plainly considers the whole of human affairs,
> reading and writing are the endeavors of a corrupt Confucianist
> while plowing fields and weeding paddies are tasks befitting a farmer. . . .
> Shall the great man not pass the local examination, the metropolitan examination, . . .
> and, as the top passer, the palace examination at the spacious grounds of Ch'undangdae? . . .
> First appointed as a sixth-rank royal messenger, he holds in turn the junior sixth-rank Military Training Agency office (Chubu)
> the magistracies of counties large and small, . . .
> Completing the tour of duty in border regions, shall he not become a junior second-rank provincial military official (Pangŏsa)?
> Shall he not serve in succession as the southern and northern Hamgyŏng provincial army commanders (Nambyŏngsa, Pukpyŏngsa)
> and as the Supreme Commander of Three Provincial Naval Forces (Samdo Sugun T'ongjesa), . . .
> before, with unanimous approval, being appointed as the Military Training Division Commander (Hullyŏn Taejang),
> and by heaven's immeasurable grace becoming the Minister of War?
> Taking up the royal command and practicing military encampment strategies,
> the Blue Dragon and White Tiger banners will be arrayed left and right,
> and the Red Sparrow and Black Warrior banners will be spread to the front and rear.[20]
> When he has brought together the Five Military Divisions and commanded the Three Armies (Samgun),
> the strategies he possessed all his life will have been thoroughly tested.

The determination embodied in the poem so impressed the father that he granted his permission. Not only did the son eventually pass the military examination and enjoy a career as a dilligent official, his descendants also pursued military careers.[21]

It is impossible to quantify the degree of interest in the military examination among the southern aristocracy, but these cases are highly suggestive. At least some southern local *yangban* seem to have chosen the military examination as an alternative way to gain admittance to central officialdom. This trend appears to have been more widespread among the lineages that had not been producing any civil examination passers or civil officials for some time since the early Chosŏn period.

All the same, those who were the first in their descent lines to turn to the military had to cope with familial and social prejudices against martial virtue, an antipathy more pronounced among the local *yangban* of Kyŏngsang Province. Available residence data for the fifteenth and sixteenth centuries show that the less populous Chŏlla Province produced more military examination passers than Kyŏngsang Province, although both were located in the south.[22] It is notable that in the early seventeenth century, Kyŏngsang Provincial Governor Pak Kyŏng-sin (1560–1626), proposing a local military examination, criticized his citizens as follows: "Although this province neighbors the island barbarians [the Japanese], it is extremely pitiful that the people [here] do not cultivate martial virtue."[23] In 1641, King Injo noted that Chŏlla and Kyŏngsang provinces lacked, respectively, Confucian scholars and martial literati; at the same time, Chŏlla Provincial Governor Chŏng Se-gyu (1583–1661) spoke of his previous posting in Kyŏngsang Province, and observed that the region lacked *yangban* willing to become military officials. In Kyŏngsang, he contended, the *yangban* taking the military examination were ostracized by their social peers. Chŏng ultimately urged the king to employ more capable military men from the province to encourage the local aristocracy to pursue military careers.[24]

The local Kyŏngsang aristocracy's low regard for military careers persisted in spite of such expressions of concern and the efforts by various kings to change the region's cultural bias. In the late eighteenth century, after finding out that only a small number of Kyŏngsang residents had taken the recent military examination, King Chŏngjo criticized the province's local *yangban* for looking down on martial virtue:

> Yŏngnam [Kyŏngsang] is a province large in size. However, the number of those taking the [military] examination, which is a state event, is not on par with those of other provinces' large locales. Do not say that the locales of [Kyŏngsang] Province are places where learning thrives, as in the home villages of Confucius and Mencius. The martial art of archery is not a base thing. Considering that Confucius also performed archery, it must be that he was fond of it. Moreover, given that employing both literary and martial virtues is the way to preserve the state for eternity, what more can be said?[25]

The issue of cultural bias against the military examination needs to be explored in a more detailed study of attitudes toward martial virtue in a Confucian society. Nonetheless, all the contemporary observations that we have seen indicate that the local aristocracy of the south—and especially in Kyŏngsang Province—held martial endeavors and the military examination in low regard.

In addition to the cultural stigma, the logistics of taking the military examination put the southern *yangban* at a disadvantage in comparison to candidates from the capital as well as the north. The examination candidates from the south, already hindered by limited training opportunities and the greater traveling distances and time involved, were also disadvantaged by the unequal distribution of special exemptions, a privilege most commonly granted to the officers and soldiers of military regiments such as the capital's Five Military Regiments and the P'yŏngan, Hamgyŏng, and Hwanghae Provinces' Royal Cavalry Guards (Ch'in'giwi) and Special Military Officers (Pyŏlmusa). Since the special military regiments (other than those of provincial governors, army commanders, and navy commanders) were concentrated in the capital region and the north, the exemption privilege did not as readily benefit the southern aristocracy.

Yet another factor that seems to have limited the extent of southern *yangban* participation in the military examination is change in the local political hegemony. In the seventeenth century, the local hegemony of bona fide *yangban* came under challenge by nonelites commanding wealth and influence. Descended from illegitimate sons of *yangban* or even commoners, such descent groups made their ways into the registers of local agency officers—the updating of which the irate old aristocracy simply discontinued after the seventeenth century in most locales.[26]

To be sure, the old *yangban* still found ways to preserve their prestige and wealth. Though the growing prominence of various new social elements may have affected the power dynamics in local administration, alienation from central politics and decreased influence in local administration reinforced sociocultural conservatism on the part of the older *yangban* aristocracy—that is, those who were once represented on the registers of local agency officers. The older families came to stress

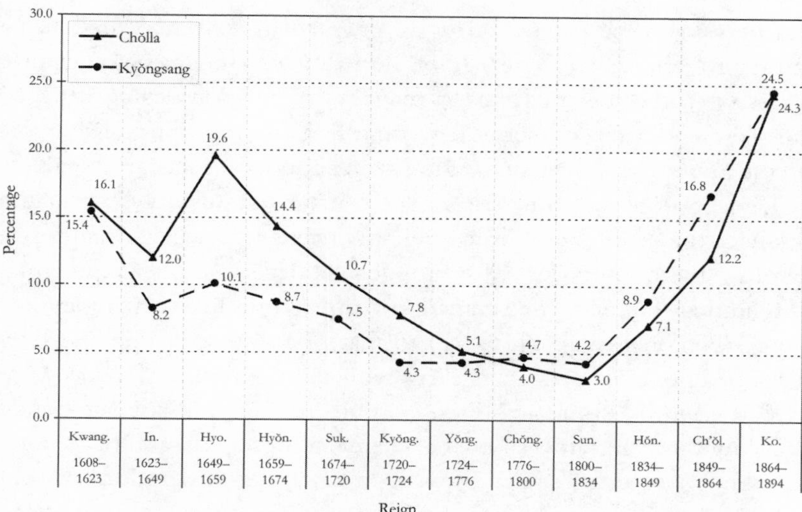

Figure 3.2 Military Examination Passers from Chŏlla and Kyŏngsang Provinces, 1608–1894. Abbreviations: Kwang. = Kwanghaegun, In. = Injo, Hyo. = Hyojong, Hyŏn. = Hyŏnjong, Suk. = Sukchong, Kyŏng. = Kyŏngjong, Yŏng. = Yŏngjo, Chŏng. = Chŏngjo, Sun. = Sunjo, Hŏn. = Hŏnjong, Ch'ŏl. = Ch'ŏlchong, Ko. = Kojong. Source: Military examination rosters; *Chosŏn sidae sach'an ŭpchi*; *Han'guk kŭndae ŭpchi*; *Chosŏn hwanyŏ sŭngnam*; *Kyonam kwabangnok*; *Honamji*; other local gazetteers; and genealogies.

organizations and activities generative of stronger lineage consciousness. The older *yangban* families manifested their strengthened status consciousness by compiling genealogies, residing in same-surname (*tongsŏng*) villages, and establishing various cultural edifices, such as private academies, shrines (*sau*), and other buildings for educational, social, and ritual purposes.[27]

Nonetheless, even in the most culturally conservative regions in Kyŏngsang Province, some new families with growing socioeconomic clout managed to creep into close social connection with the aristocracy. A few even formed marriage ties with the older local *yangban* lineages. For example, a Namp'yŏng Mun lineage of Kimhae, represented in the local agency officer register only after the late eighteenth century, was able to marry a daughter into the aforementioned Ch'angnyŏng Cho (previously Namp'yŏng Cho) lineage, traditionally one of the prominent local *yangban* descent groups of Kimhae. By the late nineteenth century, both groups (if the distinction between old aristocracy and new elite can be said to have persisted) were engaged in collective fundraising efforts to set up modern schools in Kimhae.[28] Such social change leaves open the possibility that a military examination degree attracted the old aristocracy and social newcomers at different times depending on the political circumstances at the center and local social dynamics.

Late Chosŏn fluctuations in the percentages of military examination passers from Chŏlla and Kyŏngsang provinces are revealing (Figure 3.2). Both southern provinces suffered a general decline in their representation among the military examination passers, a decline which persisted from Hyŏnjong's reign (1659–74) to that of Sunjo (1800–34). This decreased representation is congruent with the nonstatistical evidence as marshaled in the foregoing discussion on the southern aristocracy and social mobility. In terms of overall examination success and officeholding, the link between central officialdom and the southern local *yangban* weakened.

All the same, the local aristocracy of the south retained its membership in the cohesive, highest-level social status group, the *yangban,* which also included capital-based descent lines of central civil officials or central military officials. Within a descent group, a relatively close genealogical distance tied the three types of *yangban* together, at least among those who did not have to declare an offspring of a non-*yangban* mother in the intervening generations. The three were also linked by marriage ties and the exchange of adoptive heirs, though by the nineteenth century the latter appears to become uncommon. These in-group behaviors are discussed in detail in Chapter 4, which argues that the distance separating the *yangban* from other social status groups was greater than that between any two *yangban* subgroups.

After Sunjo's reign, both Chŏlla and Kyŏngsang provinces enjoyed a resurgence in the representation of their native sons among the successful military examination candidates, and the phenomenon apparently was not attributable to local *yangban.* On the contrary, the proliferation of southern military examination graduates in the nineteenth century may be linked to the increased participation—and success—of more marginal members of the local aristocracy, or even of non-aristocratic social elements of the south.

Though more social upstarts were passing various examinations, it was clearly birth that confirmed an individual's status as a *yangban*, regardless of the number of examination passers produced by his descent group. Nonetheless, a licentiate examination, which was really a qualifying test for the civil examination and normally did not lead to an appointment, retained its special appeal among local *yangban,* and many struggled for decades to earn a licentiate degree.[29] Although lacking this degree certainly was not cause for consigning an individual to the ranks of the commoners, to possess it was to demonstrate to all around that the degree holder had attained a high level of Confucian cultivation.[30]

To invest effort in a degree not linked to a government appointment is a practice explicable via Bourdieu's concept of cultural capital. According to Bourdieu, cultural capital can be realized in three states—embodied, objectified, and institutional.[31] Aspiring licentiates had to prepare for the examination by learning from an early age how to read and understand various texts, progressing from elementary primers to the established canon of Confucian classics. Because the moral values taught in those texts had to be internalized in order to be at the student's command, successful students achieved the embodied state of cultural capital. This process of personal cultivation prepared the individual for the next, objectified, state, in which he could use a specific, concrete object to facilitate and demonstrate his refinement. For a licentiate examination candidate, wearing dress befitting his vocation and performing proper Confucian rituals served as an expression of his objectified cultural capital; of course, none of these material objects had an intrinsic value to someone who did not understand what they meant. Once both the objectified and embodied states had been attained, an examination candidate could rise to the institutional state by earning the degree, which signified to all that the state had recognized his cultural competence. Since successfully undergoing all three stages was beyond the means of most nonelites, the candidate who succeeded commanded respect as a certified literatus—a status perfectly befitting a member of the aristocracy, which, at least ideally, was defined by Confucian moral terms.

The dominance of southern *yangban* in education and culture was not paralleled by great success in the licentiate examinations. In late Chosŏn, local aristocrats of the south were increasingly unlikely to hold a degree, rank, or office.[32] Since it was birth that defined membership in the aristocracy, it is even possible that the majority, if not most, of *yang-*

ban men did not bother with the licentiate exatmination. All the same, more scholarly types who were willing to devote decades to studying for the licentiate examination could be found among the *yangban* as well as the non-*yangban* with cultural capital.[33] The fact that learned aristocrats continued to take and pass the licentiate examination helped the degree retain its prestige. This is precisely the difference between the continuing prestige of the degree and the devalued distinction of getting one's name recorded in the local agency officer roster—something that the aristocrats stopped updating when it became flooded with the names of upstarts. Of course, the difference made the licentiate degree especially appealing to the nonaristocrats with cultural capital. We can better understand the potentials and limits of education by looking at other local elites.

The Kaesŏng Elite

Kaesŏng's social history during Chosŏn was unique, conforming to the pattern of neither the southern nor northern regions. Compared to the local aristocracy of southern Korea, the elites of Kaesŏng and the north had to cope with much more conscious, institutionalized discrimination by the center. In early Chosŏn, the government did not even permit the residents of Kaesŏng, the capital of the dynasty supplanted by Chosŏn, to compete in any examination. Even after the state lifted this ban, the native sons who earned a degree did not receive important positions in central officialdom. Kaesŏng residents compensated for their exclusion from the central political structure by turning to commercial activities that extended their influence over trade, even beyond Korea. Nonetheless, in late Chosŏn, the Kaesŏng elite continued to pursue examination degrees, with notable success.

When the Chosŏn dynasty succeeded the Koryŏ in 1392, Kaesŏng remained the kingdom's capital for two more years, until King T'aejo's court moved to Seoul in 1394. King Chŏngjong returned to Kaesŏng in 1398, but King T'aejong transferred the capital, yet again, to Seoul in 1405. Upon this final transfer, Seoul remained the capital until the end of Chosŏn.

As the former capital, Kaesŏng acquired distinctive social characteristics. Above all, many Koryŏ loyalists and their descendants chose not to serve the Chosŏn dynasty and continued to live in and around Kaesŏng. An apocryphal legend tells of 72 loyalists who, refusing to serve in the Chosŏn government, allegedly were killed when the enraged agents of the new regime set fire to their village in Tumun-dong, near Kaesŏng; the story is less important as historical narrative than as a popular, symbolic explanation of the fate of the valiant Koryŏ loyalists and the subsequent social history of their city.[34] For example, King Yŏngjo, after honoring the memory of the Tumun-dong loyalists during his 1745 visit to Kaesŏng, noted that because many of the descendants of the worthies from Tumun-dong lived as lowly merchants and not as as reputable scholars or officials, he wanted to appoint them to offices.[35] All the same, it was clear that the identity of Kaesŏng residents as rebels against the new dynasty was not just symbolic: the Chosŏn state barred them from all state examinations until 1470. In a 1606 conversation about the character of Kaesŏng residents, the newly appointed Kaesŏng Special Mayor (Yusu), Sin Chap (1541–1609), had to tell King Sŏnjo that literati were looked down upon and that those who entered officialdom generally could not attain anything more than low-level posts.[36] This apparently negative attitude toward scholarly life—belied by the elites' relative success in passing the civil examination—appears to reflect the fact that education still could not give them meaningful access to the locus of power.

The elite of Kaesŏng compensated for their political disenfranchisement by pursuing careers as merchant-financiers rather than as central officials. In early Chosŏn, Kaesŏng-based merchants began creating a network of trading offices and allied merchants throughout Korea, an arrangement that empowered them as commercial middlemen.[37] By late Chosŏn, they were making great profits by wholesaling—buying up goods in large quantities and reselling them at appropriate moments. Backed by agreements with key suppliers throughout Korea, Kaesŏng merchants even overwhelmed the government-licensed merchants of Seoul.[38] The most important merchandise for Kaesŏng merchants was Korean ginseng, which was popular even in Japan and China, but they were also involved in the export of cotton and cotton cloth to Japan, in return for copper and silver; the former supplied coinage, whereas the latter attracted the attention of some policy makers as a source of alternate silver currency.[39] The city's dominant commercial role continued until the economic penetration of Korea by its trading partners after 1882, which ultimately hurt indigenous mercantile interests. Kaesŏng merchants failed to survive the transition to the modern capitalistic system of twentieth-century Korea.[40]

Kaesŏng's distinctive economic role is matched by its pattern of examination success. The residences of about 80 percent of Chosŏn civil examination degree holders are known; of these 11,698 graduates, 5,264 came from Seoul (45.0 percent); the other locales best represented among the civil examination passers were Chŏngju (285 graduates, 2.4 percent), Andong (203 graduates, 1.7 percent), Ch'ungju (201 graduates, 1.7 percent), P'yŏngyang (145 graduates, 1.2 percent), Wŏnju (112 graduates, 1.0 percent), Yangju (112 graduates, 1.0 percent), Kaesŏng (111 graduates, 1.0 percent), and Suwŏn (104 graduates, 0.9 percent). Thus, in terms of the absolute number of civil examination graduates it produced during the dynasty, Kaesŏng ranks among the ten most successful locales, along with other larger counties near Seoul, such as Yangju and Suwŏn, regional centers (P'yŏngyang), and counties especially known for culture and education (Andong and Chŏngju). Yet in spite of this civil examination success, Kaesŏng failed to produce a proportionate number of civil officials occupying more important positions in the central government.[41]

Kaesŏng's pattern of licentiate examination success reveals even more distinctive characteristics. The city enjoyed greater success in this arena than it did in the civil examinations. According to Mark Peterson, Kaesŏng residents account for 696 out of about 47,000 classics and literary licentiates for whom residence information is available (about 1.5 percent).[42] Not only was Kaesŏng's share of the overall licentiates disproportionately greater, but it was also typified by much greater descent group diversity in comparison to the civil examination passers from the city. Peterson is thus moved to inquire how the elite of Kaesŏng attained the level of cultural competence required to earn the licentiate degrees. Leaving this question unanswered, he suggests that the answer may be found in Kaesŏng's economic resources.[43]

James Palais notes that merchants and artisans, as well as their descendants, were all barred from the state examination and from holding office, but I have found no such restriction in any law code.[44] His observations are based perhaps on the social commentaries of Practical Learning writers, which diverge from the law codes. It is possible that the government or the aristocracy may have penalized opportunistic merchants, who exploited local populations and profited from supplying government agencies with tribute goods, by excluding them in the same way that it did those guilty of stealing from the state treasury: a permanent exclusion from officeholding.[45]

This category did likely encompass many Kaesŏng merchants, but apparently the restriction did not apply to their sons so long as they themselves were not caught engaging in such activities. Moreover, numerous late Chosŏn observations suggest a connection, real or not, between commerce and education. For example, in 1606, when King Sŏnjo conversed with Sin Chap before his departure to take up his new post as Kaesŏng Special Mayor, Sin claimed that among the brothers of one family in Kaesŏng, all those other than the ones honing their literary skills earned a good living in street merchant enterprises.[46] The *Veritable Records* furthermore note that, as of 1660, "almost all" of those known as literati in Kaesŏng were sons of merchants.[47] Together, these contemporary observations suggest that by the seventeenth century, the merchant elite of Kaesŏng was also producing men of literary talent who passed the civil and licentiate examinations.

Since the educated elite of Kaesŏng, backed by wealth, enjoyed success in the highly regarded civil and licentiate examinations, it is not difficult to imagine that its less erudite yet more athletic representatives turned to the military examination. In fact, Kaesŏng residents were even more successful in the military examination, accounting for 2,174 out of the 30,636 military examination passers for whom I was able to determine residence (7.1 percent). Among them, several characteristics are noticeable.

First, most of the known Kaesŏng passers earned a military examination degree in late Chosŏn. The fact that only 48 men earned their degrees before 1600 suggests either that the compilers of the four extant lists I have consulted did not have adequate information on the earlier passers, or that Kaesŏng's military examination success dramatically increased in late Chosŏn.[48] My experience working with local gazetteers that document military examination passers tells me that in other areas, early Chosŏn is covered quite well.[49] Moreover, the relative completeness of the four lists, as verified by the military examination rosters, suggests that the dearth of military examination passers before

1600 indeed reflects the low degree of military examination success for Kaesŏng residents at the time.[50] Further evidence comes from Sŏnjo's 1606 conversation with Sin Chap about the character of Kaesŏng residents, in which the two agreed that they generally did not train in martial skills.[51] When the king pressed him for more explanation, Sin noted that this tendency was natural, given the general inability of even men of literary talent from Kaesŏng to attain anything more than low-level posts in the central government. Since the Kaesŏng elite was marginalized in officialdom due to the city's past harboring of Koryŏ loyalists, we may also surmise that it took some time for the Chosŏn state to trust Kaesŏng men enough to recruit them through the military examination. In fact, during this conversation, Sŏnjo stressed the importance of encouraging more Kaesŏng residents to train in martial skills, as the city's proximity to Seoul made it important for defending the capital against invasions.[52] By 1693, we find the censor-general complaining about frequent special examinations administered for local residents, even though, he reasoned, the city's location enabled them to compete in numerous examinations held in Seoul.[53]

Second, many successful Kaesŏng candidates hailed from descent groups that produced military examination passers not just among siblings and cousins but, in many cases, over generations. At least 486 out of 2,174 graduates had one or more military examination degree holders among patrilineal ancestors or kinsmen (22.4 percent), and among the 486 graduates were 268 men whose fathers had passed the military examination. Such a family's degree of military examination success was not comparable to that of central military official lines producing scores of degree holders (as we have seen in Chapter 2), but these Kaesŏng families definitely outperformed the southern local *yangban* lineages that turned to the military examination in late Chosŏn.

Third, many graduates went by a surname entirely unknown in other parts of Korea, including at least one such surname using Kaesŏng as its ancestral seat. Almost none of these unique surnames appear in the geographical treatise included in the *Veritable Records* of Sejong's reign, a fact suggesting that they came into use after early Chosŏn or were introduced to Korea through foreign emigrants. Peterson's study of the licentiates from Kaesŏng also notes a similar pattern. He hypothesizes that there may have been a link between the licentiate-producing elite of Kaesŏng and the foreigners involved in the city's merchant activities, some of whom perhaps settled down in Korea.[54]

Fourth, the careers of Kaesŏng military examination graduates were less impressive than those of southern local aristocrats. Out of 2,174 military examination graduates from Kaesŏng during the entirety of the Chosŏn period, at least 483 (22.2 percent) received a central official rank or post, whereas at least 3,722 out of 6,994 military examination graduates from Chŏlla and Kyŏngsang Provinces did so (53.2 percent). If the late Chosŏn period alone is considered, then the disparity is not as gross: whereas 1,689 out of 4,446 military examination graduates from the south between 1608 and 1894 are known to have received a rank or an office from the central government (38.0 percent), 400 out of 1,852 graduates from Kaesŏng accomplished this feat (21.6 percent). The late Chosŏn numbers are significant in that unlike the southern aristocracy, which was politically marginalized, the Kaesŏng elite's degree of participation remained essentially unchanged. Considering that the dominance of *yangban* descent groups based in western central Korea (including Seoul) became more pronounced in the same period, the fact that the successful military examination candidates from Kaesŏng were hardly affected in comparison to those from the south reinforces the conclusion that the city's economic influence, cultural capital, and strategic importance enabled its elite to more than hold their own in the central bureaucracy, albeit at the margins.

The Northern Elites of P'yŏngan and Hamgyŏng Provinces

The northern elites of P'yŏngan and Hamgyŏng Provinces were handicapped less by the doubts of the Chosŏn state and the aristocracy about the north's loyalty than by the perception that they were not *yangban.* This notion, held by the central and southern aristocrats, was based in part on the prevalent perception that Confucian learning spread relatively late in the north.[55] In spite of the lag, the northern elites of late Chosŏn attained high levels of both cultural sophistication and martial talent, and the eighteenth-century monarchs sought to tap into this talent in an effort to bolster royal power. These kings, along with some supportive central officials, extended advancement opportunities to northern residents, but the result was increased examination success without meaningful inroads into Seoul's political power structure. Talented northern men had to be content with local elite status itself. In times of crisis some worked with an increasingly well-educated or martially trained cohort of nonelites to organize an uprising against the center.

Like the residents of the capital and its surrounding areas, northern residents enjoyed an advantage when competing in the military examination. Many special military regiments were located in these regions, such as the Royal Cavalry Guard (Ch'in'giwi) and the Special Military Officers (Pyŏlmusa), in addition to the troops of Seoul's Five Military Regiments (Ogunyŏng), provincial governors, provincial army commanders, and provincial navy commanders. Thus, the officers and soldiers stationed in these regions could readily utilize the increasingly common privilege of skipping the preliminary stage of a military examination, whereas it was harder for the southern residents, other than those *hallyang* devoted to martial training, to compete successfully in the military examination.[56]

The location of military regiments helps to explain the relatively greater military examination successes enjoyed by residents of the north. At the same time, we need to consider how the broader social context in the north allowed the military examination to serve certain functions. The limited accessibility of local documents due to the division of Korea since 1945 and the subsequent Korean War (1950–53)—which was especially destructive for the western part of North Korea due to intensive American bombing—has hampered the reconstruction of the social history of the north during Chosŏn. Fortunately some recent studies have shed much light on the social history of P'yŏngan and Hamgyŏng Provinces. The picture that emerges is that of a local society far different from the south, as well as from Seoul and its immediate environs, in terms of the origins, evolution, and characteristics of local elites, their treatment by the central government and *yangban,* and their reactions to that treatment.

The central government and *yangban* officials generally discriminated against the northwest, regarding even its local elite as socially and culturally inferior and ill-equipped for serving in the government. According to O Su-ch'ang's study of the social history of the P'yŏngan Province, a careful analysis that is both broad in scope and meticulous in detail, the aristocracy of the capital and the south alike viewed the region as lacking cultural sophistication and, in particular, devoid of a strong Confucian ethos. This perception, lingering in spite of the rapid spread of Confucian education in the region in the seventeenth century, provided a powerful rationale for barring P'yŏngan men from significant positions in the central government. This changed in the late seventeenth century, when kings and some supportive officials sought to promote more men from the region. Persisting through the eighteenth century, this policy dramatically increased the number of both civil and military examination graduates among the candidates from P'yŏngan Province.[57] Many such degree earners derived from local social elements that had achieved some measure of cultural sophistication and economic wealth; the latter in particular attracted the state's attention. All the same, even the civil and military examination graduates from the region generally did not receive more important positions in the central bureaucracy. The Hong Kyŏng-nae rebellion of 1812 clearly demonstrated that P'yŏngan Province had social elements with untapped talent, including martial capabilities, that could turn against the existing order.[58]

Located to the east of P'yŏngan Province, Hamgyŏng Province was deemed even more backward a region by the central government and the aristocracy. According to a recent study by Kang Sŏk-hwa, the Chosŏn administrative jurisdictions and military installations did not extend to the Tumen River—the commonly assumed northern boundary—before the early eighteenth century. The famous 1712 Korea-China border agreement negotiations secured Chinese recognition of complete Korean control of all territories south of the river, thus providing an impetus for the Chosŏn government to develop the entire Hamgyŏng region more actively. The program entailed establishing or renovating various monuments related to the royal family in the dynasty's ancestral locales, the creation of the locally recruited Royal Cavalry Guards, and the administration of special military examinations for residents. In spite of the state's desire to stress the region's "ever-martial" (*sangmu*) social atmosphere, it could not stop the spread of more sophisticated literary culture and Confucian learning, spearheaded by the local elite's educated literati (*munsa*), who increasingly sought royal charters for their new private academies. Greater cultural sophistication also led to the appearance of numerous treatises and local gazetteers reflecting a growing consciousness of neighboring Manchuria as an historically Korean territory.[59]

These studies of Hamgyŏng and P'yŏngan Provinces by Kang and O have their strengths and weaknesses. They somewhat overstate the nationalistic awareness of the residents of both provinces and the particular class consciousness of the northwesterners, but the general arguments are built on a large body of primary sources providing much solid evidence. The emerging big picture is clear: in northern Korea, as in the south, locally prominent lineages asserted and maintained their privileged social status. To do this, they almost invariably claimed southern origins via fifteenth- or sixteenth-century ancestors who relocated to the north. In the genealogies of northern descent lines I have examined, the most commonly offered explanation involves their ancestors' banishment (*yubae*) to the north during the early Chosŏn political crises of the late fifteenth and early sixteenth centuries. Such ancestors are generally presented as central officials or scholars.[60]

Interestingly, many putative ancestors of northern lines are missing from the genealogies published by the allegedly related descent lines based in central and southern Korea. Quite common are cases of obvious chronological problems, depending on the edition of the genealogy one is consulting. For example, the Miryang Pak lineage of Chŏngju, descended from Pak Hŭng-dun does not appear in any southern editions of Miryang Pak genealogies that should record it if the claim were true. Moreover, Hŭng-dun himself, supposedly an inspector-general, does not appear in any official histories such as the *Veritable Records*—something which is inconceivable given the importance of the post during the era of literati purges. I strongly suspect that with the relatively late Confucianization of the region and the delayed spread of the culture of genealogy compilation, northern descent groups, such as the Chŏngju lineage in question, had great difficulty in tracing their genealogies. They worked with a limited body of records and, when necessary, had to imagine connections to the capital or to the southern *yangban* of early Chosŏn. Given that the early Chosŏn migrants that the state relocated from the south to the north tended to be commoner peasants, soldiers, or convicts (among other nonelite social elements), it is quite likely that some genealogies contained forgeries.

Regardless of their real or imagined descent, the northern elites harbored a status consciousness that became more pronounced in late

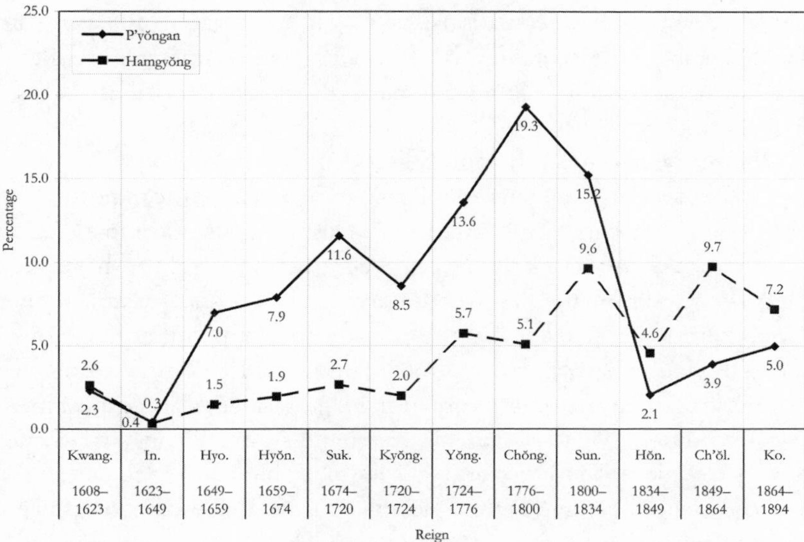

Figure 3.3 Military Examination Passers from P'yŏngan and Hamgyŏng Provinces, 1608–1894. Abbreviations: Kwang. = Kwanghaegun, In. = Injo, Hyo. = Hyojong, Hyŏn. = Hyŏnjong, Suk. = Sukchong, Kyŏng. = Kyŏngjong, Yŏng. = Yŏngjo, Chŏng. = Chŏngjo, Sun. = Sunjo, Hŏn. = Hŏnjong, Ch'ŏl. = Ch'ŏlchong, Ko. = Kojong. Source: Military examination rosters; *Chosŏn sidae sach'an ŭpchi*; *Han'guk kŭndae ŭpchi*; *Chosŏn hwanyŏ sŭngnam*; *Kyonam kwabangnok*; *Honamji*; other local gazetteers; and genealogies.

Chosŏn. With the spread of Confucian learning, values, and customs in the region, local elites viewed themselves as *yangban* or at least received recognition as such in their locales. Despite the refusal by the central and southern aristocrats to treat the northern elites as such, thereby excluding them from the center, statements by central officials and southern local *yangban* acknowledging the existence of *yangban* in the north are not unknown. For example, in 1653, when reporting on some of the most notorious criminals arrested in his jurisdiction, the governor of P'yŏngan Province referred to a local man as a *yangban* and criticized him for seeking an office by flattering influential individuals.[61] Clearly, the governor was deeming the behavior beneath the dignity of an aristocrat.

Considering all of these factors, it seems natural that the northerners' examination success increased only later in the dynasty. Out of 27,367 late Chosŏn military examination degree holders from 1608 to

1894, the residence information is available for 26,209 (95.8 percent); the changing representation of P'yŏngan and Hamgyŏng residents among the successful military examination candidates is illustrated by Figure 3.3.

Before the seventeenth century, residents of the north were underrepresented among the successful military examination candidates. An individual from Ŭiju who passed the military examination in 1620 (allegedly thanks to a powerful political connection) is said to have been the first man from the city to pass any kind of a state examination.[62] Even considering that the statement came from a political detractor of the examination passer's patron (the infamous Yi I-ch'ŏm), it seems that central officials at the time regarded the Ŭiju resident's accomplishment as extraordinary. That such an important and sizable P'yŏngan Province border city did not produce any successful examination candidates until the early seventeenth century clearly tells us that northerners were newcomers to the process of entering government service through the examination. Wagner's study on northern civil examination participation also shows that the region's increased success—especially the impressive performance by the residents of Chŏngju, which produced the greatest number of civil examination passers after Seoul—was a late Chosŏn phenomenon.[63]

Since the civil examination enjoyed greater prestige than the military examination, considering how northern residents fared in the civil examination can help us determine the role of its military counterpart. As Wagner observes, the late Chosŏn state seems to have utilized the civil examination to mollify the region's educated yet politically marginalized residents. This practice may seem puzzling in light of the fact that, as is shown in another study by Wagner, a small number of Seoul-based *yangban* descent lines increasingly dominated the civil examination at the expense of southern local *yangban*.[64] The apparent contradiction is resolved when we make an important distinction: the locals who suffered were mainly southern local *yangban,* as we have seen earlier in the chapter. In contrast, northern elites enjoyed increased success in the civil examination.[65]

In light of the fact that the state essentially awarded a large number of civil examination degrees to northern residents without sharing any meaningful political power with them, the military examination system also piques our curiosity about how the center used the military examination to further its ends. To assess the patterns of northern elites' military examination success, we must take note of the local application, in the eighteenth century, of King Yŏngjo's Policy of Impartiality (T'angp'yŏngch'aek), as well as its variant continued by King Chŏngjo. In keeping with their effort to be less dependent on the powerful, Seoul aristocracy, both monarchs highly valued and actively promoted P'yŏngan men of exceptional martial skills. Although often grouped with Hamgyŏng Province during the period's frequent court discussions on the north, P'yŏngan Province was actually the more important of the two regions, as far as the central government's efforts to tap local martial talent were concerned. Vigorous efforts, undertaken by both kings, to institutionalize local martial training and recruitment of northwestern military men led to their assignments as royal guards. The government even transferred the management of the Muyŏlsa—which honored the memory of past worthies who had served the state with their martial talent—in P'yŏngyang from local Confucian students to state-registered martial skill trainees, or "warriors" (*musa*), despite stiff opposition from the former.[66]

These policies help us make sense of the northwest's increased military examination success in the eighteenth century, much of which coincided with the reigns of the two monarchs. The region traditionally was known for its martial spirit, a resource that the aforementioned policies certainly were meant to utilize. At the same time, the highly commercialized economy of P'yŏngan Province encouraged local men with martial talent from more affluent families to seek markers of state-sanctioned social status. Increasingly over the course of late Chosŏn, merchants acquired military posts—especially the largely honorary mid-level or higher sinecures in the Five Guards hierarchy—and this pattern became especially pronounced in P'yŏngan Province.[67]

Hamgyŏng Province also received favorable treatment by monarchs. The policies of King Sukchong, which were further elaborated by Yŏngjo and Chŏngjo, accommodated the region's local martial talent and used it to bolster royal power. The most typical measure was the creation of a province-based unit of the Royal Cavalry Guards (Ch'in'giwi). As we have seen, such special military units enabled local residents to participate in various regiments' martial talent competitions and potentially to win the privilege of skipping preliminary stages in a future military examination. This route to advancement was widely available for the residents of Hamgyŏng and P'yŏngan, but much more limited in the south.[68]

The central government instituted many new local military competitions under rulers from Sukchong to Yŏngjo (between 1674 and 1776). Appendix B is not a comprehensive list, but it is nonetheless revealing for several reasons. Above all, the period covered by the list includes the emergence of central military official descent lines as well as efforts by kings to strengthen royal regiments with local martial talent. The timing suggests that whereas the central military official lines served the interests of powerful civil officials and whatever faction happened to hold power, the northern military men protected the king—at least according to the designs of royal policy.

The list also shows that the central government favored the northwest as far as local military competition opportunities were concerned. This pattern emerges when we move roughly north to south down the Korean Peninsula, noting the number of new local military competitions created for each province: Hamgyŏng (zero), P'yŏngan (six), Hwanghae (four), Kyŏnggi (two), Kangwŏn (two), Ch'ungch'ŏng (one), Chŏlla (one), and Kyŏngsang (three). Even though the three southernmost provinces (Ch'ungch'ŏng, Chŏlla, and Kyŏngsang) made up the most populous part of the country, their combined total of five new local military competitions is outnumbered by the six created for a single northern province, P'yŏngan. As Chŏng Hae-ŭn also points out, there was a solid connection between the importance of military regiments in the northwest, the capital, and Kyŏnggi Province and the strong overall representation of these regions among the late Chosŏn military examination graduates, as is discussed further in Chapter 5.

Though benefiting from greater opportunities to pass the military examination, northern residents, upon earning the degree, generally found themselves stymied in their quest to obtain offices. The more persistent among them visited Seoul in pursuit of a meaningful post, through whatever connections, lobbying, and bribery they could manage. To be sure, men of exceptional martial skills from P'yŏngan and Hamgyŏng Provinces could be appointed as, respectively, Northwestern Special Military Officers (Sŏbuk Pyŏlburyo Kun'gwan) and Northeastern Special Military Officers (Tongbuk Pyŏlburyo Kun'gwan), even before passing the military examination. Though not official posts in the regular nine-rank bureaucratic hierarchy, these assignments provided a good position from which to pass the military examination and even to obtain a regular military office afterward, hence joining officialdom.[69]

All the same, there were simply too many men aspiring to military posts in a central bureaucracy that remained essentially unchanged in size until the 1880s. Northern residents confronted an officialdom increasingly dominated by a small number of capital *yangban* descent lines—a barrier that even the southern local *yangban* could not overcome. The impediment was institutionalized in that the government customarily excluded men from the north, along with the illegitimate sons of *yangban* fathers, from registration as royal messenger candidates, an exclusion that also precluded appointments as concurrent military official-royal messenger (Mugyŏm Sŏnjŏn'gwan), bailiff (Ch'amgun), recruiter (Kwŏn'gwan), battalion commander (Pujang), and palace sentinel (Sumunjang). As we have seen, registration as a royal messenger candidate was the key point from which a military examination passer could launch a successful official career, and the registered candidates tended to be from central military official lines.[70]

The late Chosŏn kings starting with Sukchong sought to end the custom of excluding northerners from the royal messenger candidacy, but even into the nineteenth century repeated royal orders to this effect were not meaningfully implemented. During Sukchong's reign some military examination graduates from the northwest were able to attain posts of junior sixth-rank—the minimum level one had to attain in order to harbor any hope of advancing to more important positions in Chosŏn officialdom—but almost none received a district magistrate post. Even during the reign of Chŏngjo, who continued his grandfather Yŏngjo's efforts to promote martially talented northwesterners by assigning them to special royal guard units, those few military examination graduates from P'yŏngan Province who actually received an office generally could not advance beyond palace sentinel, battalion commander, frontier garrison commander, or port commander. In the end, royal policies geared toward fostering and recruiting the martially talented northwesterners failed to find them more influential roles in the central political arena.[71]

Furthermore, the gains in military examination success made by the northern elites during the seventeenth and eighteenth centuries did not continue far into the nineteenth century. As Figure 3.1 shows, the Hamgyŏng Province's share of all military examination passers produced during the 1800–34 period (9.6 percent) was more or less the peak level under which the nineteenth-century figures fluctuated (between 4.6 and 9.7 percent), whereas the P'yŏngan Province's share plummeted from a peak of 19.3 percent between 1776 and 1800 to a low of 2.1 percent between 1834 and 1849. These numbers square with the findings of earlier studies, suggesting that the center's effort to accommodate northern residents through the military examination reached its limit by about 1800. Hamgyŏng's nineteenth-century record is one of stagnation, while P'yŏngan's drop most likely reflects the adverse impact of the 1812 Hong Kyŏng-nae rebellion. The native sons of both provinces probably had little additional incentive to hone their martial skills, and this must have been especially true for P'yŏngan residents, whose region now bore the stigma of rebellion. Settling in the end for regional elite status, as did southern local *yangban*, the northwestern elite in particular, as well as the northern elites as a whole, probably saw more to gain through education and scholarship rather than martial training.[72]

Summation

In late Chosŏn, local elites turned to the military examination. The patterns of military examination success, along with the value of the examination as a sociopolitical resource, varied according to region. As an ascriptive status group, the southern *yangban* wielded local political influence by assisting the centrally appointed magistrate in governing the county while maintaining a social hierarchy that they dominated. Excluded from the central political structure, some turned to military careers in the seventeenth and eighteenth centuries, but most did not transform themselves into a kind of military aristocracy, as did many Seoul *yangban* descent lines. Meanwhile, wealthy social newcomers began challenging the *yangban*-dominated local administrative and social systems. In this context, the local aristocracy of the south focused even more on cultural activities, through which they further stressed their superior status based on birth anyway. Since an examination degree certainly was not a prerequisite for *yangban* status, it appealed mainly to those who had other reasons to desire one. Compared to the licentiate examination degree that signified the Confucian educational credentials of the degree holder, the military examination degree's efficacy as a certification of cultural capital was more limited.

The Kaesŏng elite faced more conscious, institutionalized discrimination by the center and its aristocracy. The Chosŏn state initially barred the residents of Kaesŏng, the capital of the previous dynasty, from the examination; even after the lifting of the ban those earning a degree generally did not receive important positions in the central government. The members of the Kaesŏng elite compensated for their marginalized status by assuming a dominant commercial role in the liberalized economy of late Chosŏn. Nonetheless, they continued, from the seventeenth century on, to compete successfully in the examination, especially the military contest. Along with the lofty court ranks and offices more readily available to the wealthy, a military examination degree carried prestige as a state-sanctioned marker of status, which was more important to the Kaesŏng elite than to the southern local aristocracy whose status was defined by birth.

The northern elites of P'yŏngan and Hamgyŏng Provinces suffered from the belief, held among central and southern aristocrats, that the north had no *yangban.* This perception in part derived from the prevalent notion that the region was culturally backward. The problem was also political in nature, because the aristocracy used it to rationalize the continued exclusion of northern men from the central political arena. As acknowledged by the northern elites themselves, Confucian learning spread relatively late in the north, although the seventeenth century witnessed remarkable advances in this regard as well as in commercial success. Eighteenth-century kings and some central officials, in their efforts to bolster royal power, tried to promote talented men from the north, and the martially skilled native sons found advancement opportunities through the comparatively abundant competitions held by numerous local military regiments. In this milieu, northern elites enjoyed impressive examination success in the seventeenth and eighteenth centuries, but the existing central political structure did not allow them meaningful participation. Frustrated, northern elites generally had to be content with local elite status, although some collaborated with increasingly better-educated or martially trained nonelites in subversive movements such as the Hong Kyŏng-nae rebellion. P'yŏngan Province's military examination success rate, adversely affected by this unsuccessful uprising, plummeted in the nineteenth century, whereas the pattern for Hamgyŏng Province was that of stagnation.

Varied patterns of local elite participation in the military examination provoke the question of whether the large number of military examination passers and the creation of new military units throughout the country improved the defense structure. Before the 1890s, we cannot speak of sustained, significant military activity among local elites in terms of militia formation or professionalization. The overall military system seems to have shifted its emphasis from recruitment and training to taxation; the number of troops on duty at any moment was not so important, and the state failed to expand the number of full-time troops on its payroll. The late Chosŏn military examination did not have much relation to this shift. Instead, it functioned as a state-sanctioned status credential for men of martial talent regardless of whether they were actually performing military duty.

FOUR

Yangban *Cohesiveness and the Chosŏn Dynasty*

As emerging status boundaries sharpened in late Chosŏn, the *yangban* status group itself became internally differentiated, cleaving in the seventeenth and eighteenth centuries into distinct central civil official, central military official, and local *yangban* kinship groups. Oligarchic central civil official descent lines based in Seoul and its surrounding areas dominated court politics, and the central military official lines played supporting roles. In contrast, local elites throughout Korea, including the southern *yangban,* experienced exclusion from the central political arena.

Did this differentiation lead to the dissolution of the *yangban* aristocracy into three discrete social status groups? In answering this and related questions, we need to remember that scholars of Chosŏn social history regard *yangban* not so much as a body of incumbent central officials as an ascriptive status group. Song Chun-ho, for example, once noted that regardless of branch affiliation, military examination passers and military officials drawn from local *yangban* were regarded as social equals by other local *yangban,* because they all qualified as such in the most fundamental way—by birth.[1] By extension, the same was true for the generally officeless local *yangban* as a whole.

Throughout late Chosŏn, personal ties and cultural exchanges continued to bind the central and southern *yangban* together, in spite of obvious differences in their political stature. The two groups maintained a mutually beneficial relationship. For a southern aristocratic lineage based in a remote provincial county, such ties meant access to the latest news on court politics and foreign affairs, a personal introduction to the new county magistrate or provincial governor, or even an arranged marriage with a Seoul *yangban* family. In return, local *yangban* provided their associates in the capital with gifts, supplementing the latter's official salaries, which were too small to maintain expensive lifestyles in Seoul.[2]

Of course, these ties do not prove that central civil officials, central military officials, and southern local aristocrats constituted one cohesive status group, the *yangban*. After all, it is possible that among the three, only the central civil officials retained membership in the bona fide aristocracy, with the others interacting as social inferiors or subordinates, in the same way many hereditary local functionaries and technical specialists were able to engage in intellectual exchanges with bona fide *yangban*.[3] In such relationships, a *yangban* and a *chungin* could respect each other as intellectual equals, but the disparity in status must have been experienced as real. Furthermore, clear differences in career patterns and political power among central civil official, central military official, and southern local *yangban* make it tempting to declare that the three were distinct status groups.[4]

Even the officeholding capital *yangban* lacked cohesion. Hereditary political cleavages, bloody purges, and the factionalization of local private academies for scholars and officials all indicate that cohesiveness was not the primary feature of *yangban* society, particularly when it came to politics. Economically, however, we see greater—if not total—unity. Central and local aristocrats alike defended their economic privileges in land and slave ownership, as well as their exemption from military service. For sure, some *yangban* officials took the side of the state in increasing revenues to finance the government—even going against the general interests of the *yangban* at times—but such public-minded reformers did not fare well. In sum, differences in factional loyalties and intellectual lineages could supersede the more or less common economic interests of central and local *yangban*.[5]

To determine whether the central civil officials, central military officials, and southern local aristocracy belonged to one cohesive social status group, the *yangban,* additional criteria are necessity. To that end, I will analyze marriage and adoption practices, genealogical proximity, and the state's treatment of the aristocracy and others especially as regards purchased ranks and offices. This chapter argues that the status boundary separating the aristocracy from the rest of society was far clearer and more rigid than any of the differentiations between various *yangban* subgroups in terms of their branch affiliation or extent of participation in the central political structure.

Marriage Ties

Marriage practices suggest that a high degree of social homogeneity characterized the central military aristocracy. By the nineteenth century, the majority of military examination graduates from prominent military lines had marriage ties to spouses from other such descent lines, though not matching the degree of de facto exclusivity typical of marriages among the technical specialist *chungin.* A high intraprofessional marriage rate among central military officials leaves unanswered the question of whether they, along with southern local aristocrats, retained membership in a cohesive *yangban* status group; the practice nevertheless clearly suggests that a distinct military aristocracy emerged in the course of the late Chosŏn period.

A military examination graduate genealogy (*mubo*) is an informative source for analyzing marriage patterns in that it records the degree, rank, or office (if any) of the graduate's father-in-law and maternal grandfather. In his recent study of prominent central military official descent lines of late Chosŏn, Chang P'il-gi analyzes about 3,700 military examination passers recorded in these genealogies—meaning that most of them were from western central Korea, due to the elitist nature of these sources. Chang points out that these military aristocrats maintained a highly restricted marriage sphere over generations, contracting marriages almost entirely among themselves.[6]

Since his study does not provide more detailed statistics on marriage patterns, I performed my own analysis to determine just how exclusive this marriage practice may have been in comparison to that of the technical specialist *chungin.* According to my findings, central military officials generally formed marriage ties among themselves. Among my sample of prominent central military official descent lines recorded in a nineteenth-century military examination graduate genealogy, anywhere from about 55 to 90 percent of the passers had a maternal grandfather or a father-in-law who held the same degree or became a military official (Table 4.1).

Table 4.1
Intraprofessional Marriages
among Nineteenth-Century Military Examination Passers

Descent group	Graduates recorded	Intraprofessional marriage cases	Percentage
P'yŏngyang (Cho)	40	36	90.0
Tŏksu (Yi)	64	43	67.1
Nŭngsŏng (Ku)	74	48	64.9
Chŏnŭi (Yi)	21	13	61.9
P'yŏngsan (Sin)	63	36	57.1
Suwŏn (Paek)	38	21	55.3
Miryang (Pak)	20	11	55.0

SOURCE: "Mubo," Changsŏgak collection (2-1741).
NOTE: Descent groups consist of ancestral seats followed by surnames in parentheses.

Table 4.2
Intraprofessional Marriages
among Nineteenth-Century Interpreter Examination Passers

Descent group	Graduates recorded	Intraprofessional marriage cases	Percentage
Hanyang (Yu)	17	17	100.0
Kyŏngju (Ch'oe)	20	19	95.0
Haeju (O)	13	12	92.3
Chŏnju (Yi)	46	42	91.3
Miryang (Pak)	11	10	90.9
Ch'ŏllyŏng (Hyŏn)	40	36	90.0
Chŏngŭp (Yi)	8	7	87.5

SOURCE: *Yŏkkwa p'alsebo.*
NOTE: Descent groups consist of ancestral seats followed by surnames in parentheses.

To put the practice in perspective, I also looked at the marriage patterns of technical examination degree holders—specifically, the rate of marriage among technical specialist descent lines. A genealogy of nineteenth-century interpreter examination passers, extending over eight generations, shows that between roughly 88 and 100 percent of interpreter examination (*yŏkkwa*) degree holders from prominent Seoul *chungin* lines had a technical examination passer or a technical specialist as his father-in-law or maternal grandfather (Table 4.2).

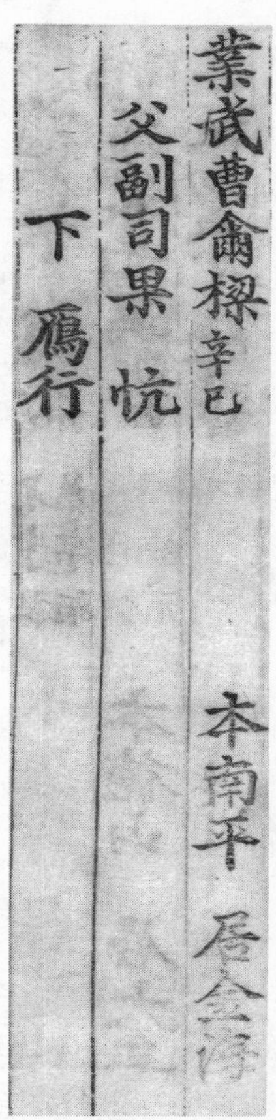

業武曹爾樑 辛巳 本南平 居金浮

父副司果 忼

下 爲行

Figure 4.1 Cho I-ryang as Recorded in the 1672 Special Military Examination Roster. Note: At the age of 32 *se*, he is attributed the service status of *ŏmmu* ("military vocation man"). Cho placed 376th among 554 third-tier (*pyŏng-kwa*) passers, a group ranked below 46 of the second tier and a single passer of the first tier. Although both the civil and military examination rosters are contained in the bound volume, the title on the cover page only mentions the civil examination. From *Imja-nyŏn pyŏlsi munkwa pangmok*. Courtesy of Harvard-Yenching Library, Harvard University.

The marriage data at hand shows that a high degree of social homogeneity characterized both the central aristocratic military men and technical specialists in late Chosŏn. At the same time, the intraprofessional marriage rate of roughly 60 percent among the central military official descent lines does not amount to the near exclusivity described by Chang P'il-gi in his study of late Chosŏn military lines in Seoul.[7] This rate is also much lower than the de facto exclusivity characterizing the marriage practice among technical specialists, of whom over 90 percent married into other technical specialist lines.[8]

In fact, civil-military marriage ties among central officials seem to have continued through the seventeenth century. For example, Kang-dong Magistrate Cho I-ryang (1641–88), a 1672 military examination graduate from the Namp'yŏng Cho lineage of Kimhae (see Figure 4.1), married his son to a granddaughter of Confucian Academy Lecturer (Chikkang) Kwak Yung, a 1627 civil examination graduate from the Hyŏnp'ung Kwak lineage residing in Hyŏnp'ung, and a nephew of the famed local militia commander during the Korean-Japanese war, Kwak Chae-u (1552–1617). Similarly, Paek Hŭi-jang (1644–1730), a Suwŏn Paek military examination graduate (1666) from Chinju, married his son to a granddaughter of Second Censor Ha Chin (1597–1658), a civil examination graduate (1633) from the same locale. Likewise, Provincial Army Deputy Commander (Pyŏngma Chŏlchesa) Chŏng Sa-sŏ (1569–1678), a Yŏnil Chŏng military examination graduate (1594) from Chinju, married his daughter to a son of Second Censor Kang Ing-mun (1568–?), who was a Chinju Kang civil examination graduate (1606) from Hapch'ŏn.[9]

In the nineteenth century, marriage ties between central military official and central civil official descent lines became less common. Among the nineteenth-century military examination degree holders whose records are included in my database, the degree subject of the father-in-law or maternal grandfather is ascertainable in 329 cases The breakdown shows 280 military examination graduates, 42 literary licentiates, 4 classics licentiates, 3 civil examination graduates, and no technical examination graduates. Given that the 329 nineteenth-century military examination graduates represent only about 7 percent of 4,718 nineteenth-century degree holders included in my database, the subject distribution data at hand has to be used with caution. Furthermore, almost all of the 329 cases are those of successful candidates from the military aristocracy.

We may also surmise that the military examination passers from less distinguished descent groups were even less likely to have a maternal grandfather or father-in-law who had passed any kind of an examination. After all in late Chosŏn, all types of state examinations were increasingly dominated by a relatively small segment of the population. Considering how these patterns had been crystallized by the nineteenth century, the evidence of those pre-1800 military examination graduates who formed marriage ties with civil examination graduates suggests that the seventeenth century was still a transition period as far as the late Chosŏn emergence of distinct civil and military official lines was concerned.

Adoption

In late Chosŏn, adoption was necessary to continue an heirless descent line. In contrast to the trend toward exclusivity that was typical of marriage practices, the adoption of heirs continued among the central civil official, central military official, and southern aristocratic lines. Throughout late Chosŏn, giving and taking adoptive sons—ideally, the adoptee would be a close agnate—remained an "in-group" behavior connected to status consciousness.[10] Once adoption practice became more common, *yangban* fathers began to look even among distant agnatic kinsmen for an heir with talent and good physical appearance, bypassing closer but less endowed relatives, as well as any natural sons by concubines.[11] The exclusion of illegitimate sons from consideration was the result of the Chosŏn social practice that stripped them of the right to inherit aristocratic prerogatives from their fathers. Without a doubt, what was imperative was a mutual recognition, between the family providing an adoptive heir and the family receiving one, that both were of same social status.

Some years ago, I noticed a case of a nineteenth-century adoption involving two remotely related lines within a single descent group, the Tŏksu Yi. One was descended from the famous admiral, Yi Sun-sin, and was a central military official line in late Chosŏn, whereas the other was descended from the famed sixteenth-century Neo-Confucian scholar Yi I, and was known mostly for civil officials. The two Tŏksu Yi lines had to trace their pedigrees all the way back to the late Koryŏ period to find a common ancestor, but the fact that neither the great genealogical distance nor the difference in branch affiliation was a stumbling block for the adoption arrangement between the two suggests that they perceived each other as belonging to the same social status group. Furthermore, both lines had an illegitimate son somewhere in the intervening generations and thus lacked full *yangban* credentials. This case makes me wonder if the central civil official, central military official, and southern aristocratic descent lines of bona fide *yangban* pedigree—that is, no illegitimacy in intervening generations—also exchanged adoptive heirs among themselves, perceiving one another as social equals. Let us examine a couple of examples typical of countless other similar cases from late Chosŏn.

The Namp'yŏng Cho descent group discussed in Chapter 3 included a capital line and a Kimhae-based branch. Sixth Rank Military Officer (Sagwa) Cho Kang (1622–66), who appeared in the register of Kimhae local agency officers (1641) and was the first from the Kimhae line to pass the military examination (1656), became the posthumous adoptive heir to a distant uncle in Seoul who had died without a son. In comparison to the Kimhae branch that had been producing degreeless officeholders for several generations preceding Cho Kang, the capital line could boast a more illustrious history. Moreover, through marriages, its direct ancestors included the first four kings of the Chosŏn dynasty, Chief State Councillor Sin Suk-chu (1417–75), Minister of Personnel Pak Chung-sŏn (1435–81), and Security Council Superintendent (Chungch'uwŏn P'ansa) Sŏng Tal-saeng (1376–1444)—who was the top passer of the first military examination (1402). Thus, the adoption would not have been possible if the Seoul line did not regard the Kimhae line as a social peer.

For another telling example of adoption representing in-group behavior, we can turn to the case of Kapsin Coup (1884) activist Kim Ok-kyun (1851–94). As is well known, Kim was born into an Andong Kim family living in Kongju in Ch'ungch'ŏng Province. Although none of his recent forebears held any important office, as a young boy Kim was adopted by a distant uncle in Seoul, Magistrate Kim Pyŏng-gi (1814–?), whose recent ancestors included important central civil officials.[12] This particular case shows that a shared status identity bound together a central civil official descent lines and its local *yangban* kinsmen.

All those directly descended from a genealogical apex figure, and whose line was free of any illegitimate sons in the intervening generations, would have felt a sense of membership in a single, cohesive kin group, with or without adoption. As Mark Peterson has shown, a family in need often brought in an adoptee from such a distant relative that one wonders if they knew any more about each other than that a well documented genealogical link existed.[13] Given that no late Chosŏn *yangban* would even have considered adopting a male from a genealogically related descent line that had been tainted by an illegitimate-son ancestor—not to mention from any technical specialist, local functionary, commoner, or slave line—the in-group exchange of adoptive heirs among the central civil official, central military official, and southern aristocratic descent lines shows that the three considered one another to be of the same social status, the *yangban.*

Branch Affiliation Diversity

By the end of the eighteenth century, Korea had become a lineage society with extended families organized on the principle of patrilineal descent. Although the growing population made it more difficult for descent groups to keep track of even their *yangban* members scattered throughout the country and record all of them in periodically updated genealogies, such groups continued to make an effort to demonstrate the relationship among various branches descended from a common ancestor. These records clearly show that late Chosŏn *yangban* descent lines could easily comprise both civil and military official branches, as well as the southern local aristocratic lines that generally produced no examination graduates, rank holders, or officials. Within a descent group, central military official and southern aristocratic descent lines could share a common ancestor with the civil official lines. In fact, the genealogical and social proximity among the three groups was close in late Chosŏn, and the apical figure tended to have lived sometime between the fourteenth and seventeenth centuries. Of course, there could not be any illegitimate son in the intervening generations.

Even the central civil official lines that dominated court politics from 1800 to 1864, a period that witnessed four consecutive accessions of a minor to the throne, had closely related military official and local *yangban* branches.[14] For example, Kim Ik-sun (?–1812), who was a military examination graduate (1789) and the grandfather of the famous wandering poet, Kim Pyŏng-yŏn (also known as Kim Satkat, 1807–63), was one of many Andong Kim military men descended from Kim Sang-hŏn (1570–1652), a renowned anti-Qing Westerner statesman, and several of his cousins. In the nineteenth century, the royal in-law Andong Kim civil officials of Seoul were also descendants of these cousins.[15]

For another example of a late Chosŏn *yangban* lineage with both civil and military official descent lines, we may turn to the Hamjong Ŏ descent group. Both Finance Minister (T'akchibu Taesin) Ŏ Yun-jung (1848–96), who was the famous Kabo Reform (1894–96) statesman, and Governor's Military Aide (Chunggun) Ŏ Chae-yŏn (1823–71), the military commander killed on Kanghwa Island while fighting valiantly against American troops, were Hamjong Ŏ. Whereas Yun-jung was a civil examination graduate from a Patriarch faction civil official descent line that had provided the second queen for King Kyŏngjong (r. 1720–24), Chae-yŏn was a military examination graduate from a military line. Based in and around Seoul, both lines were descended from Minister of Personnel Ŏ Hyo-ch'ŏm (1405–75), a 1429 civil examination graduate. The descendants of some of his first cousins constituted the local aristocratic Hamjong Ŏ lineages based in Kimhae and other counties in southern Kyŏngsang Province. In 1871, Yun-jung wrote a preface for a new edition of the Hamjong Ŏ genealogy, which, of course, recorded all three types of descent lines—that is the central civil officials, central military officials, and southern local aristocrats.[16]

Yet another example of how the central civil official, central military official, and southern local *yangban* branches of a descent group saw themselves as sharing a relatively recent common ancestry is the Miryang Pak descended from Pak Ch'ung-wŏn (1507–81), whose Seoul-based line had previously produced some merit subjects as well as victims of the 1519 Literati Purge.[17] Ch'ung-wŏn passed the civil examination in 1531 and attained the post of Fifth State Councillor (Uch'ansŏng). His four sons had varied success in their careers. The eldest son, Pak Kye-hyŏn (1524–80), passed the civil examination and eventually became the minister of war. He carried on the descent line's political prominence, which culminated in his grandson, Chief State Councillor Pak Sŭng-jong, and great-grandson, Pak Cha-hŭng, the daughter of whom was married to Kwanghaegun's crown prince. The line's political prominence came to an end when, upon Kwanghaegun's dethronement in 1623, Sŭng-jong, Cha-hŭng, and the daughter all committed suicide. After this disaster, only a few of the direct male descendants of Kye-hyŏn passed any examination, mostly as local *yangban* of Chŏlla Province in the nineteenth century. Kye-hyŏn's first younger brother, Pak Ŭng-hyŏn (1532–?), was neither a degree holder himself nor the founder of a descent line of any examination success. Kye-hyŏn's second younger brother, Pak Yong-hyŏn (1536–?), and Yong-hyŏn's son both passed the military examination, but they did not give rise to a military line. Instead, a few of their direct descendants, residing in Seoul or Ch'ungch'ŏng Province, passed the civil and licentiate examinations. It was the third younger brother, Pak Ho-hyŏn (1550–81), who founded a line that not only enjoyed great examination success but also chose a particular branch affiliation. Known among his descendants are at least 4 civil examination graduates, 24 licentiates, and 46 military examination graduates. Regardless of the examination subject or branch affiliation, most descendants lived in Seoul or various counties in western central Korea—a pattern that is hardly surprising in light of their continuing examination success and political participation until the end of the dynasty.

Both a central civil official line and a central military official line can be found among the even more closely related patrilineal descendants of an apical figure. A case in point is the Disciple faction Haeju O line, descended from Left Kyŏngsang Provincial Army Commander (Kyŏngsang-chwado Pyŏngma Chŏltosa) O Chŏng-bang (1552–1625), a top passer of the military examination in 1583. Although the son, O Sa-gyŏm, was not an examination graduate, three out of Sa-gyŏm's four sons passed the civil examination between 1612 and 1646. The eldest son became the founder of a central civil official line producing 13 civil examination graduates from 1649 to 1891, whereas the three younger sons all founded central military official lines that featured, respectively, at least 4, 13, and 41 known military examination graduates during the remainder of the dynasty. The line descended from the second son was not as strictly military in branch affiliation as the two others: besides the 4 military examination graduates, this line of descent produced at least 2 civil examination graduates (1665, 1892). In contrast, the two youngest brothers both founded lines strictly oriented toward the military branch. In sum, the case of the Haeju O line descended from O Chŏng-bang illustrates how a mid-Chosŏn military official could become the apical ancestor of both central civil and central military lines within the same descent group.[18]

Marriage alliances, the exchange of adoptive heirs, and the compilation of genealogies all demonstrate how descent lines maintained status boundaries in their social practice. Now let us turn to a consideration of how the aristocracy used the state to the same end, and of the consequences of this for the rest of the society.

The Government Sale of Ranks and Offices

Although the aristocracy increasingly allowed social newcomers to attain state-sanctioned status markers such as court ranks and offices, the elite continued to distinguish itself from the rest of the population. Notwithstanding its need for additional revenue, the *yangban*-controlled state insisted that status distinctions be a factor in determining the price (generally measured in a quantity of grain) of various ranks and offices, and restricted the availability of some to non-*yangban* purchasers. These regulations represent yet further evidence that the status boundary between a *yangban* and a non-*yangban* was deemed significant, whereas differences in the bureaucratic role or the degree of participation in the central bureaucracy among the central civil official, central military official, and southern aristocratic descent lines were not.

The concept of buying one's way up was not new. As early as the sixteenth century, the government made illegitimate sons and the low-born—previously all barred from the examination—eligible to compete if they submitted a specified amount of grain. This sort of manumission by purchase was too expensive for most slaves.[19] Beginning in 1583, the extraction of such contributions from illegitimate sons wishing to participate remained a source of resentment and humiliation for such candidates, given that those cultured and educated enough to compete tended to be sons of *yangban* fathers. After a series of debates, the state formally ended the practice in 1696, enabling illegitimate sons thereafter to take the examination without payment.[20]

In the seventeenth century, the sale of ranks and offices provided a new way for those of means to acquire a state-sanctioned status marker. The most eager purchasers were wealthy commoners and marginalized *yangban*. Faced with frequent famines and revenue shortages, the government resorted to what many *yangban* officials saw as a necessary evil: beginning in 1661, the court decided to conduct such transactions in accordance with detailed regulations.[21] The ranks and offices available for sale during this period can be divided into three categories, as described in various government documents: supernumerary offices (*kasŏljik*); ranks for the elderly of age 60 *se* and above; and ranks and offices posthumously honoring the dead (*ch'ujŭng*).[22] Upon submitting a specified amount of grain or other payment, the purchaser received for himself or his deceased ancestor a formal appointment certificate stating that the government was granting the purchased rank or office. Because the space for the appointee's name was left blank for the local authority to fill in, such a document was known as a "nameless appointment certificate" (*kongmyŏngch'ŏp*), although grain donors winning the special attention of the court could receive a more personalized copy.[23] In times of hardship—such as a severe famine pressuring the government to secure more grain for relief efforts—hundreds of nameless appointment certificates could be printed and delivered to a province or locality. Sometimes the local authority had to return leftover certificates to the central government so they could be properly destroyed.[24]

The prices of ranks and offices generally reflected prestige differentials. They were set in terms of a quantity of rice, the *sŏk* (equivalent to roughly 5.12 American bushels, or 47.6 American gallons); purchasers could also pay with silver or bolts of cloth. Of course, the exact price of each office or rank fluctuated, as did the number of blank appointment certificates issued. All depended on the needs of the government, as determined by the severity of famine, and the estimated availability of grain among potential donors.[25] For the most part, the price range was narrowest for various ranks granted to the elderly (ranging, in the mid-seventeenth century, from three to five *sŏk* of rice). These ranks also required the smallest amount of grain, with the price decreasing in accordance with advancing age. According to a regulation dated 1660, the price charged for the upper senior third civil rank was five *sŏk* of rice for those aged 60 to 69 *se*, and three *sŏk* for those at least 70; the regulations dated 1661 and 1690 show that these prices remained the same, with a lower price of four *sŏk* for those between 70 and 89 *se* and two *sŏk* for those 90 or above.[26] Interestingly, all three regulations allowed those elderly already holding the upper senior third civil rank to pay additional *sŏk* of rice (two or three, depending on the regulation) for a junior second civil rank.[27]

In spite of these regulations governing price, it became increasingly common in late Chosŏn for the state to grant ranks for free to those of advanced age. Nonetheless, the government distinguished between the *yangban* and non-*yangban* elderly in setting the minimum age requirement for such ranks. Two court discussions in 1706 dealt with the issue of granting ranks to the elderly of Cheju Island and Seoul. In both cases, the state made a status distinction: the *yangban* elderly had to be at least 80 *se,* whereas commoners had to be at least 90.[28]

Compared to the ranks sold to the elderly, the government charged a much wider range of prices for posthumous honors and supernumerary posts. According to regulations from 1660, 1661, and 1690, the price of a rank or an office purchased as a posthumous honor started at 4 *sŏk* of rice and could go up to 25 *sŏk* for the highest ranks and offices available. Supernumerary offices for the purchasers themselves were even more expensive. In the mid-seventeenth century, the price ranged from 12 to 50 *sŏk* of rice. Unlike the ranks for the elderly that were less expensive or even free, posthumous honors and supernumary posts were subject to differential pricing and even some restrictions, depending on whether the purchaser was a *yangban.* Moreover, commoners and lowborn owing military service to the state were ineligible for a supernumerary post, and the ritual performance of expressing gratitude to the king (*saŭn*) was reserved only for *yangban* purchasers of certain high-level supernumerary posts.[29]

It is difficult to calculate what portion of income the price of a rank or office represented for a purchaser. Popular lore suggests that at the end of the dynasty, someone capable of claiming a rice harvest of 10,000 *sŏk* was considered very wealthy; a cultivator harvesting 1,000 *sŏk* was still deemed well-off. If we were to assume that in late Chosŏn agricultural production increased substantially, then we can surmise that a wealthy cultivator harvesting 600 *sŏk* of rice in the seventeenth century can be deemed comparable to a wealthy cultivator harvesting 1,000 *sŏk* in the nineteenth century in terms of relative wealth in society.[30] Even a more conservative estimate of the increase in productivity and total food production from 1660 to the dynasty's end suggests that the office in question was worth a month's income for a wealthy cultivator capable of claiming an annual harvest total of 1,000 *sŏk,* whether during the seventeenth century or around 1900.[31] Clearly, then, individuals from descent lines far removed from central political power, and yet recorded with such posts in their respective genealogies, were no ordinary peasants or poor *yangban.*

In spite of its efforts to distinguish between *yangban* and non-*yangban* purchasers, the state often failed to prevent non-*yangban* from buying state-sanctioned status markers that were technically restricted by the regulations. For example, in the summer of 1683, officials informed King Sukchong that his previous order to grant an interpreter the supernumerary senior third-rank post of fifth minister-without-portfolio (Ch'ŏmji Chungch'ubusa) in exchange for fifty *sŏk* of rice could not be carried out, as the existing regulation reserved such supernumerary posts only for *yangban*. In response, Sukchong ordered the bureau concerned to change the reward for the interpreter, who, judging from the entire discussion, seems to have been a technical specialist *chungin*.[32]

Months later, in a much more detailed statement, Minister of War Nam Ku-man spoke of some confusion surrounding the issue of granting supernumerary posts to non-*yangban* grain donors. Apparently there was disagreement over whether granting a Military Colony Staff Officer (Tunjŏn Kun'gwan) and an interpreter high-ranking supernumerary posts had violated the regulations keeping such posts off limits to non-*yangban*. Sukchong sided with Nam, who suggested that—as he had heard that in the past there had been no restrictions against commoners purchasing supernumerary posts—the State Council should reconsider the whole question, set new regulations, and execute them with the king's approval, rather than leaving it up to the agency concerned to act on its own.[33] These and many other similar discussions indicate that nonaristocrats somehow continued to buy the kinds of ranks and offices that were supposedly reserved for *yangban*.

Moreover, despite the state's efforts to maintain status distinctions, purchased ranks and offices in general became devalued in the eyes of *yangban*. For example, in 1684, the Office of Famine Relief (Chinhyulch'ŏng) reported that a military officer living in the province of Ch'ungch'ŏng (referred to as Kongch'ung at the time) who had provided some 60 *sŏk* of grain for the hungry, petitioned for permission to return the Board of Personnel document granting him the upper senior third civil rank, which was commonly given to those submitting grain. He is said to have protested that he had not fed the famished in expectation of such a rank, and that such a thing was shameful for a *yangban*. In the end, the Office of Famine Relief argued that the state could not ignore a man of merit. Noting that the amount of mixed grain the righteous military officer had donated was comparable to 24 *sŏk* of rice, the Office recommended to Sukchong that the original rank bestowal certificate be taken back and replaced by another one appointing him to the supernumerary civil senior third-rank post of government arsenal second secretary (Kun'gisijŏng). The king concurred.[34] Although this post was also available for purchase at the time, the court clearly saw it as something a *yangban* would consider more prestigious, and thus more compatible with his social status, than the upper senior third civil rank much more commonly purchased by wealthy commoners.

Ranks and offices sold by the state tended to be titular in character, without involving actual appointment or incumbency. Thus, most bona fide *yangban,* whose social status was ascriptive in nature, had little incentive to purchase them, although the state awarded many such ranks and offices to those unselfish aristocrats who merely wanted to help the state and the people in time of need. In contrast, more non-*yangban* grain donors must have been attracted to the rewards embodied in the ranks or office themselves. It is likely that the *yangban*-commoner distinction was clear to most people in society. Especially from the aristocracy's vantage point, there was nothing a non-*yangban* could do to make himself into one. Even commoners, to whom purchased ranks and offices may have been more awe-inspiring, would have been hard pressed to believe that the acquisition of such trappings by their own kind meant elevation toward *yangban* status. The fact that purchased ranks and offices were still held by at least some *yangban,* if not many, made them retain prestige, especially in the eyes of nonelites.

The Sacrosanct Aristocracy

Nineteenth-century central military officials felt comfortable with their station in life and continued to defend the status quo, which guaranteed them aristocratic status, political responsibilities, and cultural roles. Both the state and central civil official descent lines appreciated the services of capable military men, and their expertise assumed even greater importance during the period of internal uprisings and imperialist incursions. Unlike technical specialists and hereditary local functionaries who, in spite of their cultural attainments and valuable services to the state, were frustrated with the status constraints that prevented them from playing more important roles in officialdom, the military examination passers of *yangban* backgrounds certainly were not agents of change. Their continuing membership in the aristocracy was dependent not so much on degrees, ranks, or offices as on the integrity of the status hierarchy.

Technical specialists and hereditary local functionaries deserve attention in a discussion of status group satisfaction with the existing order because their cases offer a comparison with the military aristocracy's attitudes toward the late Chosŏn system. While demanding equal opportunities in the *yangban*-dominated central officialdom, technical specialists themselves became more socially exclusive. In late Chosŏn, a small number of such descent lines, generally based in Seoul, monopolized the technical specialist posts in the central government for generations. Capable technical specialists received high ranks and offices because their expertise was valued by both *yangban* officials and kings, who were generally committed to the principle of promoting men of virtue and talent.[35] Aware of the vital importance of their skills and services to the state, hereditary technical specialists developed their own unique status consciousness, which they manifested through sociocultural activities such as compiling genealogies—like the *Record of Surname Origins* (*Sŏngwŏnnok*) and various eight-generation genealogies (*p'alsebo*) of technical examination graduates, such as the *Eight-Generation Genealogy of Interpreter Examination Graduates* (*Yŏkkwa p'alsebo*)—as well as examination rosters, family histories, and literary collections that focused on their own accomplishments.[36]

Outside Seoul, hereditary local functionaries also increasingly developed their own unique status consciousness.[37] As is discussed in detail in Chapter 5, many late Chosŏn local functionaries attained such a high level of education and cultural sophistication that many were able to cultivate sociocultural ties with some of the most renowned *yangban* Confucian scholars of their time. A *yangban* contact was crucial for any functionary entertaining the hope of passing the state examination and, with a *yangban* patron's recommendation, receiving a post in the central government. At the same time, educated local functionaries began to demand more respect from the *yangban* aristocracy. Rather than just emphasizing their unique history and the importance of their duties to the state, local functionary intellectuals stressed common origins with *yangban*. This argument was based on historical truth, in that the Koryŏ dynasty had set up an examination system enabling local functionaries passing the examination to enter central government service and to join the central aristocracy, the *yangban*, whose descendants of course preferred to ignore their local functionary origins. Furthermore, local functionary intellectuals claimed that, like the *yangban,* they honored Confucian virtues and rituals. Accordingly, along with other types of hereditary functionaries such as those who served in various government offices in the capital (*kyŏngajŏn*), hereditary local functionaries demanded that they be treated with appropriate Confucian etiquette by the aristocracy.[38]

Regardless of the argument, the aristocracy continued to look down upon technical specialists and local functionaries. To be sure, there were exceptional cases—like the relationship of mutual respect between Pak Kyu-su (1807–76), a member of a Patriarch-faction capital *yangban* line, and O Kyŏng-sŏk (1831–79), a *chungin* interpreter, both of whom visited China on many occasions.[39] Such relationships allowed select technical specialists to play an important role, capitalizing on the decision by King Kojong (r. 1864–1907) to open Korea to Japan and the West, and participating in the Enlightenment Movement of the 1870s and 1880s, which, among other goals, sought to acknowledge the importance of technical expertise. All the same, the complexities of Korean sociolinguistic practice alone must have allowed, for example, a *yangban* student to treat his *chungin* teacher as an intellectual superior without entirely abandoning a form of speech still suggesting his superior social status. We can easily imagine that most *yangban* continued to prefer the ideal of a generalist Confucian scholar to what they deemed the petty skills of technical specialists and the daily administrative chores of local functionaries.

Unlike hereditary local functionaries, who were despised by many *yangban* and excluded from central officialdom, technical specialists were full participants, and some even attained nontechnical positions, such as a magistracy, generally held by the aristocrats. At the same time, *yangban* officials not only kept technical specialists from assuming the more important positions, but also subjected them to strict performance evaluations. Technical specialists were vulnerable to punishments for even relatively minor scandals or crimes, especially the physicians who were responsible for the health of the king and other royals.[40]

Technical specialists and functionaries were men of education, sophistication, and, often, significant wealth, whose potentials could not be fully realized due to status constraints. Clearly frustrated, many were quick to hide their origins by seizing opportunities to claim ancestral seat designations that sounded more plausibly like those of *yangban*. In the personal resumes they submitted in the Kwangmu Reform era (1897–1905), many government officials from technical specialist and local functionary backgrounds claimed descent group affiliations different from those recorded in older documents, such as the technical examination graduate and functionary rosters.[41] For the most part, though, my own experience working with Korean genealogies informs me that the majority of Seoul *chungin* simply stopped participating in genealogy compilations and updates beginning with the late nineteenth century, to such an extent that modern genealogy editions could hope to offer only spotty coverage of their descendants. The reasons for this attitude seem to range from desire to hide less savory origins to contempt toward backward premodern customs—although those of commoner descent, even to this day, continue to make their ways into *yangban* genealogies through various means.[42]

In comparison to technical specialists and hereditary local functionaries, central military official lines occupied a secure, comfortable position in the *yangban*-dominated political and social systems of late Chosŏn. Military aristocrats manifested their distinctive group identity by compiling their own eight-generation genealogies of military examination graduates (*mubo*) in the same way the civil examination passers did. In recording the successful military examination candidates from prominent military *yangban* descent lines, such a genealogy not only excluded graduates from commoner backgrounds but also illegitimate sons, technical specialists, and local functionaries. The fact that only some 3,700 out of perhaps more than 50,000 nineteenth-century military examination passers appear in the extant military examination graduate genealogies speaks to this selectivity.[43]

Unlike the genealogies of technical specialists, those of the central military aristocracy reflect their awareness of continued membership in the *yangban* status group honoring the ideal of a "Confucian general" (Ko. *yujang*, Ch. *rujiang*). In a culture that kept martial virtue at bay, this was the only ideal that a military man could realistically pursue. A Confucian general—more than just a warrior or soldier who was physically impressive or skilled with weapons—had to be a cultured scholar overall, and necessarily applied his erudition in devising effective strategies for conducting war on the battlefield.[44] Thus, it is significant that all the extant official portraits of military officials, including all those mentioned in this study, show them in a court dress rather than armor. What follows are some illustrative examples of capable, highly regarded military men who were more than just warriors.

Cho U-sŏk (1782–1863), a *yangban* military man, was self-confident about the value of his expertise and knowledge. Hailing from a prominent P'yŏngyang Cho military line based in Seoul, in 1855 he authored a military treatise, the *Essentials of Military Preparedness* (*Mubi yoram*). In this work, Cho proudly demonstrates what he knows about military administration, weaponry, and war tactics.[45] He selects materials found in Chinese military strategy texts from the ancient Warring States down to the late Ming period and adopts them to suit Korea's needs. This also means that his discussion of European weapons such as cannons, for example, is limited to those known to the Chinese in the mid-seventeenth century—in fact, the "red barbarian cannons" (*hongip'o*) the Koreans used against the French invaders in 1866 and the Americans in 1871. Perhaps to our disappointment, Cho does not address the issue of the inferiority of Korean weapons to Western firearms, nor does he advocate converting archers and spearmen to musketeers, refurbishing weapons, copying or buying foreign weapons, or inviting foreign military specialists to Korea. Overall, he did not react to Western arms the way the Japanese *samurai* did later, and we are forced to look for the significance of the *Mubi yoram* elsewhere. In early Chosŏn, the state, rather than a private citizen or a military officer, would have compiled and published comparable military manuals, so Cho's work was a departure. He displayed what would be called classical military knowledge—surely important to being a Confucian general—and we must grant that his horizon did not encompass the looming Western military threat.

Of course, their private authorship of military manuals does not prove that late Chosŏn military officials were prouder of who they were than were hereditary technical specialists or local functionaries. What we need is an indication that the aristocracy as a whole appreciated capable military men. In that regard, the evidence is somewhat ambiguous. As discussed in Chapter 3, Kang Ŭng-hwan, the first representative of his Chinju Kang lineage of Mujang to pass the military examination, had to overcome his father's initial disapproval to pursue a military career. The main force behind his successful efforts at persuasion was a long poem that expressed his desire to serve the country through martial virtue. On the other hand, consider the following praise of a military man, Sŏ Yu-dae (1732–1802). It is noteworthy that even though the *Veritable Records* becomes more laconic in its coverage of various events from the late eighteenth century, it still paid glowing tribute to some military men:

> Military Training Division Commander Sŏ Yu-dae died. The queen dowager came forth during the royal lecture (*kyŏngyŏn*) and stated: "Before reaching his old age, this military commander was a seasoned general. Suddenly he met this fate." She greatly lamented his death for a long time. Sŏ Yu-dae was a man of Talsŏng, and he was a descendant of Lord Munjŏng, Sŏ Sŏng. Distinguished in appearance and surpassing others in strength, he earned his military examination degree through a special recommendation. When he accompanied a diplomatic mission to the *bakufu,* the Japanese all called him "*shōgun*." Far and wide he monitored the border against the Manchus, but since he was tolerant and generous by nature, no soldier complained [about his strict observance of regulations]. He was referred to as a general of good fortune (*pokchang*).[46]

After passing the military examination in 1759, Sŏ remained a key military man during the last quarter of the eighteenth century. He served four times as the Anti-Manchu Division Commander (Ch'ongyungsa), seven times as the Royal Division Commander (Ŏyŏng Taejang), three times as the Military Training Division Commander, and seven times as the Forbidden Guard Division Commander (Kŭmwi Taejang). Not only did he have a successful military career as a wise general, he was known for excellent calligraphy and enjoyed collecting the works of famous calligraphers.[47] It is not surprising that he achieved recognition as a Confucian general.

Most *yangban* military men had a career with more ups and downs than Sŏ Yu-dae's, and the case of Yi Chu-guk (1721–98) is typical (Figure 4.2). Descended from Chŏngjong, the second Chosŏn king, Yi passed the military examination at 20 *se* and proceeded to hold a series of high-level provincial and central military posts.[48] During the final two decades of his career, he went through an amazing cycle of dismissals and reappointments. He was blamed for the unruly conduct of his soldiers (who were pallbearers for a royal funeral), failure to store

Figure 4.2 Portrait of Yi Chu-guk at 64 *Se* (1784). The embroidered double-tiger chest plate denotes his status as a military official of upper-level (*tangsang*) senior third rank. Although still reflecting the conventions of stylized earlier Chosŏn portraiture, the realism that was becoming more widely employed from the late eighteenth century in Korea is also evident. Private possession of Kim Wŏn-jŏn; reproduced in Yi Kang-ch'il, ed., *Yŏksa inmul ch'osanghwa taesajŏn,* 415.

enough military grain, and mismanagement of naval vessels. When he was censured, the punishment ranged from a simple dismissal to banishment to a remote island. Amazingly, though, he was reappointed to an important military post after each punishment, and he eventually became the minister of war, a rare achievement even for the military examination passers from central military official lines of descent.[49] His reinstatements suggest that the state deemed his overall professional expertise more valuable than the seriousness of whatever mistakes he made, although we should not overlook the real likelihood that he had personal and political connections to powerful civil officials.

In contrast to Yi Chu-guk, Sŏ Yu-dae, Kang Ŭng-hwan, and Cho U-sŏk, who all exemplify more purely martial values, military men

Figure 4.3 (*left*) Portrait of Sin Hŏn at 61 *Se* (1870). Compared to the earlier portrait of Yi Chu-guk, realism is more pronounced in this painting. The overall character of the subject is that of a wise old Confucian scholar-official, whose military connection is signified by the double-tiger chest plate. Courtesy of Korea University Museum, Korea University. (*right*) Photograph at 67 *Se* (1876). The raw realism of the medium brings out the haggard, frail qualities of an elderly man. Sin dons the double-crane chest plate of a high-level civil office that he was holding at the time. Personal possession of Chang Sŏng-gil; reproduced at http://www.koreanphoto.co.kr/political/jungchi/19.htm.

with more diverse interests and areas of talent were not unheard of in late Chosŏn. Sin Hŏn (1810–84), for example, was a military official, scholar, statesman, calligrapher, and painter all at once (Figure 4.3).[50] He is best remembered as the chief of the Korean delegation at both the 1876 Korean-Japanese Treaty and the 1882 Korean-American Treaty. A member of the P'yŏngsan Sin military line descended from the elder brother of Sin Rip (commander at the 1592 Battle of T'an'gŭmdae), Sin Hŏn passed the military examination in 1828 and went on to hold various high-ranking offices.[51] He belonged to the political circle headed by Second State Councillor Pak Kyu-su, an official known for his astute observations of superior Western weapons, who advocated opening Korea to full modern diplomatic and commercial relations with all foreign countries, rather than just with China. Sin studied under Practical Learning notables, like Chŏng Yag-yong and Kim Chŏng-hŭi (1786–1856), and he himself produced numerous treatises on the military, history, geography, agriculture, and epigraphy.[52] His intellectual curiosity even extended to Buddhism: while serving in 1844 as the right Chŏlla provincial navy commander (Chŏlla-udo Sugun Chŏltosa), he maintained close personal ties to the prominent abbot of a local monastery.[53]

It was the "opening of Korea" that provided the climactic opportunity for Sin to fully exercise his abilities as a Confucian general. When the Hŭngsŏn Taewŏn'gun (1821–98)—the de facto regent during the minority of his son King Kojong—pursued an isolationist policy that resulted in French and American attacks, Sin played a limited role in actual battles. After the Taewŏn'gun stepped down in 1873, it became clear that Sin was not destined to fight against the "ocean barbarians" (*yangi*) of the West, as did his fellow military men. Instead commencing his personal rule, Kojong adopted a more accommodating stance toward the nations beyond the Sinitic horizon, and this set the stage for Sin's historic role in the signing of Chosŏn Korea's first two modern treaties. The fact that he, a military man, was put in this position was more an indication of the court's low regard for nations other than China than of the perceived importance of an occasion that should have involved more politically influential civil officials as Korea's representatives.[54] Nonetheless, Sin's career epitomizes the ultimate achievement of a late Chosŏn military official—that is, of the Confucian general within the constraints of court politics dominated by the descent lines of oligarchic civil officials.

If dutifully serving the monarch as a Confucian general was a realistically attainable ideal for *yangban* military men, it seems unlikely that they were disillusioned with the system as a whole. Instead, we find such individuals duly performing their duties. Thus, P'yŏngan Provincial Army Commander Pak Ki-p'ung, a collateral descendant of Chief State Councillor Pak Sŭng-jong, and other commanders leading the government troops against Hong Kyŏng-nae's rebel armies in 1812 were generally from the capital military aristocracy. And when engaging the Western troops on Kanghwa Island, central military officials, such as Left Vanguard Commander (Chwasŏnbongjang) Yang Hŏn-su (1866,

Chŏngjok Fort) and the aforementioned Ŏ Chae-yŏn (1871, Kwangsŏng Garrison), led their troops and fought courageously against the technologically superior intruders, despite antiquated weaponry.

Summation

This chapter examined several social institutions connected with status in order to determine whether the central civil official, central military official, and southern aristocratic kinship groups regarded one another as members of the *yangban* aristocracy. This question is important because some recent literature sees even the southern local *yangban* as a separate group without the connections or power of previous times. Other studies have portrayed the central military official lines of descent as belonging to a status group lower than the central civil official lines.

My evidence refutes these contentions. Although marriage ties among the three types of *yangban* seem to have weakened during late Chosŏn, a relatively close genealogical relationship and the exchange of adoptive heirs among the three such segments within a descent group show that they deemed one another social equals. Furthermore, it was *yangban* status in the ascriptive sense—not degrees or branch affiliation—that the aristocracy-controlled state most rigidly considered when weighing the social status of potential buyers of government ranks and offices.

Not surprisingly, late Chosŏn central military officials continued to defend the existing system, which of course the aristocracy dominated. Military examination graduates from capital *yangban* descent groups could hope for and achieve the ideal of Confucian general. They were not unhappy with the status quo in the way, for example, educated technical specialists and local functionaries were. As much as they believed in the importance of their services and maintained in-group behaviors designed to exclude those beneath them, technical specialists and local functionaries struggled in vain to shake off the constraints placed by the aristocracy upon their advancement opportunities in officialdom.

Thus, we find that in the nineteenth century, the military aristocracy of Seoul continued to serve the state well in fighting against domestic rebels and imperialist infiltrators. Ultimately, the success of the military examination system, in the sociopolitical sense, seems to have prevented *yangban* degree holders from advocating or supporting changes in the Korean military system that might have enabled it to stand up to the West or Japan. However, a more complete answer to the question of disaffection requires considering the nonelite military examination passers.

FIVE

Nonelites and the Military Examination

The late Chosŏn state opened up the military examination to nonelites, less as the result of a deliberate policy decision than as an unintended consequence of a desperate effort to deal with military crises. During the Jurchen border raids prior to 1592 and the Korean-Japanese war from 1592 to 1598, the government administered large-scale military examinations more frequently, but successful candidates still tended to be from *yangban* backgrounds. In contrast, the so-called 10,000-men military examinations in the early seventeenth century—held to cope with the growing Manchu military threat—awarded the degrees to many candidates of non-*yangban* backgrounds.

Even after the Korean-Manchu wars of 1627 and 1637 and the Chosŏn government's eventual abandonment of any hope of revenge, the frequent large-scale military examinations did not cease. They retained their original function of recruiting members of the aristocracy to the military branch of officialdom, but it seems that the late Chosŏn military examination system also served the social function of mollifying those nonelites beyond the locus of power.

By "nonelites," I refer to non-*yangban*; that is, those that the *yangban* did not recognize as their social equals. Making up the vast majority of the population, the category of nonelites included the following groups: (1) the broadly defined *chungin*, among whom were not only technical specialists (such as government interpreters, physicians, statute experts, astronomers, painters, calligraphers, and musicians) but also other intermediate status groups neither aristocrat nor commoner, such as noncommissioned military officers, functionaries working for central or local government agencies, and illegitimate sons of *yangban*; (2) commoners, comprising mostly peasants but also the descendants of illegitimate sons and a growing number of artisans and merchants; and (3) lowborn, consisting of slaves and those belonging to the denigrated semihereditary occupation groups, such as entertainers and shamans.[1]

The social function of the late Chosŏn military examination system was different for nonelites than it was for the aristocracy, since the degree's perceived significance depended on status. Nonetheless, the dim job prospects of most examination graduates did not negate the popular appeal of the degree itself, which kept its prestige in large part thanks to the fact that aristocrats also possessed it. Examination degrees, along with ranks and offices in the central government, were useful accoutrements for a status-conscious individual imitating the appearance of a *yangban*. Furthermore, these trappings, ostensibly demonstrating a connection to state power, granted their possessors important practical benefits, such as removal from the army draft register (*kunjŏk*), and thus exemption from conscript duty or the military cloth tax.[2] Although from the middle of the eighteenth century even bona fide *yangban* had to assume a greater burden through the village cloth tax (*tongp'o*) and household cloth tax (*hop'o*), exemption from the military cloth tax continued until 1870 or 1871 to be a symbol of *yangban* status.[3]

An analysis of the military examination's functions for nonelites must begin with the earliest instances of nonelite participation. I focus on three types of primary sources for this information—contemporary observations, legal measures, and examination rosters—before considering broader issues regarding nonelites and late Chosŏn social change. On the basis of this evidence, I ultimately argue that the upward social mobility of nonelites through the military examination had a clear limit. Despite such restrictions, a variety of popular cultural genres perpetuated the appeal to ordinary people of a military examination degree by fueling their imaginations about military heroes

Anecdotal and Legal Evidence of Nonelite Participation in the Seventeenth Century

Anecdotal and legal evidence shows the state's repeated vascillation as it wrestled with the aspirations of the lowborn for degree status. The initial appearance, in 1628, of laws prohibiting the lowborn and other nonelite elements from competing in the military examination shows that the phenomenon was becoming a serious concern for the state and aristocracy alike. Whereas the 1469 *Great Code of State Administration*—the basis of the institutions and practices of the sixteenth century—barely took nonelites into account, the 1746 *Amended Great Code* (*Sok taejŏn*) provides a detailed explanation of various barred groups and punishments for their illegal participation, suggesting that by then nonelite participation in the military examination had become an undeniable reality.

Well before the appearance of these laws, the state manipulated the examination degree's popular appeal to recruit desperately needed manpower, even relaxing restrictions on lowborn taking the examination. When King Sŏnjo ordered a local military examination during his sojourn in Yŏngyu in 1593, the change is said to have allowed both public and private slaves to take the examination. Thus, when Yi Hang-bok (1556–1618), a respected statesman of the era, got no response upon calling for his slave, he is said to have remarked to his guests that the slave must have gone out to take the examination, eliciting laughter from all the assembled.[4]

To what extent did lowborn participate in the military examination at the time? According to Sim's studies (which use court histories and rosters of the passers of large-scale military examinations), passers in this period included non-*yangban* candidates of slave background, as well as local functionaries and illegitimate sons, but military examination degree holders continued to be predominantly *yangban*.[5] It seems that aristocratic observers at the time exaggerated the extent of upward social mobility available to commoners and slaves in wartime.

Both primary and secondary sources show that more meaningful nonelite participation began later, in the early seventeenth century, during Kwanghaegun's reign.[6] According to Yi Su-gwang's commentary on the military examination system of his time, the scale of the competition had become so large since the Japanese invasions that a military examination roster could easily record thousands of successful candidates. Many such passers were said to have lacked archery skills or to have come from lowborn backgrounds. Since the government had granted degrees only in an effort to raise the morale of the people, the degree holders were of no practical use to the military.[7]

At the time, rapid Jurchen military expansion and the possible dispatch of reinforcements to Ming China necessitated military examinations on a larger scale. Among them were such 10,000-men examinations as the 1618 courtyard examination that selected some 3,200 men, the 1619 special examination that awarded between 3,000 and 10,000 degrees, and the 1621 courtyard examination that recruited 4,031 men. Officials estimated the necessary troop strength for shoring up the defense of the northern border at around 40,000. Kwanghaegun himself thought that it would not be difficult to raise a trained army of over 100,000 men through less rigorous military examinations—an expedient measure reminiscent of the steps his sixteenth-century predecessors had taken to quickly man the northern garrisons.[8]

Depending on circumstances, the government allowed some lowborn to take the military examination; many more tried to compete illegally by misrepresenting themselves. In July 1620, the Board of War pointed out that it had already ordered the removal from the roster of lowborn and illegitimate sons who had somehow illegally passed the recent preliminary test of a large-scale military examination. It further recommended to Kwanghaegun that the recording clerks colluding with such candidates all be punished.[9] This was just one of many such discussions that took place during the year. Regardless of the state's efforts, though, the lowborn continued to compete. In 1622, a report from the Office of the Inspector-General (Sahŏnbu) noted that the previous year's military examination roster contained many names of passers and fathers that clearly were fabrications.[10]

After the overthrow of Kwanghaegun and his Northerner (Pugin) statesmen in 1623, the new court of King Injo, comprising a Westerner majority, sought more rigorously to reverse the trend of illegal participation by nonelites. In 1628, the government stipulated that all runners (*najang, chorye*), grain transport workers (*chojol*), government-guest assistants (*ilsu*), slaves, and illegitimate sons who took the military examination without permission were to be sent off with their families to border regions, and that no amnesty measure was to free them from this punishment.[11] Moreover, compared to the illegitimate sons and others on the list who had to bear the tax and service burdens, slaves received especially harsh treatment: a forced draft as marines.[12]

At the same time, even those nonelites who legally earned a military examination degree became targets of the aristocracy's efforts to separate them from regular officeholders and examination graduates of *yangban* status. For example, a year after the 1637 Namhan Fort courtyard military examination awarded the degree to more than 5,000 men, including hundreds of manumitted slaves (*myŏnch'ŏn*) who had gained their freedom for defending the Fort, the State Tribunal (which handled criminal cases involving *yangban* officials and examination graduates) recommended that cases involving military examination degree holders without a regular office be handled instead by the Board of Punishments. In the end, though, both Second State Councillor Ch'oe Myŏng-gil and Third State Councillor Sin Kyŏng-jin argued that the tradition of privileging all examination graduates could not be ignored, and the king rejected the State Tribunal's recommendation.[13]

Such respect for military examination passers only continued to provide incentives for illegal competition by nonelites, and the government's efforts during and immediately after Injo's reign failed to stem the tide. In 1665, the court of King Hyŏnjong barred from the military examination all manumitted slaves who were not officially assigned to an auxiliary soldier unit.[14] This measure essentially targeted runners, grain transport workers, and government-guest assistants; all were legally commoners yet had to bear socially denigrated service burdens. The grain transport workers protested by arguing that even marines, who were commoners socially treated as lowborn, were allowed to take the military examination, and the government finally lifted the ban in 1672.[15] Moreover, in 1676, King Sukchong approved a measure allowing illegitimate sons who had passed the military examination without the grain submission required of them simply to meet the obligation *after* the examination rather than getting their degrees taken away.[16]

By Sukchong's reign, the large number of unemployed nonelite military examination degree holders was producing a variety of social problems. A court discussion in the summer of 1678 noted that too many graduates of the 1676 examination—which awarded degrees to an all-time high of 17,652 candidates—were scoundrels of lowborn or manumitted slave backgrounds.[17] One of the outcomes of this discussion was to treat some such non-*yangban* graduates as bona fide commoners.

In the same year, the court clarified the regulation by declaring that any military examination graduate of commoner or lowborn background who committed a crime was to be deprived of the privilege of interrogation at the State Tribunal. These degreed nonelites could not be the peers of *yangban* officeholders, civil examination graduates, or military examination graduates.[18]

The measure sparked controversy, as had a similar proposal in 1638. Mindful of potential discontent over the state stripping military examination degree holders of a traditional privilege, the censor-general petitioned Sukchong to rescind the measure. Sukchong admitted that examination passers whom the state treated no differently than degreeless military examination students must surely feel wronged, and he reversed the decision.[19] In 1686, however, he changed his mind yet again about nonelite graduates, and ordered that murder cases or crimes involving the violation of Confucian moral imperatives be handled by the Board of Punishments rather than the State Tribunal. In 1692, and again during Yŏngjo's reign in 1734, the government reaffirmed that successful military examination candidates of commoner or lowborn backgrounds who committed a serious crime were subject to the jurisdiction of the Board of Punishments.[20]

Reflecting these trends, the 1746 *Amended Great Code* included regulations on the treatment of lowborn-background military examination graduates who committed a crime. These regulations are useful for understanding the overall problem of nonelite participation in the military examination. The code stipulated that a commoner or lowborn graduate suspected of a grave offense had to be interrogated without physical torture unless he refused to yield; in the latter case he was to undergo a harsher interrogation, if recommended by the Board of Punishments. Moreover, the code classified the military examination graduates of commoner and lowborn backgrounds alongside those who had obtained an office through grain submission or military merit, and assigned their criminal cases to the Board of Punishments, rather than the State Tribunal, for interrogation.[21] Having considered the relevant laws as well as popular perceptions of how these regulations failed to protect the integrity of the military examination, let us now consider the reality of nonelite participation in the examination system.

The Actual Extent of Nonelite Participation: The Examination Roster Data

An analysis of examination rosters shows that non-*yangban* status groups were heavily represented among military examination passers during the seventeenth and eighteenth centuries. Their virtual disappearance thereafter reflects not so much the decreased participation of nonelites as it does their increased success at claiming the status titles formerly reserved for bona fide *yangban*—either with the state's permission or, more commonly, through bribing clerks. Also, many late Chosŏn military examination rosters record degree holders who, though not formally designated as members of non-*yangban* status groups, had names that are absent from their respective descent group genealogies or are non-*yangban* in appearance. In fact, the rosters demonstrate greater diversity in descent group representation among the military examination passers in comparison to other state examinations. This suggests, as we will see, that candidates of commoner or lowborn backgrounds were more successful in the military examination than in other state examinations in late Chosŏn.[22]

For a clearer picture, we cannot ignore a candidate's officially recorded service (*chigyŏk*) label, taking into account that the actual social makeup of those claiming a particular status could change over time, and that the general pattern was the devaluation of titles that previously were claimed only by *yangban*. Nonetheless, some service labels continued to signify a person of non-*yangban* social status: illegitimate sons with special permission to take the examination (*hŏt'ong*); graduates of various technical examinations and students in corresponding technical specialties; government functionaries such as clerks (*sŏri*), township headmen, sons of hereditary local functionaries who had permission to take the examination (*kongsaeng*), those from local functionary families exempted from their hereditary obligations (*myŏnhyang*), and post station functionaries (*yŏngni*); commoners such as infantrymen, cavalrymen (*kibyŏng*), marines, and bow makers (*kungin*); and former lowborns such as manumitted slaves and *sogo* army soldiers.

What percentage of late Chosŏn military examination graduates do these non-*yangban* men represent? Analyzing all late Chosŏn degree holders from my database skews the data in favor of *yangban*, because the documentation of passers in local gazetteers and military examination graduate genealogies is biased in favor of aristocratic degree holders. To overcome this limitation, I analyzed only those passers from actual military examination rosters and the *Comprehensive Essentials of the Military Examination* (*Mukwa ch'ongyo*)—a total of 22,565 men in all from 1608 to 1894. In total, 1,846 degree holders were not *yangban* (8.0 percent), including those graduates having a legitimate-son brother (implying that the graduate himself was an illegitimate son), those recorded after 1696 as support taxpayers (*poin*), and passers who had purchased a rank or an office, or whose fathers had done so. Excluding Kojong's reign, for which the roster data sample is too small, the proportion of non-*yangban* passers fluctuated between 3.3 and 16.4 percent from 1608 to 1864.[23]

These figures show that more than just a trickle of nonelite candidates competed in the late Chosŏn military examination. After all, the numbers account for only those passers who were unquestionably non-*yangban*. The degree holders recorded under other service labels include a large number of nonelite individuals, as many designations originally used for *yangban* became more commonly claimed by non-*yangban* elements as well. For example, the fact that 71 out of 102 passers whose fathers are explicitly recorded as "commoners" (*yangin*) were military regiment soldiers or officers suggests that a significant percentage of the 5,528 military regiment-affiliate passers from late Chosŏn must have been non-*yangban*.[24]

Among military examination passers, the percentage of *hallyang*—men without a rank, an office, or any other service label at the time of the degree—increased dramatically, while rank or officeholders were represented fairly consistently. The percentage of *hallyang* increased from 0.6 percent in the first half of the seventeenth century to 64.4 percent in the latter half of the nineteenth century; the representation of the holders of ranks or offices fluctuated between 25 and 33.3 percent.[25]

Chŏng Hae-ŭn and I disagree on how to interpret the increased representation of *hallyang* among late Chosŏn military examination graduates. Emphasizing what they were *supposed* to be rather than the social reality at the time, Chŏng in effect understates the possibility that those appearing as *hallyang* on various documents (such as examination rosters) actually included *chungin* and commoners as well as the individuals who had previously registered as degreeless scholars. As is well known, the population of men registered on census documents as degreeless scholars increased steeply in late Chosŏn, as more and more nonelite yet wealthy individuals claimed the status through means such as bribing recording clerks.[26] Chŏng does not explicitly address this problem, but my interpretation of her findings about the increased percentage of *hallyang* among late Chosŏn military examination graduates explains the phenomenon at least in part by considering legal or false claims of *hallyang* status by originally non-*yangban* men.

As Chŏng notes, the *Amended Great Code* made special provisions for *hallyang*. It stipulated that, like military examination graduates, *hallyang* too could be recommended for an assignment at the Office of Royal Messengers (Sŏnjŏn'gwanch'ŏng), the Office of Battalion Commanders (Pujangch'ŏng), or the Namhan Fort Defense Command (Suŏch'ŏng). Thus, *hallyang* had every reason to try to pass the military examination in order to enjoy faster promotion.[27]

In late Chosŏn, the *hallyang* status label subsumed a variety of social elements. To begin with, the government made the degreeless scholars (*yuhak*) preparing for the military examination identify themselves as *hallyang*.[28] The status of degreeless scholar itself was devalued in the eighteenth and nineteenth centuries, as we will see later in this chapter, with originally non-*yangban* individuals claiming the title on household registers. Also, military examination candidates from rank- or office-holding commoner and *chungin* families seem to have been accepted into the *hallyang* category. In January 1881, for example, when the capital security force command, the Military Guard Agency (Muwiso), employed my great-grandfather, Pak T'ae-sik (1855–1933)—a Seoul *chungin* from a descent line with marriage ties to technical specialists and noncommissioned military officers—as a new Special Military Officer (Pyŏlmusa), it recorded his status at the time as *hallyang*.[29]

Not a small number of military examination candidates *falsely* claimed *hallyang* status. In 1866, the court applied the new *Great Code Reconciliation* (*Taejŏn hoet'ong*), promulgated in the previous year, in punishing a private slave who had passed the military examination as a *hallyang* by drafting him as a marine.[30] Considering that the government took note of the man only because he got caught, we can only wonder how many—or, better yet, how many more—managed to get away with it and enjoy the prestige that the degree brought.

Besides *hallyang,* the affiliates of the Five Military Divisions of Seoul and the Special Military Officers of Hwanghae and P'yŏngan Provinces also enjoyed increased representation among passers. According to Chŏng Hae-ŭn's analysis of the 16,575 late Chosŏn military examination graduates recorded in rosters, a third (5,528) were military regiment affiliates, excluding those holding a civil or military office of the regular nine-rank bureaucratic hierarchy, and two-thirds of those 5,528 men were soldiers of subofficer status. Among them must have been many non-*yangban* men, in keeping with my estimate of 8.0 percent who definitely were not *yangban* (that is, 1,846 out of the 22,565 I analyzed).[31]

The officers and soldiers of these regiments had numerous opportunities to participate in martial talent competitions. This in turn offered them a chance to win the privilege of advancing to the palace examination stage of an upcoming military examination, either by placing first overall or by earning a perfect score on one of the weapon specialty tests. Seoul residents were represented more strongly in the regular triennial competitions, whereas the candidates from P'yŏngan and Hwanghae Provinces did better in the more frequent special examinations.[32]

Among military regiment affiliates, even those of humble origins who provided meritorious wartime service could readily pass the military examination. The 1637 Namhan Fort courtyard examination is a case in point: according to Chŏng Hae-ŭn's study, this contest awarded the degree to 5,506 men, up to 85 percent of whom were such officers and soldiers. The desperate government had manumitted slaves and recruited them as soldiers during the Manchu siege of Namhan Fort earlier in the year. A large number, if not all, of the military regiment affiliates among the successful candidates were the manumitted slaves assigned to various military units after emancipation.[33]

Recorded descent group information further suggests that graduates of examinations like that of 1637 were of humble origins. In the 1637 examination roster, descent group designations such as the Kimhae Kim and Miryang Pak are represented in disproportionate numbers: respectively, the two account for 356 and 266 out of 5,506 recorded successful candidates (6.5 percent and 4.8 percent).[34] Of course, these figures cannot signify that over a tenth of the Korean population in the seventeenth century was descended patrilineally from Kim Yu-sin (595–673) or King Kyŏngmyŏng (Pak Sŭng-yŏng, r. 917–23), the eponymous ancestors of the two descent groups.[35] The large population of these two, clan-like descent groups today, as in late Chosŏn, indicates that they have become "umbrella" descent group designations adopted by those who lacked such an identifier by the end of the dynasty.[36]

Thus, in the case of the Miryang Pak, up to half of those claiming the affiliation on one military examination roster or another can be traced genealogically, while other rosters include no traceable Miryang Pak. A typical example of the former type is the 1651 special examination that produced 1,236 passers, among whom I have so far been able to trace 14 out of 46 Miryang Pak represented. Examples of the second type include the courtyard examinations of 1637 and 1784. The extant rosters of these two competitions respectively record 260 out of 5,506 degree holders and 139 out of 2,692 degree holders as Miryang Pak, but I have so far been unable to trace a single one in any existing Miryang Pak genealogy.[37] Most likely the investigation of their genealogical antecedents is futile.

The 1637 examination roster is a treasure trove for those curious about male Korean given names that depart from the more conventional one- or two-character Sino-Korean given names. There we find that many graduates bear the kind of given name no respectable *yangban* would use, even though they claim membership in the Miryang Pak. Some are obvious in meaning even to speakers of modern Korean: standing out are apparently pure Korean names like Kaettong ("dog shit"), Malttong ("horse shit"), Tut'abi (same as Tut'ŏbi, perhaps an archaic form for toad), and Kŏmdong (same as Kŏmdung, maybe meaning "blackie"). Also, many names use character combinations that no literate *yangban* would choose for a personal name. Examples like O-in ("hating virtue") and Ak-han ("evil scoundrel") seem to reflect the well-known practice of recording clerks who used the Chinese characters not for their meanings but to approximate certain Korean sounds for an illiterate person's name.

In addition to large, clan-like descent groups such as the Miryang Pak, other obscure descent groups are recorded in the 1637 Namhan Fort courtyard examination roster. The latter typically tend to use an ancestral seat–surname combination no longer found in modern times. As Chapter 3's discussion of the fate of the Namp'yŏng Cho lineage of Kimhae reveals, obscure descent groups, *yangban* or not, are unknown to us today not so much because they failed to produce direct male descendants but rather due to their descendants' adoption of a more common, traditionally recognized ancestral seat label for their surname.

All this evidence raises the ultimate question: how many nonelite candidates passed the military examination in late Chosŏn? Neither Chŏng Hae-ŭn nor I can present an exact percentage or figure, but we agree that a sizeable portion of the late Chosŏn military examination graduate population could not have been bona fide *yangban*. The aforementioned figures—ranging between 3.3 and 16.4 percent—merely show the fluctuation in the representation of graduates who were definitely not *yangban*; the actual number of all non-*yangban* military examination graduates must have been significantly greater.[38] In fact, although the 1637 Namhan Fort courtyard military examination may seem like an extreme case in that up to 85 percent of the passers were former slaves, other large-scale military examinations, especially in the eighteenth century, are known to have awarded the degree predominantly to military regiment soldiers escorting the king.

Nonelites and Late Chosŏn Social Mobility

Late Chosŏn military examination graduates came from a social base broader than ever before in the history of the military examination system. The institution's continued function as a recruitment system for the state, staffing the military branch of central officialdom, perpetuated the prestige of the degree. Nonelite candidates who passed the military examination could indeed enhance their social status, as suggested by recent studies in local history that show how originally non-*yangban* social elements, especially those with wealth, gained greater influence in local administration and commanded greater cultural competence in the course of the late Chosŏn period. These nonelite social elements, despite their continued quest for markers of higher social status and expanding access to positions of authority, nevertheless did not enjoy unfettered opportunities for upward mobility.

An obvious indication of status aspirations of nonelites was their adoption of service labels previously reserved for *yangban*, resulting in a depreciation in value of the categories *muhak* ("military student") and *ŏmmu* ("military vocation man"). Originally, the individuals recorded as *muhak* on household registration documents were local *yangban* who, in exchange for providing support duties as provincial military school (*muhak*) students for local troops, received exemption from active military duty and taxation. In the early seventeenth century, *muhak* began to include those who had failed the military examination's classics exposition tests, and then, in the late seventeenth century, *muhak* as a whole came to form a distinct social stratum between bona fide *yangban* and commoners. By the early eighteenth century, the *muhak* category came to include even commoners making a false claim of military school enrollment.[39] In the interim, the *yangban* men preparing on their own for the military examination and exempted from military and tax obligations became known as *ŏmmu.* In the late seventeenth century, *ŏmmu* retained the same privileges and status as previously, except that by then they tended to be illegitimate sons. Beginning in the eighteenth century, the government permitted the grandsons of such *ŏmmu*, as well as *ŏbyu* ("Confucian vocation men"), to be recorded on the household registration documents as degreeless scholars (*yuhak*).[40]

The economic dimension is crucial for determining to what extent these social newcomers achieved upward social mobility. The so-called "people's hidden [complaint] memorials" (*minŭnso*) that magistrates forwarded to the central government clearly show that by the late eighteenth century, the tax system did not reflect the economic realities of the time and that abuses were widespread. In spite of the previous Uniform Land Tax Law and Equal Service Law reforms, unfair, inequitable levies threatened the taxpayers' livelihoods, forcing them to look for various ways to escape their obligations. A common method was to take advantage of legal provisions exempting those who used certain service labels traditionally reserved for *yangban,* such as that of a degreeless scholar. In doing so, many made claims to such service designations by false reporting or by bribing local functionaries. Of course, this was feasible mainly for nonelites of significant economic means.[41]

If claiming service labels formerly reserved for *yangban* helped some nonelites obtain shelter from taxation, and hence presumably greater economic security, then did they also achieve higher social standing? So far, various case studies have dealt with this and related questions, with Tansŏng, a southern county in Kyŏngsang Province, serving as a favorite example, due to its large body of extant household registers. According to Kim Chun-hyŏng's recent study, Tansŏng's nonelites strove to achieve a higher social status, even though local aristocrats maintained their position into the nineteenth century. Some nonelites, including former slaves, achieved higher status as individuals, while others did so over several generations, as families. Nonelites of economic means began participating in community compact-related organizations that used to be dominated by *yangban*, acquired more slaves, and purchased court ranks, to the extent that by the mid-nineteenth century, many social newcomers claimed to be degreeless scholars. Though the old aristocracy generally refused to accept influential commoners as its own, some sociocultural exchanges were established between the groups, especially in villages where *yangban* were less populous or economically weaker. Some such commoners obtained local administrative positions, and a smaller number even acquired duty posts at private academies—the bastion of local *yangban* culture.[42]

Social mobility in Tansŏng also posed a challenge to hereditary local functionaries who were highly protective of their interests and maintained close-knit social ties. From the late seventeenth century, some commoners and marginal *yangban* assumed functionary duties. Interested parties assessed the economic advantages associated with various positions, and competition over them intensified as many county magistrates took bribes when filling vacancies. In the nineteenth century, the aristocracy's weakened control over the local agency (*hyang-ch'ŏng*) and the magistrates' unilateral appointment of functionaries exacerbated the traditional problem of local resources and population being exploited by magistrates and local functionaries.[43] Since it was fundamentally up to the magistrates to decide who filled the posts, hereditary local functionary families had no choice but to accept the new practice while seeking to further distinguish themselves from the newcomers through social and cultural activities.[44]

Nonetheless, new social elements gained not only more political power at local levels but also greater cultural capital. In nineteenth-century Wŏnju, in central Korea, for example, new descent groups enjoyed success in the licentiate examinations. During Chosŏn, Wŏnju was the fourth most successful locale in terms of its residents' licentiate examination success; until the late nineteenth century, much of this success reflected the dominance of a small number of the most powerful local *yangban* lineages. The 17 most successful descent groups (out of 86 total) each produced at least ten licentiates, accounting altogether for 72.8 percent of all licentiates from Wŏnju. During Kojong's reign, however, 14 descent groups represented in Wŏnju each produced a licentiate for the first time ever.[45]

What were the origins of the social newcomers who possessed enough cultural capital to pass an examination? Several distinct types make their appearance on late Chosŏn examination rosters, and especially those dedicated to the military competition. Above all, many came from descent lines that were *yangban* "dropouts." We know that typically, the child of a *yangban* father and a non-*yangban* mother inherited the mother's status; descendants had no choice but to marry someone of an equal or lower social status. In fact, offspring produced by a *yangban* man and a slave woman was a slave. Regardless of whether an illegitimate son and his descendants retained the memory of their aristocratic ancestry in the form of a surname and an ancestral seat label, they did not have any standing in the *yangban* father's lineage. Not surprisingly, late Chosŏn genealogies tend to stop covering an illegitimate-son descent line after a few generations.[46]

Second, a large descent group could consist of "members," real or putative, reflecting many different shades of social status. Historically, only a small percentage of descent groups, most of which traced their origins to local functionaries of the earlier Koryŏ period, ever succeeded in achieving *yangban* status. The designation really was possible only for those entering the service of the central government before the founding of the Chosŏn dynasty, which essentially rendered central officialdom inaccessible to anyone who had not already entered the service. The unsuccessful majority simply sank into obscurity if they were unable to retain their original local functionary status or to claim some connection with a large, powerful descent group.[47]

Third, recognized descent group labels were commonly claimed by upwardly mobile nonelite families in a process that spanned several generations. Initially, a widely known surname would be adopted and combined with the residence locale name used as the ancestral seat, before the latter would be replaced, a generation or two later, with a recognized ancestral seat for the given surname. Numerous studies on household registers elucidate this common late Chosŏn social phenomenon among nonelites.[48] In many cases, the members of such upwardly mobile descent lines changed the names and service labels for themselves and their ancestors to the extent that those appearing in the mid- to late nineteenth-century Tansŏng census registers for non-*yangban* often number fewer than do their antecedents of the same descent group label. More often than not, the former cannot be genealogically connected to the latter. Modern genealogies recording such lines of descent invariably use the changed names.[49]

Overall, nonelites are indeed more noticeable in late Chosŏn sources, including household registration documents and examination rosters. Their acquisition of degrees, ranks, and offices, as well as depreciation of these credentials and other status labels, leave us with little doubt about the big picture. The liberalized economy must have helped at least some, if not many, nonelites accumulate enough wealth to purchase or study for these credentials. Since the central political elite became more narrowly defined, we need to scrutinize counties outside the capital for the complex changes in its political, social, and cultural dynamics at the local level.

The Limitations of the Military Examination as a Ladder of Success

In spite of claims to the contrary by aristocratic observers, empirical evidence shows that *yangban*, as well as more marginal elites, made up the majority of late Chosŏn military examination graduates. The preponderance of degree holders and their fathers used a service label traditionally reserved for *yangban*—or at least hailed from a family that could afford to bribe a record clerk or employ other tactics to hide their real status. Since passing the military examination system demanded cultural capital, those from nonelite backgrounds faced challenges in pursuing status. These included the state's reservation of key entry-level appointments for degree holders from prominent descent lines, the cultural gulf that separated elites from nonelites, and the prolonged peace, which, compared to the earlier period of Japanese and Manchu invasions, allowed little opportunity to achieve battlefield military merits.

Among the various sources for investigating the actual social mobility of military examination passers, extant military examination rosters are valuable in that they record each passer's service label at the time of his degree. An examination degree in Chosŏn, moreover, was a state-certified marker of an individual's social status, unlike a genealogical record, which could be more easily forged. The Office of Editorial Review (Kyosŏgwan) prepared government copies of military examination rosters, and the Board of War kept the final, official copies. Besides these government copies, private copies were published by the passers or their descendants, to preserve the memory of the graduates of the same examination and their honorable accomplishments. Private publication of a roster copy involved, among others, a preparation overseer (*pangjung saekchang*), whose responsibility it was to collect the four-ancestor lists required of all examination candidates by the government at the time of the examination, as well as other relevant documents from degree holders. Regardless of whether a copy was being prepared by the government or on private initiative, it was not easy for someone to falsify details under the watchful eyes of the king, the officials, or the degree holders themselves.[50]

To understand the limits to social mobility inherent in the military examination system, we initially need to deal with the anomaly of 1637 as it is reflected in an examination roster. Chŏng Hae-ŭn's analysis of manumitted slave passers of this examination appears to demonstrate a link between the military examination and upward social mobility. The freed slaves who passed the examination, including those recorded in the source as military regiment affiliates, were distinct from earlier lowborn degree earners in that emancipation, rather than the degree itself, served as the guarantee of their elevated social status. The 1628 prohibition on public and private slaves taking the military examination not only shows that it was illegal for a lowborn to compete, but also suggests that illegal participation was widespread. In light of the earlier legal measure, it is fair to observe that the manumitted slaves passing the 1637 examination were not only free from the fear of being forced back into lowborn status, but were also entitled to retain their degrees. In fact, upon completing their prescribed terms in the auxiliary soldier units (*poch'ungdae*), the manumitted slaves with military examination degrees could assume commoner duties (*yangyŏk*) for the state, hence completing their exodus from bondage or "base" (*ch'ŏn*) existence to commoner or "good" (*yang*) status, in both the social and legal senses. Although former private slaves continued to be subject to discriminatory treatment, and even harassment, by their former masters, passing the military examination paved the way, in the long run, for their descendants to try to achieve higher social status.[51]

A nonelite individual whose claim to commoner status was insecure could emphasize his military examination degree. An incident of note dates from 1786, when a military examination passer, Ch'oe Ch'ang-nok, broke into the palace to plead his case. According to Ch'oe, a local post station wrongly listed his grandfather on its service obligation register even though the latter's mother, originally a commoner, was only a foster daughter of a station slave. Ch'oe claimed that in return for his contructing a building for the station, he was released from service obligations. Stressing that he then passed the military examination, he argued that the names of himself, father, and grandfather should all indeed be removed from the service obligation register.[52]

Although a military examination degree encouraged people on the lowborn-commoner status boundary to strengthen their claims for higher social status, the degree by itself certainly did not guarantee graduates an official appointment, much less the political power.[53] Graduates other than those from central military official lines—who were thus likely to be registered as royal messenger candidates, for example—had great difficulty obtaining a post in central officialdom. Many had to spend years or even decades serving as military regiment officers, if they were not forced to be content with the military examination degree itself. For example, according to a soldier's petition to the court in 1787, his grandfather of 80 *se* in age, who had begun the career as a marching band musician of the Military Training Division, was still performing the same duty even though "long ago" he had passed the military examination.[54] As suggested by this petition, which generally could not get the throne's attention without the helping hands of concerned officials, such graduates tried hard to secure an appointment through years of social networking and lobbying in Seoul.[55]

At least some, if not many, nonelite military examination graduates did find more significant opportunities in officialdom, albeit without being able to shake off their status constraints. A revealing example is the rise and fall of Pak Ch'ung-mang (1630–?), a slave who had somehow bought his freedom after working in a *yangban* household. When he passed his military examination as one of the 1,236 passers in 1651, the roster recorded the service labels of he and his father as, respectively, *hallyang* and a senior third military rank holder. His understandably spotty post-degree officeholding record shows him as finishing his tenure as a junior fourth-rank small-port commander (Manho) in 1672 and receiving a senior sixth-rank civil post in the Palace Catering Service (Yebinsi) in 1681—a de facto promotion, in spite of the lower rank, in the sense that he was being posted in the capital as a mid-level official. Later in the same year, however, the Office of the Censor-General (Sahŏnbu) denounced him, highlighting that his brothers were still performing lowly services, and the king dismissed him along with several other officials with a blemished pedigree.[56] Pak's downfall illustrates the limitations of a military examination degree for a nonelite official in a sphere dominated by the aristocracy.

Bona fide *yangban* did not accept such "pretenders," finding fault simply in the lifestyles of degreed social newcomers. For example, many military examination graduates of nonelite social backgrounds often passed the examination at the same time as their fathers or even grandfathers. The low regard held by bona fide *yangban* for this practice can be discerned in many court discussions. In September 1717, when a father and a son passed the Onyang special civil examination together—with the latter outperforming the former—officials argued that this ran counter to moral discipline. Previously, the dynasty's official policy was to record the son on the roster of the following examination; the simultaneous recording of a father and his son on the same roster was deemed an affront to filial piety. Although a civil examination, the Onyang case set a new precedent for all examinations: now the father and the son could be recorded together on the same roster.[57]

The elite's contempt for such simultaneous examination success makes sense in the context of a culture that stressed the special bond among the graduates of the same examination. A degree holder generally regarded anyone who passed the same examination almost as a brother, and close personal ties were maintained among them throughout their lives. Moreover, an examination passer's sons treated their father's examination colleagues with great deference, as though they were in the presence of an uncle.[58]

If we view this disjunction, between the essentials of *yangban* status and the basic skills required to pass the military examination, as a question of cultural competence, then Bourdieu's insights into symbolic manifestation can be instructive. An existing elite can have ample reason to rationalize and maintain differences between itself and the rest of the society, and Bourdieu analyzes this inclination for various groups from European preindustrial and industrialized societies. He observes that the structure of the relationship between educational level and social origin engenders differences not only in the competence acquired but also the manner in which it is applied. The manner of application may be regarded as a symbolic manifestation, the meaning and value of which ultimately depend on both the producer and consumer of the competence in question.[59]

This formulation should inform our estimation of the varying social efficacy of a late Chosŏn military examination degree. Of course, a military examination roster could record both the names of *yangban* and of commoner graduates who allegedly demonstrated a comparable degree of cultural competence as measured by the state. Nonetheless, the difference in the manner of degree acquisition and its application apparently was all-too-evident to everyone involved in the process—especially the bona fide *yangban*. Although a military examination degree symbolized both, the cultural competence measured by the aristocracy and the professional competence measured by the aristocratic state were somewhat different; the former embodied greater range that depended heavily on the possessor's social status. In this way, the state was willing to grant recognition, and thus also a sense of status attainment, without actually enabling nonelites to challenge the existing social hierarchy.

Nonelite Aspirations

Passing the military examination could improve the social status of nonelite graduates only to a limited extent, given that the existing elite found ways to distinguish itself from such aspirants. Nonetheless, the military examination degree, like the court ranks and offices commonly acquired by social climbers, was not entirely meaningless. Although successful military examination candidates of humbler social origins had no chance of winning acceptance as members of the *yangban* aristocracy, not to mention of acquiring the political power of central civil and military official descent lines, a military examination degree appealed to non-*yangban* for many reasons.

Above all, status aspirations among nonelites seem to have intensified in late Chosŏn, a desire strengthened in part by the spread of Confucian values and ideals among the common people. Combined with a strong status consciousness deeply rooted in Korean tradition, the Confucian idealization of scholarship, morality, and rituals also defined a family of higher social standing. Thus, as we have seen, more and more nonelites sought to purchase ranks and offices, adopt *yangban*-sounding descent group designations, and fabricate genealogies—to demonstrate their education, command of rituals, and descent from scholar-officials. Though no one could thus win acceptance into the ranks of the true aristocracy, such cultural trappings could strengthen an individual to a certain extent, have a bearing on his social status, and give him an identity defined by Confucian standards. In a sense, these late Chosŏn practices seems to suggest a pragmatic application of Confucius's central teachings wherein the concept of *kunja* (Ch. *junzi*) becomes redefined from a status-based to a morally based notion of the "superior man."[60]

In conjunction, Bourdieu's concept of the three distinct states embodying cultural capital can illuminate developments in late Chosŏn Korea.[61] Regardless of his social status, a candidate seeking a degree had to attain an embodied state high enough so that he could hope, in the course of the military examination, to expound upon passages from the classics as well as to demonstrate archery, horse riding, spear wielding, and other martial skills. Personal cultivation of required expertise prepared the individual for the next objectified state. For a military examination candidate, the exhibition of various martial skills functioned as a physical, or object, display of his embodied state. Once both objectified and embodied states had been attained, a military examination candidate could hope to rise to the institutional state by earning the degree itself. Success meant both the state's recognition of his cultural competence and an elevation of his social status.

Bourdieu's concept of cultural capital seems more applicable to the late Chosŏn military examination than to the licentiate or the civil examination. For one thing, the dynasty's pool of potential civil and licentiate examination takers remained relatively small, as in practical terms only the literate elite could invest decades of effort into preparing for the examination. Moreover, as we saw in Chapter 3, a *yangban* not possessing an examination degree, a rank, or an office could nonetheless maintain aristocratic social status based on ascription, even though passing the civil or licentiate examination still constituted a signal honor. On these grounds, it seems fair to note that the late Chosŏn military examination, which granted degrees to an increasingly diverse social pool of candidates, was a more plausible means of enhancing status for the general population. Indeed, the possession of cultural capital was an obligation for the late Chosŏn *yangban*, and especially the local aristocracy of the south: they had to live up to their noble birth. To a nonelite man, a military examination degree alone carried much prestige as a state-sanctioned status marker that formally certified his accumulated cultural capital.

Available evidence suggests that, despite toughened requirements, commoner participation in the military examination continued into the nineteenth century. The 1865 *Great Code Reconciliation* restored classics exposition to the military examination.[62] The state seems to have adopted a more conservative approach after the death of King Chŏngjo in 1800 and brought back the classics exposition in order to reduce, if not eliminate, commoner participation. All the same, we may surmise that although there are no statistics on the literacy rate in late Chosŏn, apparently commoners had come to possess at least a smattering of knowledge of the pertinent classics—perhaps orally, in vernacular Korean translation, or even in literary Chinese, and the state was raising the bar.

Further indirect evidence of increased literacy is the flourishing of woodblock printing shops specializing in vernacular tales, even though professional story tellers were available for the illiterate. Especially popular among them were works of military narrative fiction (*kundam sosŏl*), which attracted a broad audience toward the end of Chosŏn.[63] As we will see in the next section, the protagonists of these narratives embodied cardinal Confucian virtues, albeit often in watered-down ways, and appealed to a diverse audience across status boundaries.[64] The popularity of these works seems to reflect the growing availability of Confucian education in late Chosŏn, and the influence of that learning in increasing individuals' aspirations.

Such aspirations often were quite practical. Most commoners probably did not expect to have government employment, not to mention

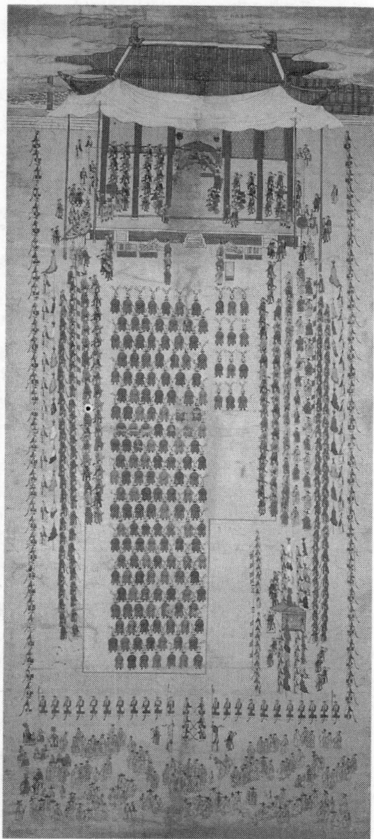

Figure 5.1 Scene of Degree Ceremony for the 1795 Suwŏn Courtyard Examination. Wearing two floral stems on their heads, successful candidates line up in the middle ground, facing the king. Only an empty throne is shown, since it was a taboo to depict the monarch in a painting other than his official portrait. Also noteworthy are the musket-holding guardsmen surrounding the venue, as well as the onlookers at the bottom of the painting. From "Naknamhŏn pangbangdo," in *Hwasŏng nŭnghaeng tobyŏng, 4 ch'ŏp.* Courtesy of Samsung Museum of Art.

political power, after earning a degree. Instead, they hoped that they could escape the military cloth tax and other onerous obligations to the state. Instrumental considerations aside, another dimension of commoners' aspirations was the genuine value accorded to the public honor of degree recipients. It must have been an emotional and triumphant moment, especially for those of humbler origins, when the examination graduates lined up, often in the king's presence, to receive the red warrant (*hongp'ae*)—the degree certificate, so named for the paper's color (Figure 5.1).[65] Even without the king's physical presence, an examination passer always received his degree certificate as a document of "royal instruction" (*kyoji*).

Reporting in 1638 on the conditions he witnessed in P'yŏngan Province, a royal messenger to the throne lucidly explained the importance of the red warrant, especially to ordinary people. His account describes soldiers mobilized in the region who had passed the previous year's local military examination and were yet without their red warrant papers, as they pleaded: "We are now set to go afar to the place of death in spite of cold. We cannot avoid this [duty], as the matter of the country is immeasurable; however, if we can still receive our red warrants for the last year's examination, then even if our bodies were to perish [upon reaching the battle site] the warrants would be an honor for our descendants. Please deliver our petition to the court."[66] The same popular sentiment toward the examination is also palpable in the 1725 argument of a royal secretary (Sŭngji) against the government's nullification of a recent courtyard examination. At the climax of his argument, he points out that since the state recruited talented men through the examination, in the people's minds passing it determined whether one's life was glorious or miserable.[67] In fact, many hapless military examination passers even got their red warrants stolen during the often chaotic process of red warrant distribution, and references to such incidents are numerous in court histories.[68]

Another indication of the degree's appeal can be found in the colorful and memorable festivities for a successful examination candidate. In addition to receiving from the king stems of flowers with which to decorate his cap, and a sun parasol for shade, every new graduate was allowed to parade around in the streets, accompanied by musicians and jesters, for three days. On rarer occasions, the king might extend a graduate's three-day festivities by another day or two as a special honor for someone he particularly favored.[69]

Even though the military examination's prestige was lower than that of its civil counterpart, ceremonies and festivities for successful candidates treated military examination graduates with due respect. In the eighteenth century, it was still customary for the graduates of both examinations to gather, on the day after the announcement of the successful candidates, at the house of the top civil examination passer, from there proceeding to the royal palace to perform the *saŭn* ritual thanking the king for his grace in bestowing the degrees upon them. On the next day, they would assemble again, this time at the top military examination passer's house, to pay homage to the Shrine of Confucius.[70]

Regardless of the examination, the state treated top passers with special respect. The person reading aloud the names of successful candidates did not dare utter the name of the best candidate; instead, the latter was referred to only as the "top passer" (*changwŏn*).[71] Anyone encountering the man on the street could not bow merely by holding his hands together and bending at the waistline, but rather needed to prostrate on the ground.[72] Such special respect also translated into a more practical benefit: in late Chosŏn, the government exempted top passers of the military examination—along with the degree holders serving in the Inner Forbidden Guards, the Concurrent Royal Stables, or the Winged Forest Guards—from frontier garrison duty.[73]

The spirit of solidarity that bound the new graduates together lasted a lifetime. Graduates of the same examination, referred to as *tongbang* (graduates of the "same roster") or *tongnyŏnbang* (graduates of the "same-year examination roster"), maintained a lasting brotherly bond expressed through such activities as gathering together on special occasions, reprinting their examination roster, and celebrating the sixtieth anniversary of their degree conferral, known as *hoebang*.[74] In fact, even the king honored such *hoebang* degree holders, regardless of their social status, as it was rare for an examination graduate—typically in his early 30s at the time he received the degree—to live a full sexagenarian calendar cycle beyond the event.[75] In June 1823, when King Sunjo (r. 1800–34) gave an audience to all those celebrating the sixtieth anniversary of passing the civil or military examination, First Royal Secretary (Tosŭngji) Yi Chi-yŏn (1777–1841) explained the custom as follows: "From the reigns of royal ancestors, there is a precedent of bestowing special grace upon the elderly, even if they are common persons. Your subject dares to admonish [your majesty], because the state must generously reward, honor, and encourage such men in particular and thus demonstrate that the noble care for those below."[76] The tradition outlived both the examination system and the dynasty: in 1919 and 1923, former emperor Sunjong

(r. 1907–10) gave an honorarium to elderly ex-officials celebrating their military examination *hoebang*.[77] Considering the prestige accorded by the monarch to the military examination degree, it should come as no surprise that nonelites, as well as more marginalized elites, continued to invest so much in earning it.

Military Ethos and Popular Culture

Culture played an important mediating role in the structure of the Chosŏn social pyramid; while society became more stratified, even the elite stratum itself became variegated. As much as everyone most likely knew where he or she "belonged," people were not entirely without means in negotiating their status—especially in the middle strata. Even the stability of a rigid, caste-like social system still relies on the ideological functions of culture, and late Chosŏn Korea offers much for us to consider in this respect. Genres of popular culture such as vernacular narrative fiction, masked dance, and *p'ansori* (which featured performances by operatic singers accompanied by drummers) not only brought various social groups together but even allowed the nonelite masses to express their status aspirations or vent their frustrations in a way the aristocracy found nonthreatening. The late Chosŏn military examination also assumed such functions.

Folk culture constitutes a space of disguised, passive resistance. Using the concept of the "hidden transcript," James Scott critiques the notion that only active struggle by nonelites against the ruling elite counts as true resistance, as well as the claim that intellectuals must lead the masses out of their state of resignation or petit bourgeois mentalities.[78] Considering more subtle forms of resistance, Scott argues that observable, ordinary interactions between elites and nonelites are shaped by a "public transcript," toward which historical sources tend to be biased, thereby affirming the dominance of the ruling class over the ruled. Since the hidden transcript that directs nonelites to express their aspirations while avoiding the oppression of the ruling elite remains excluded from official history, we are left with the false impression that a society is stable and resistant to change. Scott points out that since the ruled could not maintain a dialogue on an equal basis with the ruling class already in possession of material and institutional power, they had to engage in endless guerilla warfare rather than open battle. This struggle is none other than that articulated by the hidden transcript, the terrain of broad, lower-level politics situated on the spectrum of resistance somewhere between total passivity and open challenge.

Scott's concept of the hidden transcript helps to explain how various late Chosŏn popular cultural media, especially the genre of masked dance (*t'alch'um*), reveal social tension. Masked dance relied on humorous satire expressed through a regionally recognized set of characters and their distinctive masks. Some performances were controlled directly by the state, others were independently managed by local residents. Even in the former case, though, some scholars see a cultural production that functioned as a ritualized rebellion, since local functionaries supervised the performance and arguably represented the masses vis-à-vis the aristocracy.[79] This interpretation emerged in the 1960s and 1970s, within the context of South Korean intellectuals' criticism of authoritarian rule and the privileged elite.[80] In part due to the democratization of the country after the late 1980s, many scholars now see in the masked dance not so much a ritualized rebellion by the masses as a vehicle of social harmony, if not a safety valve. Im Chaehae points out that in a conservative, *yangban*-dominated locale such as Andong, the preeminent local *yangban* lineage of P'ungsan Yu not only sponsored masked dance productions but treated performers with respect, to the extent that a dancer enjoyed prerogatives appropriate to the social status of the character his mask represented.[81] Thus, when hiding behind the mask of, say, a *hallyang* or a wealthy aristocrat, jesters could mock and talk rudely "against" *yangban*, who still took everything as humor.[82]

The military examination system's influence extended into this realm of popular culture, even though the institution was an inherently political one that helped define and reproduce the ruling officialdom. Most nonelite participants in the military contests could not realistically expect meaningful careers in the central government, but the lure of martial heroics and glory continued to attract common people to the military examinations. The lure could be real or imagined.

Success stories told and retold among the populace were transmitted orally and in writing as *p'ansori* and vernacular fiction. By the nineteenth century, the two genres came to enjoy enormous popularity, captivating audiences across status boundaries. Legendary *p'ansori* singers, generally of humbler backgrounds, enjoyed aristocratic patronage—even translating into a military examination degree—and *yangban* authors now wrote many works of vernacular fiction.[83] Both genres feature nonelite heroes and heroines who embody cardinal Confucian virtues such as loyalty, filial piety, and female chastity, all of which once were presumed to be the monopoly of the aristocracy. Whereas *p'ansori* played a key role in oral transmission, written narrative fiction accounts produced numerous versions of a particular tale.[84] Since more narrative fictions than *p'ansori* titles have survived, I have chosen to discuss at some length how such works portray military men in a Confucian society.

Above all, those works featuring military men—namely, military narrative fiction (*kundam sosŏl*)—could celebrate heroes similar to the famous native sons performing martial heroics as honored in local gazetteers.[85] The kinds of success stories presented in local gazetteers tend to portray actual historical personalities, and most, if not all, of the details are factual in the sense that they often can be independently verified. A common motif is that of a young man of humble origins who performs amazing deeds of physical strength and courage, such as killing with his bare hands a tiger that had devoured his father or mother, cutting open the dead tiger to retrieve the parent's body for a proper burial ritual, passing the military examination, and distinguishing himself as a northern frontier garrison or port commander.[86] In fact, it was not uncommon for government officials to take note of local men with exceptional physical prowess and to recruit them. For example, in 1676 the Board of War reported that a central official on a southern tour of duty had recommended men of great strength from Tongnae and Puan for a military examination in Seoul; King Sukchong concurred.[87]

In the case of military narrative fiction, as in the stories told by *p'ansori* performers, tales of martial heroics drew on expansive realms of imagination. Exemplified by the *Tale of Hong Kil-tong* (*Hong Kil-tong chŏn*) authored by Hŏ Kyun (1569–1618), which described the adventures of a fictional illegitimate son who ultimately founded his own kingdom on a remote island, military narrative fictions came to be produced in great quantity, acquiring expanded readership and even constituting the majority of narrative fictions printed in late Chosŏn.

The protagonists appearing in military narrative fiction possess a variety of characteristics and perform heroics that are martial, religious, ideological, or political in nature. The life of a typical hero would include the following elements: a noble lineage; an extraordinary manner of birth; youthful hardship suffered in the face of wars or factional strife, often separating him from his family; meeting a patron or sponsor; the demonstration of heroic qualities through a performance of great feats during crisis; advanced years marked by great fame, nobility, and wealth; and a glorious afterlife. Among these more broadly defined elements, it is possible to identify specific motifs that appear almost invariably in a narrative fiction: the acquisition and mastery of a special sword and horse; loyalty and service to the king in times of need; a reunion with a father figure on a deserted island or in some other unusual location; and the heroism of female protagonists. Although women feature in some works as the dominant leader, their heroics are generally performed in partnership with their male lovers.[88]

Works of military narrative fiction can be divided into two subgenres, classifiable as either "historical" military narrative fiction (which uses a hero's life as the basic plot structure and a historical war as the setting) and "creative" military narrative fiction (involving a fictional military conflict). The former category includes works such as the *Record of the Imjin War* (*Imjinnok*), the *Tale of Im Kyŏng-ŏp* (*Im Kyŏng-ŏp chŏn*), and the *Tale of Lady Pak* (*Pak-ssi chŏn*). These stories are set in historical wars such as the Japanese or Manchu invasions. Both historical and fictional personalities appear in these accounts, participating in heroic narratives depicting Korean triumph over the foreign enemy. As we have seen, the wars against the Japanese and Manchus exposed fundamental problems in Chosŏn society, and humiliated the Korean people at the hands of an enemy whom they considered barbaric. Historical military narrative fictions reflected Korea's lot in the late sixteenth and early seventeenth centuries, and enabled the people to overcome their frustration at defeat through reading and hearing about the feats of their heroes and heroines.[89]

In the *Record of the Imjin War*, various versions of which evolved throughout late Chosŏn, the focus is on individuals from all walks of life who fight against the Japanese. Featured are not only actual military commanders such as Yi Sun-sin and various famous *yangban* and Buddhist monk militia leaders, but also female entertainers and mountain lads who can somehow dispose of enemy generals through wit, trickery, or magic.[90] The target audience's obvious thirst for heroes and heroines prevailing over historical miseries is understandable in light of what is known about how nonelites expressed hostility toward the court and aristocracy during the wars. Thus, in his *Book of Corrections* (*Chingbirok*), the eminent statesman Yu Sŏng-nyong (1542–1607) reflects on what went wrong for his country and even describes popular anger toward *yangban* for their cowardice and incompetence during the Japanese attack.[91]

In comparison, the more purely fictional tales depict protagonists whose adventures take place in a nonhistorical setting. Many more titles are known from this subgenre, among them the *Tale of Sŏ Tae-sŏng* (*Sŏ Tae-sŏng chŏn*), the *Tale of Yu Ch'ung-nyŏl* (*Yu Ch'ung-nyŏl chŏn*), and the *Tale of Chang Paek* (*Chang Paek chŏn*). Such works take as a theme the people's desire for better opportunities in life, their frustration with court politics, or even their desire to overthrow the whole system. Stories about a non-*yangban* hero tend to build around a protagonist, hailing from a humble background, who possesses extraordinary abilities and ultimately struggles in vain against his detractors. In contrast, a fictional military tale about a *yangban* protagonist narrates battlefield victories, personal glory, and victory for the whole country. In overcoming whatever barriers stand in the way, the hero or heroine triumphs by acquiring a power that is often supernatural; during this process, the divisions between good and evil, between this world and the afterlife, and between loyal and wicked subjects are made starkly clear. Ultimately, the heavenly order determines the outcome of all events in this world.[92]

Though they had a limited public role to play in late Chosŏn Korea, women were not excluded from this imagined realm of martial heroics. Among the most avid readers of late Chosŏn vernacular narrative fiction were women, and some works centered on women knowledgeable in battle tactics. Plot structures often featured female warriors dressed as men, fighting valiantly in battles, and ultimately saving their lovers as well as their country from danger. Even before Neo-Confucianism's spread sought their exclusion from the public sphere, women could not compete in the state examination or serve in the government, and no known legal compilation even bothers to mention women among those who are ineligible to sit for an examination or hold an office.[93] Given this kind of unquestioned discrimination in the public realm, the presence of women in military narrative fictions is all the more noteworthy.

Figure 5.2 Portrait of Im Kyŏng-ŏp Depicting Him as an Official. The somewhat mischievous expression on the subject's face seems to hint at the arguably quixotic path he chose in life. Since the court posthumously restored his ranks and offices in 1697, the portrait most likely dates from sometime thereafter. Courtesy of Tenri University Library.

Some of the most powerful accounts of martial feats appeared in vernacular narrative fictions celebrating the likes of the actual military man Im Kyŏng-ŏp (1594–1646, see Figure 5.2). Until his last breath under torture, Im held fast to his dream of avenging Chosŏn Korea's humiliation by the Manchus, and he found an honored place in the collective consciousness outside official history. He was celebrated as a larger-than-life hero in a late Chosŏn military narrative fiction, the *Tale of Im Kyŏng-ŏp* (*Im Kyŏng-ŏp chŏn*), sometimes titled the *Tale of General Im* (*Im Changgun chŏn*).[94] Various editions of the work exist, their narratives generally loosely based on what is known about his life; in addition to his actual accomplishments—such as passing the military examination and fighting against the Manchus—the work also makes liberal use of exaggerated or even fictitious details. Presenting a colorful account of Im's heroics, the *Tale* enjoyed great popularity. Its hero successfully avenged Korea, inspiring the imaginations of all men lured by martial heroics, especially the young commoner men honing weaponry skills in preparation for the military examination. According to Song Si-yŏl, who, like many Neo-Confucian *yangban,* stressed the cultural superiority of Chosŏn Korea and Ming China over the Manchus, Im's reputation was such that ordinary folk and even Buddhist monks crowded around an imposter posing as Im and advocating a war against the Manchus.[95]

Celebrated in vernacular narrative fiction and posthumously honored by the state as a loyal subject, Im also came to be worshipped as a deity by Korean shamans (Figure 5.3). From the point of view of the shamans, Im's loyalty and courage could be deployed against evil demons in the unseen world, who had the power to wreak havoc upon the lives of ordinary people.[96] Through apotheosis, Im joined Korean shamanism's pantheon, which also included other historic military men such as Ch'oe Yŏng (1316–88) and Nam I (1441–68).

Among the other deified military men, Ch'oe is well known as the major victim of a critical power struggle in the course of Yi Sŏng-gye's founding of the Chosŏn dynasty. The two official histories of Koryŏ, both compiled in early Chosŏn, are heavily biased against those who had opposed Yi, but the accounts nonetheless note Ch'oe's moral probity and martial prowess. According to a well-documented legend, Ch'oe declared his innocence before his execution, predicting that no grass would grow on his grave mound if he had indeed done nothing wrong. Not only do both official histories record people's sadness at the news of his death, but many later sources also comment on the bareness of his grave mound. Hŏ Mok (1595–1682), a Southerner-faction scholar-official, noted that people deemed Ch'oe's spirit to be potent and capable of capriciously effecting both fortune and misfortune. Because anyone disrespectful toward the spirit was said to drop dead on the spot, fearful rural folk performed rituals for him with great solemnity.[97] Overall, these popular attitudes toward Ch'oe were rooted in his fame as a distinguished battle commander and admirable character who suffered a tragic death. The resulting myth ultimately won him a place in the pantheon of Korean shamans.

Figure 5.3 Shaman Painting Depicting Im Kyŏng-ŏp as a Deity. The emphasis is on the fierce, martial qualities of a warrior ready to charge against any enemy. Source: Personal possession of Kim Kŭm-hwa; reproduced in *HMMTS*, s.v. "Im Kyŏng-ŏp changgun sin" (General Im Kyŏng-ŏp deity).

Unlike that of Ch'oe Yŏng, whose distinguished career as a general spanned decades, the apotheosis of Nam I involved a young military officer. He rose quickly through the ranks and attained the highest government posts while still in his twenties, thanks to King Sejo's patronage. During the succeeding reign of Yejong (1468–69), however, Nam's political enemies accused him of treason and executed him at the mere age of 28 *se*. Legends stressing Nam's heroic qualities are numerous; as a young boy, for example, he is credited with chasing away an evil spirit that was attempting to kill a girl, who was choking after nibbling on a peach. Her father, the dynastic foundation merit subject Kwŏn Kŭn (1352–1409), then married the revived daughter to Nam. Like both Ch'oe Yŏng and Im Kyŏng-ŏp, Nam I was a military man of heroic qualities and ultimately suffered an unjust death. He, too, came to be honored as a shamanistic deity.[98]

Nam I, Im Kyŏng-ŏp, and Ch'oe Yŏng all are military men who became gods in popular Korean religion, but what distinguishes them from other famed military men such as, say, Admiral Yi Sun-sin, who enjoyed no such status? According to Cho Hŭng-yun, the anointing of a hero deity depends not only on the the subject's accomplishments in real life, but also on social consensus: the common people must understand and accept his feats, as well as being emotionally moved by them.[99] If this is the case, then Yi Sun-sin's fame as a great military man apparently did not extend beyond the realm of the Confucian discourse that celebrated martyrs for their loyalty to the king. Perhaps his glorious naval victories against the Japanese fleets and his almost perfectly timed death while fighting the war's final naval battle—as well as the state's immediate granting of an office and a posthumous name (Ch'ungmu, "Loyal and Martial")—were too formulaic to allow any room for popular imagination. Yi's career brought him all the earthly rewards that Nam, Im, and Ch'oe were deprived of: the latters' deaths were not only untimely in that their military objectives were left unfinished, but each suffered unjustly at the hands of a wicked political adversary. In fact, while Cho Hŭng-yun prioritizes noble character and dedicated service to the country as more fundamental factors in a hero's deification, he also identifies unresolved resentment (*han*, *wŏnhan*) as an important element, as Korean shaman rituals often involve placating such resentful spirits.[100]

In the late Chosŏn cultural context, the military examination system functioned to bridge the worlds of the aristocracy and ordinary people. Shamanism—as practiced by women and the general populace—was the polar opposite of aristocratic, male-dominated, Confucianism; all the same, a broad expanse of common ground nevertheless existed between the two realms. There, a ritual often lent itself to both elite Confucian and popular religious interpretations. All the same, Confucian and popular rituals that remained distinct from each other could satisfy particular socioreligious needs.[101] The late Chosŏn military examination, too, was multidimensional—its meanings varied depending on the background of the participants, who shared in the common ideal of a wise, courageous general who faithfully served the ruler and the people. Of course, the Confucian *yangban*—literally the "two orders" of civil and military officials—were the king's "servants" (*sin*) drawn from the general population. Thus in the Confucian-influenced realm of popular culture, the military examination transcended status distinctions.

Summation

Nonelite participation in the military examination increased in the late Chosŏn period. Although the aristocracy continued to supply the kind of candidates who passed the military examination and actually went on to have meaningful official careers, the majority of degree holders recorded in the military examination rosters, or their fathers, held status titles that were used by those of less than solid *yangban* crendentials. Many rosters even record a preponderance of successful candidates who hailed from obviously nonaristocratic descent groups or had names that clearly were not those of respectable *yangban*. The roster data, then, substantiates the concerns of contemporary aristocratic observers and legal sources that too many nonelites were passing the military examination, many of them illegally.

The military examination system took on the social role of accommodating nonelites as the common people increasingly aspired to the status, lifestyle, and culture of the aristocrats who continued to compete in the contest. For this reason, even though the degree generally did not provide a route to office or political power for military examination graduates of non-*yangban* backgrounds, it retained prestige as well as helping to satisfy their aspirations for higher, officially sanctioned, social status. The Confucian cultural ethos subordinated martial virtue to literary virtue and limited the military examination degree's potency as a form of cultural capital, but passing the military examination theoretically entitled the degree holder to an appointment and symbolically set him on a path toward Confucian generalship.

At least in part, the increased influence of Confucianism fueled the desire of nonelites for upward social mobility. Not only did the state and aristocracy encourage the "Confucianization" of nonelites, Confucianism—even when practiced at a more superficial level in the manner common among nonelites—functioned as a schema that could potentially provide them with resources that could function as cultural capital. As illustrated by many nonelite heroes and heroines in *p'ansori* performances and works of vernacular narrative fiction, Confucian virtues held dear by the aristocracy were no longer the exclusive prerogatives of *yangban*.

Intensifying status aspirations among those at the margins of the power structure necessitated the emergence of common cultural media accessible to a wide array of participants. Besides vernacular narrative fiction and *p'ansori*, other genres of popular culture, such as masked dance, allowed nonelites to express their discontent, albeit in ways that the aristocracy found more or less harmless. The institution of the military examination assumed such a culturally mediating role as the social base of aspirants expanded.

CONCLUSION

The State and the Military Examination System

The late Chosŏn social status system was complex—rigid at its extremes but fluid in the middle. The status consciousness so deeply embedded in the schemas of Korean actors at the time provoked many who had the resources to try to raise their social standing. Suitable means included acquisition of proper education, mastery of "correct" rituals, development of empowering social ties, accumulation of economic wealth, and pursuit of state-granted trappings of status, such as examination degrees, ranks, and offices. The military examination was especially important; while retaining its original function as the state's primary instrument for recruiting new members for the military branch of central officialdom, it increasingly awarded degrees to a broadening social base of candidates. The military examination's dual function helped the system as a whole to satisfy the status aspirations of nonelites and marginalized elites while ensuring the stability of existing sociopolitical structures.

Representing a small percentage of the population, the capital *yangban* continued to exercise real political power, enjoy paramount social status, preserve the official culture based on Neo-Confucian values and rhetoric, and regulate the expanding resources of a predominantly agrarian economy undergoing commercialization. The state wavered between devising legal restrictions against nonelite participation in the military examination and relaxing such constraints amid the growing complaints of those excluded. Over centuries, the latter inclination prevailed.

Sewell's insights into the power dynamics of state structure can illuminate the ways that late Chosŏn actors employed their resources. A functioning state, because it can generate and mobilize a high concentration of power visible in the daily life of the population it regulates, may seem stable and durable as a structure.[1] Highly centralized states, however, risk structural crisis and transformation—if not collapse—because both the massiveness and obviousness of their resources naturally make them both the site and the stake of open struggle. An effective, powerful state, in contrast, is one that is accepted by its subjects as part of their "second nature," widely, if not universally, recognized by political actors as a power-neutral vehicle for advancing their own objectives. The durability of a state structure seems to be determined more by its depth than its power.[2]

Sewell's argument has implications for our understanding of the late Chosŏn state, which, controlled by a small segment of the aristocracy, increasingly faced challenges from those beyond the margins of power. Although political actors in the government were primarily *yangban* factions pursuing competing objectives, the state remained the legitimizing vehicle of these objectives. For the most part, the general population did not raise questions about the legitimacy of the state, which, as symbolized by the king, was the natural guardian of legal regulations and moral guidelines. If nothing else, the state recognized, to an extent, the enhanced social status of upwardly mobile nonelites, so long as no new group could marshal enough resources around an alternative vision, or set of schemas. Unlike the previous Koryŏ dynasty (which collapsed when northeastern military officers and some reformist Neo-Confucian scholar-officials amassed the material and intellectual power to overthrow a royal family whose prestige and command over resources had diminished), late Chosŏn produced no revolutionary force capable of rejecting a ruling house that, in the eyes of most aristocrats and ordinary people, commanded loyalty.[3] As much as nineteenth-century rebels and rioters resented backbreaking taxes, widespread government corruption, and status discrimination in existing social practices, few could contemplate replacing the royal house or abolishing the monarchy altogether. It was only after the Japanese annexation of Korea in 1910, and the death of the former monarch, Kojong, in 1919, that republicanism finally gained momentum.

The self-identity of Confucian Korea, as the true civilization following the "barbarian" Manchu conquest of China, burdened the late Chosŏn state with the role of the guardian of the Way.[4] Conscientious eighteenth-century monarchs such as Yŏngjo and Chŏngjo, who saw themselves, respectively, as sage king and educator of the people, played a vital role in insuring that the state would retain its sanctity as represented by the king.[5] Through more subtle means of moral persuasion subsumed under the rubric of Confucian ideology, the state exercised power over its subjects without, say, the crushing military victories typical of the Qing state of China, or the detailed, often harsh, formal laws for social order that were erratically enforced by the Tokugawa shogunate in Japan.[6] The late Chosŏn state may seem unremarkable in terms of obvious signs of power, but the fact that most nonelites evidently chose to work within the system strongly suggests that it had the kind of depth Sewell stresses. The obviousness of state power did not prevent the Qing and Tokugawa systems from falling apart, but the depth of the late Chosŏn state's power moderated the intensity of social discontent, albeit less successfully as time went on.

The dilemma of the state and its aristocratic stakeholders—that of satisfying the status aspirations of nonelites without jeopardizing the status quo—posed a challenge explicable via Bourdieu's concepts of hysteresis and autonom. Hysteresis describes the search by status-conscious social upstarts for diplomas or certificates that no longer function as vital credentials for the old elite. The hysteresis effect is stronger on those farther removed from the educational system, such as peasants, who are more likely to be attracted to trappings of depreciated value due to cultural lag; the sector of the society where these objects continue to enjoy high prestige is the autonom. As time elapses, an increasing number of those possessing devalued credentials may deliberately choose unemployment rather than settle for positions they can realistically obtain that they now deem unbefitting their station in life. Such deliberate unemployment takes place in a transition phase that can ultimately produce in social newcomers a widespread disillusionment with—and, ultimately, a total rejection of—the whole educational system as the social newcomers, too, begin to feel frustrated over devalued credentials. The autonom, the terrain wherein the hysteresis works out, can turn into a seat of discontent.[7]

The experience of Korea mirrors Bourdieu's account of a three-phase transformation: from nonelites opting for the prestige of a devalued diploma, to self-imposed unemployment, to the rejection of the whole system. Bourdieu's concepts of hysteresis and autonom explain the behavior of the status-seeking nonelites who acquired such devalued credentials as military examination degrees. As we saw earlier, the degree's efficacy depended on the social status of those who acquired it: men who passed the military examination continued to staff the military branch of central officialdom, but such recruits generally came from the central aristocracy, a small segment of the population. For this reason, the institution preserved its prestige in the eyes of nonelites, for whom military examination degrees were more attainable than any other degrees and yet still served as state-sanctioned status markers. At the same time, increased nonelite participation lowered the degree's prestige among aristocrats, especially the southern local *yangban* who, having become dissociated from the central political structure, continued to define their status through birth.

The ways in which Bourdieu's scenario of deliberate unemployment does not fit the Korean case offers insight into the dynamics of late Chosŏn society and culture. Outside the capital, credentials not directly linked to political power appealed more strongly to nonelites or marginalized elites than to true *yangban*.[8] Further, those who achieved such marks of distinction tended to be eager for admittance into officialdom. In other words, "deliberate unemployment" was more widespread among southern local aristocrats, secure in their knowledge of who they were and having little need of state-granted certifiers of social status. Local aristocrats still had too much invested in the existing social system to become a revolutionary force, whereas nonelites seeking out devalued degrees saw little reason to attack the state that issued them status credentials.[9] Contrary to Bourdieu's premise about relations between social newcomers and the state, anyone with cultural capital sufficient to earn a degree in late Chosŏn Korea viewed the state as the natural guardian of legal regulations and moral guidelines. Even peasants far removed from educational opportunities saw little reason to blame the distant head of state, the king, although corrupt aristocrats and officials abounded.

The late Chosŏn state employed the military examination degree and the military examination system as a safety valve that helped prevent the rise of potentially subversive elements among nonelites. According to Bourdieu, the overproduction and consequent devaluation of qualifications such as degrees tend to become a structural constant when theoretically equal chances of obtaining them are offered to all new generations of a social elite such as the bourgeoisie, while the access of other classes to these qualifications also increases in absolute terms.[10] Even in the late seventeenth century, after the initial impetus of the foreign military threat had disappeared, Korea saw no decline in the frequency and number of military examination passers.

Of course, earning a military examination degree or any other devalued trapping of status was beyond the means of most nonelites. By the early nineteenth century, a large number of commoners found themselves unable to bear the tax burden in spite of the reform efforts of eighteenth-century monarchs such as Yŏngjo. Many placed themselves under the protection of affluent individuals who would pay the taxes for them in exchange for slavelike labor. In more extreme circumstances, some even fled to the mountains or other barren areas, seeking, at least temporarily, respite from the rapacious hands of the state.[11]

Arguably, the first sign that the late Chosŏn state no longer commanded complete loyalty among a significant segment of the population was the 1812 Hong Kyŏng-nae rebellion in the northwest, an area discriminated against by the center and its aristocracy. The central and southern *yangban* continued to regard the north as culturally backward and devoid of true *yangban,* even though some kings and officials, especially in the eighteenth century, promoted both Confucian education and martial training as well as the employment of talented men from that region. These policies helped the northwest enjoy increased success in both the civil and military examinations, while providing more nonelites with education or martial skills. All the same, these developments also turned many against a center which continued to exclude them. Along with marginalized elites, nonelites with some cultural or economic capital most actively participated in the rebellion led by Hong Kyŏng-nae, himself a professional geomancer with enough Confucian education for a shot at the examination—which he ultimately failed to pass. Whereas the top local elites and functionaries generally shied away from the unsuccessful uprising, members of wealthy households (*yoho pumin*), merchants, and peasants more actively participated.

In spite of the regionalism that had spread discontent in the north, the new strategies employed by locals for dealing with exploitation by the center prevented a militant expression of more generalized discontent for half a century. For one thing, those still capable of meeting tax obligations devised collective means to cope with the levy system and its corrupt agents, the magistrates and functionaries. Above all, local taxpayers adopted a payment system based on a household's actual ability to bear the burden. Also, the local assembly (*hyanghoe*), which had previously been a *yangban* institution that advised the centrally appointed magistrate, became a more inclusive gathering of the representatives of various social groups, many of which shared an interest in combating the abuses of corrupt government agents. Rather than merely assisting the state with tax collection as it had done in the past, the reinvigorated assemblies actively voiced local complaints. Significantly, the new leadership included not just local *yangban* but also affluent commoners.[12]

Reduced *yangban* influence in local administration reflected the central government's delegation of more power to district magistrates and the local functionaries who advised them. New power dynamics in local politics, clearly visible by the eighteenth century, coincided with Yŏngjo and Chŏngjo's antifactionalist policies, which formally rejected southern local *yangban* views critical of the court. However, the new political arrangement became grossly distorted during the subsequent decades, during which weak kings ascended the throne as minors and the oligarchy of royal in-law families and their allies allowed disreputable men to win, through connections or bribery, appointments as magistrates. Corrupt appointees in turn colluded with local functionaries in pursuing private gain, through sundry abuses linked to tax collection, grain loans, and manpower mobilization. The situation deteriorated to the extent that finally, in 1862, a series of riots swept across southern and central Korea.

Hardly a well-organized rebellion against the center, the 1862 disturbances were spontaneous expressions of discontent among commoner peasants, as well as some local *yangban* and wealthy households, all of which were upset over endemic corruption and excess taxation. Not only did the center allay popular anger by punishing corrupt officials and confining the punishment of rioters to ringleaders, the Taewŏn'gun's subsequent conservative reform (1864–73) during the minority of his son, King Kojong, curtailed widespread corruption by ending royal in-law dominance and the "three administrative abuses" involving military cloth tax, land tax, and grain loans. The Taewŏn'gun's policies helped keep Korea free of rebellions for twenty years after his forced retirement in 1873, a period during which his detractors, the queen's Yŏhŭng Min kinsmen, did much to undermine his reforms. Nonetheless, the general direction of change affecting local society remained unaltered, as the traditionally *yangban*-dominated social hierarchy gave way to greater activism on the part of wealthy, taxpaying households that also included commoners. Without meaningful representation in the central political structure, these taxpayers became frustrated with the irrational, oppressive levying policies of the state and its disreputable agents.

The opening of Korea exacerbated these internal problems. In 1876, the country entered the age of modern commercial treaties with Japan, China, and the Western nations. The inability of the oligarchic central aristocracy to manage formidable new forces—various demands by foreign powers, Korea's urgent need to adopt Western institutions and ideas in a rapidly changing world, and the rural population's desire for relief from foreign economic penetration and widespread government corruption—fueled the rise of a new socioreligious movement, the Tonghak. In spite of government persecution, the Tonghak spread throughout rural communities during Kojong's reign. Finally staging a full-scale uprising in 1894, their armies repeatedly defeated the beleaguered government troops. Had it not been for Japanese military intervention, the Tonghak armies would most likely have entered Seoul and forced Kojong to concede to their three general demands: the rejection of foreign influence, an end to administrative corruption, and the abolition of many discriminatory laws and customs against specific social groups.

During the uprising, the government held its last military examination. The potency of a late Chosŏn military examination degree and other types of mollifiers depended heavily on the strength of the popular perception that the culturally or economically better-endowed social actors among nonelites had a reasonable chance of obtaining state-granted trappings of status. The social unrest of the nineteenth century suggests that those who saw no such chance had become larger in number, but their apparent inability to muster enough strength to overthrow the system shows the dynasty's practice of limited accommodation of demands for status enhancement continued to appeal to enough people even in the midst of widespread unrest.

The legacy of the military examination system even survived Korea's difficult journey to modernity. Although the late Chosŏn state had become too weak to legitimize the institution, the popular impulse toward higher status persisted. An intriguing case centers on Pak Sŏngbin (1871–1938). Hailing from a marginal *yangban,* or social newcomer, descent group based in a remote inland county in Kyŏngsang Province, Pak reportedly passed one of the last military examinations.[13] Afterward, he squandered the family wealth while sojourning in Seoul and trying to obtain office. The effort seems to have paid off: he apparently got a senior ninth military rank.[14] Getting nowhere thereafter, though, he returned to his home village, spending the rest of his life as a heavy drinker. A man of good physical stature, villagers addressed him as *sŏndal*—an informal title of respect for a military examination graduate without office.[15] Regardless of the veracity of these minutiae, Pak's life offers us a glimpse of a young man of undistinguished background seeking status through the military examination. It may have been no mere coincidence that his son, Pak Chŏng-hŭi (Park Chung Hee, 1917–79), quit his job as a small town elementary school teacher in colonial Korea in order to enter the Japanese military academy in Manchukuo. Later, he became a South Korean army general, lead the 1961 coup, and governed the country for eighteen years. Two generations of Paks bridged a period of immense transition, for where the father's ambition ended in a stunted career, the son gained national power of the kind once wielded only by the capital aristocracy. The upheavals of the twentieth century account for much of this change, but the late Chosŏn military examination even earlier fed dreams of advancement in life.

Appendixes

Appendix A

Highest Achievements of Military Examination Passers from Elite Military Lines, 1592–1894

Office/rank (Korean name, rank)	Tŏksu Yi	Nŭngsŏng Ku	P'yŏngyang Cho	Suwŏn Paek
Military office				
Military Division Commander (Taejang/Yŏngjang, 2B)	29	19	25	9
Royal Messenger (Sŏnjŏn'gwan, 3A–9B)	53	23	19	13
Five Guards Headquarters Commander/Deputy Commander (Owi Toch'onggwan/Puch'onggwan, 2A–2B)	3	6	1	4
Five Guards Headquarters Adjutant (Kyŏngnyŏk, 4B)	2	1	1	-
Other Five Guards military officers (3A–6B)	12	9	5	1
Palace Sentinel (Sumunjang, 6B)	-	-	-	1
Provincial Army/Navy Commander (Pyŏngma/Sugun Chŏltosa, 2A/3A)	34	23	27	13
Other provincial army/navy military officers (3B–4A)	4	2	5	2
Governor's Military Aide/Special Aide (Chunggun/Pyŏlgun, 2B, 3A)	3	6	1	2
Other provincial troop commanders (2A–2B)	13	11	12	1
Civil office				
Minister of War (Pyŏngjo P'ansŏ, 2A)	-	3	-	-
Minister of Punishments (Hyŏngjo P'ansŏ, 2A)	2	-	1	-
Minister of Public Works (Kongjo P'ansŏ, 2A)	2	1	-	1
Vice-Minister of War (Pyŏngjo Ch'amp'an, 2B)	1	2	3	2
Vice-Minister of Punishments (Hyŏngjo Ch'amp'an, 2B)	1	-	-	-
Vice-Minister of Taxation (Hojo Ch'amp'an, 2B)	-	-	1	-
Vice-Minister of Public Works (Kongjo Ch'amp'an, 2B)	1	1	-	-
Vice-Minister (Ch'amp'an, 2B)	-	-	-	1

Third Minister of War (Pyŏngjo Ch'amŭi, 3A)	-	1	1	-
OMWP Minister (2A–3A)	7	12	7	2
Mid-level board officers (5A–6B)	2	1	-	1
Border Defense Command Duty Officer (Pibyŏnsa Nanggwan)	1	1	2	1
MTA Second/Third Deputy Director (Chi/Tongji Hullyŏnwŏnsa, 2A–2B)	3	-	1	1
MTA Second/Third/Fourth Secretary (Hullyŏnwŏnjŏng/Pujŏng/Ch'ŏmjŏng, 3A–4B)	18	3	8	4
MTA Royal Secretary (Hullyŏnwŏn Sŭngji, 3A)	9	4	6	2
Mid-level MTA officers (5B–6B)	-	3	1	-
MTA/RPA/RHA First/Third/Fourth Secretary (Tojŏng/Pujŏng, 3A–4B)	10	1	-	5
MTA/RPA/RHA junior sixth rank officers (Chubu, 6B)	3	-	-	-
State Tribunal Third Magistrate (Tongji Ŭigŭmbusa, 2B)	1	-	-	-
State Tribunal/RHA/RSA/FMCH other officers (P'ansa/Tosa, 1B/5B)	-	1	1	-
Ritual-related duty officers (Sajiksŏryŏng/Ch'ambong, 5A, 5B/9B)	1	-	1	-
Chief/Second Magistrate of Seoul (Hansŏng P'anyun/Chwayun, 2A/2B)	2	1	3	2
Provincial Governor (Kwanch'alsa, 2B)	-	1	2	1
Defense Command Magistrate (Pusa, 2A–3B)	29	25	13	7
City/Island District Magistrate (Moksa, 3A)	3	2	1	1
County Magistrate (4B–6B)	24	33	27	12
Frontier County Magistrate (Pyŏnji, 2A–6B)	14	6	4	2
Post Station Superintendent (Ch'albang, 6B)	1	1	-	1
Civil rank only (1B–3A)	5	4	2	1

NOTE: Key to abbreviations: MTA = Military Training Agency (Hullyŏnwŏn), OMWP = Office of Ministers-without-Portfolio (Chungch'ubu), RHA = Royal House Administration (Tollyŏngbu), RPA = Royal Princes Administration (Chongch'inbu), RSA = Royal Sons-in-Law Administration (Ŭibinbu)

Appendix B
New Local Military Competitions from the Reigns of Sukchong through Yŏngjo, 1674–1776

Year	Province	Locality (if known)	Regiment
1712	P'yŏngan	–	Special Military Officers (Pyŏlmusa)
1717	Kyŏnggi	Kanghwa	Robust Righteous Soldiers (Changnyŏ-Ŭiryŏ)
1718	Hwanghae	–	Special Military Officers (Pyŏlmusa)
	Kyŏngsang	Tongnae	Special Cavalry (Pyŏlgiwi)
1719	P'yŏngan	Ŭiju	Special Military Officers (Pyŏlmusa)
	P'yŏngan	Kanggye	Special Military Officers (Pyŏlmusa)
	P'yŏngan	Sŏnch'ŏn	Special Military Officers (Pyŏlmusa)
	P'yŏngan	Ch'angsŏng	Special Military Officers (Pyŏlmusa)
	P'yŏngan	Samhwa	Special Military Officers (Pyŏlmusa)
1729	Kangwŏn	–	Special Military Officers (Pyŏlmusa): Recruitment Officers (Kwŏnmu Kun'gwan)
1736	Hwanghae	–	Enemy Pursuing and Capturing Warriors (Ch'up'o Musa)
	Kyŏngsang	–	Special Military Officers (Pyŏlmusa)
1751	Kyŏnggi	–	Select Martial Military Officers (Sŏnmu Kun'gwan)
	Ch'ungch'ŏng	–	Select Martial Military Officers (Sŏnmu Kun'gwan)
	Kyŏngsang	–	Select Martial Military Officers (Sŏnmu Kun'gwan)
	Chŏlla	–	Select Martial Military Officers (Sŏnmu Kun'gwan)
	Hwanghae	–	Select Martial Military Officers (Sŏnmu Kun'gwan)
	Kangwŏn	–	Select Martial Military Officers (Sŏnmu Kun'gwan)
	Hwanghae	–	Local Cavalry (Hyanggisa)

SOURCE: Yi Kŭng-ik, ed., *Yŏllyŏsil kisul, Pyŏljip* 10, *Kwanjik chŏn'go, Kwaje* 4, *Mugŏ.*

Reference Matter

Notes

Introduction

1. See Chapter 1 for a more detailed discussion of the term *yangban* ("two orders" of officials—civil and military). For now, readers can assume that "aristocracy" refers to the highest-level ascriptive status group in premodern Korea, although Korean scholars tend to reserve the Korean equivalent of "aristocracy" (*kwijok*) exclusively for reference to the pre-Chosŏn aristocracy of ancient and Koryŏ periods.

2. I follow Bottomore in using the term "elite" in the sense of "functional, mainly occupational, groups which have high status (for whatever reason) in a society," hence, a group enjoying a status superior to the rest of the population. Bottomore, 8, 12.

3. For a landmark study demonstrating that a narrowing segment of the ruling status group dominated important positions in the government in late Chosŏn Korea, see Wagner, "The Ladder of Success in Yi Dynasty Korea," 1–8.

4. By "roster," I am referring only to the documents recording those who passed the final stage of the examination.

5. Throughout this book, "military examination" refers only to the test that awarded the passer a special "red warrant" (*hongp'ae*), a formal degree certificate. Excluded from my consideration are: (1) the *chungsi* ("reexamination"), which periodically retested military examination graduates; (2) the *paryŏngsi* ("examination for extracting the worthy"), *tŭngjunsi* ("examination for elevating the lofty"), and *chinhyŏnkwa* ("test for promoting the wise"), which were given for similar purpose; and (3) the local military competitions (*tosi*) that also periodically tested officials and soldiers on martial skills and knowledge of military classics. Be-

cause of this problem of definition, as well as the uncertainty over whether certain military examinations were actually held, researchers disagree on the total number of military examinations conducted between 1402 and 1894. Totals according to Kim Yŏng-mo, Song Chun-ho, Ch'a Chang-sŏp, and Wŏn Ch'ang-ae are, respectively, 789, 744, 745, and 804. See Wŏn, 5, n. 7. I derive my own figure of 738 by excluding the various other military examination-like contests, and thus subtracting 62 from Chŏng Hae-ŭn's figure of 800. See Chŏng Hae-ŭn, "Chosŏn hugi mukwa kŭpcheja yŏn'gu," 18–19. The 131 extant military examination rosters do not evenly cover the period when the military examinations were administered. Whereas just two rosters are extant from 1402 to 1506, about two-thirds of the surviving rosters cover the seventeenth and eighteenth centuries. That only a dozen military examination rosters from the nineteenth century are known is somewhat puzzling. Some of the most recent rosters may still be in the private possession of individuals. At the same time, it seems that because of the revolutionary change Korea has undergone since 1894 and the disjuncture between old and new cultures, neither the state nor the degree holders' descendants could compile most of the late nineteenth-century examination rosters. The descendants in particular must have come to view such an activity as devoid of meaning in modern times.

6. Compared to those concerned with the military examination, extant rosters for other examinations are considerably more abundant: most, if not all, civil examination passers are known, whereas 186 out of 230 individual licentiate examination (*samasi, saengwŏn-chinsasi*) rosters (about 80 percent) and 177 out of 233 individual technical examination (*chapkwa*) rosters (76.4 percent) have survived. Thus, these surviving rosters account for all of the 14,607 civil examination passers, 40,649 out of 47,997 licentiate examination passers, and 7,627 out of over 12,000 technical examination passers. Ch'oe Chin-ok, *Chosŏn sidae saengwŏn-chinsa yŏn'gu,* 21–23; and Yi Nam-hŭi, "Chosŏn sidae chapkwa pangmok ŭi charyojŏk sŏngkyŏk," 124–27.

7. Yu Si-bu, vii–viii.

8. These works are Yi Hong-nyŏl; and Song Chun-ho, "Yijo hugi ŭi mukwa ŭi unyŏng silt'ae e kwanhayŏ."

9. Sim, "Chosŏn hugi mankwa ŭi unyŏng kwa kinŭng," cited in Chŏng Hae-ŭn, "Chosŏn hugi mukwa kŭpcheja," 2, n. 7.

10. Kim Yŏng-mo, chapter on "Mun-mukwa hapkyŏkcha ŭi sahoejŏk paegyŏng"; and Chŏng Hae-ŭn, "Chosŏn hugi mukwa ipkyŏkcha ŭi sinbun kwa sahoejŏk chiwi."

11. Sim, "Chosŏn Sŏnjodae mukwa kŭpcheja ŭi punsŏk"; Sim, "Imjin Waeran chung mukwa kŭpcheja ŭi sinbun kwa t'ŭksŏng"; Sim, "Imjin Waeran chung mukwa ŭi unyŏng silt'ae wa kinŭng"; Chŏng Hae-ŭn, "Pyŏngja Horan sigi

kun'gong myŏnch'ŏnin ŭi mukwa kŭpche wa sinbun pyŏnhwa"; Yi Hong-du, "Mukwa rŭl t'onghae pon Chosŏn hugi ch'ŏnin ŭi sinbun pyŏndong"; and Yi Hong-du, *Chosŏn sidae sinbun pyŏndong yŏn'gu*. The second Korean-Manchu war took place in the twelfth lunar month of 1636. All primary sources, as well as modern secondary sources in Korean, refer to the attack as having occurred in the year 1636. Throughout this study, I follow the common Western convention—adopted by such historians of premodern Korea as Duncan, Sun Joo Kim, and Palais, among others—of converting all dates in the lunar calendar to their solar equivalents. A further note on terminology: some readers may question my use of such terms as "Korean-Japanese war" and "Korean-Manchu wars" because this usage obscures the conventional historical wisdom that Korea was invaded by foreign powers and was not an equally active participant in these conflicts. Indeed, both the Japanese and the Manchus attacked Korea first; however, my stance is that neither aggressor initiated the conflict out of the blue. The Chosŏn government made certain key decisions and took actions that—as poorly chosen as they may have been—invited the invasions, and I intend my choice of terms to assign agency to both parties of each conflict rather than just the attckers. Portraying Korea as a passive actor in its military history demonstrates the pervasiveness of the Japanese colonialist "dependency argument" that has made the postcolonial generations of even the most objective scholars of Korea accept expressions such as the "Hideyoshi invasions" without raising the agency question. Also, such nomenclature seems to be a historiographical indiosyncracy rather uncommon in discussions of other wars in world history in the sense that convention generally refers to "wars" or "conflicts" without accounting for who first attacked whom or to what degree the invader overpowered the invaded.

12. Chŏng Hae-ŭn, "Mubo rŭl t'onghaesŏ pon 19 segi mukwa kŭpcheja ŭi kwanjik chinch'ul yangsang"; Chŏng Hae-ŭn, "Chosŏn hugi sŏnch'ŏn ŭi unyŏng kwa sŏnch'ŏnin ŭi sŏbanjik chinch'ul yangsang"; and Chang P'il-gi, "Chosọn hugi 'mubo' ŭi charyojŏk kŏmt'o." Although the rest of the study is not entirely devoted to late Chosŏn military examination graduates, there is an extensive discussion of the socioeconomic backgrounds and political stature of military examination passers from P'yŏngan Province in O Su-ch'ang, 205–32.

13. On some issues, postcolonial Korean scholars have advanced arguments based on inadequate evidence. For a general critique in English, see Palais, "A Search for Korean Uniqueness," 409–25.

14. Though most historians in Korea have stressed the first trend, Western scholarship has emphasized the latter. More recent South Korean macroscopic studies adopting this interpretive approach include: Yi T'ae-jin, *Han'guk sahoesa*

yŏn'gu; Yi Ki-baek, *Han'guksa sillon;* and Han, *Tasi ch'annŭn uri yŏksa.* The North Korean Marxist view is reflected in two compilations, both revised several times: Sahoe Kwahagwŏn Ryŏksa Yŏn'guso and Kogohak Yŏn'guso; and Son Yŏng-jong and Pak Yŏng-hae. For a general review of North Korean historiography, see Chŏng Tu-hŭi; and An Pyŏng-u and To Chin-sun, eds. Some representative Western works of scholarship emphasizing continuity through various periods of transition in Korean history include Duncan; Wagner, *The Literati Purges*; Palais, *Confucian Statecraft and Korean Institutions*; and Palais, *Politics and Policy in Traditional Korea.*

15. See Thompson, 9–11.

16. The following discussion is based on Weber, *Economy and Society,* 303–7, 392, 926–35, 938.

17. As discussed in other parts of the book, affluent nonelites of late Chosŏn began adopting manifestations of *yangban* status such as degrees, official ranks (*kwanp'um*), official posts (*kwanjik*), and genealogies. Noting this trend, conventional wisdom among ordinary people sees an increase in *yangban* population in late Chosŏn. However, empirical studies by historians, as well as plain common sense, dictate that the existing aristocracy could not accept such social newcomers into their ranks. No non-*yangban* could win *yangban* status.

18. In English-language works, the Korean term *sŏŏl* (or *sŏja*) is also translated as "secondary son" or, in Palais's studies, *nothos* (pl. *nothoi*), whereas *ch'ŏp* is also rendered as "secondary wife." Both "secondary son" and "secondary wife" are useful translations in that they can be used for both the Koryŏ and Chosŏn periods, when polygamy was institutionalized. All the same, I prefer the more commonly used English terms—"illegitimate son" and "concubine"—for the Chosŏn period since they convey more strongly the discriminatory aspects of these institutions. As we will see later in the study, an illegitimate son of an aristocrat was not entitled to the full social prerogatives of the father due to the lower social status of the concubine mother. On definitions of *chungin,* see Song Pok, "'Kŭndae ihaenggi chungin yŏn'gu' ŭi p'iryosŏng," 19–25.

19. This is not to say that the debate is over, and an intellectual divide separates Korean historians, such as Yi T'ae-jin and Ko Sŏk-kyu, from Korean economic historians, such as An Pyŏng-jik, and Western historians, such as Eckert. In fact, in late 2004 in South Korea, prominent Korean scholars from both sides sustained debate over this question in journals and newspapers for months.

20. I thank one of the two anonymous readers of an earlier version of this study for this point.

21. For a short English-language historiographical discussion on the Chosŏn aristocracy, see Palais, *Confucian Statecraft and Korean Institutions*, 34–41.

22. Examples include the following: Kim Yong-sŏp; Chŏng Sŏk-chong; and Kim Sŏk-hŭi.

23. Wagner illustrates this development especially well, by analyzing the changing patterns of descent group representation among civil examination passers. See Wagner, "The Ladder of Success in Yi Dynasty Korea."

24. Representative works include Wagner, *The Literati Purges*; Song Chun-ho, *Chosŏn sahoesa yŏn'gu*; and Duncan.

25. See Yi Sŏng-mu, *Chosŏn ch'ogi yangban yŏn'gu*; Han, *Chosŏn chŏn'gi sahoe kyŏngje yŏn'gu*; Yu Sŭng-wŏn; and Ch'oe Yŏng-ho, "Chosŏn wangjo chŏn'gi ŭi kwagŏ wa sinbun chedo." Yi's study portrays early Chosŏn *yangban* as a more distinct social stratum with aristocratic qualities, albeit not to the extent of Wagner, Song, and Duncan's characterizations.

26. Ch'oe Sŭng-hŭi, 355–56.

27. I base the following discussion on Sewell, 1–29.

28. Bourdieu, "The Forms of Capital," 241–58.

29. Bourdieu, *Distinction*, xiii, 142–44.

Chapter One

1. The process began in the tenth century when autonomous regional strongmen (*hojok*), who had become powerful during the final decades of Silla, were transformed into local functionaries (*hyangni*) carrying out the orders of Koryŏ central government.

2. Duncan, 20, 32–33, 61–63, 78–81, 192–93.

3. Ibid., 60–63, 80–81, 88–89, 152, 197–99, 218–20.

4. According to the widely accepted definition by Song Chun-ho, late Chosŏn *yangban* shared key characteristics. Above all, a *yangban* had to be descended from an eminent ancestor, who was either an official or a scholar at the beginning of Chosŏn, and had to demonstrate an impeccable pedigree comprising only *yangban* ancestors. Accordingly, a *yangban* man took in a woman of lower status only as a concubine, and a *yangban* father without a natural son by his wife could pass down his status only by adopting an heir among the patrilineal kin of the next generation. Second, a *yangban* descent group maintained at all costs a cultured lifestyle entailing proper Confucian rituals and education. Third, a descent group's *yangban* status had to be acknowledged for generations by the society in general and other *yangban* in particular. See Song Chun-ho, *Chosŏn sahoesa yŏn'gu*, 160–64, 242–59.

5. Chang Tong-ik, 442–84; Shultz, 9–12; and Park, "Military Officials in Chosŏn Korea," 29–32.

6. Shultz, 9–109.

7. A classic example of a late Koryŏ aristocratic descent group producing members in both branches is the Tongju Ch'oe. The man responsible for putting the family's political fortune on a solid footing, Ch'oe Yu-ch'ŏng (1095–1174), was a renowned civil official, and many among his direct descendants occupied important civil posts. Arguably the most famous among them, though, is Ch'oe Yŏng (1316–88), a military man pure and simple as well as one of the most famous generals throughout Korean history. His father, however, was a civil examination passer and a mid-level civil official, Ch'oe Wŏn-jik (n.d.). Similar aristocratic families became more common than rare in late Koryŏ. For a discussion of this trend and other characteristics of the late Koryŏ aristocracy, see Shultz, 176–78; Duncan, 120–35; and Park, "Military Officials in Chosŏn Korea," 30–41.

8. Park, "Military Officials in Chosŏn Korea," 37–40.

9. Ibid., 43–48; and Hazard, 15–28.

10. Park, "Military Officials in Chosŏn Korea," 48–63.

11. Min, 36–37.

12. *T'aejo sillok* 2: 3b.

13. Park, "Military Officials in Chosŏn Korea," 74–75.

14. *T'aejo sillok* 1: 43b, 1: 50b.

15. Han, *Chosŏn chŏn'gi sahoe kyŏngje yŏn'gu*, 52–53.

16. Min, 37.

17. Park, "Military Officials in Chosŏn Korea," 76.

18. Ibid., 77–78.

19. Ibid., 79–80.

20. Ibid., 80.

21. Ibid., 83–84.

22. Palais, *Confucian Statecraft and Korean Institutions*, 433.

23. *HMMTS*, s.v. "Owi" (Five Guards).

24. A brief explanation of the Chosŏn bureaucratic rank-office system is in order. As had been true during Koryŏ, Chosŏn maintained nine ranks with each divided into junior and senior levels. Whereas an individual could hold a court rank without an office, all officeholders held a rank to go with it. The Chosŏn central officialdom had three distinct tiers. The vast majority of officeholders never attained the sixth rank, the lowest level at which officials were eligible to attend court meetings held in royal audience, and achieving this rank was a breakthrough in one's career. The next milestone, which only a small minority of officials ever passed, was to achieve the senior third rank, divided into upper (*tangsang*) and lower (*tangha*) sub-levels. Receiving the upper senior third rank signaled admission into the top stratum of officialdom.

25. *HMMTS*, s.v. "Owi toch'ongbu" (Five Guards Headquarters).

26. Park, "Military Officials in Chosŏn Korea," 86.

27. Important studies include: O Chong-nok, "Chosŏn ch'ogi Pyŏngma Chŏltosaje ŭi sŏngnip kwa kŭ unyŏng (sang)"; O Chong-nok, "Chosŏn ch'ogi Pyŏngma Chŏltosaje ŭi sŏngnip kwa kŭ unyŏng (ha)"; and Pang.

28. Park, "Military Officials in Chosŏn Korea," 87.

29. Han, *Tasi ch'annŭn uri yŏksa,* 250–51, 254. For a more detailed discussion of the early Chosŏn military organization, see Ch'a Mun-sŏp, *Chosŏn sidae kunsa kwan'gye yŏn'gu,* 3–38, 249–52, 347–78; and Ch'a Mun-sŏp, *Chosŏn sidae kunje yŏn'gu,* 1–135.

30. As will be discussed below the preferred means for a Confucian ruler, as exemplified by monarchs of imperial China, was to govern through moral persuasion rather than laws or force. This hierarchy of three means is explained in Fairbank, 1–26, and I find it applicable to Confucian Korea of the Chosŏn period.

31. Park, "Military Officials in Chosŏn Korea," 89.

32. There were four subjects: interpreter examination (*yŏkkwa*), medicine examination (*ŭikwa*), law examination (*yulkwa*), and astronomy-geomancy examination (*ŭmyangkwa*). Ibid., 89–90. The accounting test (*chugyŏk*) somehow never assumed the status of a fully-fledged technical examination.

33. Ibid., 90–91.

34. *T'aejong sillok* 3: 3a.

35. Among the arrows listed, the *p'yŏnjŏn* was the smallest and yet had the longest range, of about one thousand paces. It was furthermore capable of penetrating armor. *HMMTS*, s.v. "Hwal" (Bows).

36. This code provided the basic legal reference for both the state and society for the subsequent two centuries or so.

37. Sim, "Chosŏn ch'ogi mukwa chedo," 36–45; and Yun Hun-p'yo, 32–41.

38. Sim, "Chosŏn ch'ogi mukwa chedo," 45.

39. Park, "Military Officials in Chosŏn Korea," 103–5. Incidentally, when T'aejong was still a teenager, he passed the Koryŏ civil examination—an achievement which thoroughly pleased his father, Yi Sŏng-gye, who was a military man from a frontier local strongman family.

40. For some of the more intense debates on polo, see *Sejong sillok* 28: 8b, 30: 15b–16a, 49: 35b–36a.

41. From then on, polo remained a regular requirement for the triennial examination candidates, until it was discarded in late Chosŏn. Sim, "Chosŏn ch'ogi mukwa chedo," 40; and Yi Sŏng-mu, *Han'guk ŭi kwagŏ chedo*, 236.

42. Park, "Military Officials in Chosŏn Korea," 108.

43. *Sejong sillok* 48: 25a–b.

44. This is not to say, however, that passing the military examination was easy. One means of estimating this difficulty would consider the average age of graduates at the time of the degree. For 743 out of the 2,177 military examination graduates from 1402 to 1591 (34.1 percent), the average age was 31.1 *se,* whereas the average age of Chosŏn civil examination passers was also in the early 30s. Although the athleticism required by the military examination would prompt us to expect teenagers and those in their 20s to constitute the majority of passers, more significant was the required classics exposition skill, which demanded a long period of intensive preparation.

45. And in 1605, the government, seeking to man northern garrisons, held a courtyard examination just for the martially talented men from outer regions. They had qualified for the second stage by passing local archery tests. Yi Kŭng-ik, *Yŏllyŏsil kisul* (hereafter *YK*), *Pyŏlchip* 10: 4.

46. Park, "Military Examination Graduates in Sixteenth-Century Korea," 5.

47. Ibid., 6–7.

48. Ibid., 8–10.

49. *Myŏngjong sillok* 27: 21a.

50. Park, "Military Examination Graduates in Sixteenth-Century Korea," 11–12.

51. Han, *Tasi ch'annŭn uri yŏksa*, 289.

52. Palais, *Confucian Statecraft and Korean Institutions*, 16.

53. Yi T'ae-jin, *Han'guk sahoesa yŏn'gu*, 91–121; and Ch'ŏn Kwan-u, "Han'guk t'oji chedosa, ha," 1430, as cited in Palais, *Confucian Statecraft and Korean Institutions*, 48.

54. Palais, *Confucian Statecraft and Korean Institutions*, 50–60, 70–75.

55. Yi Sang-baek, *Han'guksa: Kŭnse chŏn'gi p'yŏn*, 476–78, as cited in Palais, *Confucian Statecraft and Korean Institutions*, 112.

56. Palais, *Confucian Statecraft and Korean Institutions*, 15–17, 61–91.

57. Park, "Military Officials in Chosŏn Korea," 67–71, 149–53.

58. The Board of Rites oversaw the civil examination.

59. Park, "Military Examination Graduates in Early Chosŏn," 127.

60. *Sejong sillok* 49: 5b–6a.

61. The state regarded military examination graduates as a whole to be of the same caliber as the Inner Forbidden Guards. Park, "Military Examination Graduates in Early Chosŏn," 127.

62. Ibid.

63. Ibid., 128.

64. Ibid., 128–31. The statistics in this section are derived from an earlier version of my military examination graduate database, but the general conclusion has not changed.

65. Sim, "Chosŏn ch'ogi mukwa chedo," 63–71; and Yun Hun-p'yo, 52–60.

66. Park, "Military Examination Graduates in Sixteenth-Century Korea," 12–15.

67. My sixteenth-century data sample includes degree holders from 1495 to 1500 because Yŏnsan'gun's reign, which had distinct characteristics, lasted from 1494 to 1506 and held its first military examination in 1495.

68. Park, "Military Examination Graduates in Sixteenth-Century Korea," 16–19.

69. Kwŏn T'ae-hwan and Sin Yong-ha, 325; and Michell, 71–72. Kwŏn and Sin's estimates are lower than Michell's. They reason that although the official total population figure grossly underestimated the actual population, the eighteenth- and nineteenth-century records show a close correlation between the total population and household count figures. Accordingly, Kwŏn and Sin estimate corrective factors for various periods, so that the government's total population figure for a given year can be multiplied by an appropriate factor to estimate the actual population total; the method practically amounts to multiplying an official population total by 2.5. As they acknowledge, the validity of the multipliers depends heavily on consistency in census-taking method and relatively constant social variables affecting the nature of households. See Kwŏn T'ae-hwan and Sin Yong-ha, 293. Though suggesting different demographic trends and estimates for the Chosŏn period, Michell's methodology is not radically different, in that he multiplies the official total number of households by 7.95 to estimate total population. See Michell, 74.

70. Yi Sŏng-mu, *Chosŏn ch'ogi yangban yŏn'gu*, 126.

71. *Myŏngjong sillok* 7: 70b–71a.

72. Ibid., 22: 68b–69b.

73. Ibid., 30: 31a.

74. *Chungjong sillok* 99: 69a–76b. The source erroneously records the date, January 19, 1543, as "*kyŏngjin*" rather than "*kyŏngin*." My citation reflects the correction.

75. Park, "Military Examination Graduates in Sixteenth-Century Korea," 12–13.

76. Ibid., 12–14.

77. Ibid., 14.

78. In 1553, Myŏngjong ordered high officials to discuss the feasibility of at least restoring some supernumerary positions in other agencies. *Myŏngjong sillok* 15: 8b–9a.

79. Park, "Military Examination Graduates in Sixteenth-Century Korea," 14–15.

80. Yi Su-gwang, *Chibong yusŏl*, as cited in *YK*, *Pyŏlchip* 5: 77.

81. Kang Pak, *Kukp'o swaerok*, as cited in *YK*, *Pyŏlchip* 5: 77.

82. Park, "Military Examination Graduates in Sixteenth-Century Korea," 15.

83. Ibid., 19.

84. Palais, *Confucian Statecraft and Korean Institutions*, 79–88.

85. Yong-ho Choe stresses the fact that both ideologically and legally, the early Chosŏn examination system was open to all social status groups except the lowborn, and he highlights many cases of non-*yangban* who passed the civil examination. He concedes, though, that upon entering officialdom, such individuals mobilized all means to perpetuate the privilege of their descent group, making it extremely difficult for a non-*yangban* to compete successfully. See Ch'oe Yŏng-ho (Yong-ho Choe), "Chosŏn wangjo chŏn'gi ŭi kwagŏ wa sinbun chedo," 143–82.

86. I base this list, with some modifications, on Han Yŏng-u's interpretation of the *Code*'s regulations. See Han, *Chosŏn chŏn'gi sahoe kyŏngje yŏn'gu*, 256–73. The restrictions applied not only to the civil but also the military examination. Sim, "Chosŏn ch'ogi mukwa chedo," 57. Palais mentions that merchants and artisans, as well as their descendants, were also barred from taking an examination or holding an office, but his source is unclear. See Palais, *Confucian Statecraft and Confucian Institutions*, 33, 964. I will discuss this issue in greater detail in Chapter 3, in conjunction with my account of Kaesŏng merchants.

87. Park, "Military Examination Graduates in Early Chosŏn," 133–34.

88. Their exclusion is not surprising, given that many debates were fueled over even the fine points of their eligibility for the far less prestigious technical examinations. Decisions on whether to permit illegitimate sons to take the technical examinations were inconsistent. In early Chosŏn, most technical examination candidates probably came from technical specialist and clerk descent lines carried over from Koryŏ, but even into the sixteenth century it was not extraordinary for *yangban* to compete as well. In fact, 64 technical examination passers of the sixteenth century are known to have been degreeless scholars (*yuhak*), who were generally *yangban,* whereas no such technical examination passers are known after 1576. Yi Nam-hŭi, "16, 17 segi chapkwa ipkyŏkcha ŭi chŏllyŏk kwa kwallo chinch'ul," 258.

89. Yi Sŏng-mu, *Chosŏn ch'ogi yangban yŏn'gu*, 13.

90. Park, "Military Officials in Chosŏn Korea," 68–69; and Park, "Military Examination Graduates in Early Chosŏn," 135.

91. A central bureaucratic officeholder always had a rank, but a rank holder may or may not have held an office. Thus, a rank functioned much like a title. The ostensible purpose of these prebendal grants was to compensate *hallyang* for performing rotation duties in the capital guard units, but the more likely

reason was to support the livelihoods of untalented descendants of prebend holders. Palais, *Confucian Statecraft and Korean Institutions*, 44.

92. *HMMTS*, s.v. "Hallyang." For a detailed study of local military competitions (*tosi*), see Sim, "Chosŏn ch'ogi tosi wa kŭ sŏngkyŏk," 98–134.

93. Chŏng To-jŏn, "Chosŏn kyŏngguk, sang" (The Chosŏn state administration, part 1), *Sambongjip*, 214–15, as cited in Palais, *Confucian Statecraft and Korean Institutions*, 81–82, 681.

94. *HMMTS*, s.v. "Hallyang."

95. Among those whose highest achievements can be determined, 41 percent had acquired an office by the time of the degree. Park, "Military Examination Graduates in Early Chosŏn," 137; and Park (Pak), "Chosŏn ch'ogi mukwa ch'ulsin," 105.

96. About half of the highest known offices attained by the fathers were of junior fourth rank or higher. Even more significantly, one out of five fathers is known to have received a junior third rank, or higher, post. Someone holding an actual, salaried post (*siljik*)—as opposed to the large number of sinecures or even unsalaried posts—at these ranks could have his son or another beneficiary receive a protection appointment. Park, "Military Examination Graduates in Early Chosŏn," 141; and Park (Pak), "Chosŏn ch'ogi mukwa ch'ulsin," 108.

97. Out of 133 descent groups represented among the passers, 74 produced just a single passer, whereas 59 produced anywhere from 2 to 8 passers. Remarkably, 49 out of the 59 descent groups producing at least 2 military examination graduates originated in Chŏlla or Kyŏngsang Province (83.1 percent). Park, "Military Examination Graduates in Early Chosŏn," 141–50; and Park (Pak), "Chosŏn ch'ogi mukwa ch'ulsin," 110–13.

98. Yi T'ae-jin, *Han'guk sahoesa yŏn'gu*, 91–121; and Yi T'ae-jin, "14–16 segi Han'guk ŭi in'gu chŭngga wa sinyuhak ŭi yŏnghyang," 1–18.

99. The kind of lineage that emerged by late Chosŏn came to consist of those who shared the following characteristics: (1) resided in one locale for generations; (2) descended from a common ancestor first settling there; (3) performed proper ancestral rituals; (4) maintained lineage grave sites; (5) periodically published a genealogy; (6) used generational characters (*hangnyŏlcha, tollimcha*) for their names; (7) carried out adoptions within the patrilineal group; and (8) found marriage partners outside the group among other lineages of equal or higher social status. Deuchler, 6–14, 283–303.

100. Deuchler, 29–179.

101. A patrilineal group having a common great-great-grandfather shared mutual mourning obligations governed by the five mourning grades (*obok*). Song Chun-ho, *Chosŏn sahoesa yŏn'gu*, 20.

102. Park, "Military Examination Graduates in Early Chosŏn," 143–50; and Park (Pak), "Chosŏn ch'ogi mukwa ch'ulsin," 111–20. The third pattern supports Wagner's argument that what really distinguished the conservative merit subjects from the reformist Neo-Confucian scholar-officials was not so much a difference in social origins as their degree of commitment to Neo-Confucian political rhetoric and intellectual orientation. See Wagner, "Yijo Sarim munje e kwanhan chaegŏmt'o," 163–73. The Miryang Pak military examination passers of this period nicely illustrate these tendencies. Out of eight who passed the military examination, four came from Kyŏngsang Province. In fact, three out of the four were closely related to one another: the two from the same county were great-grandfather and great-grandson, whereas the third passer was the latter's fourth cousin, who lived in a nearby county. In contrast, the fourth passer lived in a county farther away and was distantly related to the other three—sharing a common ancestor who had lived in the eleventh century. Unlike the fourth passer, who had no other civil examination graduates among his close patrilineal relatives, the other three did. The great-grandfather had first cousins living in the capital, and five civil examination passers from the capital line were close relatives within the third-cousin radius. Among them were a merit subject who helped Sejo ascend the throne through a coup in the mid-fifteenth century and yet another merit subject from the late fifteenth century. This capital Miryang Pak line had all the characteristics of a conservative merit-subject faction, but it also produced Pak Hun (1484–1540), a civil examination passer and one of the reformists purged by the conservatives in 1519. Park, "Military Examination Graduates in Early Chosŏn," 148–49.

103. Sim, "Chosŏn Sŏnjodae mukwa kŭpcheja ŭi sinbun," 47–87.

104. Song Chun-ho, *Chosŏn sahoesa yŏn'gu*, 248. In Chosŏn Korea, the four ancestors were customarily referenced when certifying one's pedigree. Although the practice was inspired by a Chinese genealogical pattern, the inclusion of the maternal grandfather was uniquely Korean. See Deuchler, 40.

105. Han, *Chosŏn chŏn'gi sahoe kyŏngje yŏn'gu*, 264–73.

106. *HMMTS*, s.v. "Hallyang."

107. Ch'a Mun-sŏp, "Chungjongjo ŭi Chŏngnowi," 136–57, as cited in Palais, *Confucian Statecraft and Korean Institutions*, 434–35.

108. At the same time, the measure also allowed manumission of the lowborn providing the same military service. *Sŏnjo sillok* 17: 3a.

109. Park, "Military Examination Graduates in Sixteenth-Century Korea," 22–23.

110. On the context of the establishment of this arrangement between Korea and Japan, see Robinson, 94–115.

111. Park, "Military Examination Graduates in Sixteenth-Century Korea," 23–24.

112. Ibid., 24–25.

113. Besides the statistics from Park, "Military Examination Graduates in Sixteenth-Century Korea," studies by Sim Sŭng-gu also demonstrate this pattern. See Sim, "Chosŏn Sŏnjodae mukwa kŭpcheja ŭi punsŏk"; Sim, "Imjin Waeran chung mukwa kŭpcheja ŭi sinbun kwa t'ŭksŏng"; and Sim, "Imjin Waeran chung mukwa ŭi unyŏng silt'ae wa kinŭng."

114. Among the 1,060 military examination passers recorded on the ten extant rosters, which account for a quarter of all military examination passers from 1495 to 1591, the percentage of Inner Palace Guards ranges from 12.3 to 50 depending on the roster. Park, "Military Examination Graduates in Sixteenth-Century Korea," 5, 28–29.

115. This was true for up to 14.3 percent of those recorded on four rosters—indicating that the period's degree holders commanded the kind of erudition most likely possessed by *yangban*. Ibid., 30.

116. Among the 1,060 graduates, the Jurchen Quelling Guards account for anywhere from 0 to 18.3 percent depending on the roster, 0 to 0.9 percent in the case of functionaries, also 0 to 0.9 percent for the students of local functionary background who had permission to study for the examination, and, yet again, 0 to 0.9 percent for commoner infantrymen. Of course these numbers are small, and in fact each of the last three groups did not produce more than just one passer. Nonetheless, what we are seeing are the earliest signs of nonelite participation in the military examination. Ibid., 30–31.

117. Information is available for the fathers of 763 out of the 1,060 military examination passers. Among the 763 are civil or military officials of third rank or higher (2.1 percent), enfeoffment title recipients (1.8 percent), elite guards (13.1 percent), and degreeless scholars (18.9 percent). The rest include rank holders, military examination graduates, and licentiates. Ibid., 31–32.

118. Township headmen account for just 0.8 percent, whereas commoner infantrymen add up to a minuscule 0.1 percent. Ibid., 32.

119. Ibid., 31–33.

120. Ibid., 33–46. These patterns are obvious in the case of the Miryang Pak descended from Pak Hyŏn (ca. 1250–1336). His direct descendants not only entered both civil and military branches of officialdom but also produced statesmen across the late fifteenth-century political divide separating the conservative merit subjects and the reformist Neo-Confucian scholar-officials. From 1500 to 1599, at least 18 military, 9 civil, 4 technical, and 34 licentiate examination passers are known among Hyŏn's descendants. Every one of the 18 military examination graduates could claim a military examination

passer among his kinsmen of third-cousin distance or closer, whereas 12 could claim a civil examination passer among such relatives (66.7 percent), and 14 a licentiate examination passer (77.8 percent). Interestingly, though, only 11 percent of the military examination passers had a close kinsman who passed a technical examination. Showing early signs of internal differentiation according to branch affiliation, the Miryang Pak case also typifies *yangban* descent group segments that became more geographically dispersed by this period. Whereas the fifteenth-century degree holding descendants of Pak Hyŏn were distributed over just two provinces, the sixteenth-century degree holders resided in seven out of eight Chosŏn provinces. Ibid., 46–47. As discussed in Chapter 2, a late Chosŏn branch of this descent group segment turned to military careers.

121. Ibid., 39–40.

122. Ibid., 40.

123. Ibid., 46–49.

Chapter Two

1. For a short, scholarly discussion in English of the Korean-Japanese war, see Elisonas, 271–90.

2. By the 1570s, the dominant political rhetoric stressed moral legitimacy, and in court discussions the censorate and mid-level Board of Personnel officials most actively addressed ethical issues. The right of the mid-level Board of Personnel officials to designate their own successors ensured the former's effectiveness at policy criticism, but the integrity of this system depended on the character of concerned officials, who, in reality, tended to promote factional interests. Moreover, as the cardinal virtue of filial piety bound an individual to defend the ideas of his ancestors and teachers, factional loyalty became increasingly hereditary. Yi Sŏng-mu, "Chosŏn hugi tangjaeng ŭi wŏnin e taehan sogo," 1215–23.

3. *Sŏnjo sujŏng sillok* 23: 8b; and *Sŏnjo sillok* 43: 17a. The 1746 *Amended Great Code* (*Sok Taejŏn*), the long overdue update of the 1469 *Great Code of State Administration,* reflected the addition of a musket requirement. See *Sok Taejŏn* 4: 26b–27a.

4. Ch'a Mun-sŏp, *Chosŏn sidae kunje yŏn'gu*, 179–431.

5. Palais, *Confucian Statecraft and Korean Institutions*, 417–20; and Palais, *Politics and Policy in Traditional Korea*, 322, n. 42.

6. Palais, *Confucian Statecraft and Korean Institutions,* 88–91.

7. Ibid., 112, 809–18, 853–54, 866–68. The law also spurred the government to purchase needed goods through merchants, and hence, it stimulated commerce. Since King Sukchong stopped coining money in 1697, and more was

not minted until 1731 by King Yŏngjo, there most likely was a deflationary situation in the intervening decades. The long term trend, however, was toward a liberalized economy as private merchant activity continued to expand. Ibid., 866–76, 924–63, 980–98.

8. Ibid., 550–68; and Palais, *Politics and Policy in Traditional Korea,* 92–97.

9. The total for the period from 1402 to 1591 is drawn from Sim, "Chosŏn chŏn'gi mukwa yŏn'gu," 94. I calculate the total for the period between 1592 and 1607 by subtracting the figures for early and late Chosŏn from the known dynasty total of somewhere between 150,000 and 170,000. Chŏng Hae-ŭn's estimate of the total for late Chosŏn from 1608 to 1894 is 119,023, including 778 *chungsi* passers. See Chŏng Hae-ŭn, "Chosŏn hugi mukwa kŭpcheja," 17. My figure of 121,623 excludes *chungsi* passers, but includes 2,600 men who passed a special examination in 1882. I was able to establish that this contest produced at least 2,600 finalists, based on the recorded number of candidates during the various stages of this examination. *Sŭngjŏngwŏn ilgi* (hereafter *SI*) 2898: 31b–32a, 85b. Pagination is that of original image files available at Seoul National University's Kyujanggak website http://e-kyujanggak.snu.ac.kr/sub_index.jsp?ID=SJW [accessed 23 October 2006].

10. The two fifteenth-century cases, both held in 1460, were connected to the anti-Jurchen military campaigns.

11. An illegitimate son had to present at least two Japanese heads, whereas three or more were required from a lowborn. These men then received permission to proceed to a palace examination, eventually given after the war in 1599. There were 206 finalists. *Sŏnjo sillok* 39: 30a, 34b–35b.

12. Yi Ki, *Songwa chapki,* as cited in *YK, Pyŏlchip* 10: 3.

13. *Sŏnjo sillok* 28: 6b.

14. Yi Su-gwang, *Chibong yusŏl,* as cited in *YK, Pyŏlchip* 10: 3.

15. *Sŏnjo sillok* 27: 17b.

16. Yu Mong-in, *Ŏu yadam,* as cited in *YK, Pyŏlchip* 10: 3.

17. Yi Su-gwang, *Chibong yusŏl,* as cited in *YK, Pyŏlchip* 10: 4.

18. The military history of the period leading up to Korea's second defeat by the Manchus (formerly Jurchens) in 1637 has received thorough treatment in previous studies. For a concise English-language discussion of what went wrong for the Chosŏn military organization vis-à-vis the Manchus, see Palais, *Confucian Statecraft and Korean Institutions,* 92–101.

19. For example, early in Kwanghaegun's reign (1608–23), the government administered a military examination in Hamgyŏng Province in the north without a civil counterpart. Yi Su-gwang, *Chibong yusŏl,* as cited in *YK, Pyŏlchip* 10: 4.

20. *Kwanghaegun ilgi* 138: 8a–9a. All *Kwanghaegun ilgi* citations derive from the Chŏngjok-san edition unless noted otherwise. Actually, at the start of the

expedition in the summer of 1618, the army was 10,000 strong and consisted of 3,500 artillerymen, 3,500 archers, and 3,000 "killers" (*salsu*), comprising swordsmen, pikemen, and spearmen. Ibid., 130: 12b–13a. By the spring of 1619, when the army crossed the Yalu River and entered Manchuria, the troop strength was 13,000 men. Ibid., 137: 10a.

21. Ibid., 143: 21a, 23b–24a, 144: 13a.

22. Ibid., 144: 12b–13a.

23. *YK, Pyŏlchip* 10: 4. Another source, which offers a very selective listing of military examination passers from Kyŏngsang Province, records the total number of passers as more than three thousand. *Kyonam kwabangnok* 4, *Hobang* 1: 20a. Modern studies also put forth lower figures, such as three thousand or five thousand. See Yi Hong-nyŏl, 229; and Song Chun-ho, "Yijo hugi ŭi mukwa ŭi unyŏng e kwanhayŏ," 42.

24. *YK, Pyŏlchip* 10: 4.

25. *Injo sillok* 33: 6a–7a.

26. Toby, 415–56.

27. I base the following discussion of Northern Expedition policy on Yi Kyŏng-ch'an, 177–260; Kim Se-yŏng, 121–53; Hong, 85–108; and Paek Ki-in, 245–72.

28. Hong rebelled on the eighteenth day of the twelfth lunar month in 1811, which is January 31, 1812, according to the solar calendar. Korean-language secondary sources, reflecting the lunar calendar dates, cite the beginning year of the rebellion as 1811.

29. In 1589, the government administered an augmented examination when a Chosŏn embassy succeeded in persuading the Ming court to amend records that had incorrectly listed the name of the Chosŏn dynasty founder's father. The event was celebrated as the "rectification of the royal genealogy" (*chonggye pyŏnmyŏng*). For a complete list, see Chŏng Hae-ŭn, "Chosŏn hugi mukwa kŭpcheja," 21.

30. A "royal visitation" entailed a king's paying respect to the Shrine of Confucius (Munmyo) at the Confucian Academy. Ch'undangdae is a terrace inside the Ch'anggyŏng Palace compound.

31. Chŏng Hae-ŭn, "Chosŏn hugi mukwa kŭpcheja," 21–22.

32. Chŏng is able to determine the number of passers for 477 out of 553 military examinations from the period. Her total for late Chosŏn is 119,023, including the 778 *chungsi* passers. See Chŏng Hae-ŭn, "Chosŏn hugi mukwa kŭpcheja," 33, 35.

33. Ibid., 34.

34. Ch'oe Myŏng-gil, *Chich'ŏnjip,* as cited in *YK, Pyŏlchip* 10: 5.

35. Ibid.

36. Song's personal relations with military men also occasioned him to write for many of them "records of conduct" (*haengjang*), a kind of biography. Some such works are included in a modern collection of Chosŏn period biographies based on such obituary notices and other primary documents. See Yi Sang-ŭn.

37. *Pibyŏnsa tŭngnok* (hereafter *PT*) 28 *ch'aek*, 3: 2d–3a. As the original version of this source lacks pagination, I will indicate the original text's *ch'aek* number, followed by the volume and page numbers of the modern reprint edition.

38. On the way by which political factions manipulated military divisions during the power struggle of this period, see O Chong-nok, "Pungdang chŏngch'i wa kunyŏng," 301–7.

39. *PT* 3 *ch'aek,* 1: 465a–466a.

40. The same arrangement had been used previously, in 1637 and 1651. *PT,* as cited in *YK, Pyŏlchip* 10: 5.

41. *Sukchong sillok* 17: 21b–22a.

42. *PT,* as cited in *YK, Pyŏlchip* 10: 6.

43. *PT* 339 *ch'aek,* 18: 4a–b.

44. *Sukchong sillok* 22: 1a–2a.

45. *Sukchong sillok* 8: 55a.

46. Song Chun-ho, "Yijo hugi ŭi mukwa ŭi unyŏng silt'ae e kwanhayŏ," 26–36. In its full version, the late Chosŏn military examination system's martial skills component, as described in the 1746 *Amended Great Code,* required the following skills: (1) musket (*choch'ong*) shooting, (2) iron arrowhead (*yuyŏpchŏn*) target archery, (3) light arrow target archery (*kwanhyŏk*), (4) horseback metal whip lashing against dummy targets (*p'yŏnch'u*), and (5) horseback archery using dummy targets (*kich'u*). *Sok Taejŏn* 4: 24b–27a. Neither polo (*kyŏkku*) nor horseback archery using targets (*kisa*) was tested.

47. See Song Chun-ho, "Chosŏn hugi ŭi mukwa ŭi unyŏng e kwanhayŏ," 32–33, 35–36.

48. *Hyŏnjong kaesu sillok* 10: 2b–3a.

49. *Sukchong sillok* 6: 4b.

50. *Yŏngjo sillok* 121: 17b.

51. Song Chun-ho, "Chosŏn hugi ŭi mukwa ŭi unyŏng e kwanhayŏ," 32–33, 35–36.

52. Out of 32,327 passers included in my database, 27,367 earned their degrees during this period. Out of the 27,367, age information was available for 22,141 (80.9 percent).

53. *Sukchong sillok* 6: 5a.

54. This is not to say that everyone included in the various examination passer listings from local gazetteers was *yangban*. My experience working with this type of source over the years has taught me that those compiled toward

the dynasty's end reflect some upward social mobility in the sense that examination passers from those other than the *yangban* lines represented in the registers of local agency officers (*hyangan*) are also recorded. Chapters 3 and 5 discuss this issue in greater detail.

55. Chŏng is able to determine the graduate's service label at the time of the degree for 16,575 out of the 16,643 passers appearing in extant rosters from 1612 to 1882, excluding the 1637 Namhan Fort courtyard examination roster recording 5,506 men. See Chŏng Hae-ŭn, "Chosŏn hugi mukwa kŭpcheja," 80–82.

56. Yi Chun-gu, *Chosŏn hugi sinbun chigyŏk pyŏndong yŏn'gu,* 100–11.

57. Most likely to hold such a civil rank title were those who had no prospect of meaningful career in officialdom. Ibid., 102–13.

58. Ibid., 81.

59. *Chŏngjo sillok* 18: 52a–b.

60. Ibid., 54: 2b.

61. In an important study on Korean lineages, Shima Mutsuhiko refers to a descent group as a "clan" and its ancestral seat as "clan seat." Shima, 89. I have no objections to these English translations, especially since they make it easier for a Western reader to distinguish descent groups at the highest level—identified by the surname and the ancestral seat—from various lower-level groups such as segments, lineages, and lines. Instead of Shima's translations, however, I use "descent group" in accordance with the conventions of more recent English-language studies on premodern Korea, including Duncan.

62. This type of genealogy was produced in the nineteenth century for civil, licentiate, and technical examination passers as well. Each edition generally recorded only those passers from prominent descent lines. For more detailed description of the recording format adopted by military examination graduate genealogies (*mubo*), see Chŏng Hae-ŭn, "'Mubo' rŭl t'onghaesŏ pon 19 segi mukwa kŭpcheja ŭi kwanjik chinch'ul yangsang," 188–89; and Chang P'il-gi, "Chosŏn hugi muban kamun ŭi pŏryŏrhwa wa kŭ sŏngkyŏk," 9–11.

63. "Mubo," Changsŏgak collection (2–1741); "Mubo," Changsŏgak collection (2–1742); "Mubo," Harvard-Yenching Library collection (K2291.7/1748a); "Mujinsin p'alsebo," Harvard-Yenching Library collection (K2291.7/1748); *Mansŏng taedongbo* (hereafter *MT*); and *Ch'ŏnggu ssibo.*

64. For additional genealogical information, I consulted *Tŏksu Yi-ssi sebo* 12 (*sin-sang*): 12b–17b, 66b–102b, 13 (*sin-ha*): 1a–32b, 14 (*im-sang*): 38b–96b, 15 (*im-ha*): 1a–32a, 15 (*im-sok*): 1a–4a; *Chŏnŭi-Yean Yi-ssi chokpo* 1 (*sup'yŏn*): 36, 3 (*sang*): 6–24, 3 (*chung*): 50–197; *Nŭngsŏng Ku-ssi sebo* 10: 2b–9a, 15b–70a, 85b–102b, 11: 1a–107b, 12: 1a–108b, 125a–146b, 13: 1a–141b, 14: 1a–151b; and *P'yŏngyang Cho-ssi sebo* 1: 2a–6b, 14: 1a–2a, 4a–16b, 19b–29a.

65. Among the six descent lines, the nineteenth-century performance in relation to the last three centuries of the dynasty was as follows: 47.9 percent of 215 Tŏksu Yi military examination passers; 48.2 percent of 199 Chŏnŭi Yi passers; 36.7 percent of 196 Nŭngsŏng Ku passers; 51.6 percent of 155 P'yŏngsan Sin passers; 50.0 percent of 146 P'yŏngyang Cho passers; and 65.6 percent of 61 Suwŏn Paek passers. Other prominent military lines include those of the the Haep'yŏng Yun, the Kyŏngju Kim, the Namwŏn Yang, the Miryang Pak, and the Chŏnju Yi descent groups. Ch'a Chang-sŏp also discusses the Chinju Yu, Haeju O, Andong Kim, Prince Hyoryŏng branch Chŏnju Yi, and Kyŏngju Yi military lines; however, he does not mention the Suwŏn Paek, P'yŏngyang Cho, Kyŏngju Kim, Haep'yŏng Yun, Namwŏn Yang, and Miryang Pak military descent lines. He seems to exclude them from his analysis because he is primarily interested in the so-called "hereditary families of military merit" (*hun'gu sega*) that played more vital roles alongside the central civil aristocracy in late Chosŏn court politics. See Ch'a Chang-sŏp, 85, 200–4. I chose to analyze some military lines not discussed by Ch'a, especially those that arose due to factors other than military merit. Moreover, various editions of military examination graduate genealogies do not agree perfectly on the coverage of military examination passers, although they do not fail to include the most prominent ones such as the Tŏksu Yi, the Chŏnŭi Yi, the Nŭngsŏng Ku, and the P'yŏngsan Sin military lines.

66. For example, all members of the royal in-law "New" (Sin) Andong Kim lineage, which dominated the court for several decades during the nineteenth century, were descended from the famed anti-Qing Westerner statesman, Kim Sang-hŏn (1570–1652), and his first cousins. Han'guk Yŏksa Yŏn'guhoe 19 Segi Chŏngch'isa Yŏn'guban, *Chosŏn chŏngch'isa (1800–1863)* 1: 236–56, 327–39; and Ch'a Chang-sŏp, *Chosŏn hugi pŏryŏl yŏn'gu,* 58–62, 279–340.

67. *Myŏngjong sillok* 6: 26a.

68. For a genealogy of the descendants, see *MT* 2: 218a.

69. See Chapter 1, n. 102, for details on the early Chosŏn patterns of this descent group's examination success and political activity.

70. *HMMTS,* s.v. "Pak Sŭng-jong" and "Pak Cha-hŭng." Genealogical information comes from *Miryang Pak-ssi Kyujŏnggong p'a taedongbo* 1: 1–2, 4, 45–47, 2: 446–532, 953–1157; and *Ssijok wŏllyu* (*SW* hereafter), 143. *Ssijok wŏllyu* citations use pagination numbers from its modern reprint edition, as the originally unpublished manuscript from the seventeenth century is unpaginated. In critiquing conventional wisdom on late Chosŏn factionalism, Dong Jae Yim's discussion of the Northerner faction shows that in the seventeenth century some Northerners were able to gain positions in the regular bureaucracy and rise to middle rank, thanks in large part to connections with members of the

dominant factions. See Yim, 143–70. I thank him for his kind permission to cite this unpublished work.

71. *HMMTS,* s.v. "Yi I-ch'ŏm." Genealogical information comes from: *Kwangju Yi-ssi taedongbo* 1: 3–5, 16–17, 188–90; *SW*, 85–87; and *MT* 1: 99a-b.

72. *Tŏksu Yi-ssi sebo* 12 (*sin-sang*): 12b–17b, 66b–102b, 13 (*sin-ha*): 1a–32b, 14 (*im-sang*): 38b–96b, 15 (*im-ha*): 1a–32a, 15 (*im-sok*): 1a–4a.

73. *P'yŏngsan Sin-ssi taedongbo* 1 (*hap'yŏn*): 20–27, 2: 136–298, 3: 346–891; and *SW*, 624–25. This characteristic of the late Chosŏn royal messenger post is discussed in greater detail later in this chapter.

74. These kinship ties apparently were powerful enough to compensate for his connection to the Great Northerners (his sister was Yi I-ch'ŏm's daughter-in-law) vanquished in 1623. Yi Ki-sun, 59–63.

75. Ch'a fittingly refers to such military lines as "hereditary families of military merit" (*hunmu sega*). See Cha Chang-sŏp, 65–66, 85–88, 200–2.

76. *Yŏngjo sillok* 103: 4a.

77. *Muye tobo t'ongji*, 35–38 (reprint pagination).

78. For an English-language study on how civil examination success became concentrated in a small number of descent groups, see Wagner, "The Ladder of Success," 3–6.

79. Studies on the origins and development of the technical specialist *chungin* status group include Han, "Chosŏn sidae chungin ŭi sinbun-kyegŭpchŏk sŏngkyŏk," 179–209; Yi Sŏng-mu, "Chosŏn ch'ogi ŭi kisulgwan kwa kŭ chiwi," 193–229; and Kim Hyŏn-mok, 35–66.

80. *Sŏngwŏnnok*, 455, 464 (reprint pagination).

81. *Tŏksu Yi-ssi sebo* 12 (*sin-sang*): 12b–17b, 66b–102b, 13 (*sin-ha*): 1a–32b, 14 (*im-sang*): 38b–96b, 15 (*im-ha*): 1a–32a, 15 (*im-sok*): 1a–4a; and *SW*, 97–98.

82. *P'yŏngsan Sin-ssi taedongbo* 1 (*hap'yŏn*): 20–27, 2: 136–298, 3: 346–891; *Nŭngsŏng Ku-ssi sebo* 1: 1a–3b, 10: 1a–1b, 2b–9a, 15b–70a, 85b–102b, 11: 1a–107b, 12: 1a–108b, 125a–146b, 13: 1a–141b, 14: 1a–151b; and *SW*, 624–25, 713–15. Unlike the 1506 coup (which elevated Chungjong), Injo and his military men relatives, the Ku and the Sin, were deeply involved in the preparation for this coup. Yi Yŏng-ch'un, 135.

83. Chŏng Hae-ŭn, "Chosŏn hugi mukwa ipkyŏkcha," 224–38.

84. Quinones, "Military Officials of Yi Korea," 697–700; and Quinones, "The Prerequisites for Power in Late Yi Korea," 144–47.

85. Kang Hyo-sŏk, 1a–33a.

86. *HMMTS,* s.v. "Sin Kyŏng-jin," "Ku In-hu," and "Yi Wan."

87. For this analysis, I treated the Ministers-without-Portfolio posts as civil offices, but this demands an explanation. Dynastic law codes actually list the Office of the Ministers-without-Portfolio (Chungch'ubu) posts, along with

other clearly military posts, in the sections devoted to the matters of the Board of War, whereas civil posts are discussed in the section of details relating to the Board of Personnel. For an example, see *Taejŏn hoet'ong* 4: 4b–5a. This treatment of the Office of the Ministers-without-Portfolio posts as military offices seems to be based on the fact that the Office itself was physically located in the west, like other military agencies, in relation to the traditionally south-facing king, to the east of whom were various civil branch agencies. Such location assignment probably reflected the original function of the Koryŏ-period precursor and near namesake (in Korean), the Security Council (Chungch'uwŏn), which was the highest deliberative organ dealing with military- and security-related issues. In spite of the tradition of treating the Office of the Ministers-without-Portfolio as part of the military branch of central officialdom, however, at least two factors made it different from other military agencies. For one thing, the Office's various minister positions included those higher than the senior third rank, above which there actually were no military ranks available during the Koryŏ and Chosŏn periods. Also, the court often gave these minister positions as sinecures (*sanjik*) to powerful civil officials of retirement age, as well as increasingly to men of advanced age, those contributing grain supply during famines, and the *chungin*.

88. From 1800 to 1863, 19 out of 56 men holding military division commander posts were civil officials or protection appointees (33.9 percent). Out of these 19, a total of 7 were the royal in-law Andong Kim, whereas 21 out of 37 military appointees came from the prominent military lines as mentioned. Han'guk Yŏksa Yŏn'guhoe 19 Segi Chŏngch'isa Yŏn'guban 2: 774–6.

89. From 1593 to 1882, some protection appointees became military division commanders, but most appointees to the posts who were not civil examination passers were military examination graduates.

90. It is possible to calculate the more precise percentage figure for the military examination passers attaining a military division commandership. Out of 27,367 late Chosŏn military examination passers I have analyzed, just 123 ever held a military division commander post (0.5 percent). Since my database excludes about 3,200 out of some 3,700 degree holders recorded in extant military examination graduate genealogies (*mubo*) favoring men from the military aristocracy, we can suppose that as many as over 3,700 out of 30,567 (the sum of 27,367 and 3,200), or about 12 percent, rose to the office. However, since my database excludes roughly 90,000 late Chosŏn military examination passers, most of whom are undocumented in the kind of extant sources biased in favor of *yangban,* the actual percentage of late Chosŏn military examination graduates who became military division commanders should be closer to 0.5 percent than 12 percent. The number of passers (over 3,700) recorded in the

military examination graduate genealogies comes from Chang P'il-gi, "Chosŏn hugi muban kamun ŭi pŏryŏrhwa wa kŭ sŏngkyŏk," 7, n. 1.

91. Yi Tong-hŭi, 212–29.

92. Even the top passers, who received a sixth-rank civil office, were no exceptions, as they too harbored aspirations determined to a significant extent by their family and regional backgrounds. Chŏng Hae-ŭn, "Chosŏn hugi mukwa kŭpcheja," 199–210. Wagner related to me, during a 1992 discussion of civil examination passers, that he had found no evidence that the top passer status itself provided a decisive advantage for the career patterns of the civil examination graduates after their initial appointments. I too am left with the same impression after more than a decade of browsing through primary sources on personnel appointment.

93. Since the average age at which men passed the military examination in late Chosŏn was 32.5 *se,* it is hardly a surprise that those registered with the Office of Royal Messengers, known as "royal messenger candidates" (*sŏnch'ŏn*), not only tended to hail from the military aristocracy but passed the military examination at an earlier age. Registration with the Office was an event of great significance in an aspiring military official's career. Chŏng Hae-ŭn, "'Mubo' rŭl t'onghaesŏ pon 19 segi mukwa kŭpcheja ŭi kwanjik chinch'ul yangsang," 194. Young royal messenger candidates' career prospects were brighter than those of most other military examination passers. Sixty out of seventy-two military examination graduates who became military division commanders from 1776 to 1894 had been royal messengers (83.3 percent). Chŏng Hae-ŭn, "Chosŏn hugi sŏnch'ŏn ŭi unyŏng kwa sŏnch'ŏnin ŭi sŏbanjik chinch'ul," 156–57.

94. In his study, Ch'a identifies the factional affiliation for six of the nine prominent late Chosŏn military lines he mentions. Among the six were four Disciples (Soron), a Patriarch (Noron), and a Southerner (Namin). See Cha Chang-sŏp, 202–4.

95. After passing the military examination, his career had taken off shortly before the Korean-Japanese war, on the recommendation of the then Northerner—and later Great Northerner—leader, Chief State Councillor Yi San-hae (1539–1609), and he received key military appointments throughout Kwanghaegun's reign. He somehow survived the anti-Northerner coup that overthrew Kwanghaegun in 1623, but the new Westerner-dominated regime questioned his loyalty. Upon Yi Kwal's rebellion in 1624, he was executed along with 34 other political figures suspected of sympathy with the rebel. *HMMTS,* s.v. "Yi Si-ŏn."

96. *HMMTS,* s.v. "Yi Su-ryang."

97. *HMMTS,* s.v. "Nam T'ae-jing."

98. Yi T'ae-jin, *Chosŏn hugi ŭi chŏngch'i wa kunyŏngje pyŏnch'ŏn,* 81–318; and O Chong-nok, "Pungdang chŏngch'i wa kunyŏng," 301–7.

Chapter Three

1. An aristocratic central official descent group based in Seoul could maintain three distinct types of residence: a capital residence (*kyŏngjŏ*), a special villa (*pyŏlsŏ*), and a country residence (*hyangje*). The first was the main home located in Seoul, the second an alternate mansion generally located within a day's distance from Seoul (often near a good river route such as the Han River), and the third a house located further out in the countryside. The special villa, also known as *pyŏrŏp* ("special activities villa") and *yasŏ* ("rustic villa"), was an intermediate form of residence, a central official's pleasure retreat, if not his destination after retirement. The most politically powerful capital *yangban* continued to maintain all three types, but by the mid-eighteenth century two new types of phenomena emerged: (1) a capital *yangban* traveling back and forth only between the capital residence and a special villa located somewhere outside Seoul in western central Korea; and (2) a more localized *yangban* possessing only a country residence. Among the localized descent groups of the south, only the lineages based outside western central Korea can be considered a true local elite, in the sense of forming the most powerful social group within a locale. In contrast, the power of localized descent groups in areas such as Ch'ungch'ŏng Province, where Seoul *yangban* maintained villas, was more limited. Chŏng Sŭng-mo, 189–204.

2. Han'guk Yŏksa Yŏn'guhoe 19 Segi Chŏngch'isa Yŏn'guban 1: 165.

3. Yi T'ae-jin, "18-segi Namin ŭi chŏngch'ijŏk soet'oe wa Yŏngnam chibang," 195–96. Yŏngjo's official rejection of public discourse was in accordance with his Policy of Impartiality (T'angp'yŏngch'aek), which sought to curtail factionalism.

4. Yi Chung-hwan, *T'aengniji,* as cited in Han'guk Yŏksa Yŏn'guhoe 19 Segi Chŏngch'isa Yŏn'guban 1: 193.

5. On the origins of *chikpu* candidates and the palace examination, see Sim, "Chosŏn chŏn'gi mukwa yŏn'gu," 60–67.

6. Chŏng Hae-ŭn, "Chosŏn hugi mukwa kŭpcheja," 64.

7. Ibid. The various martial skills tests of Chosŏn can be divided into four general categories: the recruitment test (*ch'wijae*), the martial talent competition (*sijae*), the military examination (*mukwa*), and the *chungsi*. The recruitment test was relatively simple, conducted by military regiments to recruit officers and soldiers. Regiments used martial talent competitions to reward or promote them, and the competitions falling in this category included *sisa*, *naesisa*, *pyŏlsisa*, *chungil*, *chungsun*, and local military competitions (*tosi*). Unlike recruitment tests or martial talent competitions, a military examination, at least in theory, entitled the passer to an official appointment. Lastly, the *chungsi* rewarded or

promoted incumbent military officials who already had the military examination degree. Ibid., 66, n. 178.

8. Ibid., 73–74.

9. In the end, though, even this seemingly reasonable effort to limit the special treatment of those earning a perfect score in merely one weaponry subject was unsuccessful, and the state changed its position at least four times between the introduction of the measure under Chŏngjo in the late eighteenth century and the end of Ch'ŏlchong's reign in 1864 (lunar twelfth month of 1863). Ibid., 74–78. In spite of a growing gap between the capital and countryside, it is not clear whether local *yangban* stopped taking the prestigious civil examination. They may have continued to stand for the civil examinations and simply failed due to possible political and regional biases in the process of selecting successful candidates. Ideally, evidence would document fluctuations in the numbers of candidates from southern Korea who showed up to compete, but I have found extant records regarding the residences only of known passers, and no primary sources or secondary works discussing the residences of those who merely stood for the examinations. Wagner, who devoted decades of research to the Chosŏn civil examination passers, mentioned in the early 1990s that he had yet to see such a record and even doubted its existence.

10. *Injo sillok* 28: 33b.

11. Chŏng Hae-ŭn, "Chosŏn hugi mukwa ipkyŏkcha," 196, 238–40.

12. *Kimhae hyangan kŭp Kimhae ŭpchi chŏryak*, 16b–17a; and *Ch'angnyŏng Cho-ssi Sijunggong p'abo* 1: 4–6, 26–27. Both Cho Kang and his son, who also earned the degree, appear in extant military examination rosters.

13. Including their own examination rosters and their wives' natal family genealogies, eighteenth-century documents begin to record Namp'yŏng Cho men as Ch'angnyŏng Cho. Interestingly, in the early seventeenth century a licentiate examination roster had recorded a distant Seoul kinsman of the Kimhae lineage members as a Namwŏn Cho. In the eighteenth century, a member of the Kimhae lineage appeared in his wife's family genealogy as a "Ch'angwŏn" Cho. Perhaps the two cases reflect the lineage's transition-phase descent group designation, changing from Namp'yŏng to Namwŏn to Ch'angwŏn to Ch'angnyŏng.

14. Yi Su-gŏn, *Yŏngnam sarimp'a ŭi hyŏngsŏng,* 3–4; and Yi Su-gŏn, *Han'guk chungse sahoesa yŏn'gu,* 30–33. In contrast to later genealogies, the oldest extant multi-lineage genealogy, the *Ssijok wŏllyu,* which was compiled in the mid-seventeenth century, leaves various segments of a descent group unconnected to one another, noting local functionary origins or any conflicting versions of pedigree information. Thus, for example, in the cases of the Ch'angnyŏng Cho and Ŭisŏng Kim descent groups, the *Ssijok wŏllyu* records for each two

versions of its Koryŏ-period genealogy and even suggests that the version showing more obvious signs of a local functionary descent line is probably more accurate. *SW*, 259–60, 668–69.

15. *Paek-ssi taedongbo* 1: 23–24, 7: 1–17, 89–106, 265–70; and *SW*, 663.

16. Kim Chun-hyŏng, "Chosŏn hugi Tansŏng chiyŏk ŭi sahoe pyŏnhwa wa sajokch'ŭng ŭi taeŭng," 75; and Chŏng Hae-ŭn, "Chosŏn hugi mukwa kŭpcheja," 87–88.

17. I base the discussion of Kang Ŭng-hwan's family background and career on Song Chun-ho, *Chosŏn sahoesa yŏn'gu*, 376–415.

18. Pratt and Rutt, 204.

19. This is my translation of the Korean text given in Yi T'ae-gŭk, 202–3. The original work is somewhat more rhetorical than poetic, and so I chose a more literal rendition. The poem consists of 64 lines, each a couplet of two multi-syllabic verses, and reflecting this format in the translation posed a problem. Separating, in English, two verses of a couplet line was not feasible, as doing so would not allow proper syntax. I was, however, able to keep each line intact, and an indentation in the translation marks a line that is really a continuation of the previous one. I thank John Frankl for helping me with the translation.

20. These banners represent, respectively, east, west, south, and north.

21. For example, the Board of Personnel commended him for effective relief measures and for donating his salary during a famine. *Chŏngjo sillok* 13: 40b–41a. Both Ŭng-hwan and his son, Chae-ho, are recorded as Mujang-resident military examination passers in *Honamji* 2: 103b.

22. Park, "Military Officials in Chosŏn Korea," 205.

23. *Kwanghaegun ilgi* 130: 27a.

24. *PT* 6 *ch'aek* 1: 464d–465b.

25. *Chŏngjo sillok* 39: 27a.

26. Kim In-gŏl, 767–92; An Pyŏng-uk, "The Growth of Popular Consciousness," 4–19; Kim Hyŏn-yŏng, 411–47; Paek Sŭng-jong, "18–19 segi Chŏlla-do esŏ ŭi sinhŭng seryŏk ŭi taedŭ," 1339–67; and Han'guk Yŏksa Yŏn'guhoe Chosŏn Sigi Sahoesa Yŏn'guban, 283–308.

27. Representative studies highlighting these trends include Song Chun-ho, "Sinbunje rŭl t'onghaesŏ pon Chosŏn hugi sahoe ŭi sŏngkyŏk ŭi ilmyŏn," 1–62; Fujiya Kawashima, 20–24; and Chŏng Chin-yŏng, 335–43.

28. Lists of various types of educational and cultural institutions established by local *yangban* during the colonial period are found in a modern edition of the Kimhae local gazetteer, the *Kugyŏk Kimhae ŭpchi*. For genealogical information on the marriage ties formed with newer families (such as the Namp'yŏng Mun) by the nineteenth-century Ch'angnyŏng Cho (formerly Namp'yŏng Cho)

lineage of Kimhae, see *Ch'angnyŏng Cho-ssi Sijunggong p'abo* 2: 50–51. *Yangban* identity persisted after 1945 among many descendants living in their ancestral locales, meaning that the pattern of social change toward the end of Chosŏn varied tremendously among different descent groups and locales throughout Korea. Song Chun-ho, "Sinbunje rŭl t'onghaesŏ pon Chosŏn hugi sahoe ŭi sŏngkyŏk ŭi ilmyŏn," 57–62.

29. Song Chun-ho, "Chosŏn hugi ŭi kwagŏ chedo," 89.

30. Ch'oe Chin-ok, *Chosŏn sidae saengwŏn-chinsa yŏn'gu,* 265.

31. I base the following discussion on Bourdieu, "The Forms of Capital," 243–48.

32. Kawashima, 11–16.

33. In the *Record of Surname Origins* (*Sŏngwŏnnok*), capital *chungin* licentiates are concentrated toward the end of the dynasty. This was especially true among those *chungin* lines not as exclusively oriented toward technical specialties.

34. Various traditional sources such as Sŏng Sa-je's *Biographies of Tumun-dong Teachers* (*Tumun-dong sŏnsaeng silgi*) and Chang Sŏk-chin *Memorabilia of Tumun-dong* (*Tumun-dong yusa*) do not agree completely on the names of the loyalists.

35. *Yŏngjo sillok* 127: 60b.

36. *Sŏnjo sillok* 203: 10a.

37. O Sŏng, "Hanmal Kaesŏng chibang ŭi ho ŭi kusŏng kwa hoju," 1708, 1725.

38. Kuksa P'yŏnch'an Wiwŏnhoe 33: 172, 348.

39. O Sŏng, *Chosŏn hugi sangin yŏn'gu,* 24–53; Kang Man-gil, 120–32; Kuksa P'yŏnch'an Wiwŏnhoe 33: 172, 348–52; and Palais, *Confucian Statecraft and Korean Institutions,* 857–61, 974–78.

40. Kaesŏng merchants were simply overwhelmed by the wave of modern merchants and goods arriving with imperialism toward the end of the dynasty. Eckert, 8–11.

41. The *Genealogy of Examination Graduates from Chunggyŏng* [*Kaesŏng*] (*Chunggyŏng kwabo*), an eight-generation pedigree record (*p'alsebo*) of examination passers from Kaesŏng, records 124 civil examination graduates as well as each man's final or most notable office. Among the offices listed, 49 were provincial assignments such as a county magistracy (39.5 percent), and only 18 were third-rank civil posts or higher (14.5 percent). *Chunggyŏng kwabo* 1: 1a–14a. These patterns suggest that as a whole, even the residents passing the civil examination hardly achieved a significant presence in the central government, despite the city's proximity to Seoul, large population, and economic stature.

42. Kaesŏng men account for 559 out of 40,649 degree holders (1.4 percent), according to more recently published licentiate data. Han'guk Chŏngsin Munhwa Yŏn'guwŏn.

43. Peterson, "Hyangban and Merchant in Kaesŏng," 4–15.

44. Palais, *Confucian Statecraft and Korean Institutions*, 33, 964.

45. The exclusion was in effect by the late fifteenth century and continued to be upheld by subsequent law codes, including the 1865 *Great Code Reconciliation*. See *Taejŏn hoet'ong* 3: 1a–b.

46. During the same conversation, Sŏnjo noted that whereas in the past he had never heard of anyone in Kaesŏng mastering literary skills, now there were some. *Sŏnjo sillok* 203: 10a. As one of the most prominent families of the late Chosŏn military aristocracy that we saw in Chapter 2, the P'yŏngsan Sin military men were descendants of either Sin Chap, actually a civil official, or Sin Rip, his military official younger brother.

47. *Hyŏnjong kaesu sillok* 4: 54a.

48. The four lists are found in various late Chosŏn editions of the Kaesŏng local gazetteer. The lists in the 1782 and 1855 gazetteers appear to be updates to the list in the 1648 edition. In contrast, the list in the 1802 gazetteer excludes many passers recorded in earlier editions while including some not recorded earlier. See *Songdoji* (1648), *Songdoji* (1782), *Songdo sokchi* (1802), and *Chunggyŏngji* (1855).

49. Park, "Local Elites, Descent, and Status Consciousness in Nineteenth-Century Korea," 212–13.

50. Just 8 out of all 375 Kaesŏng residents who appear in the military examination rosters through 1648 also appear on the 1648 list (2.1 percent); 181 roster-recorded graduates appear in the 1782 list (48.2 percent); 110 appear in the 1802 list (29.3 percent); and 340 in the 1855 list (90.6 percent).

51. *Sŏnjo sillok* 203: 10a.

52. Ibid.

53. *Sukchong sillok* 25: 23b–24a.

54. Peterson, "Hyangban and Merchant in Kaesŏng," 12–15.

55. O Su-ch'ang, 157–58.

56. Chŏng Hae-ŭn, "Chosŏn hugi mukwa kŭpcheja," 124–40.

57. After Seoul, it was Chŏngju, a northwestern county of commercial significance, that produced the greatest number of civil examination passers during the Chosŏn period.

58. O Su-ch'ang, 331–41.

59. Such an interest in Manchuria on the part of Hamgyŏng residents coincided with more relaxed Qing control of the Chosŏn-Qing border region and the subsequent migration of Koreans into Manchuria. Kang Sŏk-hwa, "Chosŏn hugi Hamgyŏng-do ŭi chiyŏk palchŏn kwa pukpang yŏngt'o ŭisik," 217–21.

60. For example, a local elite Miryang Pak lineage based in Chŏngju in P'yŏngan Province, producing several civil examination passers and licentiates

in the nineteenth century, claimed descent from a certain Pak Hŭng-dun, who is said to have been an inspector-general before banishment to the north during a literati purge of Yŏnsan'gun's reign (1494–1506). These claims are made in reference to his descendants recorded in later sources such as the *Comprensive Genealogy of Korean Gentlemen* (*Chosŏn sinsa taedongbo*), the *Korean Pedigrees and Generations* (*Han'guk kyehaengbo*), and the Chŏngju local gazetteers—all of which reflect the upward social mobility some descent groups achieved in late Chosŏn.

61. *PT* 16 *ch'aek* 2: 364a–365c. In her recent study of the Hong Kyŏng-nae rebellion, Sun Joo Kim offers an in-depth examination of the way the central government and *yangban* aristocrats discriminated against the northwestern elite, and how the latter sought to negotiate status vis-à-vis the center. In explaining the origins of the rebellion, Kim observes that compared to the highly educated local elite, the residents of marginal elite or lower status were more actively involved—even driven by popular prophetic beliefs. See Sun Joo Kim, 27–69, 133–42. I thank her for permitting me to cite her unpublished book manuscript. For a recent English-language discussion of the fate of northern residents during Korea's transition to the modern era, see Hwang, "From the Dirt to Heaven," 135–78; and Hwang, *Beyond Birth,* 273–89.

62. *Kwanghaegun ilgi* 154: 5a.

63. Wagner, "The Civil Examination Process as Social Leaven," 22–27.

64. Wagner, "The Ladder of Success," 3–6.

65. Wagner, "The Civil Examination Process as Social Leaven," 23–25.

66. O Su-ch'ang, 99–126.

67. Ibid., 205–9.

68. Kang Sŏk-hwa, "Chosŏn hugi Hamgyŏng-do ŭi Ch'in'giwi," 24–60.

69. Moreover, the fact that they were assigned to a special royal guard unit—the Dragon and Tiger Division (Yonghoyŏng)—clearly illustrates the throne's special concern for them.

70. Also, from Chŏngjo's reign, even the military examination graduates registered as messenger candidates still had to serve at least six months in the Inner Forbidden Guards before receiving an initial official appointment.

71. O Su-ch'ang, 210–32.

72. The individuals who belonged to the top stratum of the northwestern elite, especially those holding civil examination degrees or central offices, were generally reluctant to participate in the rebellion, even though they strongly resented the discriminatory practices of the central aristocracy. Sun Joo Kim, 151–57.

Chapter Four

1. Song Chun-ho, *Chosŏn sahoesa yŏn'gu,* 159.

2. In a recent case study of a southern local *yangban* lineage that maintained such ties to an eminent capital *yangban,* Chŏn Kyŏng-mok contends that moral virtues, scholarly fame, and local social connections were insufficient means for maintaining the aristocratic status of a late Chosŏn local *yangban* descent group not producing examination passers or central officials. He concludes that ties to the capital aristocracy were vitally important for the local aristocracy. See Chŏn Kyŏng-mok, 247–90. Chŏn seems to overstate the importance of such ties, while underestimating the fundamentally ascriptive nature of *yangban* status in late Chosŏn society. Nonetheless, his identification of close interactions between local and central aristocrats provides a logical explanation for the end-of-the-dynasty phenomenon whereby many local *yangban* used personal connections to capital *yangban* statesmen to gain ranks and offices.

3. Such relations between local functionaries and *yangban* are discussed in Yi Hun-sang, "Chosŏn hugi ŭpch'i sahoe ŭi kujo wa cheŭi," 47–94.

4. In what may be the first English-language study treating late Chosŏn military officials as a distinct social category, Kyung Hwang argues that *muban* were separate from civil official descent lines and cannot be considered as even a lower-ranking partner to them within the ruling status group, the *yangban.* In fact, he ties military men together with illegitimate sons, technical specialists, and local functionaries as "secondary status groups" in analyzing their expanding roles during the dynasty's final decades as well as the Japanese colonial period. See Hwang, *Beyond Birth,* 290–354. Late Chosŏn military officeholders hailed from diverse social backgrounds, and as we shall see later in this chapter, those from the central military aristocracy retained membership in a cohesive *yangban* status group that, of course, also included the central civil aristocracy and the southern local aristocracy. Hwang's study oversimplifies the late Chosŏn social landscape, wherein an individual holding a military office or a descent line producing many military officeholders could be of any ascriptive social status. The *Comprehensive Genealogy of Ten Thousand Surnames* (*Mansŏng taedongbo*), which offers a highly selective record of mostly *yangban* descent lines, and the *Record of Surname Origins* (*Sŏngwŏnnok*), covering Seoul *chungin* lines, both include many descent lines that produced predominantly military examination passers and officeholders. Of course, late Chosŏn household registration records, too, show obviously commoner families that produced such men.

5. Palais, "Confucianism and the Aristocratic/Bureaucratic Balance in Korea," 455–67; and Palais, *Politics and Policy in Traditional Korea,* 279–82.

6. Chang P'il-gi, "Chosŏn hugi muban kamun ŭi pŏryŏrhwa wa kŭ sŏngkyŏk," 91–159, 162–63.

7. Ibid., 175.

8. For quantitative data on the marriage connections of technical examination passers, see Ch'oe Chin-ok, "Chosŏn sidae chapkwa sŏlhaeng kwa ipkyŏkcha punsŏk," 37–45.

9. *Ch'angnyŏng Cho-ssi Sijunggong p'abo* 1: 26–7; *P'osan Kwak-ssi sebo* 16: 63b; *Paek-ssi taedongbo* 7: 8-9; *Yŏngil Chŏng-ssi sebo* 1: 47–51; *SW*, 338, 620, 663; and *MT* 1: 243a, 2: 114b–115a, 235a–b, 238b, 243b–244a.

10. For a critical English-language analysis of Chosŏn adoption practice, including a discussion of the kinship boundaries within which heirs were sought, see Peterson, *Korean Adoption and Inheritance,* 163–90.

11. Ibid., 100–6, 173–78.

12. Genealogical information comes from *Andong Kim-ssi sebo* 3: 341, 344, 350–51, 394–95, 518–19; and *SW*, 213.

13. Peterson, *Korean Adoption and Inheritance,* 173–78.

14. The fourth such ruler, Kojong, ascended the throne on a day of the twelfth lunar month of 1863, which converts to January 1864.

15. *Andong Kim-ssi sebo* 3: 341, 344, 350–51, 394–95, 518–19; and *SW*, 213. Kim Ik-sun was the Sŏnch'ŏn defense command magistrate (Pusa) when he surrendered to a rebel force during the Hong Kyŏng-nae rebellion. For a concise biography of Kim Pyŏng-yŏn, see *HMMTS,* s.v. "Kim Pyŏng-yŏn."

16. *HMMTS,* s.v. "Ŏ Yun-jung," "Ŏ Chae-yŏn," and "Ŏ Hyo-ch'ŏm." Genealogical information comes from *Hamjong Ŏ-ssi sebo* 1: 1a–5a, 3: 1a–1b, 7b–8b, 8: 4b–8a, 9: 31a–33b, 14: 15a–16b, 15: 34b–36b, 20: 4b; and *SW*, 777.

17. I based the following discussion of Pak Ch'ung-wŏn and his descendants on *Miryang Pak-ssi Kyujŏnggong-p'a taedongbo*; *MT* 1: 215a–217a; Edward W. Wagner and Song Chun-ho, *CD-ROM Poju Chosŏn munkwa pangmok*; Edward W. Wagner and Song Chun-ho, "Yijo sama pangmok chipsŏng"; and my own military examination graduate database.

18. The following discussion of the O Chŏng-bang line is based on *MT* 2: 103a–106b and my military examination graduate database.

19. Chŏn Hyŏng-t'aek, *Chosŏn hugi nobi sinbun yŏn'gu,* 31, 207–9, 267, as cited in Palais, *Confucian Statecraft and Korean Institutions,* 227–29, 1059, n. 83, 1059–60, n. 84.

20. Song Chun-ho, "Chosŏn sidae ŭi kwagŏ wa yangban mit yangin (I)," 114–16.

21. For an expression of this sentiment, see *PT* 37 *ch'aek*, 3: 678c–679b.

22. For various dynastic codes' regulations on these honors for the elderly and the dead, see *Taejŏn hoet'ong* 1: 68a–69b.

23. Regulations on the format for various types of appointment certificates are found in *Taejŏn hoet'ong* 3: 64b–66a

24. For instance, in early 1837, the court authorized issuing of 500 blank appointment certificates as a part of its effort to solicit rice donations to relieve food shortage in Kyŏngsang region. *Hŏnjong sillok* 3: 12b.

25. *PT* 21 *ch'aek*, 2: 702a–703c.

26. The senior third rank was divided into upper (*tangsang*) and lower (*tangha*) levels.

27. *PT* 20 *ch'aek*, 2: 646a–b; 21 *ch'aek*, 2: 702a–b; and 44 *ch'aek*, 4: 315d.

28. *PT* 57 *ch'aek*, 5: 597c–d, 5: 610b.

29. *PT* 20 *ch'aek*, 2: 646b–647a; 21 *ch'aek*, 2: 702b–703c; and 44 *ch'aek*, 4: 315c–316b.

30. According to this argument, a greater variety of rice strains, better fertilizers, and improvement in seedling transfer and other rice-farming techniques increased agricultural output. Kuksa P'yŏnch'an Wiwŏnhoe 33: 32–42; *PT* 20 *ch'aek,* 2: 646d.

31. For a more conservative estimate, see Palais, *Confucian Statecraft and Korean Institutions,* 362–67.

32. *PT* 37 *ch'aek*, 3: 624b.

33. *PT* 37 *ch'aek*, 3: 668c–d.

34. *PT* 38 *ch'aek*, 3: 742b.

35. Yi Nam-hŭi, "Chosŏn sidae (1498–1894) chapkwa ipkyŏkcha ŭi chillo wa kŭ ch'ui," 246–69.

36. Yun Chae-min, 333–44.

37. Remarkably, in at least some locales such as Namwŏn, local functionaries have kept their own associations into the modern era. Honda, 23–72.

38. Yi Hun-sang, *Chosŏn hugi ŭi hyangni,* 235–46; and Yi Hun-sang, "Chosŏn hugi ŭpch'i sahoe ŭi kujo wa cheŭi," 47–94.

39. Sin, 186–94.

40. Yi Nam-hŭi, "Chosŏn sidae (1498–1894) chapkwa ipkyŏkcha ŭi chillo wa kŭ ch'ui," 271.

41. Some extant ones are collected together in a reprint edition of the Resumes of Korean Empire Bureaucrats (*Taehan Cheguk kwanwŏn iryŏksŏ*).

42. One of my new research projects is to examine the rise and transformation of Seoul *chungin* descent lines in the late Chosŏn and early modern periods, as well as their place in contemporary South Korean genealogical discourse, which is dominated by the commoner-descent majority subscribing to social fantasies about their ancestry.

43. Chang P'il-gi, "Chosŏn hugi muban kamun ŭi pŏryŏrhwa wa kŭ sŏngkyŏk," 7, n. 1.

44. According to Winston Lo, the military man ideal that was most acceptable to both the Chinese elite and the state was a Confucian general (*rujiang*)

or civilian commander whose effectiveness as a practitioner of war (*bingjia*) derived from a broad knowledge. See Lo, 15–20. I find that much of this also was true in late Chosŏn Korea.

45. The *Mubi yoram* text I used is the 1982 Ilchogak edition, with a preface by Yi Pyŏng-do. Genealogical information comes from *P'yŏngyang Cho-ssi sebo* 1: 2a–6b, 14: 1a–2a, 4a–5b, 20b; *SW*, 297–98; and *MT* 2: 82a–84b.

46. *Sunjo sillok* 4: 35b.

47. *HMMTS*, s.v. "Sŏ Yu-dae."

48. *MT* 1: 13b–15a.

49. *Chŏngjo sillok* 48: 31b; and *HMMTS*, s.v. "Yi Chu-guk."

50. The majority of the primary source references record him by his previous name, Sin Kwan-ho. In 1868, the Board of Personnel reported the name change, and King Kojong approved. *SI* 2724: 69a.

51. "Mubo," Changsŏgak collection edition (2–1741), 2: 35a; and *MT* 2: 44a, 45b, 48a.

52. Kim Chŏng-hŭi read through the famous *Illustrated Gazette of the Maritime Nations* (*Haiguo tuzhi*) by Wei Yuan (1794–1857) of China. Unlike Pak Kyu-su, Kim ignored Wei's call to fight the Westerners by learning their military technology and other skills. I would like to thank an anonymous reviewer of the earlier version of the manuscript of this book for the observation.

53. *HMMTS*, s.v. "Sin Hŏn."

54. Sin Hŏn's performance during the negotiation of the 1876 Korean-Japanese Treaty was not impressive, as he had a limited knowledge of modern diplomacy. The 1882 Korean-American Treaty was actually crafted by the Chinese and the American negotiator in China, who then sent the finalized document to King Kojong for approval. Again, I thank an anonymous reviewer of my manuscript for this information.

Chapter Five

1. An anonymous reviewer of this study noted that by the eighteenth century, the *chungin* constituted an "elite" in themselves. Studies demonstrating that late Chosŏn *chungin,* especially the technical specialists of Seoul, accumulated considerable economic and cultural capital are too numerous to cite, and by no means am I downplaying their importance by treating them as a "nonelite." Rather, I am emphasizing that the divide separating the *yangban* aristocracy from the rest of the society was more fundamental between any boundaries distinguishing lower status groups.

2. These benefits are described in a memorial to the throne in 1676. See *Sukchong sillok* 5: 20b.

3. Palais, *Politics and Policy in Traditional Korea,* 97–109, 275–76.

4. Yu Mong-in, *Ŏu yadam,* as cited in *YK, Pyŏlchip* 10: 3.

5. Sim, "Imjin Waeran chung mukwa ŭi unyŏng silt'ae wa kinŭng," 69–122; and Sim, "Imjin Waeran chung mukwa kŭpcheja ŭi sinbun kwa t'ŭksŏng," 109–46.

6. Yi Hong-du sees significant fluctuation in the level of lowborn participation during the period from 1592 to 1720. The initial peak, between 1592 and 1623, is said to have been followed by the nadir, between 1623 and 1659, then by another peak between 1674 to 1720. See Yi Hong-du, "Chosŏn hugi ch'ŏnin ŭi sinbun pyŏndong," 269–307.

7. Yi Su-gwang, *Chibong yusŏl,* as cited in *YK, Pyŏlchip* 10: 4.

8. *Kwanghaegun ilgi* 143: 21a–b, 144: 12b–13a, 15a–b.

9. *Kwanghaegun ilgi,* T'aebaek-san edition, 153: 92. The *kwŏn* number, 153, is printed on the original text which, however, is not paginated. The modern reprint edition supplies its own page numbers, in this case, 92.

10. *Kwanghaegun ilgi,* Chŏngjok-san edition, 174: 2a.

11. *Sugyo chimnok* 4 (*Pyŏngjŏn, Chegwa*), as cited in Chŏng Hae-ŭn, "Chosŏn hugi mukwa kŭpcheja," 38.

12. Those of Hamgyŏng Province, which had no naval unit, were sent off to the most distant military outposts within the province. *Sugyo chimnok* 4 (*Pyŏngjŏn, Chegwa*), as cited in Chŏng Hae-ŭn, "Chosŏn hugi mukwa kŭpcheja," 38.

13. *Injo sillok* 36: 41b–42a. As noted in Chapter 1, in 1430, Sejong followed a recommendation by the Board of Rites to treat the examination passers charged with a crime as incumbent officials, hence entitling them to an initial interrogation by the State Tribunal.

14. *Sugyo chimnok* 4 (*Pyŏngjŏn, Chegwa, Sungjŏng mujin sŭngjŏn*), as cited in Chŏng Hae-ŭn, "Chosŏn hugi mukwa kŭpcheja," 38.

15. *Injo sillok* 19: 61b, 23: 13b; and *Sugyo chimnok* 4 (*Pyŏngjŏn, Chegwa, Kanghŭi imja sŭngjŏn*), as cited in Chŏng Hae-ŭn, "Chosŏn hugi mukwa kŭpcheja," 38.

16. *Sukchong sillok* 5: 9b.

17. *SI* 265: 14a.

18. *Sinbo Sugyo chimnok* 5 (*Hyŏngjŏn, Ch'udan, Kanghŭi muo sŭngjŏn*), as cited in Chŏng Hae-ŭn, "Chosŏn hugi mukwa kŭpcheja," 42.

19. *Sukchong sillok* 7: 16b.

20. Chŏng Hae-ŭn, "Chosŏn hugi mukwa kŭpcheja," 42.

21. *Sok Taejŏn* 5: 1b–2a. All this meant that if the accused admitted his guilt, he would not be tortured. In other words, even a truly innocent person could be subject to torture if he or she insisted on innocence while the interrogators disagreed. Obviously, this was not much of a relief for the accused, although those charged and tried by the State Tribunal also had to face the same thing.

22. According to Chŏng Hae-ŭn, the percentage of the total number of passers from the most successful descent groups—each accounting for at least one percent of all graduates of the same subject—was 50.4 percent for the technical examinations, 40.5 percent for the civil examination, 38.6 percent for the licentiate examinations, and 30.2 percent for the military examination. See Chŏng Hae-ŭn, "Chosŏn hugi mukwa kŭpcheja," 147.

23. Chŏng's data shows that among the 16,528 late Chosŏn passers for whom the father's occupation is known, at least 648 (3.9 percent) had a father who was recorded on the son's roster with a non-*yangban* service label. See Chŏng Hae-ŭn, "Chosŏn hugi mukwa kŭpcheja," 54–55, 164, 278–79. In light of her exclusion of 5,506 passers of the 1637 Namhan Fort courtyard examination (among whom were 564 manumitted slaves) and the illegitimate-son passers whose fathers were *yangban*, my independently derived number of 8.0 percent makes sense. She analyzes this examination separately from the rest due to its unusually large scale and the disproportionate number of passers of lowborn background.

24. Ibid., 90, 279.

25. Ibid., 80–82. Here I use Chŏng's data on the degree holders' occupations at the time of earning their degrees, because my own military examination passer database includes additional passers from sources other than extant rosters—meaning that the occupation information is not available in most such cases.

26. Chŏng Hae-ŭn, "Chosŏn hugi mukwa kŭpcheja," 87–89.

27. Nonetheless, such *hallyang* recommendees were still subject to restrictions on how far they could advance in the bureaucracy. Ibid., 89–90.

28. Ibid., 84.

29. *Chigugwanch'ŏng ilgi* 7: 189b. His family background information comes from genealogies and examination rosters. In May 1882, Pak went on to pass a large-scale military examination that recruited some 2,600 men, among whom 2,061 were *chikpu* candidates. *SI* 2898: 31b–32a, 85b, 2899: 14a–b. This military examination contrasts sharply with the companion civil examination, which selected only 23 men. Including the famous Phillip Jaisohn (Sŏ Chae-p'il, 1866–1951), 18 civil examination passers appear in the *Comprehensive Genealogy of Ten Thousand Surnames* (*Mansŏng taedongbo*), a highly selective genealogy covering mostly aristocratic descent lines and including "fully two-thirds" of all Chosŏn civil examination passers. Wagner, "The Ladder of Success," 3. Interestingly, the *Daily Records of the Royal Secretariat* (*Sŭngjŏngwŏn ilgi*) lists all 23 civil examination passers but mentions only the top passer of the military examination by name. See *SI* 2899: 14a–b. According to the *Daily Records of the Military Guard Agency* (*Chigugwanch'ŏng ilgi*), Pak T'ae-sik and several other Military Guard Agency–affiliated officers were actually presented to the king, while all other

military examination passers stood outside the gate during the ceremony. See *Chigugwanch'ŏng ilgi* 9: 54b.

30. *Ilsŏngnok* 12816, *ch'aek* 0047, image 0063. This is an online image file of the original Kyujanggak text available at http://e-kyujanggak.snu.ac.kr/sub_index.jsp?ID=ILS [accessed 6 October 2006].

31. The number of regiments represented among the passers increased from 22 to 72, and the state's creation of new regiments throughout late Chosŏn seems to account for the increase. All the same, certain regiments tended to be more strongly represented than others. Moreover, the central regiment affiliates were represented almost equally as well as those of the regiments from the rest of Korea, although the percentage of provincial regiments represented was higher than that for the central ones at the sub-officer level. Chŏng Hae-ŭn, "Chosŏn hugi mukwa kŭpcheja," 90–102.

32. Ibid., 85–86.

33. Reasoning that most passers from Kyŏnggi Province, representing 75.2 percent of the graduates, apparently were lowborns serving as Royal Division Soldiers or *sogo* army soldiers controlled by the Anti-Manchu Division, Chŏng concludes that most military duty personnel originally had been slaves. In particular, including 564 passers recorded in the roster as manumitted slaves (10.2 percent), she concludes that up to 85 percent of the 1637 military examination passers were former slaves. See Chŏng Hae-ŭn, "Pyŏngja Horan sigi kun'gong myŏnch'ŏnin ŭi mukwa kŭpche wa sinbun pyŏnhwa," 76–93.

34. These figures are highly significant in light of the fact that the Kimhae Kim and Miryang Pak continue to be the two most populous descent group designations in South Korea today. According to the country's 2000 census, the two descent groups respectively number 4,124,934 (9.0 percent) and 3,031,478 (6.6 percent) out of 45,985,289 South Koreans. T'onggyech'ŏng, "Haengjŏng kuyŏk (si-do)/ sŏngssi-pon'gwan pyŏl kagu mit in'gu." http://kosis.nso.go.kr/cgi-bin/sws_999.cgi?ID=DT_1INOOSC&IDTYPE=3&A_LANG=1&FPUB=3&ITEM=&CLASS1=S.000 [accessed 9 October 2006]. This follows the pattern of the two previous census surveys, dating from 1960 and 1985. *Han'guk sŏngssi taegwan,* 46–47, 62, 270–71, 276; and *Sŏngssi ŭi kohyang,* 225, 745. Interestingly, O Sŏng's study of Kyŏnggi Province census documents from the late nineteenth and early twentieth centuries shows that the Kimhae Kim and Miryang Pak ranked first and third in population among household heads (*hoju*). See O Sŏng, *Han'guk kŭndae sangŏp tosi yŏn'gu,* 179. It seems that the overall representation pattern of the most populous descent group designations had crystallized by the dynasty's end, if not much earlier.

35. Actually, some Kimhae Kim claim descent from King Kyŏngsun (r. 927–35), who was the last king of Silla, or Kim Ch'ung-sŏn, a Japanese officer

who defected during the Korean-Japanese war of 1592–98. Both groups' populations are much smaller than the vast majority of the Kimhae Kim that claim descent from Kim Yu-sin.

36. Although taking an overly critical stance toward genealogy consciousness among modern Koreans, Yi Ki-baek offers an insightful and stimulating discussion of the place occupied by genealogies in South Korean society. See Yi Ki-baek, "Chokpo wa hyŏndae sahoe," 108–17.

37. The actual number of passers recorded in the 1637 roster is 5,506. For an explanation of the discrepancy between the number of those who passed and those actually recorded in the roster, see Chŏng Hae-ŭn, "Horan sigi kun'gong myŏnch'ŏnin," 75–76.

38. During a conversation in October 2002, I asked Chŏng what percentage of late Chosŏn military examination passers were not *yangban*; she stated that her intuitive feeling was that de facto *yangban* made up roughly 30 percent of all late Chosŏn passers, with the remainder comprising those from "intermediate" and nonelite social strata.

39. Yi Chun-gu, "Chosŏn hugi ŭi 'muhak' ko," 49–81.

40. Yi Chun-gu, *Chosŏn hugi sinbun chigyŏk pyŏndong yŏn'gu,* 34–92, 125–64.

41. An Pyŏng-uk, "19 segi hyanghoe wa millan," 10–36.

42. Kim Chun-hyŏng, "Chosŏn hugi Tansŏng chiyŏk ŭi sahoe pyŏnhwa wa sajokch'ŭng ŭi taeŭng," 95–116.

43. Ibid., 116–32. In his earlier study of Ulsan, another locale for which a large body of late Chosŏn household registers is extant, Kim Chun-hyŏng presents the same picture. See Kim Chun-hyŏng, "Chosŏn hugi Ulsan chiyŏk ŭi hyangnich'ŭng pyŏndong." His argument on the new functionaries is based on the paradigm advanced by Kim P'il-tong, "Chosŏn hugi chibang isŏ *chip*tan ŭi chojik kujo, part 1," 79–116; and Kim P'il-tong, "Chosŏn hugi chibang isŏ *chip*tan ŭi chojik kujo, part 2," 87–116.

44. Yi Hun-sang, *Chosŏn hugi ŭi hyangni,* 42–44, n. 4. Yi Hun-sang and Kim Chun-hyŏng disagree on the question of which nineteenth-century social phenomenon was more important: increasing new functionary presence in local administration or the old local functionary families' successful assertion of superiority over such newcomers. The extent to which newcomers challenged the indigenous functionaries' positions must have varied significantly from one locale to another.

45. Chang Yŏng-min, 209–38.

46. Such entries tend to have less detailed information than do those for *yangban* kinsmen; they also often lack any mention of whether the line became extinct. All the same, I have noticed while working with genealogies that in the descent lines traceable back to early or mid-Chosŏn, illegitimate sons are

documented better than those descended from later lines. This suggests that earlier illegitimate sons were less stigmatized by the aristocratic genealogy compilers. Interestingly, the early Chosŏn illegitimate sons passing the technical examination rarely gave rise to hereditary technical specialist lines, whereas their mid-Chosŏn counterparts often did; in contrast, the late Chosŏn illegitimate sons rarely passed an examination other than the military examination, and their descendants generally were not degree holders. Throughout the Chosŏn period, illegitimate sons pleaded their case to the government, gradually winning the right to compete in all the examinations and holding even the most prestigious offices previously reserved for those from prominent *yangban* descent lines. Song Chun-ho, "Chosŏn sidae ŭi kwagŏ wa yangban mit yangin (I)," 113–23. Nonetheless, until the 1880s they were unable to expand their presence in the central bureaucracy at the decision-making levels. For a recent English-language discussion of this development, see Hwang, *Beyond Birth,* 232–47.

47. Yi Su-gŏn, *Han'guk chungse sahoesa yŏn'gu,* 346–52.

48. For an English-language discussion of the various transition stages that individual households could undergo in the process of upward social mobility, see Somerville, 11–12.

49. For some highly illustrative genealogical charts of commoner descent groups that gradually changed their occupation labels, personal names, and even ancestral seat designations, see Kim Chun-hyŏng, "Chosŏn hugi Tansŏng chiyŏk ŭi sahoe pyŏnhwa wa sajokch'ŭng ŭi taeŭng," 278–90.

50. Chŏng Hae-ŭn, "Chosŏn hugi mukwa kŭpcheja," 7–9.

51. Chŏng Hae-ŭn, "Horan sigi kun'gong myŏnch'ŏnin," 93–99.

52. For the crime of violating the palace compound, the court subjected him to the standard punishment: 60 lashes with a cane, loss of appointment certificates, and banishment for one year. *Ilsŏngnok* 12811, *ch'aek* 0218, image 0013 available at http://e-kyujanggak.snu.ac.kr/sub_index.jsp?ID=ILS [accessed 6 October 2006].

53. Both Chŏng Hae-ŭn's detailed analysis of over ten thousand military examination passers from 1674 to 1800 and Kenneth Quinones' study of military officials from 1864 to 1910 show that nonelite military examination graduates and their descendants did not gain membership in the existing bureaucratic elite. See Chŏng Hae-ŭn, "Chosŏn hugi mukwa ipkyŏkcha," 187–243, and Quinones, "Military Officials of Yi Korea," 691–700.

54. Following the regulation stipulating that soldiers performing 45 or more years of satisfactory service receive a court rank, King Chŏngjo rewarded the petitioner's grandfather accordingly. *Ilsŏngnok* 12811, *ch'aek* 0232, image 0160 available at http://e-kyujanggak.snu.ac.kr/sub_index.jsp?ID=ILS [accessed 6 October 2006].

55. Chŏng Hae-ŭn, "Chosŏn hugi mukwa kŭpcheja," 210–55.

56. *Sinmyo pyŏlsi munkwa pangmok* 23a; *Sukchong sillok* 12: 27b; and *SI* 226: 34a, 281: 57b; 285: 53a.

57. *Sukchong sillok* 60: 25b, 44b–45a.

58. *Sungjŏng sam kapsin Kangdobu pyŏlkwa pangmok* preface, as cited by Chŏng Hae-ŭn, "Chosŏn hugi mukwa kŭpcheja," 9.

59. Bourdieu, *Distinction,* 65–66.

60. Song Ch'an-sik, 622–30; and Paek Sŭng-jong, "Wijo chokpo ŭi yuhaeng," 67–85.

61. As we saw in Chapter 3, cultural capital has three dimensions: the embodied state, the objectified state, and the institutional state. Bourdieu, "The Forms of Capital," 243–48.

62. *Taejŏn hoet'ong* 4: 40a.

63. For a study of the origins, spread, and decline of woodblock-printed works of narrative fiction, see Han'guk Ko Sosŏl Yŏn'guhoe, 223–97.

64. *Sosŏl* can also refer to a modern novel or a late Chosŏn narrative fiction, but the latter is more comparable to, for example, a medieval European romance.

65. According to the *Great Code of State Administration,* civil and military examination passers alike received a red warrant of the same format, whereas licentiates and technical examination graduates got a white warrant (*paekp'ae*). *Kyŏngguk taejŏn* 3: 53a. Degree certificate formats remained relatively unchanged to the end of the dynasty, as reflected in the last comprehensive legal code. *Taejŏn hoet'ong* 3: 66a–b.

66. *PT* 5 *ch'aek,* 1: 388d–389a.

67. Yi Man-sŏng, *Haengho ilgi,* as cited in *YK, Pyŏlchip* 9: 23–24.

68. For example in 1873, the court ordered reissuing of the red warrants for two such passers as well as ordering the Seoul Police Command (P'odoch'ŏng) to catch the thief. *Ilsŏngnok* 12816, *ch'aek* 0135, image 0009 available at http://e-kyujanggak.snu.ac.kr/sub_index.jsp?ID=ILS [accessed 9 October 2006].

69. King Sejo did just that for his nephew, the Yŏngsun'gun, who placed first in a *chungsi.* Yi Su-gwang, *Chibong yusŏl,* as cited in *YK, Pyŏlchip* 9: 9; and Yi Ik-chin, *Myŏngsinnok,* as cited in *YK, Pyŏlchip* 9: 10.

70. *YK, Pyŏlchip* 9: 25.

71. The ceremony was concerned less with announcing who passed the examination as it was with ranking the participants. Thus, even without the name read, everyone present would have known who the top passer was, since all other names had been called by that point.

72. Sim Su-gyŏng, *Ch'ŏngch'ŏn kyŏnhannok,* as cited in *YK, Pyŏlchip* 9: 25.

73. For references to this exemption, see *PT* 49 *ch'aek,* 4: 730c–d; and 64 *ch'aek,* 6: 411d.

74. Sim Su-gyŏng, *Ch'ŏngch'ŏn kyŏnhannok,* as cited in *YK, Pyŏlchip* 9: 25.

75. As far as I know, the 1865 *Great Code Reconciliation* (*Taejŏn hoet'ong*) was the first codification to refer specifically to honoring the *hoebang* graduates of all examinations. The addition presumably reflected the custom that had taken root. *Taejŏn hoet'ong* 1: 68b.

76. *Sunjo sillok* 26: 20a–b.

77. The recipients were all former Chosŏn official of high rank. Sunjong seems to have personally honored them as an expression of respect for tradition and care toward those he knew rather than as a broader action that would have involved all such individuals. *Sunjong sillok purok* 10: 16a, 14: 3b.

78. I base the following discussion on Scott, 2–9, 19–23, 45–62, 71–96, 150–79, 184–206.

79. For example, see Yi Hun-sang, *Chosŏn hugi ŭi hyangni,* 149–74.

80. Yun Kwang-bong, 390.

81. See Im, 267–68.

82. Ibid., 268–69.

83. Pak Yu-jŏn and Pak Man-sun, both legendary *p'ansori* singers active in the nineteenth century, are said to have passed the military examination thanks to the Taewŏn'gun's patronage. Chŏng No-sik, 43, 57–59.

84. For a brief English-language introduction to the *p'ansori* genre, see Tong-il Cho (Cho Tong-il), "The General Nature of *P'ansori,*" 10–21.

85. In modern Korean-language scholarship, military narrative fictions are also known as "hero narrative fictions" (*yŏngung sosŏl*). On the ground that such works almost invariably utilize a war as an occasion during which the heroic protagonist rises to glory, Sŏ Tae-sŏk regards military narrative fiction as a more inclusive category than hero narrative fiction, although he concedes that neither term is perfect. See Sŏ, 11–14.

86. The tiger can easily be replaced with, for example, a marauding party of Japanese soldiers. Over the years, I have seen such variations on the theme in oral tales from Koyang in Kyŏnggi Province, Puyŏ in Ch'ungch'ŏng Province, and Kimhae in Kyŏngsang Province.

87. *PT* 250 *ch'aek,* 13: 254d.

88. Sŏ, 228–40; and Cho Tong-il, *Han'guk munhak t'ongsa* 3: 470–75.

89. Cho Tong-il, *Han'guk munhak t'ongsa* 3: 462–63.

90. The details and plot structure vary tremendously, depending on the version. I examined two different versions: Lee; and "Imjinnok."

91. The version I consulted is Yu Sŏng-nyong, *The Book of Corrections,* trans. Byonghyon Choi.

92. Sŏ, 220–31; and Cho Tong-il, *Han'guk munhak t'ongsa* 3: 462–75.

93. Sŏ, 231–40.

94. *HMMTS,* s.v. "Im Kyŏng-ŏp." The version of the *Tale of General Im* that I consulted is a nineteenth-century Seoul print edition (Kyŏng *p'anbon*) from *Im Changgun chŏn,* trans. Kim Ki-hyŏn, 219–93.

95. Cho Tong-il, *Minjung yŏngung iyagi,* 277.

96. Not all such military men were deified, as we shall see in the following discussion.

97. Hŏ Mok, *Misu kiŏn,* as cited in *YK, Pyŏlchip* 4: 77.

98. *Kukcho kisa,* as cited in *YK* 6: 4.

99. Cho Hŭng-yun, *Han'guk ŭi mu,* 105.

100. Cho Hŭng-yun, *Mu wa minjok munhwa,* 300–3; and Cho Hŭng-yun, *Han'guk mu ŭi segye,* 247.

101. Walraven, 188–92.

Conclusion

1. A study stressing stability of premodern Korean sociopolitical structure is Palais, "Confucianism and the Aristocratic/Bureaucratic Balance in Korea."

2. Sewell, 24.

3. For this interpretation of the fall of Koryŏ, see Duncan, 8–9, 154–55, 200–1.

4. For an English-language discussion of this aspect of late Chosŏn culture, see Haboush, 23–24.

5. The images Yŏngjo and Chŏngjo projected as rulers are discussed in detail in Haboush, 29–82, and Chŏng Ok-cha, 45–86, 123–46.

6. I am not suggesting that the Qing state primarily depended on military conquests to control its subjects, but its command of adequate resources for such accomplishments, before the nineteenth-century rebellions, seems remarkable—even in comparison to Europe. For a stimulating comparative discussion on state formation and transformation in China and Europe, see Wong, 71–104. As for Japan, my point is that the Tokugawa state power was more "obvious" than its late Chosŏn counterpart, although the former certainly did not find it easy to deal with the broad socioeconomic changes that were taking place in Japanese society. For a relevant discussion on the Tokugawa state's dilemma of whether to capitalize on or suppress these changes, see Totman, 316–47.

7. Bourdieu, *Distinction,* 142–44.

8. Park, "Local Elites, Descent, and Status Consciousness in Nineteenth-Century Korea," 216–23.

9. Yi T'ae-jin, who has done extensive research on the nature of the Chosŏn state in the final decades of the dynasty, explained to me during our conversation on 3 August 2001 that in pushing ahead with his reform agendas, Kojong seems to have trusted talented non-*yangban* more than those from prominent aristocratic families.

10. Bourdieu, *Distinction,* 147.

11. An Pyŏng-uk, "19 segi hyanghoe wa millan," 37–44.

12. Ibid., 65–118.

13. Pak did not come from a distinguished family. According to the five-volume 1970 edition of the Koryŏng Pak genealogy (*Koryŏng Pak ssi taedongbo*), not a single one of his direct ancestors passed any examination, and none held a court rank or an office after the early seventeenth century. Furthermore, even though the descent group is said to have been based in Sŏngju since 1504, its members do not appear in various editions of Sŏngju local gazetteers' listings of late Chosŏn local notables. Finally, recorded information on wives shows that marriage connections were with families of no distinction. Significantly, the data is sparse—a pattern opposite of prominent *yangban* descent group genealogies, which tend to provide detailed information on the wife's patrilineage. Some details regarding Pak's career also require an explanation. According to descendents and villagers, he passed the military examination, but I have not been able to verify this independently with examination rosters, military examination graduate genealogies, local gazetteers, or other documents. Nonetheless, I see no reason to dismiss the claim. Known nineteenth-century military examination rosters are few in number, whereas military examination graduate genealogies and local gazetteers are highly selective in coverage, generally favoring men from the Seoul military aristocracy.

14. The Koryŏng Pak genealogy records him as the magistrate of Yŏngwŏl county in Kangwŏn Province, but I could not find him in any of the searchable databases on this period's magistrates, including the *Records of Daily Reflections* (*Ilsŏngnok*), *Records of Capital Offices* (*Kaksa tŭngnok*), and *Official Gazette* (*Kwanbo*). Since the magistrate appointment records for this period are complete, with the possible exception of the months of the Tonghak uprising in 1894, it seems that Pak either never received the appointment or did not assume the granted post. Had he done so, the appointment would have been remarkable, as it was a senior third-rank civil office—a meteoric rise for a relatively young man, only in his 30s, merely holding a junior ninth military rank. Interestingly, while explaining that he could not assume the magistracy due to the Tonghak uprising, some accounts state that he led troops to suppress the rebels and others claim that he joined them. This disagreement seems to reflect the changing assessment of the Tonghak movement—whereby it has been increasingly understood

as a revolution instead of a rebellion—in post-1945 South Korean discourse. Written accounts on Pak emerged during the authoritarian rule of his son, Park Chung Hee (Pak Chŏng-hŭi), and many clearly try to flatter the latter. Those exaggerating Pak Sŏng-bin's achievements sought to choose the right side as far as the Tonghak movement was concerned. Overall, the least embellished description of his life is none other than a published memoir by the son. See Pak Chŏng-hŭi (Park Chung Hee), 84–95.

15. Pak Chŏng-hŭi.

Works Cited

An Pyŏng-u and To Chin-sun. *Pukhan ŭi Han'guksa insik* (North Korean understanding of Korean history). 2 vols. Seoul: Han'gilsa, 1990.

An Pyŏng-uk (Pyŏng-uk An). "The Growth of Popular Consciousness and Popular Movement in the 19th Century: Focus on the *Hyanghoe* and *Millan*." *Korea Journal* 28 (April 1988): 4–19.

———. "19 segi ŭi hyanghoe wa millan" (19th-century local assemblies and popular uprisings). Ph.D. diss., Sŏul Taehakkyo, 2000.

Andong Kim-ssi sebo (Genealogy of the Andong Kim). 7 vols. 1959.

Bottomore, T. B. *Elites and Society*. New York: Basic Books, 1964.

Bourdieu, Pierre. *Distinction: A Social Critique of the Judgment of Taste*. Trans. Richard Nice. Cambridge, MA: Harvard University Press, 1984.

———. "The Forms of Capital." In *Handbook of Theory and Research for the Sociology of Education*, ed. John G. Richardson, 241–58. Westport, CT: Greenwood Press, 1986.

Ch'a Chang-sŏp. *Chosŏn hugi pŏryŏl yŏn'gu* (Studies on late Chosŏn elite families). Seoul: Ilchogak, 1997.

Ch'a Mun-sŏp. *Chosŏn sidae kunje yŏn'gu* (Studies on the military system in the Chosŏn period). Seoul: Tan'guk Taehakkyo Ch'ulp'anbu, 1973.

———. *Chosŏn sidae kunsa kwan'gye yŏn'gu* (Studies on military-related matters in the Chosŏn period). Seoul: Tan'guk Taehakkyo Ch'ulp'anbu, 1996.

Chang P'il-gi. "Chosŏn hugi 'mubo' ŭi charyojŏk kŏmt'o" (An examination of the value of '*mubo*' as a source). *Chosŏn sidae sahakpo* 7 (December 1998): 149–76.

———. "Chosŏn hugi muban kamun ŭi pŏryŏrhwa wa kŭ sŏngkyŏk" (The late Chosŏn transformation of military official families into a power elite and its nature). Ph.D. diss., Yŏngnam Taehakkyo, 1999.

Chang Sŏk-chin. *Tumun-dong yusa* (Memorabilia of Tumun-dong). N.p., 1917.

Chang Tong-ik. "Koryŏ chŏn'gi ŭi sŏn'gun: kyŏnggun kusŏng ŭi ihae rŭl wihan il siron" (The military recruitment in early Koryŏ: a preliminary discussion for understanding the composition of the capital army). In *Koryŏsa ŭi che munje* (Various problems in Koryŏ history), ed. Pyŏn T'ae-sŏp, 442–84. Seoul: Samyŏngsa, 1986.

Chang Yŏng-min. "Chosŏn sidae Wŏnju kŏju samasi kŭpcheja wa yangban sahoe" (Wŏnju-resident licentiate examination passers and *yangban* society in the Chosŏn period). In *Chosŏn sidae ŭi sahoe wa sasang* (Society and thoughts in the Chosŏn period), ed. Chosŏn Sahoe Yŏn'guhoe (Chosŏn Society Research Association), 209–39. Seoul: Chosŏn Sahoe Yŏn'guhoe, 1998.

Ch'angnyŏng Cho-ssi Sijunggong p'abo (Genealogy of Sijunggong branch of the Ch'angnyŏng Cho). 2 vols. Pusan: Ch'angnyŏng Cho-ssi Sijunggong-p'a Ut'aegong Chongmunhoe, 1985.

Chigugwanch'ŏng ilgi (Daily records of the Military Guard Agency). 9 vols. (*ch'aek*). Original edition at Changsŏgak collection (K2–3375), Academy of Korean Studies. No date.

Cho Hŭng-yun. *Han'guk ŭi mu* (Korea's shamanism). Seoul: Chŏngŭmsa, 1983.

———. *Mu wa minjok munhwa* (Shamanism and national culture). Seoul: Minjok Munhwasa, 1994.

———. *Han'guk mu ŭi segye* (World of Korean shamanism). Seoul: Minjoksa, 1997.

Cho Tong-il (Tong-il Cho). "The General Nature of *P'ansori*." *Korea Journal* 26.4 (April 1986): 10–21.

———. *Han'guk munhak t'ongsa* (A survey history of Korean literature), vol. 3. Second edition. Seoul: Chisik Sanŏpsa, 1991.

———. *Minjung yŏngung iyagi* (Tales of popular heroes). Seoul: Munye Ch'ulp'ansa, 1992.

Cho U-sŏk. *Mubi yoram* (Essentials of military preparedness). Seoul: Ilchogak, 1982.

Ch'oe Chin-ok. "Chosŏn sidae chapkwa sŏlhaeng kwa ipkyŏkcha punsŏk" (An analysis of the technical examination administration and passers in the Chosŏn period). In *Chosŏn sidae chapkwa hapkyŏkcha ch'ongnam* (Compendium of Chosŏn-period technical examination passers), ed. Yi Sŏng-mu, Ch'oe Chin-ok, and Kim Hŭi-bok, 11–47. Sŏngnam: Han'guk Chŏngsin Munhwa Yŏn'guwŏn, 1990.

———. *Chosŏn sidae saengwŏn-chinsa yŏn'gu* (A study of the classics-literary licentiates in the Chosŏn period). Seoul: Chimmundang, 1998.

Ch'oe Sŭng-hŭi. "Chosŏn hugi yangban ŭi sahwan kwa kase pyŏndong: Sŏnsan muban'ga No Sang-ch'u ŭi sarye rŭl chungsim ŭro" (Officeholding and changing family fortune among late Chosŏn *yangban*: The case of No Sang-ch'u from a military family of Sŏnsan). *Han'guksa ron* 19 (1988): 355–84.

Ch'oe Yŏng-ho (Yong-ho Choe). "Chosŏn wangjo chŏn'gi ŭi kwagŏ wa sinbun chedo" (The examination and social status systems in the early Chosŏn dynasty period). *Kuksagwan nonch'ong* 26 (1991): 143–82.

Chŏn Hyŏng-t'aek. *Chosŏn hugi nobi sinbun yŏn'gu* (A study of slave status in late Chosŏn). Seoul: Ilchogak, 1989.

Chŏn Kyŏng-mok. *Ko munsŏ rŭl t'onghaesŏ pon Uban-dong kwa Uban-dong Kim-ssi ŭi yŏksa* (Uban-dong and the Uban-dong Kim as seen through old documents). Chŏnju: Sina Ch'ulp'ansa, 2001.

Chŏng Chin-yŏng. "Chosŏn hugi tongsŏng ch'ollak ŭi hyŏngsŏng kwa paltal" (The formation and development of same-surname villages in late Chosŏn). *Yŏksa pip'yŏng* 28 (Spring 1995): 335–43.

Chŏng Hae-ŭn. "Chosŏn hugi mukwa ipkyŏkcha ŭi sinbun kwa sahoejŏk chiwi: Sukchong-Chŏngjo yŏn'gan ŭi 'mukwa pangmok' punsŏk ŭl chungsim ŭro" (The social status and social standing of military examination passers in late Chosŏn: an analysis of the 'military examination rosters' from the reigns of Sukchong through Chŏngjo). *Ch'ŏnggye sahak* 11 (1994): 187–243.

———. "'Mubo' rŭl t'onghaesŏ pon 19 segi mukwa kŭpcheja ŭi kwanjik chinch'ul yangsang" (Patterns of 19th-century military examination graduates' entry into officialdom as seen through '*mubo*'). In *Chosŏn sidae ŭi sahoe wa sasang* (Society and thoughts in the Chosŏn period), ed. Chosŏn Sahoe Yŏn'guhoe (Chosŏn Society Research Association), 185–208. Seoul: Chosŏn Sahoe Yŏn'guhoe, 1998.

———. "Pyŏngja Horan sigi kun'gong myŏnch'ŏnin ŭi mukwa kŭpche wa sinbun pyŏnhwa: 'Chŏngch'uk chŏngsi mukwa pangmok' (1637 nyŏn) ŭl chungsim ŭro" (Military examination passing and social status change of manumitted slaves with military merit during the Pyŏngja War period: the 'Chŏngch'uk courtyard military examination roster' [1637]). *Chosŏn sidae sahakpo* 9 (June 1999): 71–104.

———. "Chosŏn hugi sŏnch'ŏn ŭi unyŏng kwa sŏnch'ŏnin ŭi sŏbanjik chinch'ul yangsang" (The late Chosŏn administration of royal messenger recommendation and the patterns of recommendees' appointment to western-order posts). *Yŏksa wa hyŏnsil* 39 (March 2001): 127–60.

———. "Chosŏn hugi mukwa kŭpcheja yŏn'gu" (A study of late Chosŏn military examination passers). Ph.D. diss., Han'guk Chŏngsin Munhwa Yŏn'guwŏn, 2002.

Chŏng No-sik. *Chosŏn ch'anggŭksa* (A history of Chosŏn singing drama). Reprint edition. Seoul: Hyŏngil Ch'ulp'ansa, 1974.

Chŏng Ok-Cha. *Chŏngjo ŭi susangnok* Iltŭngnok *yŏn'gu* (A study of the *Record of Daily Obtainments*, Chŏngjo's record of reflections). Seoul: Ilchisa, 2000.

Chŏng Sŏk-chong. *Chosŏn hugi sahoe pyŏndong yŏn'gu* (A study of late Chosŏn social change). Seoul: Ilchogak, 1983.

Chŏng Sŭng-mo. "Kyŏngjŏ, hyangje, pyŏlsŏ wa Chosŏn hugi munhwa ŭi chiyŏksŏng" (Capital residences, country residences, special villas, and the regional characteristics of late Chosŏn culture). In *Han'guksa e issŏsŏ chibang kwa chungang* (The periphery and the center in Korean history), ed. Chŏng Tu-hŭi and Edward J. Shultz, 189–204. Seoul: Sŏgang Taehakkyo Ch'ulp'anbu, 2003.

Chŏng Tu-hŭi. "Pukhan ŭi yŏksahak ch'egye kaegwan" (A general survey of historical scholarship in North Korea). *Tonga yŏn'gu* 33 (June 1997): 97–146.

Ch'ŏnggu ssibo (Genealogy of Ch'ŏnggu [Korean] families). 30 vols. Ch'ŏkch'ŏmdae, 1926.

Chŏngjo sillok (Veritable records of King Chŏngjo). In *Chosŏn wangjo sillok*.

Chŏnŭi-Yean Yi-ssi chokpo (Genealogy of the Chŏnŭi-Yean Yi). 10 vols. Seoul: Chŏnŭi-Yean Yi-ssi Taedongbo Kanhaeng Wiwŏnhoe, 1979.

Chosŏn hwanyŏ sŭngnam (An all-around geographical survey of Korea). 16 vols. Seoul: Han'guk Inmun Kwahagwŏn, 1998.

Chosŏn sidae sach'an ŭpchi (Privately compiled Chosŏn-period town gazetteers). 55 vols. Seoul: Han'guk Inmun Kwahagwŏn, 1989.

Chosŏn sinsa taedongbo (Comprehensive genealogy of Korean gentlemen). Seoul: Asea Munhwasa, 1985.

Chosŏn wangjo sillok (Veritable records of the Chosŏn dynasty). 48 vols. Seoul: Kuksa P'yŏnch'an Wiwŏnhoe, 1955–58.

Chunggyŏng kwabo (Genealogy of examination graduates from Chunggyŏng [Kaesŏng]). Kaesŏng: Sungyang Munyesa, 1918.

Chunggyŏngji (Chunggyŏng [Kaesŏng] town gazetteer). In *Chosŏn sidae sach'an ŭpchi*, vols. 4–5 (q.v.).

Chungjong sillok (Veritable records of King Chungjong). In *Chosŏn wangjo sillok*.

Deuchler, Martina. *The Confucian Transformation of Korea: A Study of Society and Ideology*. Cambridge, MA: Council on East Asian Studies, Harvard University, 1992.

Duncan, John B. *The Origins of the Chosŏn Dynasty*. Seattle, WA: University of Washington Press, 2000.

Eckert, Carter J. *Offspring of Empire: The Koch'ang Kims and the Colonial Origins of Korean Capitalism, 1876–1945*. Seattle, WA: University of Washington Press, 1991.

Elisonas, Jurgis. "The Inseparable Trinity: Japan's Relations with China and Korea." In *The Cambridge History of Japan*, vol. 4: *Early Modern Japan*, ed. John Whitney Hall, 235–300. Cambridge, UK: Cambridge University Press, 1991.

Fairbank, John K. "Introduction: Varieties of the Chinese Military Experience." In *Chinese Ways in Warfare*, ed. Frank A. Kierman, Jr. and John K. Fairbank, 1–26. Cambridge, MA: Harvard University Press, 1974.

Haboush, JaHyun Kim. *A Heritage of Kings: One Man's Monarchy in the Confucian World*. New York: Columbia University Press, 1988.

Hamjong Ŏ-ssi sebo (Genealogy of the Hamjong Ŏ). 7 vols. (28 *kwŏn*). Seoul, 1871.

Han Yŏng-u. *Chosŏn chŏn'gi sahoe kyŏngje yŏn'gu* (Studies in early Chosŏn society and economy). Seoul: Ŭryu Munhwasa, 1983.

———. "Chosŏn sidae chungin ŭi sinbun-kyegŭpchŏk sŏngkyŏk" (Social status-class characteristics of *chungin* in the Chosŏn period). *Han'guk munhwa* 9 (1988): 179–209.

———. *Tasi ch'annŭn uri yŏksa* (Our history revisited). Seoul: Kyŏngsewŏn, 1997.

Han'guk Chŏngsin Munhwa Yŏn'guwŏn (Academy of Korean Studies). *CD-ROM Sama pangmok* (CD-ROM licentiate examination rosters). Seoul: Sŏul Sisŭt'em, 2001.

Han'guk Ko Sosŏl Yŏn'guhoe (Korean Classical Narrative Fiction Research Association), ed. *Ko sosŏl ŭi chŏjak kwa chŏnp'a* (Writing and propagation of classical narrative fictions). Seoul: Asea Munhwasa, 1994.

Han'guk kŭndae ŭpchi (Modern Korean local gazetteers). 64 vols. Seoul: Han'guk Inmun Kwahagwŏn, 1991.

Han'guk kyehaengbo (Korean pedigrees and generations). Seoul: Pogosa, 1992.

Han'guk sŏngssi taegwan (Compendium of Korean surnames). Seoul: Ch'angjosa, 1971.

Han'guk Yŏksa Yŏn'guhoe 19 Segi Chŏngch'isa Yŏn'guban (19th-Century Political History Research Group, Organization of Korean Historians). *Chosŏn chŏngch'isa (1800–1863)* (Chosŏn political history (1800–1863)). 2 vols. Seoul: Ch'ŏngnyŏnsa, 1990.

Han'guk Yŏksa Yŏn'guhoe Chosŏn Sigi Sahoesa Yŏn'guban (Chosŏn Social History Research Group, Organization of Korean Historians). *Chosŏn ŭn chibang ŭl ŏttŏkk'e chibae haennŭn'ga* (How did Chosŏn rule the countryside?). Seoul: Ak'anet, 2000.

Hazard, Benjamin H. "The Wakō and Korean Responses." In *Papers in Honor of Professor Woodbridge Bingham: A Festschrift for His Seventy-fifth Birthday,* ed. James B. Parsons, 15–28. San Francisco, CA: Chinese Materials Center, Inc., 1976.

Honamji (Honam [Chŏlla] gazetteer). 6 vols. Chŏngŭp. Preface dated 1934.

Honda Hiroshi. "Rizoku to mibun tentō no keisei: Nangen chiiki no jirei kara" (Functionary families and the formation of status tradition: the case of Namwŏn region). *Kankoku-Chōsen no bunka to shakai* 3 (2004): 23–72.

Hong Chong-p'il. "Sambŏnnan ŭl chŏnhu han Hyŏnjong Sukchong yŏn'gan ŭi Pukpŏllon: T'ŭkhi yurim kwa Yun Hyu rŭl chungsim ŭro" (The Northern Expedition debate before and after the rebellion of the Three Feudatories during the reigns of Hyŏnjong and Sukchong: the Confucian literati and Yun Hyu). *Sahak yŏn'gu* 27 (June 1977): 85–108.

Hŏnjong sillok (Veritable records of King Hŏnjong). In *Chosŏn wangjo sillok.*

Hwang, Kyung Moon. "Bureaucracy in the Transition to Korean Modernity: Secondary Status Groups and the Transformation of Government and Society, 1880–1930." Ph.D. diss., Harvard University, 1997.

———. "From the Dirt to Heaven: Northern Koreans in the Chosŏn and Early Modern Eras." *Harvard Journal of Asiatic Studies* 62.1 (June 2002): 135–78.

———. *Beyond Birth: Social Status in the Emergence of Modern Korea.* Cambridge, MA: Harvard University Asia Center, 2004.

Hyŏnjong kaesu sillok (Revised veritable records of King Hyŏnjong). In *Chosŏn wangjo sillok.*

Ilsŏngnok (Record of daily reflections). Online image files of the original text. Seoul: Sŏul Taehakkyo Kyujanggak Han'gukhak Yŏn'guwŏn, 2002. http://e-kyujanggak.snu.ac.kr/sub_index.jsp?ID=ILS.

Im Chae-hae. *Han'guk minsok kwa chŏnt'ong ŭi segye* (The world of Korean folk cultural tradition). Seoul: Chisik Sanŏpsa, 1991.

Im Changgun chŏn (Tale of General Im). Kim Ki-hyŏn, trans. In *Han'guk kojŏn munhak chŏnjip* (Collection of classical Korean literature), ed. Koryŏ Taehakkyo Minjok Munhwa Yŏn'guso (National Culture Research Institute, Korea University), 15: 219–93. Seoul: Koryŏ Taehakkyo Minjok Munhwa Yŏn'guso, 1995.

Imja-nyŏn pyŏlsi munkwa pangmok (1672 Special Civil Examination Roster). No place, no date.

"Imjinnok" (Record of the Imjin War). In *Han'guk kojŏn munhak 100* (Korean classical literature 100), ed. Kim Ki-dong and Chŏn Kyu-t'ae, vol. 15, *Paekhaksŏn chŏn, Kŭmu T'aeja chŏn, Imjinnok* (Tale of Paekhaksŏn, Tale of Prince Kŭmu, Record of Korean-Japanese War), 95–224. Seoul: Sŏmundang, 1984.

Injo sillok (Veritable records of King Injo). In *Chosŏn wangjo sillok.*

Kang Hyo-sŏk. *Chŏn'go Taebang* (Reference for old Korea). Revised and expanded edition. Kyŏngsŏng: Hanyang Sŏwŏn, 1925.

Kang Man-gil. *Chosŏn hugi sangŏp chabon ŭi paltal* (Development of commercial capital in late Chosŏn). Seoul: Koryŏ Taehakkyo Ch'ulp'anbu, 1973.

Kang Sŏk-hwa. "Chosŏn hugi Hamgyŏng-do ŭi chiyŏk palchŏn kwa pukpang yŏngt'o ŭisik." (The late Chosŏn regional development in Hamgyŏng Province and the understanding of northern frontier territory). Ph.D. diss., Sŏul Taehakkyo, 1996.

———. "Chosŏn hugi Hamgyŏng-do ŭi Ch'in'giwi" (The late Chosŏn Hamgyŏng Province Royal Cavalry Guards). *Han'guk hakpo* 89 (Winter 1997): 24–60.

Kawashima, Fujiya. "A Study of the *Hyangan*: Kin Group and Aristocratic Localism in the Seventeenth- and Eighteenth-Century Korean Countryside." *Journal of Korean Studies* 5 (1984): 3–38.

Kim Chun-hyŏng. "Chosŏn hugi Ulsan chiyŏk ŭi hyangnich'ŭng pyŏndong" (A study of the change of Ulsan local functionary stratum in late Chosŏn). *Han'guksa yŏn'gu* 56 (1987): 33–88.

———. "Chosŏn hugi Tansŏng chiyŏk ŭi sahoe pyŏnhwa wa sajokch'ŭng ŭi taeŭng" (Late Chosŏn social change and *sajok* stratum's responses in Tansŏng area). Ph.D. diss., Sŏul Taehakkyo, 2000.

Kim Hyŏn-mok. "Chosŏn chunggi chapkwa ipkyŏkcha ŭi sinbun kwa sŏngkyŏk: 16 segi chapkwa tanhoe pangmok ŭi punsŏk" (The social status and characteristics of the mid-Chosŏn technical examination passers: an analysis of the individual 16th-century examination rosters). *Yŏksa hakpo* 139 (1993): 35–66.

Kim Hyŏn-yŏng. "Chosŏn hugi hyangch'on sahoe chunginch'ŭng ŭi tonghyang: sŏŏlch'ŭng ŭi hwaltong ŭl chungwim ŭro" (Movements of *chungin* in late Chosŏn local society: the activity of illegitimate sons). In *Han'guk kŭndae ihaenggi chungin yŏn'gu* (Studies on *chungin* during the period of transition to modernity in Korea), ed. Yŏnse Taehakkyo Kukhak Yŏn'guwŏn, 411–47. Seoul: Tosŏ Ch'ulp'an Sinsŏwŏn, 1999.

Kim In-gŏl. "Chosŏn hugi hyangch'on sahoe kujo ŭi pyŏndong" (Structural changes in the late Chosŏn rural village society). In *Pyŏn T'ae-sŏp Paksa hwagap kinyŏm sahak nonch'ong* (Festschrift for Dr. Pyŏn T'ae-sŏp), 767–92. Seoul: Samyŏngsa, 1985.

Kim P'il-tong. "Chosŏn hugi chibang isŏ chiptan ŭi chojik kujo (sang): sahoesajŏk chŏpkŭn" (The organizational structure of late Chosŏn local functionary and clerk groups (part *sang*): a social historical approach). *Han'guk hakpo* 28 (September 1982): 79–116.

———. "Chosŏn hugi chibang isŏ chiptan ŭi chojik kujo (ha): sahoesajŏk chŏpkŭn" (The organizational structure of late Chosŏn local functionary and clerk groups (part *ha*): a social historical approach). *Han'guk hakpo* 29 (December 1982): 87–116.

Kim Se-yŏng. "Chosŏn Hyojongjo Pukpŏllon yŏn'gu" (A study of Northern Expedition debate during Chosŏn Hyŏnjong's reign). *Paeksan hakpo* 51 (August 1998): 121–53.

Kim Sŏk-hŭi. "18–19 segi hogu ŭi silt'ae wa sinbun pyŏndong: sillye Ŏnyanghyŏn hojŏk taejang ŭl chungsim ŭro" (Actual conditions of households and social mobility in the 18th and 19th centuries: the case of Ŏnyang prefecture household register document collection). *Pusan Taehakkyo inmun nonch'ong* 26 (1984): 343–86.

Kim, Sun Joo. *A Region Protests: Marginalized Elite, Regional Discrimination, and the Tradition of Prophetic Belief in the Hong Kyŏngnae Rebellion of 1812.* Seattle, WA: University of Washington Press, 2007.

Kim Yŏng-mo. *Chosŏn chibaech'ŭng yŏn'gu* (Studies of the Chosŏn ruling elite stratum). Seoul: Ilchogak, 1977.

Kim Yong-sŏp. *Chosŏn hugi nongŏpsa yŏn'gu* (Studies in the late Chosŏn agrarian history). Seoul: Ilchogak, 1976.

Kimhae hyangan kŭp ŭpchi chŏryak (Kimhae local agency officer register and abridged gazetteer). Preface dated 1912.

Kojong-Sunjong sillok (Veritable records of Emperors Kojong and Sunjong). 4 vols. Seoul: T'amgudang, 1986.

Koryŏng Pak-ssi taedongbo (Comprehensive genealogy of the Koryŏng Pak). 5 vols. Taejŏn: Hoesangsa, 1970.

Kugyŏk Kimhae ŭpchi (Translated Kimhae town gazetteer). Trans. Kwŏn Chŏng-sŏk. Kimhae: Kimhae Munhwawŏn, 1984.

Kuksa P'yŏnch'an Wiwŏnhoe (National Institute of Korean History). *Han'guksa* (History of Korea), vol. 33: *Chosŏn hugi ŭi kyŏngje* (Late Chosŏn economy). Kwach'ŏn: Kuksa P'yŏnch'an Wiwŏnhoe, 1997.

Kwanghaegun ilgi (Daily records of King Kwanghaegun). Chŏngjoksan edition. In *Chosŏn wangjo sillok.*

Kwanghaegun ilgi (Daily records of King Kwanghaegun). T'aebaeksan edition. In *Chosŏn wangjo sillok.*

Kwangju Yi-ssi taedongbo (Comprehensive genealogy of the Kwangju Yi). Seoul: Kwangju Yi-ssi Taedongbo P'yŏnch'an Wiwŏnhoe, 1988.

Kwŏn T'ae-hwan and Sin Yong-ha. "Chosŏn wangjo sidae in'gu ch'ujŏng e kwanhan il siron" (A preliminary discussion on estimating population during the Chosŏn dynasty period). *Tonga munhwa* 14 (1975): 287–330.

Kyonam kwabangnok (Record of examination graduates from Kyonam [Kyŏngsang]). 9 vols. Kyŏngsan: Kyŏngsan Inswaeso, Yujo Kondon, 1936.

Kyŏngguk taejŏn (Great code of state administration). Seoul: Ilchisa, 1978.

Lee, Peter H., trans. *The Record of the Black Dragon Year.* Seoul: Institute of Korean Culture, Korea University, 2000.

Maengsan kunji (Maengsan county gazetteer). 1936. In *Han'guk kŭndae ŭpchi,* vol. 61 (q.v.).

Mansŏng taedongbo (Comprehensive genealogy of ten thousand surnames). 3 vols. Seoul: Mansŏng Taedongbo Kanhaengso, 1931–33.

Michell, Tony. "Fact and Hypothesis in Yi Dynasty Economic History: The Demographic Dimension." *Korean Studies Forum* 6 (Winter-Spring 1979/1980): 65–93.

Min Hyŏn-gu. "Chosŏn ch'ogi ŭi sabyŏng" (Early Chosŏn private armies). In *Che sipsam-hoe Tongyanghak haksul hoeŭi kangyŏn ch'o* (Proceedings from the Thirteenth Oriental Studies Conference), 31–39. Seoul: Tan'guktae Tongyanghak Yŏn'guso, 1983.

Miryang Pak-ssi Kyujŏnggong-p'a taedongbo (Comprehensive genealogy of Kyujŏnggong branch the Miryang Pak). 16 vols. Seoul: Miryang Pak-ssi Kyujŏnggong-p'a Taedongbo P'yŏnsuhoe, 1980.

"Mubo" (Genealogy of military examination graduates). 3 vols. Bound photocopy of the original at Changsŏgak collection (2-1741), Academy of Korean Studies. No date.

"Mubo" (Genealogy of military examination graduates). 2 vols. Bound photocopy of the original at Changsŏgak collection (2-1742), Academy of Korean Studies. No date.

"Mubo" (Genealogy of military examination graduates). 2 vols. Manuscript at Harvard-Yenching Library (Rare Book TK2291.7/1748a), Harvard University. Ca. 1900.

"Mujinsin p'alsebo" (Eight-generation genealogy of military *yangban*). Manuscript at Harvard-Yenching Library (Rare Book TK2291.7/1748), Harvard University. No date.

Mukwa ch'ongyo (Comprehensive essentials of the military examination). Seoul: Asea Munhwasa, 1974.

Muye tobo t'ongji (Comprehensive illustrated manual of martial skills). Seoul: Hangmun'gak, 1970.

Myŏngjong sillok (Veritable records of King Myŏngjong). In *Chosŏn wangjo sillok*.

Nŭngsŏng Ku-ssi sebo (Genealogy of the Nŭngsŏng Ku). 16 vols. (16 *kwŏn*). Preface dated 1906.

O Chong-nok. "Chosŏn ch'ogi Pyŏngma Chŏltosa ŭi sŏngnip kwa kŭ unyŏng (sang)" (Establishment of provincial army commanders and their function in early Chosŏn (part *sang*)). In *Chindan hakpo* 59 (1985): 77–114.

———. "Chosŏn ch'ogi Pyŏngma Chŏltosa ŭi sŏngnip kwa kŭ unyŏng (ha)" (Establishment of provincial army commanders and their function in early Chosŏn (part *ha*)). In *Chindan hakpo* 60 (1985): 101–23.

———. "Pungdang chŏngch'i wa kunyŏng" (Partisan politics and military divisions). *Yŏksa pip'yŏng* 29 (Summer 1995): 301–7.

O Sŏng. *Chosŏn hugi sangin yŏn'gu* (A study of late Chosŏn merchants). Seoul: Ilchogak, 1989.

———. "Hanmal Kaesŏng chibang ŭi ho ŭi kusŏng kwa hoju: Nam-bu Tojo-ri hoju ŭi chigŏp punp'o wa kwallyŏn hayŏ" (The composition of households and the household heads in Kaesŏng region at the end of Korean Empire: occupation distribution among the household heads of Tojo-ri, Nam-bu). In *Yi Ki-baek Sŏnsaeng kohŭi kinyŏm Han'guk sahak nonch'ong* (Festschrift for Mr. Yi Ki-baek), 2: 1708–33. Seoul: Ilchogak, 1994.

———. *Han'guk kŭndae sangŏp tosi yŏn'gu: Kaesŏng, Inch'ŏn ŭi hojŏk taejang punsŏk ŭl chungsim ŭro* (A study of commercial cities in modern Korea: an analysis of the household registration collections for Kaesŏng and Inch'ŏn). Seoul: Kukhak Charyowŏn, 1998.

O Su-ch'ang. *Chosŏn hugi P'yŏngan-do sahoe palchŏn yŏn'gu* (A study on the social development in late Chosŏn P'yŏngan Province). Seoul: Ilchogak, 2002.

Paek Ki-in. "18 segi Pukpŏllon kwa tae Ch'ŏng pangŏ chŏllyak" (The 18th-century Northern Expedition debate and anti-Qing defense strategies). *Kunsa* 41 (December 2000): 245–72.

Paek Sŭng-jong. "18–19 segi Chŏlla-do esŏ ŭi sinhŭng seryŏk ŭi taedŭ: T'aein-hyŏn Kohyŏllae-myŏn ŭi sŏryu" (Emergence of newly risen forces in Chŏlla Province in the 18th–19th centuries: the illegitimate sons of Kohyŏllae-myŏn, T'aein Prefecture). In *Yi Ki-baek Sŏnsaeng kohŭi kinyŏm Han'guk sahak nonch'ong* (Festschrift for Mr. Yi Ki-baek), 2: 1339–67. Seoul: Ilchogak, 1994.

———. "Wijo chokpo ŭi yuhaeng" (Popularity of fabricated genealogies). *Han'guksa simin kangjwa* 24 (1999): 67–85.

Paek-ssi taedongbo (Comprehensive genealogy of the Paek). 13 vols. Seoul: Paek-ssi Taedongbo P'yŏnch'an Chungang Wiwŏnhoe, 1959.

Pak Chŏng-hŭi (Park Chung Hee). "Na ŭi ŏrin sijŏl" (My youthful times). *Wŏlgan Chosŏn* 4 (May 1984): 84–95.

Pak Yŏng-jin. See Park, Eugene Y.

Palais, James B. *Politics and Policy in Traditional Korea.* Cambridge, MA: Council on East Asian Studies, Harvard University, 1975.

———. "Confucianism and the Aristocratic/Bureaucratic Balance in Korea." *Harvard Journal of Asiatic Studies* 44.2 (1984): 427–68.

———. "A Search for Korean Uniqueness." *Harvard Journal of Asiatic Studies* 55.2 (1995): 409–25.

———. *Confucian Statecraft and Korean Institutions: Yu Hyŏngwŏn and the Late Chosŏn Dynasty.* Seattle, WA: University of Washington Press, 1996.

Pang Sang-hyŏn. *Chosŏn ch'ogi sugun chedo* (The early Chosŏn navy system). Seoul: Minjok Munhwasa, 1991.

Park, Chung Hee. See Pak Chŏng-hŭi.

Park, Eugene Y. "Military Officials in Chosŏn Korea, 1392–1863." Ph.D. diss., Harvard University, 1999.

———. "Military Examination Graduates in Early Chosŏn: Their Social Status in the Fifteenth Century." *The Review of Korean Studies* 3.1 (July 2000): 123–56.

———. (Pak Yŏng-jin). "Chosŏn ch'ogi mukwa ch'ulsin ŭi sahoejŏk chiwi: T'aejong-Sŏngjong yŏn'gan ŭi kŭpcheja rŭl chungsim ŭro" (The social status of early Chosŏn military examination graduates: passers from the reigns of T'aejong through Sŏngjong). *Yŏksa wa hyŏnsil* 39 (March 2001): 100–26.

———. "Military Examination Graduates in Sixteenth-Century Korea: Political Upheaval, Social Change, and Security Crisis." *Journal of Asian History* 35.1 (2001): 1–57.

———. "Local Elites, Descent, and Status Consciousness in Nineteenth-Century Korea: Some Observations on the County Notable Listings in the *Chosŏn Hwanyŏ Sŭngnam*." In *Han'guksa e issŏsŏ chibang kwa chungang* (The periphery and the center in Korean history), ed. Chŏng Tu-hŭi and Edward J. Shultz, 205–25. Seoul: Sŏgang Taehakkyo Ch'ulp'anbu, 2003.

Peterson, Mark A. "Hyangban and Merchant in Kaesŏng." *Korea Journal* 19 (December 1979): 4–18.

———. *Korean Adoption and Inheritance: Case Studies in the Creation of a Classic Confucian Society*. Ithaca, NY: Cornell East Asia Program, 1996.

Pibyŏnsa tŭngnok (Record of the Border Defense Command). 28 vols. Seoul: Kuksa P'yŏnch'an Wiwŏnhoe, 1982.

P'osan Kwak-ssi sebo (Genealogy of the P'osan [Hyŏnp'ung] Kwak). 9 vols. (18 *kwŏn*). Seoul: Aksegwan, 1925.

Pratt, Keith, and Richard Rutt. *Korea: A Historical and Cultural Dictionary*. Surrey, UK: Curzon Press, 1999.

P'yŏngsan Sin-ssi taedongbo (Comprehensive genealogy of the P'yŏngsan Sin). 6 vols. Seoul: P'yŏngsan Sin-ssi Taejongjung, 1976.

P'yŏngyang Cho-ssi sebo (Genealogy of the P'yŏngyang Cho). 5 vols. (21 *kwŏn* and 1 *purok*). 1791.

Quinones, C. Kenneth. "The Prerequisites for Power in Late Yi Korea: 1864–1894." Ph.D. diss., Harvard University, 1975.

———. "Military Officials of Yi Korea: 1864–1910." In *Che 1–hoe Han'gukhak kukche haksul hoeŭi nonmunjip* (Papers of the 1st International Conference on Korean Studies), 691–700. Sŏngnam: Han'guk Chŏngsin Munhwa Yŏn'guwŏn, 1980.

Robinson, Kenneth R. "From Raiders to Traders: Border Security and Border Control in Early Chosŏn, 1392–1450." *Korean Studies* 16 (1992): 94–115.

Sahoe Kwahagwŏn Ryŏksa Yon'guso (History Research Institute, Social Science Academy). *Chosŏn chŏnsa* (A comprehensive history of Korea). 33 vols.

and 2 appendices. P'yŏngyang: Kwahak Paekkwa Sajŏn Ch'ulp'ansa, 1979–83.

Scott, James C. *Domination and the Arts of Resistance: Hidden Transcripts.* New Haven, CT: Yale University Press, 1990.

Sejong sillok (Veritable records of King Sejong). In *Chosŏn wangjo sillok.*

Sewell, William H., Jr. "A Theory of Structure: Duality, Agency, and Transformation." *American Journal of Sociology* 98.1 (July 1992): 1–29.

Shima, Mutsuhiko. "In Quest of Social Recognition: A Retrospective View on the Development of Korean Lineage Organization." *Harvard Journal of Asiatic Studies* 50.1 (June 1990): 87–129.

Shultz, Edward J. *Generals and Scholars: Military Rule in Medieval Korea.* Honolulu, HI: University of Hawaii Press, 2000.

Sim Sŭng-gu. "Chosŏn ch'ogi mukwa chedo" (The early Chosŏn military examination system). *Pugak saron* 1 (1989): 1–73.

———. "Chosŏn ch'ogi tosi wa kŭ sŏngkyŏk" (The early Chosŏn local military competition and its characteristics). *Han'guk hakpo* 60 (1990): 98–134.

———. "Chosŏn chŏn'gi mukwa yŏn'gu" (A study of the early Chosŏn military examination). Ph.D. diss., Kungmin Taehakkyo, 1994.

———. "Chosŏn Sŏnjodae mukwa kŭpcheja ŭi punsŏk: 1583–1584 nyŏn ŭi taeryang sich'wi pangmok ŭl chungsim ŭro" (An analysis of military examination passers during Chosŏn Sŏnjo's reign: the large-scale recruitment examination rosters from 1583–1584). *Yŏksa hakpo* 144 (1994): 47–87.

———. "Imjin Waeran chung mukwa kŭpcheja ŭi sinbun kwa t'ŭksŏng: 1594 nyŏn (Sŏnjo 27) ŭi pyŏlsi mukwa pangmok ŭl chungsim ŭro" (The social status and special characteristics of the military examination passers during the Korean-Japanese war: the 1594 (Sŏnjo 27) special examination roster). *Han'guksa yŏn'gu* 92 (March 1996): 109–46.

———. "Imjin Waeran chung mukwa ŭi unyŏng silt'ae wa kinŭng" (The actual condition of the administration of the military examination and its functions during the Korean-Japanese war). *Chosŏn sidae sahakpo* 1 (April 1997): 69–122.

Sin Yong-ha. *Han'guk kŭndae sahoe sasangsa yŏn'gu* (Studies on modern social ideology in Korea). Seoul: Ilchisa, 1987.

Sinmyo pyŏlsi munkwa pangmok (1651 Special Civil Examination Roster). No place, ca. 1656.

Sŏ Tae-sŏk. *Kundam sosŏl ŭi kujo wa paegyŏng* (The structure and context of military narrative fiction). Seoul: Ihwa Yŏja Taehakkyo Ch'ulp'anbu, 1985.

Sok taejŏn (Amended great code). Seoul: Asea Munhwasa, 1983.

Somerville, John N. "Stability in Eighteenth Century Ulsan." *Korean Studies Forum* 1 (1976–77): 1–18.

Son Yŏng-jong and Pak Yŏng-hae. *Chosŏn t'ongsa* (A survey history of Korea). Vol. 1. P'yŏngyang: Sahoe Kwahak Ch'ulp'ansa, 1987.

Song Ch'an-sik. *Chosŏn hugi sahoe kyŏngjesa ŭi yŏn'gu* (Studies in late Chosŏn socio-economic history). Seoul: Ilchogak, 1997.

Song Chun-ho. "Chosŏn sidae ŭi kwagŏ wa yangban mit yangin (I): munkwa wa saengwŏn-chinsasi rŭl chungsim ŭro hayŏ" (The examination system, *yangban*, and commoners of the Chosŏn period (I): the civil examination and the classics-literary licentiate examinations). *Yŏksa hakpo* 69 (March 1976): 101–35.

———. "Yijo hugi ŭi mukwa ŭi unyŏng silt'ae e kwanhayŏ: Chŏng Tasan ŭi oransŏl ŭl chungsim ŭro" (On the actual condition of military examination administration in the late Yi dynasty period: Chŏng Tasan's explication of five chaotic abuses). *Chŏnbuk sahak* 1 (February 1977): 19–44.

———. *Chosŏn sahoesa yŏn'gu: Chosŏn sahoe ŭi kujo wa sŏngkyŏk mit kŭ pyŏnch'ŏn e kwanhan yŏn'gu* (Studies in the social history of Chosŏn: studies on the structure and characteristics of Chosŏn society and its change). Seoul: Ilchogak, 1987.

———. "Sinbunje rŭl t'onghaesŏ pon Chosŏn hugi sahoe ŭi sŏngkyŏk ŭi il-myŏn" (A facet of the nature of late Chosŏn society as seen through the social status system). *Yŏksa hakpo* 133 (March 1992): 1–62.

———. "Chosŏn hugi ŭi kwagŏ chedo" (The late Chosŏn examination system). *Kuksagwan nonch'ong* 63 (1995): 37–191.

Song Pok. "'Kŭndae ihaenggi chungin yŏn'gu' ŭi p'iryosŏng" (The need for 'Studies on *chungin* during the period of transition to modernity'). In *Han'guk kŭndae ihaenggi chungin yŏn'gu* (Studies on *chungin* during the period of transition to modernity in Korea), ed. Yŏnse Taehakkyo Kukhak Yŏn'guwŏn, 17–52. Seoul: Tosŏ Ch'ulp'an Sinsŏwŏn, 1999.

Sŏng Sa-je. *Tumun-dong sŏnsaeng silgi* (Biographies of Tumun-dong teachers). N.p., 1809.

Songdoji (Songdo [Kaesŏng] gazetteer). 1648 edition. In *Chosŏn sidae sach'an ŭpchi*, vol. 2 (q.v.).

Songdoji (Songdo [Kaesŏng] gazetteer). 1782 edition. In *Chosŏn sidae sach'an ŭpchi*, vol. 3 (q.v.).

Songdo sokchi (Songdo [Kaesŏng] gazetteer continuation). In *Chosŏn sidae sach'an ŭpchi*, vol. 3 (q.v.).

Sŏngssi ŭi kohyang (Homes of surnames). Seoul: Chungang Ilbosa, 1989.

Sŏngwŏnnok (Record of surname origins). Seoul: Osŏngsa, 1985.

Sŏnjo sillok (Veritable records of King Sŏnjo). In *Chosŏn wangjo sillok*.

Sŏnjo sujŏng sillok (Revised veritable records of King Sŏnjo). In *Chosŏn wangjo sillok*.

Ssijok wŏllyu (Origins of descent groups). Seoul: Pogyŏng Munhwasa, 1991.

Sukchong sillok (Veritable records of King Sukchong). In *Chosŏn wangjo sillok*.

Sŭngjŏngwŏn ilgi (Daily records of the Royal Secretariat). Online image files of the original text. Seoul: Sŏul Taehakkyo Kyujanggak Han'gukhak Yŏn'guwŏn, 2002. http://e-kyujanggak.snu.ac.kr/sub_index.jsp?ID=SJW.

Sunjo sillok (Veritable records of King Sunjo). In *Chosŏn wangjo sillok*.

Sunjong sillok purok (Appendix to veritable records of Emperor Sunjong). In *Kojong-Sunjong sillok*.

Taehan Cheguk kwanwŏn iryŏksŏ (Resumes of Korean Empire bureaucrats). Seoul: Kuksa P'yŏnch'an Wiwŏnhoe, 1972.

T'aejo sillok (Veritable records of King T'aejo). In *Chosŏn wangjo sillok*.

Taejŏn hoet'ong (Great code reconciliation). Seoul: Pogyŏng Munhwasa, 1985.

T'aejong sillok (Veritable records of King T'aejong). In *Chosŏn wangjo sillok*.

Thompson, E. P. *The Making of the English Working Class*. London: V. Gollancz, 1963.

Toby, Ronald P. "Carnival of the Aliens: Korean Embassies in Edo-Period Art and Popular Culture." *Monumenta Nipponica* 41.4 (1986): 415–56.

Tŏksu Yi-ssi sebo (Genealogy of the Tŏksu Yi). 16 vols. Preface dated 1898.

T'onggyech'ŏng (Korean National Statistical Office). "Haengjŏng kuyŏk (si-do)/sŏngssi-pon'gwan pyŏl kagu mit in'gu" (Administrative district [city-province]/number of households and population according to surname–ancestral seat). Taejŏn: T'onggyech'ŏng, 1996–2006. http://kosis.nso.go.kr/cgi-bin/sws_999.cgi?ID=DT_1INOOSC&IDTYPE=3&A_LANG=1&FPUB=3&ITEM=&CLASS1=S.000.

Totman, Conrad. *Early Modern Japan*. Berkeley, CA: University of California Press, 1993.

"Tŭngdannok" (List of Five Military Division commanders). In Kang Hyo-sŏk, *Chŏn'go Taebang*.

Wagner, Edward W. *The Literati Purges: Political Conflict in Early Yi Korea*. Cambridge, MA: Council on East Asian Studies, Harvard University, 1974.

———. "The Ladder of Success in Yi Dynasty Korea." *Occasional Papers on Korea* 1 (1974): 1–8.

———. "The Civil Examination Process a Social Leaven: The Case of the Northern Provinces in the Yi Dynasty Korea." *Korea Journal* 17 (1977): 22–27.

———. "Yijo Sarim munje e kwanhan chaegŏmt'o" (A re-evaluation of the problem of the Yi dynasty Sarim). *Chŏnbuk sahak* 4 (1980): 163–73.

Wagner, Edward W., and Song Chun-ho. *CD-ROM Poju Chosŏn munkwa pangmok* (CD-ROM Annotated Chosŏn civil examination rosters). CD-ROM. Seoul: Tongbang Midiŏ, 2001.

———. "Yiji sama pangmok chipsŏng" (Collection of Yi-dynasty licentiate examination rosters). Unpublished collection of photocopied candidate entries from rosters.

Walraven, Boudewijn. "Popular Religion in a Confucianized Society." In *Culture and the State in Late Chosŏn Korea*, ed. JaHyun Kim Haboush and Martina Deuchler, 160–98. Cambridge, MA: Harvard University Asia Center, 1999.

Weber, Max. *Economy and Society: An Outline of Interpretive Sociology*. Ed. Guenther Roth and Claus Wittich, trans. Ephraim Fischoff. New York: Bedminster Press, 1968.

Wŏn Ch'ang-ae. "Chosŏn sidae munkwa kŭpcheja yŏn'gu" (A study of Chosŏn period civil examination graduates). Ph.D. diss., Han'guk Chŏngsin Munhwa Yŏn'guwŏn, 1997.

Wong, R. Bin. *China Transformed: Historical Change and the Limits of European Experience*. Ithaca, NY: Cornell University Press, 1997.

Yi Chun-gu. "Chosŏn hugi ŭi 'muhak' ko" (An inquiry on the late Chosŏn '*muhak*'). *Taegu sahak* 23 (1983): 49–81.

———. *Chosŏn hugi sinbun chigyŏk pyŏndong yŏn'gu* (Studies on the late Chosŏn changes in social status and occupation-service). Seoul: Ilchogak, 1993.

Yi Hong-du. "Mukwa rŭl t'onghae pon Chosŏn hugi ch'ŏnin ŭi sinbun pyŏndong" (Late Chosŏn social mobility among the lowborn as seen through the military examination). *Minjok munhwa* 19 (1996): 269–307.

———. *Chosŏn sidae sinbun pyŏndong yŏn'gu: ch'ŏnin ŭi sinbun sangsŭng ŭl chungsim ŭro* (A study of late Chosŏn social mobility: the upward social mobility of the lowborn). Seoul: Hyean, 1999.

Yi Hong-nyŏl. "Mankwa sŏlhaeng ŭi chŏngch'aeksajŏk ch'ui: Chosŏn chunggi rŭl chungsim ŭro" (Trends in the establishment and administration of the ten thousand-men examination from the perspective of policy history: the mid-Chosŏn period). *Sahak yŏn'gu* 18 (1964): 207–46.

Yi Hun-sang. *Chosŏn hugi ŭi hyangni* (Late Chosŏn local functionaries). Seoul: Ilchogak, 1990.

———. "Chosŏn hugi ŭpch'i sahoe ŭi kujo wa cheŭi: hyangni chiptan ŭi chŏngch'esŏng hollan kwa ŭpch'i cheŭi ŭi yuhŭihwa" (The late Chosŏn structure of town governance and ceremonies: the confusion in local functionary group identity and the transformation of ceremonies for town governance into entertainment). *Yŏksa hakpo* 147 (September 1995): 47–94.

Yi Kang-ch'il, ed. *Yŏksa inmul ch'osanghwa taesajŏn* (An encyclopedia of the portraits of historical personalities). Seoul: Hyŏnamsa, 2003.

Yi Ki-baek. *Han'guksa sillon* (A new history of Korea). Revised edition. Seoul: Ilchogak, 1990.

———. "Chokpo wa hyŏndae sahoe" (Genealogy and contemporary society). *Han'guksa simin kangjwa* 24 (February 1999): 107–17.

Yi Ki-sun. "Injojo ŭi panjŏng kongsin seryŏk e kwanhan yŏn'gu" (A study of the coup d'état merit subjects during Injo's reign). Ph.D. diss., Hongik Taehakkyo, 1989.

Yi Kŭng-ik. *Yŏllyŏsil kisul* (Narratives of Yŏllyŏsil [Yi Kŭng-ik]). 2 vols. Seoul: Chosŏn Kwangmunhoe, 1914.

Yi Kyŏng-ch'an. "Chosŏn Hyojongjo ŭi Pukpŏl undong" (The Northern Expedition movement of Chosŏn Hyŏnjong's reign). *Ch'ŏnggye sahak* 5 (December 1988): 177–260.

Yi Nam-hŭi. "16, 17 segi chapkwa ipkyŏkcha ŭi chŏllyŏk kwa kwallo chinch'ul" (Technical examination passers' prior experience and official appointment in the 16 and 17th centuries). *Minjok munhwa* 18 (1995): 241–81.

———. "Chosŏn sidae chapkwa pangmok ŭi charyojŏk sŏngkyŏk" (Characteristics of Chosŏn-period technical examination rosters as a source). *Ko munsŏ yŏn'gu* 12 (December 1997): 121–58.

———. "Chosŏn sidae (1498–1894) chapkwa ipkyŏkcha ŭi chillo wa kŭ ch'ui: 'Chapkwa pangmok' teit'ŏbeisŭ punsŏk ŭl chungsim ŭro" (The careers of Chosŏn period (1498–1894) technical examination passers and their changing patterns: an analysis of 'technical examination roster' database). In *Chosŏn sidae ŭi sahoe wa sasang* (Society and thoughts in the Chosŏn period), ed. Chosŏn Sahoe Yŏn'guhoe, 241–72. Seoul: Chosŏn Sahoe Yŏn'guhoe, 1998.

Yi Sang-ŭn. *Han'guk yŏktae inmuljŏn chipsŏng* (Collection of Korean historical biographies). 5 vols. Kwangmyŏng: Minch'ang Munhwasa, 1990.

Yi Sŏng-mu. "Chosŏn ch'ogi ŭi kisulgwan kwa kŭ chiwi: chunginch'ŭng ŭi sŏngnip munje rŭl chungsim ŭro" (Technical specialists and their status in early Chosŏn: the problem of *chungin* stratum formation). In *Hyeam Yu Hong-nyŏl Paksa hwagap kinyŏm nonch'ong* (Festschrift for Hyeam Dr. Yu Hong-nyŏl), 193–229. Seoul: Yu Hong-nyŏl Paksa Hwagap Kinyŏm Saŏphoe, 1971.

———. *Chosŏn ch'ogi yangban yŏn'gu* (A study of early Chosŏn *yangban*). Seoul: Ilchogak, 1980.

———. *Han'guk ŭi kwagŏ chedo* (Korea's examination system). Revised ed. Seoul: Chimmundang, 1994.

———. "Chosŏn hugi tangjaeng ŭi wŏnin e taehan sogo" (A brief consideration of the causes of late Chosŏn factional strife). In *Yi Ki-baek Sŏnsaeng kohŭi kinyŏm Han'guk sahak nonch'ong* (Festschrift for Mr. Yi Ki-baek), 2: 1189–227. Seoul: Ilchogak, 1994.

———, Ch'oe Chin-ok, and Kim Hŭi-bok, eds. *Chosŏn sidae chapkwa hapkyŏkcha ch'ongnam* (Compendium of Chosŏn-period technical examination passers). Sŏngnam: Han'guk Chŏngsin Munhwa Yŏn'guwŏn, 1990.

Yi Su-gŏn. *Yŏngnam sarimp'a ŭi hyŏngsŏng* (The formation of the rusticated literati faction in Yŏngnam). Kyŏngsan: Yŏngnam Taehakkyo Ch'ulp'anbu, 1979.

———. *Han'guk chungse sahoesa yŏn'gu* (Studies in the social history of medieval Korea). Seoul: Ilchogak, 1984.

Yi T'ae-gŭk. "Sae kasa chuhae sam p'yŏn" (Three new annotated sung poems). *Kugŏ kungmunhak* 25 (June 1962): 193–218.

Yi T'ae-jin. *Chosŏn hugi ŭi chŏngch'i wa kunyŏngje pyŏnch'ŏn* (Late Chosŏn politics and changes in the military division system). Seoul: Han'guk Yŏn'guwŏn, 1985.

———. *Han'guk sahoesa yŏn'gu: nongŏp kisul paltal kwa sahoe pyŏndong* (Studies in the social history of Korea: the development of agricultural technology and social change). Seoul: Chisik Sanŏpsa, 1986.

———. "18 segi Namin ŭi chŏngch'ijŏk soet'oe wa Yŏngnam chibang" (The political decline of Southerners and the Yŏngnam region in the 18th century). *Minjok munhwa nonch'ong* 11 (1990): 195–205.

———. "14–16 segi Han'guk ŭi in'gu chŭngga wa sinyuhak ŭi yŏnghyang" (Population increase in 14th–16th century Korea and the influence of Neo-Confucianism). *Chindan hakpo* 76 (1993): 1–18.

Yi Tong-hŭi. "19 segi chŏnban suryŏng ŭi immyŏng silt'ae" (The actual condition of the district magistrate appointment in the first half of the 19th century). In *Chŏnbuk sahak* 11–12 (1989): 211–36.

Yi Yŏng-ch'un. *Chosŏn hugi wangwi kyesŭng yŏn'gu* (A study of late Chosŏn royal succession). Seoul: Chimmundang, 1998.

Yim, Dong Jae. "Factional Ties in Seventeenth Century Korea: A Reevaluation of Traditional Concepts." Ph.D. diss., Harvard University, 1976.

Yŏkkwa p'alsebo (Eight-generation genealogy of interpreter examination graduates). Bound photocopy edition at Harvard-Yenching Library (Rare Book TK2291.7/1750.4), Harvard University. No date.

Yŏngil Chŏng-ssi Mun'chunggong-p'a sebo (Genealogy of the Much'unggong branch of the Yŏngil Chŏng). 3 vols. Seoul: Yŏngil Chŏng-ssi Munch'unggong-p'a Chungang Chongmuwŏn, 1963.

Yŏngjo sillok (Veritable records of King Yŏngjo). In *Chosŏn wangjo sillok*.

Yu Si-bu. "Haeje" (Introduction). In *Mukwa ch'ongyo*, iii-ix (q.v.).

Yu Sŏng-nyong. *The Book of Corrections: Reflections on the National Crisis during the Japanese Invasion of Korea, 1592–1598*. Trans. Byonghyon Choi. Berkeley, CA: Institute of East Asian Studies, University of California, 2002.

Yu Sŭng-wŏn. *Chosŏn ch'ogi sinbunje yŏn'gu* (Studies on the early Chosŏn status system). Seoul: Ŭryu Munhwasa, 1987.

Yun Chae-min. "Chosŏn hugi sahoe pyŏndong kwa yesul: chungin munhak" (The late Chosŏn social change and art: the *chungin* literature). *Yŏksa pip'yŏng* 23 (November 1993): 333–44.

Yun Hun-p'yo. "Chosŏn ch'ogi mukwa chedo yŏn'gu" (A study of early Chosŏn military examination system). *Hangnim* 9 (1987): 1–62.

Yun Kwang-bong. "Ch'ukche ŭi yŏn'gu" (A study on festivals). In *Han'guk minsok yŏn'gusa* (A History of research in Korean folk culture), ed. Ch'oe In-hak, Ch'oe Rae-ok, and Im Chae-hae, 377–93. Seoul: Chisik Sanŏpsa, 1994.

Character List

Ak-han 惡漢
alsŏngsi 謁聖試
Andong 安東
Andong Kim 安東金
Andong Kwŏn 安東權

bakufu 幕府
Beijing 北京

cha 字
Ch'albang 察訪
Ch'amgun 參軍
Ch'amp'an 參判
Ch'amŭi 參議
Chang Paek chŏn 장백전
Chang P'il-gi 張弼基
Changnyŏ-Ŭiryŏ 壯旅義旅
Ch'angnyŏng 昌寧
Ch'angnyŏng Cho 昌寧曺
Ch'angsŏng 昌城
changwŏn 壯元
Changyongwi 壯勇衛
chapkwa 雜科
Chejo 提調
Cheju 濟州
Chi Hullyŏnwŏnsa 知訓練院事
chigyŏk 職役
Chikchehak 直提學
Chikkang 直講
chikpu 直赴
Chingbirok 懲毖錄
Ch'in'giwi 親騎衛
chin'gwan 鎭管
Chin'gwan Ch'ŏmjŏlchesa
鎭管僉節制使
Chinhyulch'ŏng 賑恤廳
Chinju 晋州
Chinju Kang 晋州姜
chinsa 進士
Cho Hŭng-yun 趙興胤
Cho I-ryang 曺爾樑
Cho In 趙寅
Cho Kang 曺伉
Cho Sik 曺植
Cho U-sŏk 趙禹錫
Cho Yu-in 曺由仁
Cho Yun-son 曺潤孫
Ch'oe Ch'ang-nok 崔昌祿
Ch'oe Myŏng-gil 崔鳴吉
Ch'oe Yŏng 崔瑩
chojol 漕卒
Chŏlchesa 節制使

ch'ŏlchŏn 鐵箭
Ch'ŏlchong 哲宗
Chŏlla 全羅
Chŏlla-udo Sugun Chŏltosa 全羅右道水軍節度使
Ch'ŏllyŏng Hyŏn 川寧玄
Ch'ŏmji Chungch'ubusa 僉知中樞府事
Ch'ŏmjŏlchesa 僉節制使
Ch'ŏmjŏng 僉正
ch'ŏn 賤
Chŏng Hae-ŭn 鄭海恩
Chŏng Sa-sŏ 鄭思恕
Chŏng Se-gyu 鄭世規
Chŏng To-jŏn 鄭道傳
Chŏng Yag-yong 丁若鏞
chŏngbyŏng 正兵
chongch'in 宗親
Chongch'inbu 宗親府
Chŏngjo 正祖
Chŏngjok 鼎足
Chŏngju 定州
Chŏngnowi 征虜衛
ch'ŏn'gŏ 薦舉
chŏngsi 庭試
Chŏngŭp Yi 井邑李
chŏn'gyo 傳教
Ch'ongyungch'ŏng 摠戎廳
Ch'ongyungsa 摠戎使
ch'ŏnin 賤人
Chŏnju Yi 全州李
ch'ŏnmin 賤民
chŏnsi 殿試
Chŏnŭi Yi 全義李
chŏnya hansa 田野閑士
ch'ŏp 妾
chorye 皂隸
ch'osi 初試
Chosŏn 朝鮮
Chubu 主簿
ch'ugaengsi 秋更試
ch'ujŭng 追贈
Ch'undangdae 春塘臺
ch'undangdaesi 春塘臺試
Ch'ungch'ŏng 忠清
Chungch'ubu 中樞府
Chungch'uwŏn 中樞院
Chungch'uwŏn P'ansa 中樞院判事
Chunggun 中軍
chŭnggwangsi 增廣試
chungin 中人
Chungjong 中宗
Ch'ungju 忠州
Ch'ungmu 忠武
ch'ungnyangkwa 忠良科
chungse 中世
Ch'ungyŏlsa 忠烈祠
Ch'up'o Musa 追捕武士
Chwach'amch'an 左參贊
Chwasŏnbongjang 左先鋒將
Chwaŭijŏng 左議政

Ha Chin 河溍
Haeju O 海州吳
hallyang 閑良
Hamgyŏng 咸慶
Hamjong Ŏ 咸從魚
Han 漢
han 恨
hangnyŏlcha 行列字
Hansŏng Chwayun 漢城左尹
Hansŏng P'anyun 漢城判尹
Hanyang Yu 漢陽劉
Hapch'ŏn 陜川
Hŏ Kyun 許稛
Hŏ Mok 許穆
hoebang 回榜
hoesi 會試
hojang 户長

Hojo 户曹
Hojo Ch'amp'an 户曹參判
hongip'o 紅夷砲
Hong Kil-tong chŏn 홍길동전
Hong Kyŏng-nae 洪景來
Hong U-wŏn 洪宇遠
hongp'ae 紅牌
Hŏnjong 憲宗
hop'o 户布
hŏt'ong 許通
Hullyŏn Pyŏltae 訓練別隊
Hullyŏn Taejang 訓練大將
Hullyŏn Togam 訓練都監
Hullyŏnwŏn 訓練院
Hullyŏnwŏn Pujŏng 訓練院副正
Hullyŏnwŏn Sŭngji 訓練院承旨
Hullyŏnwŏnjŏng 訓練院正
Hŭngsŏn Taewŏn'gun
興宣大院君
Hwanghae 黄海
hyangan 鄉案
Hyanggisa 鄉騎士
hyanghoe 鄉會
hyangni 鄉吏
Hyojong 孝宗
Hyŏngjo 刑曹
Hyŏngjo Ch'amp'an 刑曹參判
Hyŏngjo P'ansŏ 刑曹判書
Hyŏnjŏlsa 顯節祠
Hyŏnjong 顯宗
Hyŏnp'ung 玄風
Hyŏnp'ung Kwak 玄風郭

ian 吏案
Ijo 吏曹
Ijo P'ansŏ 吏曹判書
ilsu 日守
Im Chae-hae 林在海
Im Changgun chŏn 임장군전
Im Hyŏng-su 林亨秀
Im Kyŏng-ŏp 林慶業
Im Kyŏng-ŏp chŏn 임경업전
Imjin 壬辰
Imjinnok 임진록
Injo 仁祖
Inmok 仁穆
isŏ 吏胥

Jin 金
junzi 君子

Kabo 甲午
Kaesŏng 開城
Kaettong 介叱同
Kang Ing-mun 姜翼文
Kang Sŏk-hwa 姜錫和
Kang Ŭng-hwan 姜膺煥
Kangdong 江東
Kanggye 江界
kanggyŏng 講經
Kanghwa 江華
kangsŏ 講書
Kangwŏn 江原
Kapsin 甲申
kasa 歌辭
kasŏljik 假設職
kibyŏng 騎兵
kich'ang 騎槍
kigyŏk 騎擊
Kija 箕子
Kim Chŏng-hŭi 金正熙
Kim Chong-sŏ 金宗瑞
Kim Chun-hyŏng 金俊亨
Kim Ik-sun 金益淳
Kim Ok-kyun 金玉均
Kim P'il-tong 金弼東
Kim Pyŏng-gi 金炳基
Kim Pyŏng-yŏn 金炳淵
Kim Sang-hŏn 金尚憲
Kim Satkat 김삿갓, 金笠

Kim Yu-sin 金庾信
Kimhae 金海
Kimhae Kim 金海金
kisa 騎射
kisaeng 妓生
koga yujok 古家遺族
kŏjin 巨鎮
Kojong 高宗
Kŏmdong 儉同
Kŏmdung 검등
kŏmgyo 檢校
Kongch'ung 公忠
kongin 貢人
Kongjo 工曹
Kongjo Ch'amp'an 工曹參判
Kongjo P'ansŏ 工曹判書
Kongju 公州
kongmyŏngch'ŏp 空名帖
kongnap 貢納
kongnon 公論
kongsaeng 貢生
kongsin 功臣
korip 雇立
Koryŏ 高麗
Koryŏng Pak 高靈朴
Ku In-hu 具仁垕
Ku Yang 具揚
Kŭmwi Taejang 禁衛大將
Kŭmwiyŏng 禁衛營
kundam sosŏl 軍談小說
kungin 弓人
Kun'gisi Pujŏng 軍器寺副正
Kun'gisijŏng 軍器寺正
kun'gwan 軍官
kunja 君子
kunjik 軍職
kunjŏk 軍籍
kunp'o 軍布
kwajŏn 科田
Kwak Chae-u 郭再祐
Kwak Yung 郭瀜
Kwanch'alsa 觀察使
Kwanghaegun 光海君
Kwangmu 光武
Kwangsŏng 廣城
kwanjik 官職
kwanp'um 官品
Kwŏn Kŭn 權近
Kwŏn P'il-ch'ing 權必稱
Kwŏn To 權濤
Kwŏn Yul 權慄
Kwŏn'gwan 權官
kwŏnji 權知
Kwŏnmu Kun'gwan 勸武軍官
Kwŏnmuch'ŏng 勸武廳
kyoji 教旨
kyŏkku 擊球
kyŏngajŏn 京衙前
Kyŏnggi 京畿
Kyŏngguk taejŏn 經國大典
Kyŏngjong 景宗
Kyŏngju Ch'oe 慶州崔
Kyŏngmyŏng 景明
Kyŏngnyŏk 經歷
Kyŏngsang 慶尚
Kyŏngsang-chwado Pyŏngma Chŏltosa 慶尚左道兵馬節度使
kyŏngsŏng sega 京城世家
kyŏngyŏn 經筵
kyosaeng 校生
Kyosŏgwan 校書館
Kyujŏnggong 糾正公
kyunyŏkpŏp 均役法

mabyŏng 馬兵
Malttong 末叱同
Manho 萬户
mankwa 萬科
Min Yu-jung 閔維重

Ming 明
minŭnso 民隱疎
Miryang Pak 密陽朴
mokchŏn 木箭
Moksa 牧使
molgi 沒技
Mongmin simsŏ 牧民心書
muban 武班
Mubi yoram 武備要覽
mubo 武譜
Mugyŏm Sŏnjŏn'gwan 武兼宣傳官
muhak 武學
Muhoga 武豪家
Mujang 茂長
mukwa 武科
Mukwa ch'ongyo 武科總要
munban 文班
munch'ŏng 文青
munjip 文集
Munjong 文宗
Munjŏng 文定
Munjŏng 文貞
munkwa 文科
munmu ilch'e 文武一體
muŏp 武業
musa 武士
Muwiso 武衛所
Muyŏlsa 武烈祠
myŏnch'ŏn 免賤
Myŏngjong 明宗
myŏnhyang 免鄉

Naegŭmwi 内禁衛
najang 羅將
Nam I 南怡
Nam Ku-man 南九萬
Nam T'ae-jing 南泰徵
Nambyŏngsa 南兵使
Namhan 南漢
Namin 南人
Nammyŏng 南冥
Namp'yŏng Cho 南平曺
Namp'yŏng Mun 南平文
nobi 奴婢
Noron 老論
Nŭngsŏng Ku 綾城具

Ŏ Chae-yŏn 魚在淵
O Chŏng-bang 吳定邦
Ŏ Hyo-ch'ŏm 魚孝瞻
O Sa-gyŏm 吳士謙
O Su-ch'ang 吳洙彰
Ŏ Suk-kwŏn 魚叔權
Ŏ Yun-jung 魚允中
O-in 惡仁
ŏbyu 業儒
oebang pyŏlsi 外方別試
Ogunyŏng 五軍營
ŏmmu 業武
Onyang 溫陽
Owi 五衛
Owi Puch'onggwan 五衛副摠官
Owi Toch'ongbu 五衛都摠府
Owi Toch'onggwan 五衛都摠官
Owijang 五衛將
Ŏyŏng Taejang 御營大將
Ŏyŏngch'ŏng 御營廳
Ŏyŏnggun 御營軍

p'a 派
Paek Hŭi-jang 白熙章
Paek Ik-chin 白翼鎮
Paek Ik-kyŏn 白益堅
Paek Sa-su 白思粹
Pak Cha-hŭng 朴自興
Pak Chŏng-hŭi 朴正熙
Pak Ch'ung-mang 朴忠望
Pak Chung-sŏn 朴仲善
Pak Ch'ung-wŏn 朴忠元

Pak Ho-hyŏn 朴好賢
Pak Hŭng-dun 朴興遯
Pak Hŭng-wŏn 朴興元
Pak Hyŏn 朴鉉
Pak Ki-jong 朴起宗
Pak Ki-p'ung 朴基豊
Pak Kye-hyŏn 朴啓賢
Pak Kyŏng-sin 朴慶新
Pak Kyu-su 朴珪壽
Pak Pae-wŏn 朴培元
Pak Sŏng-bin 朴成彬
Pak Sŭng-jong 朴承宗
Pak Sŭng-yŏng 朴昇英
Pak T'ae-sik 朴泰植
Pak Ŭng-hyŏn 朴應賢
Pak Yong-hyŏn 朴用賢
Pak-ssi chŏn 박씨전
P'al Changsa 八壯士
p'alch'on 八寸
p'alsebo 八世譜
pangjung saekchang 榜中色掌
pangmok 榜目
pangnap 防納
Pangŏsa 防禦使
P'ansa 判事
P'ansŏ 判書
p'ansori 판소리
Pibyŏnsa 備邊司
Pibyŏnsa Nanggwan 備邊司郎官
p'o 浦
poch'ungdae 補充隊
pogyŏk 步擊
poin 保人
p'ojin 浦鎮
pokchang 福將
poksi 覆試
pon'gwan 本貫
pon'gwan ssijok 本貫氏族
pŏp 法
p'osu 砲手
Puan 扶安
Pugin 北人
Pujang 部將
Pujangch'ŏng 部將廳
Pujŏng 副正
pukpŏl 北伐
Pukpyŏngsa 北兵使
P'ungsan Yu 豊山柳
P'ungyang Cho 豊壤趙
Pusa 府使
Pyŏkp'a 僻派
Pyŏlchang 别將
pyŏlch'ŏn 别薦
Pyŏlgiwi 别技衛
Pyŏlgun 别軍
Pyŏlmusa 别武士
pyŏlsi 别試
Pyŏlsiwi 别侍衛
P'yŏngan 平安
Pyŏngjo 兵曹
Pyŏngjo Ch'amp'an 兵曹參判
Pyŏngjo Ch'amŭi 兵曹參議
Pyŏngjo P'ansŏ 兵曹判書
Pyŏngma Chŏlchesa 兵馬節制使
Pyŏngma Chŏltosa 兵馬節度使
pyŏnji 邊地
p'yŏnjŏn 片箭
P'yŏngsan Sin 平山申
P'yŏngyang 平壤
P'yŏngyang Cho 平壤趙
pyŏngyŏng 兵營

Qi Jiguang 戚繼光
Qing 青

rujiang 儒將

sabyŏng 私兵
Sado 思悼

saengwŏn 生員
saengwŏn-chinsasi 生員進士試
Sagan 司諫
Saganwŏn 司諫院
Sagwa 司果
Sahŏnbu 司憲府
Sajiksŏryŏng 社稷署令
sajok 士族
salsu 殺手
samasi 司馬試
Samdo sugun t'ongjesa 三道水軍統制使
Samgun 三軍
Samhwa 三和
samsubyŏng 三手兵
samurai 侍, 士
sangmin 常民
sangmu 常武
sasu 射手
sau 祠宇
saŭn 謝恩
se 歲
Sejo 世祖
Sejong 世宗
Seoul 서울
Shenyang 瀋陽
shōgun 將軍
shuwu 束五
sijae 試才
Sillok 實錄
Sim Sŭng-gu 沈勝求
sin 臣
Sin Cha-jun 申自準
Sin Chap 申磼
Sin Hŏn 申櫶
Sin Kyŏng-jin 申景禛
Sin Rip 申砬
Sin Suk-chu 申叔舟
Sin Yŏ-ch'ŏl 申汝哲
sinbun 身分
singnyŏnsi 式年試
sinyŏk 身役
Sirhak 實學
siwip'ae 侍衛牌
Sŏ Sŏng 徐渻
Sŏ Tae-sŏng chŏn 서대성전
Sŏ Yu-dae 徐有大
Sobuk 小北
Sŏbuk Pyŏlburyo Kun'gwan 西北別付料軍官
sogo 束五
Sŏin 西人
sŏk 石
Sok taejŏn 續大典
sokwa 小科
Sŏnch'ŏn 宣川
sŏnch'ŏn 宣薦
sŏndal 先達
Song Chun-ho 宋俊浩
Sŏng Hon 成渾
Song Si-yŏl 宋時烈
Sŏng Tal-saeng 成達生
Sŏnggyun'gwan 成均館
Sŏngjong 成宗
Sŏngju 星州
Sŏngwŏnnok 姓源錄
Sŏnjo 宣祖
Sŏnjŏn'gwan 宣傳官
Sŏnjŏn'gwanch'ŏng 宣傳官廳
Sŏnmu Kun'gwan 選武軍官
sŏŏl 庶孼
sŏri 胥吏
Soron 小論
sŏwŏn 書院
sugun 水軍
Sugun Chŏltosa 水軍節度使
sui 歲
Sukchong 肅宗
Sumunjang 守門將

Sŭngji 承旨
Sunjo 純祖
Sunjong 純宗
Suŏch'ŏng 守禦廳
Suwŏn 水原
Suwŏn Paek 水原白
suyŏng 水營

Taebuk 大北
taedongpŏp 大同法
taegan 大諫
Taejang 大將
taejangbu 大丈夫
T'aejo 太祖
Taejŏn hoet'ong 大典會通
T'aejong 太宗
taekwa 大科
T'aengniji 擇里誌
taerip 代立
taesa 代射
Taesagan 大司諫
Taesahŏn 大司憲
Taizu 太祖
Takchibu Taesin 度支部大臣
t'alch'um 탈춤
Talsŏng 達城
Tang 唐
tangnae 堂内
T'angp'yŏngch'aek 蕩平策
tangsang 堂上
T'an'gŭmdae 彈琴臺
Tanjong 端宗
Tansŏng 丹城
Toch'onggwan 都摠官
toe 되
Tojŏng 都正
Tŏksu Yi 德水李
Tokugawa 德川
tokwa 道科
tollimcha 돌림자
Tollyŏngbu 敦寧府
tongbang 同榜
Tongbuk Pyŏlburyo Kun'gwan 東北別付料軍官
Tonghak 東學
Tongin 東人
Tongji Chungch'ubusa 同知中樞府事
Tongji Hullyŏnwŏnsa 同知訓練院事
Tongji Ŭigŭmbusa 同知義禁府事
Tongnae 東萊
tongnyŏnbang 同年榜
tongp'o 洞布
t'ongsinsa 通信使
Top'yŏngŭisasa 都評議事司
Tosa 都事
tosi 都試
Tosŭngji 都承旨
Tumen 土門
Tumun-dong 杜門洞
Tunjŏn Kun'gwan 屯田軍官
Tut'abi 豆他非
Tut'ŏbi 두터비

Uch'amch'an 右參贊
Uch'ansŏng 右贊成
Ŭibinbu 儀賓府
Ŭigŭmbu 義禁府
Ŭihŭng Ch'in'gun Chwauwi 義興親軍左右衛
Ŭihŭng Samgunbu 義興三軍府
Ŭiju 義州
Ulsan 蔚山
ŭmgwan 陰官
ŭmsŏ 陰敍
ŭpchi 邑誌
Uŭijŏng 右議政
wakō 倭寇

Wangja Sabu 王子師傅
Wijang 衛將
wŏnhan 怨恨
wŏnjong kongsin 原從功臣
Wŏnju 原州

Yalu 鴨綠
yang 良
Yang Hŏn-su 梁憲洙
yangban 兩班
yangi 洋夷
yangin 良人
Yangju 楊州
yangmin 良民
yangyŏk 良役
Yebinsi 禮賓寺
Yejo 禮曹
Yejong 睿宗
Yi Chi-yŏn 李止淵
Yi Chu-guk 李柱國
Yi Chun-min 李俊民
Yi Chung-hwan 李重煥
Yi Hang-bok 李恒福
Yi Hong-du 李弘斗
Yi Hun-sang 李勛相
Yi I 李珥
Yi I-ch'ŏm 李爾瞻
Yi In-jwa 李麟佐
Yi Ki 李芑
Yi Kwal 李适
Yi Pang-wŏn 李芳遠
Yi Si-ŏn 李時言
Yi Sŏng-gye 李成桂
Yi Su-gwang 李睟光
Yi Su-ryang 李遂良
Yi Sun-sin 李舜臣
Yi Wan 李浣
Yi Wŏn-u 李元祐
yoho pumin 饒户富民
Yŏhŭng Min 驪興閔
yŏkkwa 譯科
Yŏkkwa p'alsebo 譯科八世譜
Yŏllyŏsil 燃藜室
Yŏllyŏsil kisul 燃藜室記述
Yŏngjang 營將
Yŏngjo 英祖
Yŏngnam 嶺南
yŏngni 驛吏
Yŏngŭijŏng 領議政
Yŏngwŏl 寧越
Yŏngyu 永柔
Yŏnil Chŏng 延日鄭
Yŏnsan'gun 燕山君
Yu Ch'ung-nyŏl chŏn 유충렬전
Yu Sŏng-nyong 柳成龍
Yuan 元
yubae 流配
yubanggun 留防軍
yuhak 幼學
yujang 儒將
yujangch'ŏn 儒將薦
Yulgok 栗谷
Yusu 留守

Zhejiang 浙江

Index

Adoption, 123–25
Agency, 5, 6, 11, 195*n*11
Amended Great Code (*Sok taejŏn*), 148, 151
American incursion, 140–41
Ancestral seat (*pon'gwan*), *see* Descent groups
Andong, 169
Andong Kim, "New" (Sin), 124, 125, 211*n*66. *See also* Kim Ok-kyun
Andong Kwŏn, 93
Archery, 26, 199*n*35
Aristocracy (*yangban*), 6, 9, 16, 49–50, 117, 118, 193*n*1, 197*n*4; in late Chosŏn, 1–2, 7, 13, 52, 118, 125–31 *passim*, 134, 215*n*1; military, 2, 50, 74–84, 119–23, 135–42 *passim*, 211*n*65, 221*n*4; southern, 2, 88–100 *passim*, 105–7 *passim*, 117–18, 182, 184, 221*n*2; in Koryŏ, 8, 9, 15–18 *passim*, 47, 137–41, 198*n*7; in early Chosŏn, 8–9, 15, 24, 31, 47, 48, 49; and military examination, 42–45 *passim*, 68, 70, 90, 145, 147, 179; central, 46–47, 82, 90, 106, 107, 117–18. *See also* Civil officials; Civil-military divide; Elites; Military officials; Officialdom; Status
Army, *see* Military organization
Ascriptive status, *see* Status
Augmented examinations (*chŭnggwangsi*), 59–60, 208*n*29
Autonom, 12–13, 181–82

"Base" (*ch'ŏn*), *see* Lowborn
Blank appointment certificates, *see* "Nameless appointment certificates"
Board of Punishments (Hyŏngjo), 148
Board of War (Pyŏngjo), 33
Bourdieu, Pierre, 11, 12–13, 99, 161–62, 163, 181–83
Bureaucracy, *see* Officialdom

Calendar, *see* Date conversion
Capital region, *see* Western central region
Censorate (*taegan*), 36

Central bureaucracy, *see* Officialdom
Central government, *see* State
Certificates, *see* Degree certificates; Qualifications
Ch'a Chang-sŏp, 211*n*65
Chang P'il-gi, 119
Ch'angnyŏng Cho, *see* Namp'yŏng Cho
Changwŏn, *see* Top passers
Chapkwa, *see* Technical examination
Chief State Councillor (Yŏngŭijŏng), *see* High state councillor posts
Chigyŏk, *see* Service labels, 149
Chinju Kang, 93–94. *See also* Kang Ŭng-hwan
Chinju popular uprising, *see* Riots of 1862
Chinsasi, *see* Licentiate examination
Cho Hŭng-yun, 176
Cho I-ryang, 121 fig. 4.1. *See also* Namp'yŏng Cho
Cho Kang, 124. *See also* Namp'yŏng Cho
Cho U-sŏk, 136. *See also* P'yŏngyang Cho
Cho Yun-son, 37–38
Ch'oe Ch'ang-nok, 160
Ch'oe Myŏng-gil, 61–62, 92
Ch'oe Yŏng, 174–76. *See also* Tongju Ch'oe
Choe, Yong-ho, 202*n*85
Chŏlchesa, *see* Inspecting commissioners
Chŏlla Province, 98, 105
Ch'ŏmjŏlchesa, *see* Ports
Chŏn Kyŏng-mok, 221*n*2
Chŏng Hae-ŭn, 69, 69–70, 208*n*32
Chŏng To-jŏn, 20
Chŏng Yag-yong, 65–66
Chongch'in, *see* Royal family, enfeoffed members of
Chŏngjo, King, 70, 83–84, 95, 111
Chŏngjong, King, 20–21
Chŏngju, 108, 219–20
Ch'ŏn'gŏ, *see* Recommendation system
Chŏngsi, *see* Courtyard examinations
Ch'ŏnin, *see* Lowborn
Ch'ŏnmin, *see* Lowborn
Chŏnsi, *see* Palace examination
Ch'ŏp, *see* Concubines
Ch'osi, *see* Preliminary examination
Ch'ujŭng, *see* Court ranks and offices, sale of
Chungch'ubu, *see* Office of the Ministers-without-Portfolio
Chŭnggwangsi, *see* Augmented examinations
Chungin, 7, 78, 218*n*33, 224*n*1. *See also* Technical examination; Technical specialists
Chungjong, King, 30
Chwaŭijŏng, *see* High state councillor posts
Civil examination (*munkwa*), 25, 26, 102, 107, 110, 210*n*62
Civil-military divide, 17, 18, 47, 49, 74–76, 125, 198*n*7. *See also* Aristocracy; Civil officials; Descent groups; Elites; Military officials; Officialdom; Status
Civil officials, 2, 17, 24. *See also* Aristocracy; Civil-military divide; Elites; Military officials; Officialdom; Status
Clans, *see* Descent groups
Class, 5–6, 7–8

Class mobility, *see* Status
Commoners (*yangin*, *yangmin*, *sangmin*), 7, 24, 41, 52, 147–48, 149
Concubines (*ch'ŏp*), 196*n*18
"Confucian general" (*yujang*, *rujiang*), 135–36, 137, 139–40, 223–24
Confucianism, 11–12, 163, 176, 177–78, 199*n*30
Corruption, 3, 4, 36, 82, 184
County magistrates, *see* District magistrates
Court politics, *see* Factionalism
Court ranks (*kwanp'um*), 37, 69, 198*n*24, 202*n*91
Court ranks and offices, sale of, 128–32
Courtyard examinations (*chŏngsi*), 30, 60
Criminal interrogation, 148, 225*n*21. *See also* State Tribunal
Cultural capital, 12, 13, 99, 159–62, 163–64, 177, 182

Date conversion, 195*n*11
Degree ceremony, 165–66, 230*n*71
Degree certificates, 166, 182, 230*n*65
Descent groups, 2, 157–58, 216–17, 226*n*22, 227*n*34; and civil-military divide, 17, 18, 125; producing military examination passers, 41–42, 45–46, 70–72, 104–5, 149, 152–54, 203*n*97. *See also* Descent lines; Lineages
Descent lines, 72–79 *passim*. *See also* Descent groups; Lineages
Diplomas, *see* Qualifications
Disciples (Soron), 83
District magistrates, 22, 38, 82, 184

Eastern Learning, *see* Tonghak
Economy, late Chosŏn, 7, 8, 101–2, 118, 206–7
Elderly, state's treatment of, 129, 167–68
Elites: local, 86, 87–88, 89 map 3.1; definition of, 193*n*2. *See also* Aristocracy; *individual regional elites by name*
Embodied state, 99
Equal Service Law (*kyunyŏkpŏp*), 52–53. *See also* Tax system
Essentials of Military Preparedness (*Mubi yoram*), 136
Examination, 16, 17, 25, 202*n*85; rosters (*pangmok*), 2–3, 158–59, 193*n*4, 194*n*5, 194*n*6; passers, 25, 226*n*22, 229*n*46; candidates, 128, 216*n*9. *See also* Military examination passers; *individual examinations by name*

Factionalism, 74–75; late Chosŏn, 2, 4, 63–64, 83–84, 90, 118, 211–12, 214*n*94; 16th century, 30–31, 36–37, 204*n*102, 206*n*2. *See also individual factions by name*; Officialdom
Families, *see* Descent groups; Descent lines; Lineages
Females, *see* Women
Five Guards (Owi), 21–22. *See also* Military organization
Five Military Divisions (Ogunyŏng), 51, 152. *See also* Military division commanders; Military organization; Military Training Administration
"Four ancestors" (*sajo*), 204*n*104
French incursion, 140–41

Functionaries (*sŏri*), *see* Local functionaries

Garrisons (*kŏjin*), 22. *See also* Military organization
Genealogies, 108, 125, 134–35, 216–17, 219–20, 228–29; military examination passer (*mubo*), 72, 119, 135, 210*n*62
Giddens, Anthony, 11
Government, *see* State
Government service examination, *see* Examination
Grain submission, 128–31
"Grand examinations" (*taekwa*), *see* Civil examination; Military examination
Great Code Reconciliation (*Taejŏn hoet'ong*), 151
Great Northerners (Taebuk), 75

Haeju O, 127
Hallyang, 40–41, 43–44, 68, 69, 150–51
Hamgyŏng Province, 106, 107, 111–12, 114
Hamjong Ŏ, 125–26. *See also* Ŏ Chae-yŏn; Ŏ Yun-jung
Hero narrative fiction (*yŏngung sosŏl*), 231*n*85
Hidden transcript, 168–69
Hideyoshi invasion, *see* Japan
High state councillor posts, 34
Hoesi, *see* Metropolitan examination
Hong Kyŏng-nae rebellion, 114, 183, 208*n*28, 220*n*61
Hongp'ae, *see* Degree certificates
Hullyŏn Togam, *see* Military Training Administration
Hŭngsŏn Taewŏn'gun, 140, 184–85
Hwang, Kyung Moon, 221*n*4
Hyanghoe, *see* Local assemblies
Hyangni, *see* Local functionaries
Hyŏngjo, *see* Board of Punishments
Hysteresis, 12, 13, 181–82

Illegitimate sons (*sŏŏl*), 40, 44, 52, 123–25, 128, 157, 196*n*18, 202*n*88, 228–29
Im Hyŏng-su, 74
Im Kyŏng-ŏp, 173–76 *passim*
Im Changgun chŏn, *see Tale of Im Kyŏng-ŏp*
Imjinnok, *see Record of the Imjin War*
Imjin War, *see* Japan
Im Kyŏng-ŏp chŏn, *see Tale of Im Kyŏng-ŏp*
Injo, King, 56, 146–47
Inspecting commissioners (Chŏlchesa), 18, 19
Institutionalized state, 99
Interpreter examination (*yŏkkwa*), *see* Technical examination
Irregular examinations, *see* Special examinations

Japan, 44, 50–54 *passim*, 140, 145
Junzi, *see* "Superior man"
Jurchens, 44, 54–55, 146. *See also* Manchus; Qing dynasty

Kaesŏng, 100–2, 103–5, 218*n*41, 219*n*50
Kang Sŏk-hwa, 107–8
Kang Ŭng-hwan, 93–94, 136–37. *See also* Chinju Kang
Kanghwa Treaty, *see* Japan

Kasŏljik, *see* Court ranks and offices, sale of
Kigyŏk, *see* Polo
Kim Chun-hyŏng, 228
Kim Ok-kyun, 124. *See also* Andong Kim, "New" (Sin)
Kim, Sun Joo, 220*n*61
Kimhae, 97–98
Kimhae Kim, 227–28
Kŏjin, *see* Garrisons
Kojong, King, 140, 185
Kongin, *see* Tribute tax
Kongmyŏngch'ŏp, *see* "Nameless appointment certificates"
Kongnap, *see* Tribute tax
Korean historiography, 2–4, 5, 8, 9
Korean-Japanese Treaty, *see* Japan
Korean-Japanese war, *see* Japan
Korip, *see* Substitutes
Koryŏng Pak, *see* Pak Chŏng-hŭi; Pak Sŏng-bin
Kundam sosŏl, *see* Military narrative fiction
Kunja, *see* "Superior man"
Kunp'o, *see* Military cloth tax
Kwanghaegun, King, 55, 145–46
Kwanp'um, *see* Court ranks
Kwŏn T'ae-hwan, 201*n*69
Kyŏkku, *see* Polo
Kyŏngsang Province, 90, 95, 97–98, 105
Kyunyŏkpŏp, *see* Equal Service Law

"Lesser examinations" (*sokwa*), *see* Licentiate examination
Licentiate examination (*saengwŏnchinsasi*, *samasi*), 26, 99–100, 102, 156, 157
Lineages, 203*n*99. *See also* Descent groups; Descent lines
Literacy, 164
Local assemblies (*hyanghoe*), 184
Local examination, *see* Preliminary examination
Local functionaries (*hyangni*), 40, 157; late Chosŏn, 118, 133–35, 156, 228*n*44
Local gazetteers (*ŭpchi*), 170, 219*n*48
Local military competitions (*tosi*), 112, 193*n*5, 215–16
Lowborn (*ch'ŏnin*, *ch'ŏnmin*), 7, 128, 145–49 *passim*, 225*n*6
Lunar calendar dates, *see* Date conversion

Magistrates, *see* District magistrates
Manchu invasions, *see* Manchus
Manchus, 56. *See also* Jurchens; Qing dynasty
Manho, *see* Ports
Mankwa, *see* "Ten thousand-men examinations"
Manumission, *see* Slaves
Marines (*sugun*), *see* Military organization
Marriage, 119–23
Martial skills tests, *see* Local military competitions
Martial virtue (*mu*), 19, 93–96 *passim*, 135–36, 168–77 *passim*
Masked dance (*t'alch'um*), 169
Merchants, 102–3
Metropolitan examination (*hoesi*, *poksi*), 26
Michell, Tony, 201*n*69
"Middle people," *see Chungin*
Military cloth tax (*kunp'o*), 31–32. *See also* Military service; Tax system

Military command, 18–24 *passim*. *See also* Military organization; Provincial army headquarters; Provincial navy headquarters
Military division commanders (Taejang, Yŏngjang), 81, 213*n*90. *See also* Five Military Divisions; Military command
Military divisions, *see* Military regiments
Military ethos, *see* Martial virtue
Military examination (*mukwa*), 25, 26, 39, 54, 66–67, 102–3, 166–67, 176–77, 193–94; in late Chosŏn, 2, 3, 4, 60–61, 64–65, 169, 176–77, 178; in early Chosŏn, 19, 28–29, 47–48; requirements and standard for, 28, 31, 53–54, 65, 90–91, 145, 164, 207*n*11, 209*n*46; frequency of, 29–31, 53, 54–60, 66, 84, 194*n*5; and discontent, 58, 59, 66, 141–42, 182–83
Military examination passers, 10, 33, 67, 69, 161, 167–68, 200*n*44; careers of, 34–35, 79, 82, 203*n*95; social status of, 41–48 *passim*, 82, 203*n*96, 205*n*117; residences of, 42, 46–47, 86–87; number of, 44, 64, 207*n*9, 208*n*32
Military heroes, *see* Martial virtue
Military merit, 35, 75–76, 152, 159–60
Military narrative fiction (*kundam sosŏl*), 164, 170–74, 231*n*85
Military officials, 2, 15, 17, 24, 79–80, 221*n*4. *See also* Aristocracy; Civil-military divide; Civil officials; Elites; Officialdom; Status
Military organization, 18, 19–22, 24, 38, 43, 51–52, 116. *See also* Five Guards; Five Military Divisions; Garrisons; Military command; Military regiments; Ports; Provincial army headquarters; Provincial navy headquarters
Military regiments, 69, 83–84, 106, 150, 152, 227*n*31. *See also* Military organization
Military rule, Koryŏ, 17, 18
Military service, 24, 31. *See also* Military cloth tax
Military students, *see Muhak*
Military Training Administration (Hullyŏn Togam), 51
Military vocation men, *see Ŏmmu*
Ming dynasty, 20, 207–8
Miryang Pak, 108, 153, 204*n*102, 219–20, 227*n*34; Kyujŏnggong (Pak Hyŏn) branch of, 74–75, 76–78, 126–27, 205–6*n*120, 227*n*34. *See also individual members by name*
"Miscellaneous examinations," *see* Technical examination
Mongols, 18
Mourning group (*tangnae*), 42
Mu, *see* Martial virtue
Muban, *see* Aristocracy
Mubi yoram, *see Essentials of Military Preparedness*
Mubo, *see* Genealogies
Muhak, 154–55
"Muhoga," *see* "Song of a Martial Hero"
Mujang, 93–94
Mukwa, *see* Military examination
Munjŏng, Queen, 31
Munkwa, *see* Civil examination

Muskets, 51
Myŏngjong, King, 31, 36

Nam I, 175–76
Nam Ku-man, 65
Nam T'ae-jing, 83
"Nameless appointment certificates" (*kongmyŏngch'ŏp*), 129
Namhan Fort courtyard military examination, 147, 152, 159–60, 227*n*33, 228*n*37
Namin, *see* Southerners
Namp'yŏng Cho, 92, 124, 216*n*13. *See also* Cho I-ryang; Cho Kang
Namp'yŏng Mun, 97–98
Navy, *see* Military organization
Neo-Confucianism, *see* Confucianism
Nobi, *see* Slaves
Nonelites, 13, 143–44, 168–69, 183; status aspirations of, 128–32, 150, 157–58, 177–78; among military examination passers, 146–50, 153, 154, 160–61, 166, 177, 205*n*116, 226*n*23, 228*n*38; and military examination degree; 164–66, 182, 185–86. *See also individual nonelite groups by name*
Noron, *see* Patriarchs
North, 46–47, 96, 106; local elites of, 108–10, 112–13, 219–20. *See also* Hamgyŏng Province; P'yŏngan Province
Northeast, *see* Hamgyŏng Province
Northern Expedition (*pukpŏl*) policy, 57–58. *See also* Manchus; Qing dynasty
Northerners (Pugin), 211–12*n*70
Northwest, *see* P'yŏngan Province
Nothoi, *see* Illegitimate sons (*sŏŏl*)
Novels, *see* Vernacular narrative fiction
Nŭngsŏng Ku, 188–89 appendix A
Nurhaci, 55

Ŏ Chae-yŏn, 126. *See also* Hamjong Ŏ
O Su-ch'ang, 107, 108
Ŏ Suk-kwŏn, 37
Ŏ Yun-jung, 126. *See also* Hamjong Ŏ
Objectified state, 99
Occupation, *see* Service labels
Office of the Censor-General (Sagan'wŏn), *see* Censorate
Office of the Inspector-General (Sahŏnbu), *see* Censorate
Office of the Ministers-without-Portfolio (Chungch'ubu), 212–13
Offices and ranks, *see* Court ranks and offices, sale of
Officialdom, 11, 15–18 *passim*, 25, 47, 49, 102–3, 198*n*24, 218*n*41; in late Chosŏn, 1–2, 74–75, 81, 90, 107, 112–13, 130, 134; military examination passers in, 33, 34–38, 48, 69, 105, 213*n*90. *See also* Factionalism
Official ranks (*kwanp'um*), *see* Court ranks
Ogunyŏng, *see* Five Military Divisions
Old Doctrine, *see* Patriarchs
Ŏmmu, 154–55
Origins of Descent Groups, *see Ssijok wŏllyu*
Owi, *see* Five Guards

Pak Cha-hŭng, 126. *See also* Miryang Pak
Pak Chŏng-hŭi, 186, 234*n*14. *See also* Koryŏng Pak
Pak Ch'ung-mang, 160–61
Pak Ch'ung-wŏn, 126. *See also* Miryang Pak
Pak Kye-hyŏn, 126. *See also* Miryang Pak
Pak Sŏng-bin, 186, 233–34. *See also* Koryŏng Pak
Pak Sŭng-jong, 74, 126. *See also* Miryang Pak
Pak T'ae-sik, 151, 226–27. *See also* Miryang Pak
Palace courtyard examination, *see* Courtyard examination
Palace examination (*chŏnsi*), 26
Palais, James B., 102
Pangnap, *see* Tribute tax
P'ansori, 169–70
Park Chung Hee, *see* Pak Chŏng-hŭi
Patriarchs (Noron), 83
P'o, *see* Ports
Poin, *see* Support tax payers
P'ojin, *see* Ports
Poksi, *see* Metropolitan examination
Politics, *see* Factionalism; Officialdom
Polo (*kyŏkku*, *kigyŏk*), 26–27, 28
Popular culture, late Chosŏn, 10, 168–77
Population estimates of Chosŏn Korea, 201*n*69
Port commanders (Ch'ŏmjŏlchesa, Manho), *see* Ports
Ports (*p'o*, *p'ojin*), 22. *See also* Military organization
Posthumous ranks and offices, *see* Court ranks and offices, sale of
Prebends, 202–3
Preliminary examination (*ch'osi*), 26
Private armies (*sabyŏng*), 18–20 *passim*
Production relations, 6
Protection appointment (*umsŏ*), Koryŏ, 16–17
Provincial army headquarters (*pyŏngyŏng*), 22. *See also* Military organization
Provincial navy headquarters (*suyŏng*), 22. *See also* Military organization
Provisioners, *see* Support taxpayers
Pugin, *see* Northerners
Pukpŏl policy, *see* Northern Expedition policy
Pyŏlsi, *see* Special examinations
P'yŏngan Province, 106, 107, 111, 112, 114
P'yŏngsan Sin, 75. *See also* Sin Chap; Sin Hŏn; Sin Yŏ-ch'ŏl
P'yŏngyang Cho, 188–89 appendix A. *See also* Cho U-sŏk
Pyŏngyŏng, *see* Provincial army headquarters

Qi Jiguang, *see* *Shuwu*
Qing dynasty, 57–58. *See also* Manchus; Northern Expedition policy
Qualifications, 12, 181, 183

Rebellion of the Three Feudatories, 58
Recommendation system (*ch'ŏn'gŏ*), 62

Record of the Imjin War (*Imjinnok*), 172
"Red warrants" (*hongp'ae*), *see* Degree certificates
Regional elites, *see* Elites
Regional special examinations (*tokwa*), 60
Regular examinations, *see* Triennial examinations
Resources, 11–12, 179–80
Righteousness Flourishing Three Armies Office (Ŭihŭng Samgunbu), 20–21
Riots of 1862, 184
Ritualized rebellion, 169
Royal family, enfeoffed members of (*chongch'in*), 39
Royal in-laws, 184–85
Royal messenger candidates (*sŏnch'ŏn*), 214*n*93
Rujiang, *see* "Confucian general"
Rules, *see* Schemas

Sabyŏng, *see* Private armies
Saengwŏn-chinsasi, *see* Licentiate examination
Saengwŏnsi, *see* Licentiate examination
Sagan'wŏn, *see* Censorate
Sahŏnbu, *see* Censorate
Sajo, *see* "Four ancestors"
Samasi, *see* Licentiate examination
"*Samsubyŏng*," *see* Military Training Administration
Sangmin, *see* Commoners
Schemas, 11–12, 179
Scott, James, 168–69
Secondary sons, *see* Illegitimate sons
Secondary wives, *see* Concubines
Second State Councillor (Chwaŭijŏng), *see* High state councillor posts
Sejong, King, 28
Seoul, 87 fig. 3.1, 90, 100. *See also* Western central region
Service (*chigyŏk*) labels, 69, 149–50, 154–55. *See also individual service labels by name*
Sewell, William, Jr., 11, 180
Shamanism, 174–76
Shuwu, 51–52
Sin Chap, 103, 104. *See also* P'yŏngsan Sin
Sin Hŏn, 139–40, 224*n*54. *See also* P'yŏngsan Sin
Sin Yŏ-ch'ŏl, 65. *See also* P'yŏngsan Sin
Sin Yong-ha, 201*n*69
Sinbun, 5. *See also* Status
Singnyŏnsi, *see* Triennial examinations
Slaves (*nobi*), 7, 52, 128; manumitted, 147, 152, 159–60, 227*n*33
Small Northerners (Sobuk), 74–75
Sŏ Yu-dae, 137
Sobuk, *see* Small Northerners
Social hierarchy, *see* Status
Social mobility, *see* Status
Sogo army, 51–52
Sŏin, *see* Westerners
Sŏja, *see* Illegitimate sons
Sok (measure of rice), 130
Sok taejŏn, *see Amended Great Code*
Sokwa, *see* Licentiate examination
Sŏnch'ŏn, *see* Royal messenger candidates
Song Chun-ho, 117, 197
Song Si-yŏl, 62–63

"Song of a Martial Hero" (Muhoga), 93–94
Sŏnjo, King, 103, 104
Sŏŏl, *see* Illegitimate sons
Sŏri, *see* Local functionaries
Soron, *see* Disciples
Southeast, *see* Kyŏngsang Province
Southerners (Namin), 90
Special examinations (*pyŏlsi*), 26, 27, 30, 59–60
Specialization, *see* Civil-military divide. *See also individual examinations by name*
Ssijok wŏllyu, 216–17*n*14
State, 180, 181, 232*n*6
State examination, *see* Examination
State Tribunal (Ŭigŭmbu), 33, 147–48
Status, 2, 5–9 *passim*, 98–100, 117, 202*n*85, 221*n*4; consciousness, 2, 108–9, 128–35 *passim*, 144, 150, 157–58, 163, 177–78; hierarchy, 6–7, 98, 117–19, 132, 141, 179, 221*n*4, 224*n*1; mobility, 96, 97–98, 128–32, 156–60 *passim*, 185–86, 196*n*17, 209–10, 228*n*44
Structure, 4–5, 10–11, 180
Substitutes (*korip*, *taerip*), 31
Sugun, *see* Military organization
Sukchong, King, 64–65, 113, 147–48
"Superior man" (*kunja*, *junzi*), 163
Supernumerary posts (*kasŏljik*), *see* Court ranks and offices, sale of
Support tax payers (*poin*), 24. *See also* Military cloth tax; Military service; Tax system
Surnames, *see* Descent groups
Suwŏn Paek, 92–93, 188–89 appendix A
Suyŏng, *see* Provincial navy headquarters

Taebuk, *see* Great Northerners
Taedongpŏp, *see* Uniform Land Tax Law
Taegan, *see* Censorate
Taejang, *see* Military division commanders
T'aejo, King (Yi Sŏng-gye), 18, 19, 20
Taejŏn hoet'ong, *see Great Code Reconciliation*
T'aejong, King (Yi Pang-wŏn), 20–21, 28
Taekwa, *see* Civil examination; Military examination
Taerip, *see* Substitutes
Taewŏn'gun, *see* Hŭngsŏn Taewŏn'gun
T'alch'um, *see* Masked dance
Tale of General Im, *see Tale of Im Kyŏng-ŏp*
Tale of Im Kyŏng-ŏp (*Im Kyŏng-ŏp chŏn*), 173–74
Tangnae, *see* Mourning group
Tansŏng, 93, 155–56
Tax system, 32, 52–53, 155, 184, 185. *See also individual taxes by name*
Technical examination (*chapkwa*), 25, 236, 199*n*32, 202*n*88, 210*n*62. *See also Chungin*; Technical specialists
Technical specialists, 76–78, 118, 119–22, 133, 134–35. *See also Chungin*; Technical examination
"Ten thousand-men examinations" (*mankwa*), 62, 146
Third State Councillor (Uŭijŏng), *see* High state councillor posts

Thompson, E. P., 6
"Three skills army," *see* Military Training Administration
Tŏksu Yi, 75, 79, 123–24, 188–89 appendix A. *See also* Yi Sun-sin
Tokwa, *see* Regional special examinations
Tonghak, 185, 233–34*n*14
Tongju Ch'oe, 198*n*7. *See also* Ch'oe Yŏng
Top passers, 167, 214*n*92
Tosi, *see* Local military competitions
Town gazetteers, *see* Local gazetteers
Tribute tax (*kongnap*), 32. *See also* Tax system
Triennial examinations (*singnyŏnsi*), 26–27
Tumun-dong, *see* Kaesŏng

Ŭigŭmbu, *see* State Tribunal
Ŭihŭng Samgunbu, *see* Righteousness Flourishing Three Armies Office
Ŭmsŏ, *see* Protection appointment, Koryŏ
Unemployment, deliberate, 181–82
Uniform Land Tax Law (*taedongpŏp*), 52. *See also* Tax system
Ŭpchi, *see* local gazetteers
Uŭijŏng, *see* High state councillor posts

Vernacular narrative fiction, 169–74

Wagner, Edward W., 110, 197*n*23, 204, 214*n*92
Wealthy households (*yoho pumin*), 184, 185. *See also* Status; Tax system
Weber, Max, 6
Western central region, 46, 79–80, 96. *See also* Seoul
Westerners (Sŏin), 63–64
Women, 171, 172
Wŏnju, 156–57

Yangban, *see* Aristocracy
Yangban crescent, *see* Western central region
Yangin, *see* Commoners
Yangmin, *see* Commoners
Yi Chu-guk, 137–38
Yi Hun-sang, 228
Yi I-ch'ŏm, 74–75
Yi Pang-wŏn, *see* T'aejong, King
Yi Si-ŏn, 214*n*95
Yi Sŏng-gye, *see* T'aejo, King
Yi Su-gwang, 37
Yi Sun-sin, 75. *See also* Tŏksu Yi
Yi Su-ryang, 83
Yi T'ae-jin, 233*n*9
Yim, Dong Jae, 211–12
Yoho pumin, *see* Wealthy households
Yŏkkwa, *see* Technical examination
Yŏngjang, *see* Military division commanders
Yŏngjo, King, 52–53, 75–76, 83, 111
Yŏngnam, *see* Kyŏngsang Province
Yŏngŭijŏng, *see* High state councillor posts
Yŏngung sosŏl, *see* Hero narrative fiction
Young Doctrine, *see* Disciples
Yuan dynasty, *see* Mongols
Yujang, *see* "Confucian general"

Harvard East Asian Monographs
(*out-of-print)

*1. Liang Fang-chung, *The Single-Whip Method of Taxation in China*
*2. Harold C. Hinton, *The Grain Tribute System of China, 1845–1911*
3. Ellsworth C. Carlson, *The Kaiping Mines, 1877–1912*
*4. Chao Kuo-chün, *Agrarian Policies of Mainland China: A Documentary Study, 1949–1956*
*5. Edgar Snow, *Random Notes on Red China, 1936–1945*
*6. Edwin George Beal, Jr., *The Origin of Likin, 1835–1864*
7. Chao Kuo-chün, *Economic Planning and Organization in Mainland China: A Documentary Study, 1949–1957*
*8. John K. Fairbank, *Ching Documents: An Introductory Syllabus*
*9. Helen Yin and Yi-chang Yin, *Economic Statistics of Mainland China, 1949–1957*
10. Wolfgang Franke, *The Reform and Abolition of the Traditional Chinese Examination System*
11. Albert Feuerwerker and S. Cheng, *Chinese Communist Studies of Modern Chinese History*
12. C. John Stanley, *Late Ching Finance: Hu Kuang-yung as an Innovator*
13. S. M. Meng, *The Tsungli Yamen: Its Organization and Functions*
*14. Ssu-yü Teng, *Historiography of the Taiping Rebellion*
15. Chun-Jo Liu, *Controversies in Modern Chinese Intellectual History: An Analytic Bibliography of Periodical Articles, Mainly of the May Fourth and Post-May Fourth Era*
*16. Edward J. M. Rhoads, *The Chinese Red Army, 1927–1963: An Annotated Bibliography*
*17. Andrew J. Nathan, *A History of the China International Famine Relief Commission*
*18. Frank H. H. King (ed.) and Prescott Clarke, *A Research Guide to China-Coast Newspapers, 1822–1911*
*19. Ellis Joffe, *Party and Army: Professionalism and Political Control in the Chinese Officer Corps, 1949–1964*

*20. Toshio G. Tsukahira, *Feudal Control in Tokugawa Japan: The Sankin Kōtai System*

*21. Kwang-Ching Liu, ed., *American Missionaries in China: Papers from Harvard Seminars*

*22. George Moseley, *A Sino-Soviet Cultural Frontier: The Ili Kazakh Autonomous Chou*

23. Carl F. Nathan, *Plague Prevention and Politics in Manchuria, 1910–1931*

*24. Adrian Arthur Bennett, *John Fryer: The Introduction of Western Science and Technology into Nineteenth-Century China*

*25. Donald J. Friedman, *The Road from Isolation: The Campaign of the American Committee for Non-Participation in Japanese Aggression, 1938–1941*

*26. Edward LeFevour, *Western Enterprise in Late Ching China: A Selective Survey of Jardine, Matheson and Company's Operations, 1842–1895*

27. Charles Neuhauser, *Third World Politics: China and the Afro-Asian People's Solidarity Organization, 1957–1967*

*28. Kungtu C. Sun, assisted by Ralph W. Huenemann, *The Economic Development of Manchuria in the First Half of the Twentieth Century*

*29. Shahid Javed Burki, *A Study of Chinese Communes, 1965*

30. John Carter Vincent, *The Extraterritorial System in China: Final Phase*

31. Madeleine Chi, *China Diplomacy, 1914–1918*

*32. Clifton Jackson Phillips, *Protestant America and the Pagan World: The First Half Century of the American Board of Commissioners for Foreign Missions, 1810–1860*

*33. James Pusey, *Wu Han: Attacking the Present Through the Past*

*34. Ying-wan Cheng, *Postal Communication in China and Its Modernization, 1860–1896*

35. Tuvia Blumenthal, *Saving in Postwar Japan*

36. Peter Frost, *The Bakumatsu Currency Crisis*

37. Stephen C. Lockwood, *Augustine Heard and Company, 1858–1862*

38. Robert R. Campbell, *James Duncan Campbell: A Memoir by His Son*

39. Jerome Alan Cohen, ed., *The Dynamics of China's Foreign Relations*

40. V. V. Vishnyakova-Akimova, *Two Years in Revolutionary China, 1925–1927,* trans. Steven L. Levine

41. Meron Medzini, *French Policy in Japan During the Closing Years of the Tokugawa Regime*

42. Ezra Vogel, Margie Sargent, Vivienne B. Shue, Thomas Jay Mathews, and Deborah S. Davis, *The Cultural Revolution in the Provinces*

43. Sidney A. Forsythe, *An American Missionary Community in China, 1895–1905*

*44. Benjamin I. Schwartz, ed., *Reflections on the May Fourth Movement.: A Symposium*

*45. Ching Young Choe, *The Rule of the Taewŏngun, 1864–1873: Restoration in Yi Korea*

46. W. P. J. Hall, *A Bibliographical Guide to Japanese Research on the Chinese Economy, 1958–1970*

47. Jack J. Gerson, *Horatio Nelson Lay and Sino-British Relations, 1854–1864*

48. Paul Richard Bohr, *Famine and the Missionary: Timothy Richard as Relief Administrator and Advocate of National Reform*
49. Endymion Wilkinson, *The History of Imperial China: A Research Guide*
50. Britten Dean, *China and Great Britain: The Diplomacy of Commercial Relations, 1860–1864*
51. Ellsworth C. Carlson, *The Foochow Missionaries, 1847–1880*
52. Yeh-chien Wang, *An Estimate of the Land-Tax Collection in China, 1753 and 1908*
53. Richard M. Pfeffer, *Understanding Business Contracts in China, 1949–1963*

*54. Han-sheng Chuan and Richard Kraus, *Mid-Ching Rice Markets and Trade: An Essay in Price History*

55. Ranbir Vohra, *Lao She and the Chinese Revolution*
56. Liang-lin Hsiao, *China's Foreign Trade Statistics, 1864–1949*

*57. Lee-hsia Hsu Ting, *Government Control of the Press in Modern China, 1900–1949*

*58. Edward W. Wagner, *The Literati Purges: Political Conflict in Early Yi Korea*

*59. Joungwon A. Kim, *Divided Korea: The Politics of Development, 1945–1972*

60. Noriko Kamachi, John K. Fairbank, and Chūzō Ichiko, *Japanese Studies of Modern China Since 1953: A Bibliographical Guide to Historical and Social-Science Research on the Nineteenth and Twentieth Centuries, Supplementary Volume for 1953–1969*
61. Donald A. Gibbs and Yun-chen Li, *A Bibliography of Studies and Translations of Modern Chinese Literature, 1918–1942*
62. Robert H. Silin, *Leadership and Values: The Organization of Large-Scale Taiwanese Enterprises*
63. David Pong, *A Critical Guide to the Kwangtung Provincial Archives Deposited at the Public Record Office of London*

*64. Fred W. Drake, *China Charts the World: Hsu Chi-yü and His Geography of 1848*

*65. William A. Brown and Urgrunge Onon, translators and annotators, *History of the Mongolian People's Republic*

66. Edward L. Farmer, *Early Ming Government: The Evolution of Dual Capitals*

*67. Ralph C. Croizier, *Koxinga and Chinese Nationalism: History, Myth, and the Hero*

*68. William J. Tyler, tr., *The Psychological World of Natsume Sōseki,* by Doi Takeo

69. Eric Widmer, *The Russian Ecclesiastical Mission in Peking During the Eighteenth Century*

*70. Charlton M. Lewis, *Prologue to the Chinese Revolution: The Transformation of Ideas and Institutions in Hunan Province, 1891–1907*

71. Preston Torbert, *The Ching Imperial Household Department: A Study of Its Organization and Principal Functions, 1662–1796*
72. Paul A. Cohen and John E. Schrecker, eds., *Reform in Nineteenth-Century China*
73. Jon Sigurdson, *Rural Industrialism in China*
74. Kang Chao, *The Development of Cotton Textile Production in China*

75. Valentin Rabe, *The Home Base of American China Missions, 1880–1920*
*76. Sarasin Viraphol, *Tribute and Profit: Sino-Siamese Trade, 1652–1853*
77. Ch'i-ch'ing Hsiao, *The Military Establishment of the Yuan Dynasty*
78. Meishi Tsai, *Contemporary Chinese Novels and Short Stories, 1949–1974: An Annotated Bibliography*
*79. Wellington K. K. Chan, *Merchants, Mandarins and Modern Enterprise in Late Ching China*
80. Endymion Wilkinson, *Landlord and Labor in Late Imperial China: Case Studies from Shandong by Jing Su and Luo Lun*
*81. Barry Keenan, *The Dewey Experiment in China: Educational Reform and Political Power in the Early Republic*
*82. George A. Hayden, *Crime and Punishment in Medieval Chinese Drama: Three Judge Pao Plays*
*83. Sang-Chul Suh, *Growth and Structural Changes in the Korean Economy, 1910–1940*
84. J. W. Dower, *Empire and Aftermath: Yoshida Shigeru and the Japanese Experience, 1878–1954*
85. Martin Collcutt, *Five Mountains: The Rinzai Zen Monastic Institution in Medieval Japan*
86. Kwang Suk Kim and Michael Roemer, *Growth and Structural Transformation*
87. Anne O. Krueger, *The Developmental Role of the Foreign Sector and Aid*
*88. Edwin S. Mills and Byung-Nak Song, *Urbanization and Urban Problems*
89. Sung Hwan Ban, Pal Yong Moon, and Dwight H. Perkins, *Rural Development*
*90. Noel F. McGinn, Donald R. Snodgrass, Yung Bong Kim, Shin-Bok Kim, and Quee-Young Kim, *Education and Development in Korea*
*91. Leroy P. Jones and Il SaKong, *Government, Business, and Entrepreneurship in Economic Development: The Korean Case*
92. Edward S. Mason, Dwight H. Perkins, Kwang Suk Kim, David C. Cole, Mahn Je Kim et al., *The Economic and Social Modernization of the Republic of Korea*
93. Robert Repetto, Tai Hwan Kwon, Son-Ung Kim, Dae Young Kim, John E. Sloboda, and Peter J. Donaldson, *Economic Development, Population Policy, and Demographic Transition in the Republic of Korea*
94. Parks M. Coble, Jr., *The Shanghai Capitalists and the Nationalist Government, 1927–1937*
95. Noriko Kamachi, *Reform in China: Huang Tsun-hsien and the Japanese Model*
96. Richard Wich, *Sino-Soviet Crisis Politics: A Study of Political Change and Communication*
97. Lillian M. Li, *China's Silk Trade: Traditional Industry in the Modern World, 1842–1937*
98. R. David Arkush, *Fei Xiaotong and Sociology in Revolutionary China*
*99. Kenneth Alan Grossberg, *Japan's Renaissance: The Politics of the Muromachi Bakufu*
100. James Reeve Pusey, *China and Charles Darwin*

101. Hoyt Cleveland Tillman, *Utilitarian Confucianism: Chen Liang's Challenge to Chu Hsi*
102. Thomas A. Stanley, *Ōsugi Sakae, Anarchist in Taishō Japan: The Creativity of the Ego*
103. Jonathan K. Ocko, *Bureaucratic Reform in Provincial China: Ting Jih-ch'ang in Restoration Kiangsu, 1867–1870*
104. James Reed, *The Missionary Mind and American East Asia Policy, 1911–1915*
105. Neil L. Waters, *Japan's Local Pragmatists: The Transition from Bakumatsu to Meiji in the Kawasaki Region*
106. David C. Cole and Yung Chul Park, *Financial Development in Korea, 1945–1978*
107. Roy Bahl, Chuk Kyo Kim, and Chong Kee Park, *Public Finances During the Korean Modernization Process*
108. William D. Wray, *Mitsubishi and the N.Y.K, 1870–1914: Business Strategy in the Japanese Shipping Industry*
109. Ralph William Huenemann, *The Dragon and the Iron Horse: The Economics of Railroads in China, 1876–1937*
*110. Benjamin A. Elman, *From Philosophy to Philology: Intellectual and Social Aspects of Change in Late Imperial China*
111. Jane Kate Leonard, *Wei Yüan and China's Rediscovery of the Maritime World*
112. Luke S. K. Kwong, *A Mosaic of the Hundred Days:. Personalities, Politics, and Ideas of 1898*
*113. John E. Wills, Jr., *Embassies and Illusions: Dutch and Portuguese Envoys to K'ang-hsi, 1666–1687*
114. Joshua A. Fogel, *Politics and Sinology: The Case of Naitō Konan (1866–1934)*
*115. Jeffrey C. Kinkley, ed., *After Mao: Chinese Literature and Society, 1978–1981*
116. C. Andrew Gerstle, *Circles of Fantasy: Convention in the Plays of Chikamatsu*
117. Andrew Gordon, *The Evolution of Labor Relations in Japan: Heavy Industry, 1853–1955*
*118. Daniel K. Gardner, *Chu Hsi and the "Ta Hsueh": Neo-Confucian Reflection on the Confucian Canon*
119. Christine Guth Kanda, *Shinzō: Hachiman Imagery and Its Development*
*120. Robert Borgen, *Sugawara no Michizane and the Early Heian Court*
121. Chang-tai Hung, *Going to the People: Chinese Intellectual and Folk Literature, 1918–1937*
*122. Michael A. Cusumano, *The Japanese Automobile Industry: Technology and Management at Nissan and Toyota*
123. Richard von Glahn, *The Country of Streams and Grottoes: Expansion, Settlement, and the Civilizing of the Sichuan Frontier in Song Times*
124. Steven D. Carter, *The Road to Komatsubara: A Classical Reading of the Renga Hyakuin*
125. Katherine F. Bruner, John K. Fairbank, and Richard T. Smith, *Entering China's Service: Robert Hart's Journals, 1854–1863*

126. Bob Tadashi Wakabayashi, *Anti-Foreignism and Western Learning in Early-Modern Japan: The "New Theses" of 1825*
127. Atsuko Hirai, *Individualism and Socialism: The Life and Thought of Kawai Eijirō (1891–1944)*
128. Ellen Widmer, *The Margins of Utopia: "Shui-hu hou-chuan" and the Literature of Ming Loyalism*
129. R. Kent Guy, *The Emperor's Four Treasuries: Scholars and the State in the Late Chien-lung Era*
130. Peter C. Perdue, *Exhausting the Earth: State and Peasant in Hunan, 1500–1850*
131. Susan Chan Egan, *A Latterday Confucian: Reminiscences of William Hung (1893–1980)*
132. James T. C. Liu, *China Turning Inward: Intellectual-Political Changes in the Early Twelfth Century*
*133. Paul A. Cohen, *Between Tradition and Modernity: Wang T'ao and Reform in Late Ching China*
134. Kate Wildman Nakai, *Shogunal Politics: Arai Hakuseki and the Premises of Tokugawa Rule*
*135. Parks M. Coble, *Facing Japan: Chinese Politics and Japanese Imperialism, 1931–1937*
136. Jon L. Saari, *Legacies of Childhood: Growing Up Chinese in a Time of Crisis, 1890–1920*
137. Susan Downing Videen, *Tales of Heichū*
138. Heinz Morioka and Miyoko Sasaki, *Rakugo: The Popular Narrative Art of Japan*
139. Joshua A. Fogel, *Nakae Ushikichi in China: The Mourning of Spirit*
140. Alexander Barton Woodside, *Vietnam and the Chinese Model: A Comparative Study of Vietnamese and Chinese Government in the First Half of the Nineteenth Century*
*141. George Elison, *Deus Destroyed: The Image of Christianity in Early Modern Japan*
142. William D. Wray, ed., *Managing Industrial Enterprise: Cases from Japan's Prewar Experience*
*143. T'ung-tsu Ch'ü, *Local Government in China Under the Ching*
144. Marie Anchordoguy, *Computers, Inc.: Japan's Challenge to IBM*
145. Barbara Molony, *Technology and Investment: The Prewar Japanese Chemical Industry*
146. Mary Elizabeth Berry, *Hideyoshi*
147. Laura E. Hein, *Fueling Growth: The Energy Revolution and Economic Policy in Postwar Japan*
148. Wen-hsin Yeh, *The Alienated Academy: Culture and Politics in Republican China, 1919–1937*
149. Dru C. Gladney, *Muslim Chinese: Ethnic Nationalism in the People's Republic*
150. Merle Goldman and Paul A. Cohen, eds., *Ideas Across Cultures: Essays on Chinese Thought in Honor of Benjamin L Schwartz*
151. James M. Polachek, *The Inner Opium War*
152. Gail Lee Bernstein, *Japanese Marxist: A Portrait of Kawakami Hajime, 1879–1946*

*153. Lloyd E. Eastman, *The Abortive Revolution: China Under Nationalist Rule, 1927–1937*

154. Mark Mason, *American Multinationals and Japan: The Political Economy of Japanese Capital Controls, 1899–1980*

155. Richard J. Smith, John K. Fairbank, and Katherine F. Bruner, *Robert Hart and China's Early Modernization: His Journals, 1863–1866*

156. George J. Tanabe, Jr., *Myōe the Dreamkeeper: Fantasy and Knowledge in Kamakura Buddhism*

157. William Wayne Farris, *Heavenly Warriors: The Evolution of Japan's Military, 500–1300*

158. Yu-ming Shaw, *An American Missionary in China: John Leighton Stuart and Chinese-American Relations*

159. James B. Palais, *Politics and Policy in Traditional Korea*

*160. Douglas Reynolds, *China, 1898–1912: The Xinzheng Revolution and Japan*

161. Roger R. Thompson, *China's Local Councils in the Age of Constitutional Reform, 1898–1911*

162. William Johnston, *The Modern Epidemic: History of Tuberculosis in Japan*

163. Constantine Nomikos Vaporis, *Breaking Barriers: Travel and the State in Early Modern Japan*

164. Irmela Hijiya-Kirschnereit, *Rituals of Self-Revelation: Shishōsetsu as Literary Genre and Socio-Cultural Phenomenon*

165. James C. Baxter, *The Meiji Unification Through the Lens of Ishikawa Prefecture*

166. Thomas R. H. Havens, *Architects of Affluence: The Tsutsumi Family and the Seibu-Saison Enterprises in Twentieth-Century Japan*

167. Anthony Hood Chambers, *The Secret Window: Ideal Worlds in Tanizaki's Fiction*

168. Steven J. Ericson, *The Sound of the Whistle: Railroads and the State in Meiji Japan*

169. Andrew Edmund Goble, *Kenmu: Go-Daigo's Revolution*

170. Denise Potrzeba Lett, *In Pursuit of Status: The Making of South Korea's "New" Urban Middle Class*

171. Mimi Hall Yiengpruksawan, *Hiraizumi: Buddhist Art and Regional Politics in Twelfth-Century Japan*

172. Charles Shirō Inouye, *The Similitude of Blossoms: A Critical Biography of Izumi Kyōka (1873–1939), Japanese Novelist and Playwright*

173. Aviad E. Raz, *Riding the Black Ship: Japan and Tokyo Disneyland*

174. Deborah J. Milly, *Poverty, Equality, and Growth: The Politics of Economic Need in Postwar Japan*

175. See Heng Teow, *Japan's Cultural Policy Toward China, 1918–1931: A Comparative Perspective*

176. Michael A. Fuller, *An Introduction to Literary Chinese*

177. Frederick R. Dickinson, *War and National Reinvention: Japan in the Great War, 1914–1919*

178. John Solt, *Shredding the Tapestry of Meaning: The Poetry and Poetics of Kitasono Katue (1902–1978)*
179. Edward Pratt, *Japan's Protoindustrial Elite: The Economic Foundations of the Gōnō*
180. Atsuko Sakaki, *Recontextualizing Texts: Narrative Performance in Modern Japanese Fiction*
181. Soon-Won Park, *Colonial Industrialization and Labor in Korea: The Onoda Cement Factory*
182. JaHyun Kim Haboush and Martina Deuchler, *Culture and the State in Late Chosŏn Korea*
183. John W. Chaffee, *Branches of Heaven: A History of the Imperial Clan of Sung China*
184. Gi-Wook Shin and Michael Robinson, eds., *Colonial Modernity in Korea*
185. Nam-lin Hur, *Prayer and Play in Late Tokugawa Japan: Asakusa Sensōji and Edo Society*
186. Kristin Stapleton, *Civilizing Chengdu: Chinese Urban Reform, 1895–1937*
187. Hyung Il Pai, *Constructing "Korean" Origins: A Critical Review of Archaeology, Historiography, and Racial Myth in Korean State-Formation Theories*
188. Brian D. Ruppert, *Jewel in the Ashes: Buddha Relics and Power in Early Medieval Japan*
189. Susan Daruvala, *Zhou Zuoren and an Alternative Chinese Response to Modernity*
*190. James Z. Lee, *The Political Economy of a Frontier: Southwest China, 1250–1850*
191. Kerry Smith, *A Time of Crisis: Japan, the Great Depression, and Rural Revitalization*
192. Michael Lewis, *Becoming Apart: National Power and Local Politics in Toyama, 1868–1945*
193. William C. Kirby, Man-houng Lin, James Chin Shih, and David A. Pietz, eds., *State and Economy in Republican China: A Handbook for Scholars*
194. Timothy S. George, *Minamata: Pollution and the Struggle for Democracy in Postwar Japan*
195. Billy K. L. So, *Prosperity, Region, and Institutions in Maritime China: The South Fukien Pattern, 946–1368*
196. Yoshihisa Tak Matsusaka, *The Making of Japanese Manchuria, 1904–1932*
197. Maram Epstein, *Competing Discourses: Orthodoxy, Authenticity, and Engendered Meanings in Late Imperial Chinese Fiction*
198. Curtis J. Milhaupt, J. Mark Ramseyer, and Michael K. Young, eds. and comps., *Japanese Law in Context: Readings in Society, the Economy, and Politics*
199. Haruo Iguchi, *Unfinished Business: Ayukawa Yoshisuke and U.S.-Japan Relations, 1937–1952*
200. Scott Pearce, Audrey Spiro, and Patricia Ebrey, *Culture and Power in the Reconstitution of the Chinese Realm, 200–600*
201. Terry Kawashima, *Writing Margins: The Textual Construction of Gender in Heian and Kamakura Japan*
202. Martin W. Huang, *Desire and Fictional Narrative in Late Imperial China*

203. Robert S. Ross and Jiang Changbin, eds., *Re-examining the Cold War: U.S.-China Diplomacy, 1954–1973*
204. Guanhua Wang, *In Search of Justice: The 1905–1906 Chinese Anti-American Boycott*
205. David Schaberg, *A Patterned Past: Form and Thought in Early Chinese Historiography*
206. Christine Yano, *Tears of Longing: Nostalgia and the Nation in Japanese Popular Song*
207. Milena Doleželová-Velingerová and Oldřich Král, with Graham Sanders, eds., *The Appropriation of Cultural Capital: China's May Fourth Project*
208. Robert N. Huey, *The Making of 'Shinkokinshū'*
209. Lee Butler, *Emperor and Aristocracy in Japan, 1467–1680: Resilience and Renewal*
210. Suzanne Ogden, *Inklings of Democracy in China*
211. Kenneth J. Ruoff, *The People's Emperor: Democracy and the Japanese Monarchy, 1945–1995*
212. Haun Saussy, *Great Walls of Discourse and Other Adventures in Cultural China*
213. Aviad E. Raz, *Emotions at Work: Normative Control, Organizations, and Culture in Japan and America*
214. Rebecca E. Karl and Peter Zarrow, eds., *Rethinking the 1898 Reform Period: Political and Cultural Change in Late Qing China*
215. Kevin O'Rourke, *The Book of Korean Shijo*
216. Ezra F. Vogel, ed., *The Golden Age of the U.S.-China-Japan Triangle, 1972–1989*
217. Thomas A. Wilson, ed., *On Sacred Grounds: Culture, Society, Politics, and the Formation of the Cult of Confucius*
218. Donald S. Sutton, *Steps of Perfection: Exorcistic Performers and Chinese Religion in Twentieth-Century Taiwan*
219. Daqing Yang, *Technology of Empire: Telecommunications and Japanese Expansionism, 1895–1945*
220. Qianshen Bai, *Fu Shan's World: The Transformation of Chinese Calligraphy in the Seventeenth Century*
221. Paul Jakov Smith and Richard von Glahn, eds., *The Song-Yuan-Ming Transition in Chinese History*
222. Rania Huntington, *Alien Kind: Foxes and Late Imperial Chinese Narrative*
223. Jordan Sand, *House and Home in Modern Japan: Architecture, Domestic Space, and Bourgeois Culture, 1880–1930*
224. Karl Gerth, *China Made: Consumer Culture and the Creation of the Nation*
225. Xiaoshan Yang, *Metamorphosis of the Private Sphere: Gardens and Objects in Tang-Song Poetry*
226. Barbara Mittler, *A Newspaper for China? Power, Identity, and Change in Shanghai's News Media, 1872–1912*
227. Joyce A. Madancy, *The Troublesome Legacy of Commissioner Lin: The Opium Trade and Opium Suppression in Fujian Province, 1820s to 1920s*

228. John Makeham, *Transmitters and Creators: Chinese Commentators and Commentaries on the Analects*
229. Elisabeth Köll, *From Cotton Mill to Business Empire: The Emergence of Regional Enterprises in Modern China*
230. Emma Teng, *Taiwan's Imagined Geography: Chinese Colonial Travel Writing and Pictures, 1683–1895*
231. Wilt Idema and Beata Grant, *The Red Brush: Writing Women of Imperial China*
232. Eric C. Rath, *The Ethos of Noh: Actors and Their Art*
233. Elizabeth Remick, *Building Local States: China During the Republican and Post-Mao Eras*
234. Lynn Struve, ed., *The Qing Formation in World-Historical Time*
235. D. Max Moerman, *Localizing Paradise: Kumano Pilgrimage and the Religious Landscape of Premodern Japan*
236. Antonia Finnane, *Speaking of Yangzhou: A Chinese City, 1550–1850*
237. Brian Platt, *Burning and Building: Schooling and State Formation in Japan, 1750–1890*
238. Gail Bernstein, Andrew Gordon, and Kate Wildman Nakai, eds., *Public Spheres, Private Lives in Modern Japan, 1600–1950: Essays in Honor of Albert Craig*
239. Wu Hung and Katherine R. Tsiang, *Body and Face in Chinese Visual Culture*
240. Stephen Dodd, *Writing Home: Representations of the Native Place in Modern Japanese Literature*
241. David Anthony Bello, *Opium and the Limits of Empire: Drug Prohibition in the Chinese Interior, 1729–1850*
242. Hosea Hirata, *Discourses of Seduction: History, Evil, Desire, and Modern Japanese Literature*
243. Kyung Moon Hwang, *Beyond Birth: Social Status in the Emergence of Modern Korea*
244. Brian R. Dott, *Identity Reflections: Pilgrimages to Mount Tai in Late Imperial China*
245. Mark McNally, *Proving the Way: Conflict and Practice in the History of Japanese Nativism*
246. Yongping Wu, *A Political Explanation of Economic Growth: State Survival, Bureaucratic Politics, and Private Enterprises in the Making of Taiwan's Economy, 1950–1985*
247. Kyu Hyun Kim, *The Age of Visions and Arguments: Parliamentarianism and the National Public Sphere in Early Meiji Japan*
248. Zvi Ben-Dor Benite, *The Dao of Muhammad: A Cultural History of Muslims in Late Imperial China*
249. David Der-wei Wang and Shang Wei, eds., *Dynastic Crisis and Cultural Innovation: From the Late Ming to the Late Qing and Beyond*
250. Wilt L. Idema, Wai-yee Li, and Ellen Widmer, eds., *Trauma and Transcendence in Early Qing Literature*
251. Barbara Molony and Kathleen Uno, eds., *Gendering Modern Japanese History*

252. Hiroshi Aoyagi, *Islands of Eight Million Smiles: Idol Performance and Symbolic Production in Contemporary Japan*
253. Wai-yee Li, *The Readability of the Past in Early Chinese Historiography*
254. William C. Kirby, Robert S. Ross, and Gong Li, eds., *Normalization of U.S.-China Relations: An International History*
255. Ellen Gardner Nakamura, *Practical Pursuits: Takano Chōei, Takahashi Keisaku, and Western Medicine in Nineteenth-Century Japan*
256. Jonathan W. Best, *A History of the Early Korean Kingdom of Paekche, together with an annotated translation of* The Paekche Annals *of the* Samguk sagi
257. Liang Pan, *The United Nations in Japan's Foreign and Security Policymaking, 1945–1992: National Security, Party Politics, and International Status*
258. Richard Belsky, *Localities at the Center: Native Place, Space, and Power in Late Imperial Beijing*
259. Zwia Lipkin, *"Useless to the State": "Social Problems" and Social Engineering in Nationalist Nanjing, 1927–1937*
260. William O. Gardner, *Advertising Tower: Japanese Modernism and Modernity in the 1920s*
261. Stephen Owen, *The Making of Early Chinese Classical Poetry*
262. Martin J. Powers, *Pattern and Person: Ornament, Society, and Self in Classical China*
263. Anna M. Shields, *Crafting a Collection: The Cultural Contexts and Poetic Practice of the* Huajian ji 花間集 *(Collection from Among the Flowers)*
264. Stephen Owen, *The Late Tang: Chinese Poetry of the Mid-Ninth Century (827–860)*
265. Sara L. Friedman, *Intimate Politics: Marriage, the Market, and State Power in Southeastern China*
266. Patricia Buckley Ebrey and Maggie Bickford, *Emperor Huizong and Late Northern Song China: The Politics of Culture and the Culture of Politics*
267. Sophie Volpp, *Worldly Stage: Theatricality in Seventeenth-Century China*
268. Ellen Widmer, *The Beauty and the Book: Women and Fiction in Nineteenth-Century China*
269. Steven B. Miles, *The Sea of Learning: Mobility and Identity in Nineteenth-Century Guangzhou*
270. Lin Man-houng, *China Upside Down: Currency, Society, and Ideologies, 1808–1856*
271. Ronald Egan, *The Problem of Beauty: Aesthetic Thought and Pursuits in Northern Song Dynasty China*
272. Mark Halperin, *Out of the Cloister: Literati Perspectives on Buddhism in Sung China, 960–1279*
273. Helen Dunstan, *State or Merchant? Political Economy and Political Process in 1740s China*
274. Sabina Knight, *The Heart of Time: Moral Agency in Twentieth-Century Chinese Fiction*

275. Timothy J. Van Compernolle, *The Uses of Memory: The Critique of Modernity in the Fiction of Higuchi Ichiyō*
276. Paul Rouzer, *A New Practical Primer of Literary Chinese*
277. Jonathan Zwicker, *Practices of the Sentimental Imagination: Melodrama, the Novel, and the Social Imaginary in Nineteenth-Century Japan*
278. Franziska Seraphim, *War Memory and Social Politics in Japan, 1945–2005*
279. Adam L. Kern, *Manga from the Floating World: Comicbook Culture and the* Kibyōshi *of Edo Japan*
280. Cynthia J. Brokaw, *Commerce in Culture: The Sibao Book Trade in the Qing and Republican Periods*
281. Eugene Y. Park, *Between Dreams and Reality: The Military Examination in Late Chosŏn Korea, 1600–1894*